Gregory L. Freeze is Assistant Professor of History, Brandeis University.

The Russian Levites

Russian Research Center Studies, 78

The Russian Levites

Parish Clergy in the Eighteenth Century

Gregory L. Freeze

BIP-90

Harvard University Press
Cambridge, Massachusetts
and London, England
1977

Printed in the United States of America
Publication of this book has been aided by a grant from the
Andrew W. Mellon Foundation.

Library of Congress Cataloging in Publication Data
Freeze, Gregory L   1945-
  The Russian Levites.
  (Russian Research Center studies; 78)
  Bibliography: p.
  Includes index.
  1. Orthodox Eastern Church, Russian—Clergy—History.
2. Clergy—Russia—History. I. Title. II. Series:
Harvard University. Russian Research Center. Studies; 78.
BX540.F73   281.9'3   76-30764
ISBN 0-674-78175-9

To Karen

Preface

By the 1860s one group in Imperial Russia was so distinct and isolated that contemporaries routinely described it as a caste. It was hereditary, culturally separate from other groups in society, and unique in its education and manner of life; no other word seemed adequate to describe the phenomenon. To be sure, all the traditional estates had a special juridical status and way of life; yet none was as rigidly hereditary and socially separate as the parish clergy, the estate of married priests and sacristans who served in the parish churches and carried the Church's mission to lay society. The Russian priest invariably came from clerical origins, married the daughter of another cleric, and passed his life in the cocoon of ecclesiastical society and culture. Church journals, priests' memoirs, secular newspapers, reform commissions—all affirmed that the clergy were a unique social group, with an iron-clad hereditary order and striking isolation from the rest of society. The image of a hereditary religious caste impelled some to call the parish clergy Levites, after the clan of priests in the Old Testament. That epithet even found expression in state law: faced with a war emergency in 1797, Emperor Paul addressed the clergy as Levites and ordered that some clerics be conscripted into the army and serve as Biblical Levites had done in their day.

The clergy's castelike structure, so manifest and distressing for nineteenth-century observers, first arose in the eighteenth century, as medieval Muscovy became modern Imperial Russia. It was a formative epoch for the Russian state, marking the rise of secular absolutism and dynamic new policies bound to violate the traditional prerogatives of the clergy. The eighteenth century also signaled the formation of *sosloviia* (estates),[1] as medieval ranks (*chiny*) coalesced into larger social aggregates with specific service roles and statuses. It was also a century of dramatic cultural change, as secularization and new subcultures recast the traditional forms of life and thought. Secularism affected all strata of society, as nobles imitated Western culture, as peasants and townspeople substituted secular diversions for Church liturgies. Secularism meant not the appearance of worldliness, for medieval man knew well the delights of irreligious diversion; it was, rather, a sharpened consciousness of the tension between the "sacred and profane" that was new and disturbing. The aristocrat Shcherbatov spoke alarmingly about the corruption of morals in society, and the conservative Old Believers invented a term to describe these changes—*obmirshchenie*, "becoming worldly." Simultaneously, distinct soslovie subcultures began to replace the regional cultures that had been formed in the deep past and that had been left untouched by the forced political centralization of medieval Muscovy. The new estates acquired cultural identities that transcended region or locale and reinforced their cohesion and self-awareness.

These changes affected the clergy no less than other groups, but the results were strikingly different. There was, to be sure, much in common. Like other sosloviia, the clergy had emerged from various medieval ranks into a separate social estate. Like other sosloviia, it acquired a specific service role in the Petrine state, with an appropriate juridical status and economic support. Like other sosloviia, it developed a special subculture that distinguished it from the rest of society. But unlike all other sosloviia, it became more like a caste than a loosely structured estate. The principal task of this book is to discover why this was so and how the clergy's social condition affected the fate of Orthodoxy in modern Imperial Russia.

Although primary sources are rich and varied, the clergy has been all but ignored by Russian historiography. There are excellent histories of other social groups—the nobility (Romanovich-Slavatinskii and Raeff), the townspeople (Kizevetter and Ryndziunskii), and the peasantry (Semevskii's classic and numerous Soviet studies). No comparable work exists on the parish clergy, and the vast pool of archival and printed sources has remained untapped. It is a striking lacuna in descriptions of the social mosaic.

---

1. The *soslovie*, in Russian historiography, has represented something between a European estate (*Stand* or *état*) and a caste; it was more rigidly closed than an estate, but more internally diverse than a caste. I will use the conventional translation of "estate" for *soslovie* and "clerical estate" for *dukhovnoe soslovie*, and let the analysis flesh out the full meaning of the term.

Yet that piece of the mosaic is important for a fuller understanding of Imperial Russian society and culture. A study of the parish clergy will enable us to grasp more perceptively the problems and weaknesses of the Orthodox Church in prerevolutionary Russia. The parish priest was the Church's representative in the village; the linchpin of a parish community, he played a decisive role in determining the Church's status and influence in a postmedieval society. How he discharged his role, how competently he met the challenges of Old Belief (*raskol*) and disbelief, how he ranked on the ladder of social prestige—all this had a direct effect upon the authority of the Church in a consciously secular world. A proverb current in the eighteenth century aptly observed that "as the priest is, so too is the parish."[2] Historians have explained the Church's decline in Imperial Russia as due to the Petrine church reforms or, in still vaguer generalities, as due to secularization. A closer scrutiny of the clergy may reveal more serious problems in the infrastructure of the Church, providing a new perspective on how the Church actually functioned and interacted with government and society at the lowest levels.

A study of the clergy, moreover, can enrich our general understanding of Russian society. The priest came into daily contact with people from all social groups, for the Church was an inclusive social field, bringing together men of all ranks and statuses. V. I. Semevskii, the great historian of the peasantry, noted that a study of social relationships in the parish could add a new perspective on peasant and nobleman; the same can also be said of the townsmen. Moreover, a close scrutiny of the clergy is essential for understanding the many individuals who left the clerical estate and entered the bureaucracy, the arts and letters, the professions, and later the revolutionary intelligentsia. Steeped in the peculiar subculture of the clerical soslovie, the personalities of such individuals were profoundly affected by formative experiences at home and in the seminary. That special background was often the butt of anticlerical humor, especially among the noblemen who resented the *parvenus* in the bureaucracy. One popular anecdote described several bureaucrats of clerical origin seeking relief from the summer heat by swimming in a nearby river. Just as they emerged *au naturel* from the water, a peasant who had lost his way happened to come by and turned to ask for directions. "Not knowing who they were, [he was at first perplexed] but then discerned what

2. Eighteenth-century usage of the proverb is attested in the manuscript collections of V. N. Tatishchev and A. I. Bogdanov (B. N. Putilov, ed., *Poslovitsy, pogovorki, zagadki v rukopisnykh sbornikakh XVIII-XX vv.* [Moscow, Leningrad, 1961], pp. 54, 85).

breed they were and cried out: 'Hey churchmen, listen!' "[3] It was indeed a special crucible that produced such figures as Speranskii, Kliuchevskii, and Chernyshevskii; to interpret data about these bureaucrats and intellectuals of clerical origin, it is important to understand the ecclesiastical society from which they came. Finally, the parish clergy offer an instructive case for understanding the dynamics of soslovie formation and cohesion. The traditional statist school provided a purely legalistic explanation for the origins of sosloviia; that explanation, however, cannot account for developments in the Russian hinterland, where government fiat often had scant effect.

A study of the Orthodox clergy can also clarify broader problems best explored by comparative analysis. One is the process of secularization, a term which was first used at Westphalia in 1648 to describe the confiscation of church lands and which has come to have assorted meanings—the decline of established religion, the separation of society and state from the Church, the desacralization of thought and institutions. A study of the clergy and parish can suggest what secularization meant and how it developed in Imperial Russia. Moreover, such a study can broaden the comparative framework for analyzing the Church in modern Europe and the problem of ecclesiastical development amidst cultural and political change. Finally, the social history of the parish clergy is of considerable sociological interest, particularly with regard to the problems of social mobility and caste in the newer comparative definitions.

It is important to register a caveat: this book is but a reconnaissance, a preliminary expedition into uncharted social terrain. It makes no pretension to definitiveness; inferences, conclusions, even raw data may prove erroneous. But this rough map may guide later researchers through the unfamiliar thickets of Church law, unwritten custom, and erratic statistics.

The standard American system of transliteration has been used, with the customary exceptions for well-known names and terms. Spelling has been modernized, with certain exceptions; for example, Pereiaslavl'-Zalesskii was Pereslavl in the eighteenth-century (to distinguish it from Pereiaslavl'-Borisopol') and I have followed the eighteenth-century spelling here. Dating follows the Old-Style Julian calendar, which in the eighteenth century lagged eleven days behind that of

3. "Zapiski M. P. Veselovskogo," in Rukopisnyi otdel, Gosudarstvennaia publichnaia biblioteka im. M. E. Saltykova-Shchedrina, fond 550, F. IV, delo 861, list 385 ob.

the West. For the sake of clarity, Church refers to the institution, church to a specific parish church.

This volume owes much to the generosity of others. I am particularly indebted to Marc Raeff, who gave valuable suggestions for the revision of the original manuscript. My work has profited much from the thoughtful criticisms and comments of John Alexander, Bernard Barber, Daniel Brower, Robert Crummey, Georges V. Florovsky, Nancy Frieden, Charles Halperin, Andrzej Kamiński, Brenda Meehan-Watters, Alexander Muller, Walter Pintner, Donald Treadgold, and Isser Wolloch. It goes without saying that the final responsibility is mine; in some cases I have stuck to my original views, perhaps *po svoemu uporstvu* (out of stubbornness), to use a cherished phrase of eighteenth-century bishops for describing parish priests.

During two years of research in the Soviet Union I received useful counsel from my two Soviet advisers, M. T. Beliavskii and N. G. Sladkevich. My sincerest thanks are also due to the staffs and officers of several Soviet archival institutions, particularly Tsentral'nyi gosudarstvennyi istoricheskii arkhiv SSSR. Support for research was generously provided by the International Research and Exchanges Board, the Foreign Area Fellowship Program, and the Russian Research Center of Harvard University. Preparation was facilitated by grants from Brandeis University and the Ford Foundation.

Part of Chapter 7 was previously published in "Social Mobility and the Russian Parish Clergy in the Eighteenth Century," *Slavic Review* (December 1974).

Finally, for unstinting support, for selflessly deferring her own important research, for risking life and limb as my severest critic and editor, I am indeed grateful to my colleague and wife, Karen.

Contents

1 The Parish Clergy   1

2 Parish Clergy in a Secular Empire   13

3 The Hierarchy and the Parish Clergy   46

4 The New World of the Seminary   78

5 The Structure and Economics of Clerical Service   107

6 The Clergy and the Parish Community   147

7 A Separate Society and Culture   184

Conclusion   218

Abbreviations   225

Notes   228

Bibliography   298

Index   319

Tables

1	Church distribution among central dioceses	8
2	Seminary enrollments, 1739	84
3	Growth of seminary enrollments, 1766-1808	88
4	Structure of seminary enrollments, 1790s	88
5	Sources of seminarian support, 1790s	90
6	Grade achieved at departure from school, 1790s	91
7	Structure of the seminary curriculum	92
8	Types of churches, 1779	108
9	Number of urban churches, 1747 and 1783	113
10	Changes in average size of parishes, 1740-83	114
11	*Dukhovnyi Shtat*, the clerical registry of 1722	115
12	Average size of parish church landholdings, 1735-40	129
13	Size of parishes in Pereslavl and Pereslavl uezd, 1767	133
14	Size of parishes in Suzdal Diocese, 1781	134
15	Staffing shortages in central dioceses, 1747	139
16	Staffing patterns according to rank, 1747	140
17	Staffing patterns in central dioceses, 1784	142
18	Moscow staffing before and after redistribution, 1782 and 1784	143
19	Legal and actual fees for church rites	166
20	"Legal" income from rites	167
21	Former poll-tax registrants in the clergy, 1784	200
22	Social origins of pupils in seminaries and church schools, 1720s-40s	202

The Russian Levites

The Parish Clergy

1

The eighteenth century was a seminal period in the rise of modern Imperial Russia. Though harbingers of change can be discerned earlier, it was not until the eighteenth century that these diverse changes fused to create a wholly new polity, society, and culture. The tsar discarded a medieval political theology, borrowed unabashedly from Western political writings, and assumed a role and style befitting a modern secular ruler. Peter the Great and his successors also laid the foundations for the Imperial bureaucracy that was so essential for the state, so loathsome to the people. Instead of a chaotic hodgepodge of *prikazy* (central offices) and provincial satrapies that merely plundered the citizenry without executing the tsar's will, the state acquired a new administrative system with entirely new levels of control, coherence, and rationality. In a word, the modern secular state descended upon Russia, and its appearance augured ill for such traditional institutions as the Orthodox Church.

This century was furthermore an age of important social and economic change. The pace, to be sure, was languid and uneven; Russia did not suddenly burst into rapid modernization, and indeed the fetters of serfdom bound the peasantry ever more firmly. Yet the heavily restricted social system allowed for considerable adaptation and change. New cities sprang to life, the pitted roadways bustled with trade, and factories began to appear in ever larger numbers. Even rural Russia responded to the new forms of economic activity and social organization. Passport in hand, peasants began moving into the towns and cities to share in the new commercial market. Even the nobility deigned to exploit these tempting economic opportunities, by opening factories or by seeking to transform their estates into agricultural enterprises.

Still more striking changes swept through elite and popular culture. Seventeenth-century Muscovy belonged to an age of icons and Church Slavonic: it had known the bitter agony of fierce religious controversy, and from the Time of Troubles it burned with spiritual fervor. But Peter the Great's shocking festivities in the "Most Holy Drunken Sobor of Fools and Jesters," replete with unmistakable parodies of the Church, heralded a new age of challenge and retreat for the traditional religious culture. Internally the Church was racked by schism as the Old Belief spread relentlessly throughout the peasantry and townspeople. Moreover, Western culture and mores, now essential symbols of noble status, introduced the first seeds of atheism and Freemasonry. Above all, a pervasive secularism seeped into all strata of society; high or low, the laity accepted new values and life styles, from the gentry's new belletrism to the billiards of the *raznochintsy* (common townspeople).[1] In a word, the eighteenth century sounded the death knell for medieval Muscovy and heralded the birth of Imperial Russia.

These changes affected the Russian Orthodox Church perhaps more profoundly than any other institution. In Muscovite Russia from the fifteenth through the seventeenth centuries, the Church had been an institution of paramount importance. It possessed enormous wealth (about one third of all the land), wielded great influence in the theocratic politics of Muscovy, and held a virtual monopoly over culture and art. In the eighteenth century, however, this awesome power all but vanished. Peter the Great replaced the patriarch with the Holy Synod in 1721; instead of a single omnipotent patriarch (who might cherish claims to political power, as had Nikon in the mid-seventeenth century), a collegial board now governed the Church, which became a part of the general state structure. Though the Synod maintained considerable operational autonomy throughout the eighteenth century, the secular government held ultimate authority over the Church; by the early nineteenth century the actual administration of the Church had come to be controlled by the lay overseer of the Synod, the overprocurator. The Church's economic power similarly disappeared. Peter had audaciously exploited Church property, and his successors kept a tight control over these resources; the coup de grâce came in the 1760s, when the state finally sequestered Church lands and peasants. Henceforth the Church was placed on a state budget that crippled its activities, thwarted significant reform, and made the ecclesiastical hierarchy dependent upon the secular authorities.

However important the institutional changes in the Church, even more significant were those recasting the social foundations of the Church—its primary servitors, the parish clergy. In the eighteenth century the parish clergy underwent a fundamental transformation, acquiring a new social profile and different service patterns that sharply distinguished it from its Muscovite forebears. Particularly important was the formation of the *dukhovnoe soslovie*, the hereditary clerical estate. In contrast to the celibate monastic clergy, the parish clergy had to be married before ordination and thus the clerical population embraced not only the serving clergy but also their wives, children, and sundry relatives; in the eighteenth century that population became locked inside the *dukhovnoe soslovie* to form a rigid caste-like order, a development of momentous importance for the Church and society. At the same time, the clergy experienced radical changes in juridical status, economic condition, and social role; these changes too had direct and significant consequences for the clergy and Church. Altogether the result was a festering social problem that plagued the Church until 1917 and seriously impaired its ability to adjust to a post-medieval society and culture.

The parish clergy (also called the white or secular clergy) formed a large and complex service group. Standing apart from the monastic (or black) clergy, they were the main worldly servitors of the Church, providing spiritual and pastoral services for the laity in churches, chapels, and cathedrals. The parish clergy were divided into an upper stratum of ordained clergy (*sviashchennosluzhiteli*) and a lower stratum of churchmen or sacristans (*tserkovnosluzhiteli* or, less formally, *tserkovniki*). The ordained clergy, who had received the sacrament of ordination from the bishop and thus were empowered to administer sacraments, consisted of three main ranks—archpriest, priest, and deacon. The lower stratum of churchmen held a distinctly lower status in both Church and state law; divided into the ranks of *d'iachok* and *ponomar'*, they were responsible for guarding the church buildings, ringing the bells, keeping the church clean, and aiding in church services (by reading and singing). The sacristan, though not ordained, had to be installed and confirmed by the bishop; traditionally, his service was a full-time occupation and a kind of apprenticeship, preparing him to ascend to the priesthood. Together with their families, the priests and sacristans formed a group that would undergo fundamental changes in the eighteenth century, emerging as that distinctive social group, the *dukhovnoe soslovie*.

A systematic study of the parish clergy's transformation must examine several related problems. One task is to consider the clergy's relationship to the new secular polity; it is important to consider the full complex of service obligations, modified juridical status, and social policy that for the first time affected a group traditionally outside the state's jurisdiction. A second problem concerns the new relationship between priest and bishop, a relationship strained by differing interests and loyalties; by the nineteenth century a profound social cleavage separated the white and black clergy, and it is essential that the origins and structure of this intraclerical conflict be examined closely. A third task is to examine the impact of a new institution in the Russian Church —the seminary. Muscovy lacked formal ecclesiastical education; the rise of the seminary was of extraordinary importance in determining the social and cultural structure of the parish clergy by the end of the eighteenth century. A fourth task is to study the new system of clerical service, a combination of bureaucratic controls on both churches and appointments that had profound consequences for the behavior and stability of the parish clergy. A fifth problem concerns the relationship between the clergy and the parish community. The secular clergy of Muscovy had been dependent employees of powerful parish communities and landlords; a close study of the changing structure of the parish and clergy-parish relations can illuminate the tensions and conflicts that permeated the clergy's prescribed religious and social roles. The final problem is to explain the rise of the *dukhovnoe soslovie,* to chart the social and cultural dynamics that transformed the clergy into the closed, hereditary estate, unique in Imperial Russia.

These problems have received very little attention in the existing historiography. Prior to the 1860s historical literature on the Church was written mainly by the monastic elite, who ignored the parish clergy and dealt instead with the history of the monasteries and the hierarchy. Only during the period of the "great reforms," when a parallel movement developed within the Church, did the white clergy begin to receive serious study.[2]

It was in this atmosphere that P. V. Znamenskii published his lengthy history of the parish clergy in Imperial Russia.[3] A pioneering and comprehensive study, it attempts to treat all the diverse regions of the Russian Empire and, to a large degree, exhausts the published sources available at the time. However, it cannot be considered a satisfactory treatment. Above all, such an old work has fundamental conceptual weaknesses, overlooking some basic questions and patterns; nor can its impressionistic methodology satisfy a modern social historian. It also suffers from a narrow source base; Znamenskii used no archives and relied mainly upon the *Polnoe sobranie zakonov* (Complete Collection of Laws), which cannot be the basis of social history. And on some crucial issues he has a tendency to project back into the eighteenth century his picture of the nineteenth-century clergy, notwithstanding some important developments (for example, in education) at the beginning of the nineteenth century. Besides Znamenskii's monograph, several lesser works also appeared in this period; though some of these are still of value, they generally use little archival material and follow Znamenskii both in sources and in analysis.[4] When the reform atmosphere dissipated in the 1870s, so too did interest in the lower clergy. For the balance of the prerevolutionary period, only a few scattered studies treated the general problem of the clergy, and the voluminous body of archival and printed sources remained unexplored.[5]

Even less attention has been devoted to the clergy since 1917. Apart from propagandistic tracts or summary accounts, Soviet historians have produced only two serious works on the Church in the eighteenth century. The most recent, O. F. Kozlov's dissertation on the Petrine church reforms, relies heavily upon published sources and prerevolutionary monographs; it contributes little to an understanding of the parish clergy.[6] An impressive piece of archival research is Kadson's dissertation on the Church during the Pugachev rebellion of 1773-75. However, though he compiles a wealth of detail on the clergy's revolutionary and counterrevolutionary acts, he adds little new data on the clergy and relies upon Znamenskii for social information about the group.[7] Nor have the parish clergy received much attention from Western historians. The most extensive treatment is in Igor Smolitsch's encyclopedic *Geschichte der russischen Kirche*. Though this work provides a convenient compilation of data from prerevolutionary monographs, its discussion of the clergy merely summarizes Znamenskii, introducing little new in sources, methodology, or analysis.[8] In short, the Russian clergy is still an unexplored area of social history, and the large body of relevant archival and published sources has been virtually untapped.

The present study is limited to several dioceses of central Russia—what eventually became the dioceses of Moscow, Iaroslavl, Vladimir, Riazan, Tula, and Kaluga. Although reference will occasionally be made to other areas of the empire for comparative purposes and for defining Synodal policy, the focus here is on the central dioceses. When one goes beyond the general legal documents to highly particularistic materials and massive statistical data, it is essential to limit the scope if the sources are to be analyzed closely and carefully. The central dioceses have not been chosen because they were "typical"; the empire was far too diverse to allow for that. Rather, this central region was selected because of its special importance: it was the original crucible for the formation of the new soslovie, which appeared first in central Russia and did not spread to the Ukraine or outlying provinces until much later. The central region, furthermore, is intersected by several separate dioceses; this provides a valuable comparative framework, needed to correct possible distortions due to the idiosyncracies of a single bishop or a particular diocesan administration. This area

also offers extraordinary social diversity. It ranged from the great
metropolitan center of Moscow to the tiny blacksoil hamlets of Riazan
diocese; its social composition included almost every conceivable type
of noble, townsman, and peasant. It was also the area most intensely
affected by the new wave of modernization and change—urbanization, industrialization, enhanced regulation from above, and acculturation. Finally, this focus can overcome the peculiar Moscow-Kiev-
Irkutsk bias of historiography: while Znamenskii had relatively good
information on Moscow, Irkutsk, and Kiev, he had very little social
information on the central provinces outside Moscow and was un-
aware that the contiguous central provinces often developed quite differently from the highly urbanized Moscow area.

The materials for this region are extremely rich and varied. The
chief archival collection, which forms the basis for this book, is the
old Synodal archive, now located at the Central State Historical Archive in Leningrad. Apart from some published portions, this archive
has been used little and contains a wide variety of sources and information. First, it holds the Synod and state policy papers on the clergy,
documents that reveal clearly the institutional rivalries and the diverg-
ing perspectives on the clergy's social problems. Second, it contains
periodic census reports and other statistical data on the clergy. Although administrative reorganizations complicate and limit the use of
this material, it is fairly reliable and highly useful for composing a social profile of the clergy. Third, the archive holds the reports submitted by the diocesan seminaries, including registers of the students
and their social origins; these records are valuable, especially as the
seminary increased its importance in staffing the clergy. Finally, the
Synodal archive preserves countless petitions and judicial cases of parish clergy. Whether petty or sensational, such cases give a needed
counterweight to the rhetoric of legislation and the muteness of statistical data and clarify the attitudes prevailing in the clergy and parish.[9]

The Central State Archive of Ancient Acts contains another set of
relevant materials, of which the most important is the archive of the
Moscow Synodal Chancellery. Especially in the first half of the eighteenth century, when diocesan administration was still poorly developed, the Chancellery's responsibility over the central eparchies made
it an important center for data collection and even policy making. Its
role was especially important in areas such as Vladimir province, most
of which was under the direct administration of the Synod until the
1740s. Many important materials in the Chancellery's archive, such as
priests' petitions and consistory reports, never reached the Synod;
these give a clear record of local administration and contain invalu-
able descriptive material. As in the case of the Synodal archive, these
materials on the clergy have not been used by previous historians.[10]

Eighteenth-century printed sources are also extensive. Especially interesting are the church-script publications—ordination certificates,
instruction manuals and pamphlets, seminary catechism textbooks,
sermons, and instructions for clerical elders and ecclesiastical superintendents. One must use these with caution, bearing in mind their purpose, origin, and degree of distribution. Nevertheless, they do reflect
social conditions, illuminate the clergy's prescribed social role, and
show how the church elite perceived the problems of local religious
life. An important supplement to ecclesiastical sources is a variety of
secular publications—government documents, gentry memoirs, instructions to stewards, ethnographic materials, and literary sources.
These yield sparse but valuable information. Significantly, there is relatively little on the clergy in literary sources.[11]

Although it proved impossible to utilize the holdings of provincial
archives, this gap is to a large degree filled by published sources and
monographs.[12] Particularly valuable are the diocesan serials (eparkhial'nye vedomosti); appearing weekly or biweekly in most dioceses
from the 1860s until 1917, these serials often published documents
from diocesan archives or research based on them.[13] Additional materials are presented in the publications (Trudy) of the provincial archival commissions. Established in the late nineteenth century, the
commissions frequently published archival documents and excellent
pieces of local history, often with a special interest in church history.[14]
Moreover, there are a number of excellent monographs on dioceses
and seminaries; drawing heavily upon the diocesan archives, they present much useful information on the diocesan administration, parish
clergy, and religious life in the provinces.[15] These printed sources and
central archives, unfortunately, cannot fully compensate for the lack
of provincial archival materials; only the latter would make possible
an intensive analysis using quantitative methods to obtain precise
measurements of demographic change, family structure, and career
patterns. However, the sources do permit the study of most questions
and shed some light on those problems requiring further study in provincial archives.

The administrative history of the central dioceses is exceedingly
complex. As the eighteenth century opened, most of central Russia
belonged to one massive diocese, the patriarchal region, a vast ecclesiastical empire of nearly 4,000 churches. But there were also some
small dioceses (Rostov, Kolomna, Suzdal, Riazan) with several hundred churches in each (Table 1). After the Synod was established in
1721, it assumed responsibility for the old patriarchal region, which
was renamed the Synodal region in 1721. A new Moscow diocese replaced the Synodal region in 1742, but because it too was unmanage-
ably large, it was divided two years later into several smaller dioceses

Table 1. Church distribution among central dioceses

Area	1700	1736	1764	1784	1799
Patriarchal (Synodal)					
Region	3,150	4,832	-	-	-
Kolomna diocese	500	733	870	909	1,180
Moscow diocese	-	-	1,085	1,356	1,011
Pereslavl diocese	-	-	643	568	-
Riazan diocese	955	1,208	905	847	1,002
Rostov diocese	731	760	837	903	909
Suzdal diocese	402	502	619	596	-
Vladimir diocese	-	-	696	1,094	1,083

Sources: Pokrovskii, Russkie eparkhii, 2:26, n.1; 439-447; 840-851; prilozhenie 2; Shimko, pp. 274-276.

—Moscow, Vladimir, and Pereslavl. This new structure of central dioceses, though subject to minor adjustments, held fast until the 1780s. Then, in the wake of earlier provincial reforms, the government realigned the dioceses to coincide with the new boundaries of state provinces. Like the diocesan reforms of Joseph II in the Habsburg lands, the diocesan reform in Russia was intended to establish a more unified Church-state administration. The government made further changes in the late 1790s, creating a diocesan structure that survived throughout the nineteenth century with only minor alterations.[16]

The government repeatedly changed the boundaries of its provincial administration. It first made fundamental provincial reforms in 1718-19, when Peter created a single Moscow guberniia in central Russia. After further modifications in 1727, this guberniia included all areas of central Russia (divided into provintsii and uezdy) until 1775. Then Catherine's provincial reform of 1775-85 once again made radical changes in this system; it not only divided the guberniia into smaller autonomous provinces but also redefined the boundaries of the basic unit—the uezd (district). The new provincial system, with minor modifications, was left unchanged in central Russia throughout the nineteenth century. For our purposes, however, it is important to note that one cannot compare raw data (even at uezd levels) for the periods before and after 1775-85. Since the basic units are different, a direct comparison of quantitative data is impossible.[17]

This central region formed the core of old Muscovy. Its nucleus was the rising principality of Moscow, which had triumphed by 1500 as the new capital and center of the Great Russian state. Moscow had

gradually absorbed the bordering principalities that once were its formidable competitors for hegemony in the northeast; like Moscow,
they too had once erected an inspiring ensemble of princely kremlins
and episcopal cathedrals. For the white clergy this historic legacy had
considerable importance: central Russia inherited a number of old religious capitals like Rostov and Vladimir where the superabundance of
churches was not matched by subsequent economic or political development.[18] Of these medieval ecclesiastical centers only Moscow
achieved a worldly status commensurate with its religious claims; elsewhere Church authorities faced the difficult task of redistributing
churches—and clergy—to fit economic and social reality. Furthermore, because of their proximity to the Muscovite court, many
churches in the central region caught the eye of the tsar, who rewarded
them with annual stipends (*ruga*) that formed a vital supplement to
their income. When the secular rulers of the eighteenth century sharply
reduced the stipends, these churches suffered great hardships. It was
also the central churches, especially the cathedrals of the Moscow
Kremlin, that had received populated estates for their support; the
secularization of Church lands in 1764 took these away too. Thus, precisely because this area formed the very core of medieval Russia, its
adjustment to a modernizing world and secularizing polity would
prove far more painful than in the outlying provinces of the empire.

The clergy were affected not only by the special burden of historical
legacy but also by their immediate social environment. They obtained
all their economic support (in land and income) from the local parish
and received no state salary to moderate their direct economic dependence upon the parish. Consequently, the clergy shared the fate—
good or bad—of their parishioners. A catastrophe for the laity—fire,
plague, drought—meant a ruined parish; church annals are filled with
the dreary epitaphs of "dead churches and parishes," where the population was decimated and the church boarded shut.[19] Existence in the
central region was harsh; the population, still overwhelmingly peasant (91 to 95 percent),[20] subsisted on a marginal economy, often visited
by crop failures and blight. It was not merely the result of severe climate or crude agricultural methods; the land itself was poor, stubbornly refusing to yield its fruits in sufficient bounty. Renowned as
the "non-blacksoil zone,"[21] this area had irregular, low yields, the land
sometimes barely returning the seed-grain. An eighteenth-century
writer, M. M. Shcherbatov, calculated that because of the marginality
"famine would occur even with the slightest crop failure."[22] Even into
the distant past, the chronicles recorded a grim history of calamity
and suffering.[23]

This traditional problem was compounded in the eighteenth century by a new disturbing development: unrelieved demographic growth. The Muscovite area had recovered first from the ravages of the Time of Troubles, and by the late seventeenth century it was the thriving nucleus of the empire.[24] The population responded to this prosperity and the region became a center of steady, uninterrupted growth—with a yearly increase of 0.38 percent in the eighteenth century. Significantly, the population of the central provinces participated little in the migration to the east and south; the level of attrition through illegal serf flight was also exceptionally low. By the late eighteenth century, the result was a ponderous population density, by far the highest in the empire.[25] Accordingly, peasants in central Russia had the smallest average allotments of arable land—often from 2.5 to 3.5 dessiatines per male soul.[26]

The result was a popular belief in land shortage, and cries of land hunger began to resound as early as the mid-eighteenth century.[27] The academician and traveler, Lepekhin, drew this observation in 1768 during his research journeys through Vladimir province: "You rarely find a village where the peasants consider themselves to have a satisfactory amount of arable land; everywhere they are complaining about the land shortage."[28] Similar reports flowed into the Free Economic Society in the 1760s when it undertook a systematic survey through local correspondents. A reply from Vladimir, for example, stressed that "in this province there are more cultivators than land suitable for farming." A correspondent in Kaluga reported that the local peasants could make ends meet only if the harvest was above average. Otherwise, "if it is an average harvest, then many cannot subsist on their grain but must purchase it wherever it is cheaper; the cause of their poverty is the lack of land, which, moreover, is not of good quality."[29] As a result, many peasants were compelled to abandon their villages in search of seasonal or permanent employment; the number of peasants who departed on passports to hire themselves out was to increase unremittingly in the second half of the eighteenth century.[30]

This bleak picture had significant implications for the Church and for the parish clergy. It meant that, notwithstanding pockets of economic boom, the parishioners were still too poor to increase, or even to sustain, the material support voluntarily given to the local priest and sacristan. This augured ill for the parish clergy, as they desperately sought to emulate the "cultured nobility" and to elude identification with the lower classes. Furthermore, with land in short supply, many parishes were reluctant to apportion land for their clergy and indeed were eager to encroach upon land once given to the church. Predictably, the land-hungry peasant of central Russia firmly opposed the surveyors who came after 1754 with the intent of measuring off land for the clergy.

The central area included almost every kind of peasant category, from the much-oppressed landlord's serf to the freer state and Church peasants. As data from the first census in the 1720s show, each uezd often had some of each type living side-by-side.[31] The dominant category was the landlord's serf, but there were also sizable contingents of Church and state peasants. Thus the social structure of rural parishes was diverse; a "peasant" parish could be the nest of a single magnate, the common enterprise of several petty nobles, or a peasant commune free from nobles altogether. It is important to determine how such parishes developed in the eighteenth century—and, in particular, how they related to the parish clergy. The concentration of nobility in the central provinces was particularly important; their serf-owner mentality and new cultural styles posed a direct threat to the clergy's status.

Though the central provinces were still overwhelmingly rural, they began to show signs of quickening urbanization. The merchants and townspeople composed only 3 percent of the population of Russia, but a significant part of this group (32 percent) was concentrated in the central zone.[32] The great majority were in Moscow, a metropolis numbering approximately 175,000 inhabitants in 1788-95. It was a thriving economic center, a focus of national trade; encircled by artisans' and factory workers' suburbs, it was the main site of textile factories and other industrial enterprises. It was also the center of new opportunities, from Moscow University to the expanding business in publications.[33] In a word, Moscow was an exceptional phenomenon: its vast numbers of parish churches had a solid base of economic support, and the city offered an extraordinary array of attractive occupations.

Other cities in the central provinces bore little resemblance to Moscow, and they represented a wide variety of urban types. One type was a genuine economic center; though not common, a city like Serpukhov or Kaluga had a population of several thousand, included rich merchants and shopkeepers, boasted a few manufactories, and was the commercial center of the province.[34] A second type of city was more frequent. With a population of several hundred or at most one or two thousand, such towns were mainly occupied with trade and had little small-goods production and few factories.[35] These towns often had a distinct agrarian flavor, for much of the population spent half their time tilling garden plots on the outskirts of the town. For example, a relatively advanced town like Suzdal reported a population of 1,640 in the 1760s, with a small elite group of merchants; but "for the most part the rest of the townspeople support themselves by harvesting the yields of their gardens and, when these fail, by hiring themselves out as laborers."[36] Thus, though many towns of the central-industrial zone could claim a factory and handful of wealthy merchants, the bulk of the population was extremely poor and semi-peasant by occupation. Finally, a third type of town was the purely administrative city, which held no economic importance whatsoever but was officially designated as a city by the government. Such administrative cities proliferated after the provincial reforms of 1775, when the number of official cities in central Russia increased from 75 to 114 overnight.[37] Many of these new cities were like the tiny town of Zvenigorod, where "the merchants have no handicrafts or enterprises except for agriculture."[38] On the other hand, some towns with intensive economic activity were still designated villages, despite a busy marketplace and textile industry. Thus a serf village like Ivanovo had an impressive complex of textile factories and serf millionaires like the Grachevs, while some officially designated cities (Pokrov, Sudogda, Zvenigorod) had no economic significance.[39]

This structure of cities in eighteenth-century Russia has several important implications for our analysis of the parish clergy. Above all, in mapping out the social environment of the parish clergy, one must be cautious in making comparisons of urban and rural parishes. Moscow was in a class by itself; the picture of social relations here must not be heedlessly extended to the surrounding provincial towns. Similarly, within the provincial cities it is important to distinguish real economic centers from stagnant towns and especially from fictitious administrative cities (such as Zvenigorod or Sudogda). Moreover, much important commercial and industrial activity took place outside the city and on rural gentry estates. Hence one must treat with caution the archival materials that follow the official categories of "city" and "uezd" in arranging data. It is also important to note that, like the village parishes, many urban parishes were deeply impoverished. Few towns could afford stone buildings, and almost every home was built of wood; thus, even though the central cities did increase in size and economic importance, most afforded only a very weak base of support for the dependent parish clergy.[40] Each city had a few rich parishes with high-salaried officials and prosperous merchants, but most parishes were sure to include that mass of indebted shopkeepers, poor artisans, and immigrant peasants.

The clergy would thus develop in the eighteenth century amidst a new social environment, where fundamental changes were reshaping secular society, state institutions, and the economy. These developments directly affected the parish clergy, creating new demands and tensions for a Church that was built upon traditional relations, institutions, and social patterns. The final result would be an important deterioration in the clergy's stability, status, and role, developments bearing considerable significance for the Church. The following chapter will examine a powerful force that assumed an unprecedented role in the clergy's lives: the new secular state of Petrine Russia.

Parish Clergy in a
Secular Empire

2

In retrospect, the rise of the secular state in modern Europe seems ineluctable and uncomplicated—the defeat of the Church by a secular authority that pursues its own immediate aims without regard to otherworldly values and religious institutions. In fact, political secularization was a long and complex process, a gradual evolution toward an unsuspected destination. Paradoxically enough, it was born in the heat of religious strife, as the reformation and counter-reformation of the sixteenth century encouraged secular authorities to assume a new role in Church affairs. They did so not merely to enhance their own power or to seize ecclesiastical property (although that too occurred); rather, they were seeking to resolve religious controversy, to assert confessional integrity in their own domain, and to steel the faithful by excoriating bad mores and bad clergy. Protestant princes, unhindered by the papacy, went furthest, each claiming to be *summus episcopus*; yet their Catholic cousins did not lag far behind, in fact (though not in theory) assuming unprecedented powers over ecclesiastical property and organization, and even influencing papal decisions on matters of dogma. This first phase thus institutionalized secular control over the Church. In the eighteenth century, *le siècle éclairé*, secularity attained new dimensions as the state shed the religious concern but retained its power over the Church. Political rulership in this enlightened age became consciously secular, sacrificing Church interests and unabashedly pursuing *raison d'état*. It was an age capable of religious tolerance, for the new confession was the state itself; in the words of Joseph II, there should be but "one religion—that of directing all citizens equally toward the good of the state."[1]

Nowhere did the new political secularity clash so harshly with the traditional political culture as in "Holy Russia." Whatever the crude realities behind court politics in old Muscovy, its political culture was intensely liturgical, permeated with religious myth: Muscovy was the "Third Rome," its sovereign a pious saintly prince with clear overtones of divinity.[2] That myth achieved optimal expression with Aleksei Mikhailovich (1645-76), a tsar whose daily life was filled with religious toil and ritual—prayers, vigils, and meetings with revered holy men.[3] Yet secularity was already intruding ever more insistently, as the state encroached on Church property and privilege and for the first time formulated political crime. In 1680 it admonished subjects not to compare the tsar to God—an ukase testifying as much to the new secularity as to popular religiosity.[4] Full realization of secularity, however, came only in the reign of Aleksei's own son, Peter the Great. Peter—the self-taught carpenter, drummer, European traveler, admirer of Samuel Pufendorf, dynamic lawgiver, fearless warrior—shattered the traditional image of the pious, retiring tsar, and in its place fashioned a new conception of rulership: the dynamic, prescriptive emperor. In an unmistakable affront to medieval myth, Peter called himself a "Christian autocrat" instead of Orthodox tsar, drew explicitly upon European political theory and laws, indulged in bizarre parodies of traditional rulership (*kniaz'-kesar'*), adopted the Latin title *Imperator*, and deleted some stereotyped but symbolically important phrases from the liturgy.[5] Appropriately enough, in popular mentality Peter emerged as the countermyth to the saintly tsar: "Antichrist," an image widespread among diverse strata of his realm.[6]

However dramatic Peter's symbolic secularity, the process of political secularization did not end with him. To be sure, Peter placed himself beyond ecclesiastical judgment, declaring that the sovereign "is not obliged to answer for his actions to anyone on earth, but as a Christian Autocrat rules his lands and states in accordance with his own will and benevolence."[7] But Peter was in fact more the seventeenth-century German prince, who asserts new power over the Church but does so in the name of the faith. With his minutely detailed decrees, Peter sought to regularize and improve the Church, not simply exploit it; he had no use for European religious dogma, ordering the Synod to translate only part of his admired Pufendorf (on the duties of man and the citizen) but not the second section on the Christian faith "because I see no need or use for it."[8] Peter's prolific legislation, at once modern and traditional, further reflected his contradictory status. As a man in an age of rationalism, Peter issued laws that were tediously didactic; filled with such phrases as "because," "for that reason," "in order that," Peter's laws tried to convince his readers of the utility of changes, the harm of custom. This rationality, a regular part of Petrine laws, was unknown in the laconic decrees of Peter's own father, Aleksei Mikhailovich. But the traditional sovereign in Peter concluded laws just as his father did: with an appeal to fear (*strakh*), not to reason. If Peter had a strong grasp on the eighteenth century, he nonetheless still had both feet firmly planted in the seventeenth.

That traditionalism, religious sensibility, even the appeal to terror gradually faded with Peter's successors. Its attrition was at first irregular and slow in the reigns of Peter's immediate successors, but it had completely vanished by the time of Catherine the Great (1762-96). To be sure, she did not formally cut herself free from traditional religious moorings; she secularized Church lands and peasants but nominally for "the Church's own good"; her legislation, like Peter's, was still liberally sprinkled with references to divine providence and her own God-given authority.[9] But Catherine was the consummately secular monarch, ruling with a clear sense of *raison d'état*, wholly unfettered by religious sensibility. Catherine's conception of rulership differed from Peter's in still another way: whereas Peter tried to determine every facet of development through prolix, prescriptive regulations, Catherine sought greater initiative and diversity from her subjects as she directed their energies toward the "greatest of all good."[10]

Secularity and absolutism, whether Petrine or Catherinian, augured ill for the Church and clergy. For, if the medieval tsar respected Church prerogatives and interests (however reluctantly), his successors in the eighteenth century felt no such constraints, a change most dramatically revealed in the case of Church landholding. For two hundred years the Muscovite tsar had vainly sought to encroach on this vast wealth; only in the eighteenth century did secular rulers first plunder and eventually sequester Church lands and peasants.[11] The government was interested not only in Church property but also in its service people. "Looking at the clerical ranks," Peter saw "much disorder and great poverty," and his successors also complained, often and bitterly, that "many clergy lead a life unbecoming their rank, quarrelling, fighting, and drinking without measure," even tending to "lead the simple people astray" from the true Christian path.[12] Whether through Petrine regulation or Catherinian "enlightened absolutism," the state expected more effective service from the clergy, although the definition of that service would change considerably. For the first time the parish priest, even in the most remote village, stood in the shadow of secular authority.

Yet the triumph of secular absolutism did not mean a sudden eclipse of Church authority and influence. To the contrary, precisely because secular absolutism was evolving, it still allowed for dynamic change in Church-state relations. Whatever the harsh rhetoric of a Petrine law or the soothing rationalization of a Catherinian manifesto, the actual

relationship between Church and state changed significantly throughout the eighteenth century and indeed even into the nineteenth. It is
quite misleading to argue, as have both Soviet and Western historians,
that the Church's influence suddenly ended in 1721 with the Synodal
reform, a magic Petrine act that made the Church "an integral part of
the Russian state structure and administration."[13] Peter's reform did
settle any doubts about the sovereign's authority over the Church, if
indeed the strangling of Filipp in 1569 or removal of Nikon in 1667
had left any doubts. But it did not define the state's relationship to the
Church. Instead, it created two realms, the Synodal (or ecclesiastical)
command (Sinodal'naia or dukhovnaia kommanda) and the secular
command (svetskaia kommanda); the Synod and Senate were at the
center, the bishop and governor in the provinces. The unifying element was the sovereign's person; in the end he resolved their disputes
and periodically altered their relative status. For lack of interest or
time, the civil government accorded routine operational autonomy
to the Church; when state and Church interests diverged, however,
that parallelism gave rise to direct conflict and competition. In the
eighteenth century this system of Church-state relations begot intense
controversy over such issues as property, clerical status, poll taxes,
and religious tolerance; in the nineteenth it enabled the Church to reestablish its authority such that even a Pobedonostsev could not claim
the authority of a Protasov.[14]

This evolution of political secularity and Church-state relations was
particularly evident in the case of the parish clergy, as the government
began to redefine their place in society. At stake were essentially three
issues. The first was the clergy's juridical status: as the state enlarged
its authority over the Church, how was it to define the status of the
clergy in civil law? A second issue was the proper service for the parish
clergy: as the state transformed society into service sosloviia, how did
it define the appropriate obligations of the clergy and how did this definition change from Peter's Polizeistaat to Catherine's enlightened absolutism? A third question concerned the status of the whole clerical
soslovie, not just the priests and churchmen, but their numerous and
sundry dependents: how did the state seek to marshal them into "useful" state service? An analysis of these questions will enable us to assess data on political disaffection among the clergy and to evaluate
more broadly the impact of state policies on the burgeoning crisis of
the clergy.

Juridical Status: Old and New Elements

Before the Church reforms of Peter the Great, the parish clergy enjoyed a privileged juridical status: they were under Church, not state,

jurisdiction. Despite occasional exceptions, the priest served only the Church, which "in old Russia was a unique institution, juridically independent from state authority."[15] As a result, the clergy were outside of civil law; exempt from state service and taxation, they were the subjects of the "ecclesiastical government."[16] In the eighteenth century, however, as the secular state intervened in Church affairs and adopted measures directly concerning the parish clergy, it *volens-nolens* had to define their legal status. The government implicitly altered the clergy's status as it resolved three issues: the clergy's corporate status, their composition and structure, and their special judicial privileges. All three issues were of considerable moment, determining not only the clergy's legal status but their social prestige as well.

THE CLERGY'S CORPORATE STATUS

How did the state define the clergy's corporate status? What did the group represent in eighteenth-century law? The historical literature routinely describes the clergy as simply another soslovie, unqualifiedly applying the term *dukhovnoe soslovie* (clerical soslovie) to the eighteenth-century clergy.[17] But to use such terminology for the eighteenth century, at least without qualification, is highly anachronistic. The term soslovie acquired currency only in late nineteenth-century historiography, and even the Digest of Russian Laws of 1835 used the term sparingly and in different senses.[18] In the eighteenth century the term was not used in the sense of social estate but only to describe an assembly, group, or even whole population.[19] To my knowledge the term *dukhovnoe soslovie* was not used in any eighteenth-century documents.

Instead, government legislation referred to the clergy as the clerical rank (*dukhovnyi chin*), or simply cited the clergy (*dukhovenstvo*) or a specific rank, such as priest. Most often, particularly in general formulations, it used *chin* (rank), which was the standard Muscovite term for the group.[20] That Peter preserved this traditional terminology is somewhat surprising, for the Petrine state was highly innovative in legal language and borrowed heavily from foreign sources, especially the German.[21] More important, the government treated the clergy as a group of servicemen in the Synodal command, men occupying a *chin*; it did not address the clergy as a collective social group, only as a corps of ecclesiastical officers bearing a special *chin*. Nor did the government even try to integrate this traditional clerical *chin* into its new hierarchy for *chiny*, the Petrine Table of Ranks; significantly, as it adapted European models for the new table, it deliberately omitted sections that defined the equivalent ranks for bishops and priests.[22] In a word, the government adhered to the traditional Muscovite conception of the clergy as a *chin* and did not try to formulate social policy on the clergy as a social estate. Hence it made no attempt to establish corporate institutions for the clergy in the late eighteenth century, as was done for the nobility and townspeople.

It is, to say the least, a striking anomaly that the secular state was so cautiously traditional in adhering to this conception of the clergy as a *chin*. It did so for a number of reasons. First, the state claimed ultimate authority over the Church and clergy, but as a practical matter it left routine administration to the Church. Unless government interests were at stake, civil authorities ordinarily accepted the terminology and views contained in Synodal decisions and tended to absorb, quite uncritically, the traditional ecclesiastical language and concepts of the Church.[23] Nor indeed was it an easy matter for laymen to comprehend the arcane intricacies of the Synodal command; as Ia. P. Shakhovskoi (one of the more conscientious lay over-procurators of the Synod) recalled, he had to study long and hard to learn the special rules governing the Church.[24] Furthermore, while Peter felt secure enough to order changes and explicitly argue their rationality, his successors deliberately sought to avoid leaving the impression of change, routinely avowing that their new laws only reaffirmed a decree of "our father, Peter the Great," even when such was far from the case.[25] Most important, the state found it exceedingly convenient to retain the traditional conception of clerical *chin*, for such a view limited ecclesiastical privilege to those holding clerical ranks, not their multitudinous dependents. In practice, to be sure, a cleric's son was a subject in the Synodal command; the government detained runaway sons and promptly returned them to the appropriate Church authorities.[26] Yet the *chin* provided a useful distinction between the clergy and the legally undefined clerical soslovie. It was precisely this distinction that enabled the state, without formally violating clerical privilege, to draft the clergy's sons into the army or to assign them to the civil service.

The conception of *chin* also caused the peculiar juridical isolation of the clergy, as the state separated them from lay society. The government implicitly posited this unique status in its manifestoes, which juxtaposed civil and clerical ranks as distinct service orders. Such a distinction was consistent with the categories of secular (*svetskaia*) and Synodal commands, to which each rank belonged.[27] But, more broadly, the distinction symbolized the clergy's exclusion from the ranks of civil society. This juridical apartness, moreover, explains partly why the secular clergy were excluded from the Legislative Commission of 1767-68, which Catherine II had convoked to compose a new law code for the empire. While she invited most social groups (not only nobles and townspeople, but even state peasants and certain

minorities) to send delegates, two important groups were not represented—the parish clergy and the landlords' serfs.[28] Catherine simply
regarded the clergy as a staff of ecclesiastical officers, not a true soslovie; accordingly, she saw no reason to invite them to a commission
that would write a civil law code for secular society.[29] A subcommittee
on the "middle social categories" (srednii rod gosudarstvennykh zhite-
lei) proposed to include the urban parish clergy in this middle group of
laity. The Synod objected sharply to the idea of dividing the clergy
and insisted that the clergy should have a separate status equal to that
accorded the nobility.[30] In the end nothing came of these debates, for
the commission was abandoned, its work incomplete. In the 1780s
William Tooke perceptively observed the clergy's peculiar outcast status: "The clergy are frequently comprehended in the middle order, yet
without impropriety we may assign them, as in several other king-
doms, to a distinct class, being numerous and respectable, and having
certain privileges of its own; besides, as it is sometimes particularly
mentioned in manifestos and in several places, it is distinct from other
classes."[31]

The government also set the clergy apart in more concrete ways as
well, denying them the special privileges of the nobility and townspeople. As the nobility in the eighteenth century gradually won a monopoly on serf ownership, all other groups, including the clergy, were excluded from that distinctive privilege of the aristocracy. Apart from
court archpriests like Dubianskii (who owned eight thousand serfs),
the parish clergy rarely owned populated estates, though some did
have houseservants.[32] The only exception, a temporary one that soon
fell victim to nobles' interests, occurred in the 1720s, when excess
churchmen and clerical youths were ascribed by the poll-tax registry
to regular clergy, who were responsible for their poll taxes and were
implicitly their "owners." Although that proprietary right was circumscribed—the priest could not sell these people to landlords as serfs
—his right to own poll-tax people was tacitly recognized.[33] But in 1745
the Senate closed this gap, declaring that only the parish church—not
parish clergy—could own poll-tax registrants.[34] The Synod sought to
amend this discrimination in 1767, proposing that the clergy share the
noble privilege of owning serfs; the suggestion was ignored.[35] Although priests still had houseservants and a few even bought populated estates in the name of a local nobleman,[36] the government had
plainly set the clergy apart from the nobility—and had definitely low-
ered their status.

The government also excluded the clergy from engaging in business
and trade. The Law Code of 1649 had first prohibited such activities
by the clergy, as townspeople and merchants tried to establish a mo-

nopoly over commerce.[37] The Synod upheld such government prohibitions "in order to ensure that [the clergy] not enter into activities unbecoming their rank (and thereby forfeit due respect) and to ensure that they not be subjected to secular justice."[38] Thus it strictly forbade the clergy to engage in business or make loans, threatening to defrock violators. The bishops enforced the rules just as zealously as the Synod; the bishop of Moscow, for example, forbade his clergy to trade and punished one priest caught dealing in timber.[39] Similarly, the bishop of Suzdal began an investigation of a sacristan in Iur'ev-Pol'skii uezd in 1769, when a number of promissory notes were discovered in his possession.[40] A clerical instruction manual reiterated that it was inappropriate for the clergy to "engage in commerce or in various enterprises for profit."[41] The sentiments against clerical involvement in trade were resilient; not until the 1860s would priests and even some bishops urge a repeal of this legislation.

COMPOSITION OF THE CLERGY

Although the state adhered to traditional language and conceptions of the clerical *chin*, it could not avoid the practical problem of determining which subcategories genuinely belonged to that status. The basic issue was whether the parish clergy included only ordained clerics or also the churchmen. The Church itself, both in Muscovy and in the eighteenth century, distinguished between the ordained clergy and churchmen because of the special spiritual status of the ordained clergy: unlike the churchman, the priest received holy ordination and had the power to administer the sacraments. The Church consequently gave the priest supervisory powers over the churchman and accorded the priest other marks of preferential treatment: the priest ordinarily received twice the income of a churchman and, for the same crime, suffered less severe punishment.[42] Nevertheless, the Church regarded the churchmen as part of the parish clergy, required them to obtain episcopal confirmation, and exacted fees and service from them as regular church servitors. The state had an even more ambiguous policy. Some churchmen, as the young sons of priests, enjoyed full clerical privilege, including exemption from state service and taxes. Yet many others, quite likely of nonclerical origin, were inscribed in the state tax registries alongside peasants and townspeople.[43] In one decree the state allowed only the ordained clergy to own indentured servants, and forbade churchmen to do so.[44] As the Petrine state began to legislate actively on the clergy, it inevitably had to resolve the ambiguity of the churchman's status.

Predictably, the eighteenth-century state was disposed to resolve the question to its own advantage and therefore to require service and taxation from churchmen. Very early in his reign, Peter began to pry churchmen loose from the clerical rank and make them subject to services and taxes imposed upon the common laity. For example, in his famous edict that required his subjects to shave off their beards or pay a stiff fine, Peter specifically exempted the ordained clergy and not churchmen from the law. He also made a basic distinction when he permitted only the ordained clergy, but not churchmen or clerical children, to purchase exemption from military service.[45] Prior to 1719, however, this distinction did not become a critical issue; the taxes were a nuisance, but were unavoidable wartime measures. In any event, there was no longer a patriarch to contest Peter's narrow definition of the clergy.

The question became critically important in 1719-22, when the government established the poll-tax system that had such fundamental significance in freezing Russian social structure.[46] The poll-tax registry enrolled individual male townsmen and peasants, permanently consigning them to townsman or peasant status; only the nobility and clergy (as traditionally tax-exempt groups) were freed from this new tax on commoners. But now that the state began to make a systematic individual headcount, it had to determine who belonged to the clergy.

At first the state exempted only the ordained clergy, not the churchmen or the clergy's sons; as Peter decreed in January 1720, the registry must include "churchmen but not priests and deacons," a policy upheld in subsequent decrees.[47] In 1721 the Senate reaffirmed that ordained clergy were exempt from the poll tax, but "other church servicemen [churchmen] are not to be removed from the poll-tax registry and are to pay the poll tax along with other registrants."[48]

The Synod vigorously opposed the government's policy and sought to have churchmen as well as priests exempted from the poll tax. The Synod informed the Senate that it energetically protested against the Senate's decision to place churchmen on the poll-tax rolls and declared that "the Holy Governing Synod must, as its position requires, be concerned about the churchmen under its jurisdiction." It argued that the churchmen were simply too poor to pay the poll tax: unlike other poll-tax registrants, they had little land and no enterprises, and thus no means for paying the poll tax. If the tax was not lifted, the Synod warned, it would ruin the churchmen currently serving and in the future it would be impossible to find people willing to become churchmen. Worse still, churchmen were the main source of ordained clergy, and therefore shortages of churchmen would inevitably cause vacancies in the ranks of priests and deacons, thus depriving parishioners of Holy Services and such crucial sacraments as baptism and extreme unction. In November 1721 the Synod again raised the issue, reiterating its request that churchmen be removed from the poll-tax registry. Eventually the Synod's view prevailed, and in a decree of 24 February 1722 Peter agreed to exempt the churchmen from the poll tax. The Synod had won a major victory, and subsequently it cited this precedent to free churchmen from other taxes.[49]

Nevertheless, the state continued to regard the two groups differently, and the churchmen remained vulnerable to state demands. For example, it later became a major issue whether poll-tax registrants could enter the clergy. Starting in the 1740s, the government made a revealing distinction between the two groups: it overlooked the ordained clergy who had come from the poll-tax population (even if they had entered the clergy illegally), but demanded that churchmen return to the poll-tax rolls even though they had been formally installed.[50] Similarly, when the state conducted its devastating conscriptions of "excess clerics," it drafted only churchmen and clerical children, not ordained clergy. The government extended this policy to judicial rights, declaring in 1746 that "churchmen, who do not have priestly or monastic *chin*, are to be investigated like common people."[51] Thus, however great the religious distinction between priest and churchman, the social breach widened as a result of government policy. Little wonder that seminarians scorned appointment as churchmen, and that bishops punished poor students by installing them as churchmen "without hope of attaining the rank of ordained clergy."

JUDICIAL PRIVILEGE

At first glance Peter seems to have crudely shattered the clergy's traditional status in the courts. In medieval Russia the clergy were subject exclusively to ecclesiastical courts, except for murder and robbery.[52] If a cleric committed a spiritual misdeed or came into conflict with a layman, he was subject to investigation by ecclesiastical officials only. Initially, Peter did indeed overturn this privilege, subjecting the clergy to lay courts and justice. Unwilling to appoint a new patriarch after Adrian's death in 1700, Peter closed some patriarchal chancelleries and in the next year assigned broad powers to the Chancellery for Monastery Affairs (*Monastyrskii prikaz*), which was under a lay administrator. During the next two decades, according to Church sources, lay officials put the clergy under their jurisdiction, subjecting the defenseless clerics to great harm and abuse.[53]

It is significant that once Peter had deliberately reorganized the Church, he largely restored the clergy's former judicial privilege. Shortly after the Synod opened in 1721, it petitioned the tsar to reestablish the clergy's traditional status: suspected clergy should be investigated only by Church officials, and only after judged guilty should they be defrocked and delivered to civil authorities for punishment. Peter approved the Synod's request but reserved jurisdiction to the government for cases involving "serious matters of state," a reflection of his abiding concern about political disaffection among the clergy.[54] While the caveat on political crimes is a revealing hint of the mounting political tensions, the most remarkable feature of the decree was Peter's decision not to integrate ecclesiastical and secular justice into a single, coherent system. One factor behind his decision was the concept of *chin*: the clerical ranks were not a social group but a service order subject to a special combination of canon law and state legislation, from the *Kormchaia kniga* to the Ecclesiastical Regulation. Peter's concession to the Synod was consistent with his view of the Synodal command, an ecclesiastical administration (*vedomstvo*) best suited to discipline its subordinates.

The Petrine decree, however, proved unworkable in practice. Under Peter's formula, accused clergy were first subject to investigation and judgment by the Church, whether the case was a civil or criminal matter; only when clearly implicated were they to be tried in the lay courts. Impatient state officials, however, often did not heed such legal niceties. Either from zeal or simple disrespect for Church authority, their first impulse was to arrest a suspected priest and, in generous doses, apply torture until he confessed. Few waited for an ecclesiastical investigation; if influential nobles or merchants were involved, the lay officials were especially inclined to ignore clerical privilege. The Synod, which received a steady flow of complaints about violations, made this dismal assessment: "In the *gubernii* and *provintsii* many officials commit abuses and cause hardships for ecclesiastical subjects, i.e., clergy. Specifically, they take priests, deacons, and churchmen—not only in important but also in petty civil suits—into state chancelleries, keep them there under arrest for long periods of time, and cause them great losses and harm." Expressing outrage, the Synod demanded satisfaction from the Senate and thereafter vigilantly defended the clergy's judicial privileges.[55]

It could not, however, stem the violations. In most cases the state officials failed to consult the local consistory before arresting some clerical miscreant; usually, the issue was not actual abuse but rather a bureaucratic snub. For example, in 1730-31 a government official in Riazan seized two priests, interrogated them, and kept them under arrest without consulting the local bishop. Convinced of their guilt, the official requested that the bishop defrock them but received a curt refusal—on the grounds that the ecclesiastical office should have conducted the investigation.[56] But, as ecclesiastical sources are inclined to emphasize, some officials did subject the clergy to physical abuse and mistreatment. A flurry of such cases occurred in the late 1750s, when the government tightened controls on the sale of liquor; state officials, who suspected clergy of bootlegging, flagrantly disregarded the clergy's judicial privilege. Lay officials raided the house of a priest in Pereslavl-Zalesskii, for instance, but found nothing; nevertheless, they beat the cleric savagely, presumably hoping for a confession, and eventually carted him off to jail. Though the bishop of Pereslavl was outraged and used every means at his disposal to free the priest, the case dragged on for three years, and the archival record ends with no hint of ecclesiastical victory.[57] Such cases clearly indicate the limits of diocesan power; even an energetic bishop could not defend the parish clergy from local officials.

Alarmed by such flagrant violations, the Synod demanded satisfaction in specific cases and badgered the Senate for an unequivocal confirmation of Peter's decree.[58] Its efforts availed little, however, even in the reign of Elizabeth in the 1740s and 1750s, when the Synod exercised considerable influence at court. To be sure, the Synod obtained edicts confirming the Petrine formula; for example, in 1741 and 1746, the Senate firmly admonished its subordinate officials not to violate the clergy's judicial privilege.[59] But, as the Senate admitted, these decrees had little effect: "Some governors and *voevody* [provincial administrators], in violation of the decree of 15 March 1721, have assumed jurisdiction over the clergy (that is, priests and deacons)."[60] Foreshadowing later legislation, Elizabeth actually curtailed the clergy's privilege: in civil and criminal cases, the clergy were to be tried in joint lay-ecclesiastical courts in the presence of special church deputies (*deputaty*).[61]

Besides illegal violations, the clergy's formal privilege was jeopardized by Peter's caveat, the special provision on "serious affairs of state." That Peter assigned jurisdiction in such cases to the state and not the Church was understandable; it resulted from the experience with unruly patriarchs in the seventeenth century and the clergy's complicity in conspiracies involving the tsar's disloyal son. However necessary for political security, this provision gave the organs of political police (the *Preobrazhenskii prikaz* and later the *Tainaia kantseliariia* or Secret Chancellery) unlimited authority over the clergy. Even the Synod did not seek to protect clergy suspected of political crimes; it summarily defrocked them, without trying to ascertain the circumstances of the case.[62] The Synod did refuse to defrock priests in the "bloody chambers" of the Secret Chancellery, but it obediently did so in its own offices.[63] The diocesan authorities were equally docile. In a typical case in 1746, the Secret Chancellery ordered a consistory to arrest and deliver a priest for unspecified reasons, and the office immediately complied.[64] Regardless of their feelings, the Church authorities had no legal justification to resist and quite rightly feared provoking suspicion.

The proviso on political crimes was important not because the clergy was a hotbed of political disaffection (though there was some of that), but because clerics frequently made false declarations concerning the "Sovereign's word and deed" (slovo i delo gosudarevo). The concept of word and deed, which originated in the Law Code of 1649, required subjects to inform the government of any conspiracies or impending revolts. After declaring word and deed, the informer was to be delivered promptly to the central authorities; no one could detain or interrogate him. Not surprisingly, some of the tsar's faithful subjects found this a marvelous conduit to the throne for "true justice." Local authorities sometimes found themselves paralyzed because of false declarations of word and deed by prisoners and criminals who knew of no conspiracy but simply hoped to halt torturous interrogations or to secure a new trial.[65]

The parish clergy also made liberal use of word and deed and frequently found themselves en route to the Secret Chancellery. Only rarely did they actually have information even remotely resembling a true political crime; in most cases, they were simply trying to escape from the hands of local officials. Typical was the case of a deacon, Evfimii, in Riazan uezd. "Unable to tolerate the beatings" of tax collectors, he put an end to the abuse by declaring word and deed, even though he knew of no political conspiracy.[66] Cases of this type began to multiply during the reign of Peter the Great and then increased still more sharply in the 1730s, when the government was especially distrustful of the clergy. To halt false declarations, the government threatened offenders with flogging and defrocking.[67] After 1740 the frequency of such cases gradually declined, partly because clerics had been duly chastised and feared the political police, partly because Elizabeth's government was less credulous. The dreaded institution even became a fit subject for clerical wit, as one priest testified: "I dropped in at a tavern in Pereslavl and saw peasants [of my parish] drinking wine. I walked up to them and shouted "Word and deed of the Sovereign!" Terrified [of becoming involved in an investigation], they fled in all directions, and I drank up the wine they had left."[68] A few foolish clerics still resorted in desperation to word and deed for temporary relief, but such cases were rare.[69] By the time Peter III abolished the Secret Chancellery and word and deed in 1762, the institution had already largely expired.[70]

It was left to Catherine's government to resolve the problems created by Peter's definition of clerical privilege. The government left purely ecclesiastical questions (such as clerical discipline and the sacrament of marriage) to Church authorities, but it did seek to improve the system of investigating clergy accused in civil or criminal cases. Determined to resolve the friction, in 1766 the government clarified the rules governing joint civil-ecclesiastical trials of suspected clergy and later improved the institution of ecclesiastical deputies to expedite judicial investigation.[71] In 1791 Catherine's government established a still more elaborate network of ecclesiastical deputies, who could be readily summoned for prompt investigation.[72] Thus, though the clergy still formally belonged to the Synodal command, they were now held liable before government courts in civil or criminal matters; whether a priest had committed a crime or was sued, he could not depend upon the bishop for protection. Although the Synod conferred upon the ordained clergy an important new privilege, that of exemption from corporal punishment, the empress took away the ecclesiastical shield that had traditionally safeguarded their interests.[73]

Thus the government gradually but inexorably modified the clergy's status, a process that Peter began and Catherine completed. Formally, the government still recognized the clergy's medieval status; given the structure of Church-state relations (a "Synodal command" hitched alongside a "secular command," both under the sovereign's whip), it was quite reasonable for the state to preserve the clergy's formal subordination to the Church. However, the government did not shrink from self-serving innovations, such as its distinction between ordained clergy and churchmen and its de facto integration of parish clergy into the regular system of justice.

Serving the Secular State: Priest and Churchman

In its quest for power the Petrine state demanded service from all social groups, a traditional obligation in Muscovy now inflated by new theories of absolutism and cameralism. Service (*sluzhba*) was indeed one of Peter's favorite words, appearing often in his laws and private correspondence and figuring prominently in his own self-image and behavior.[74] His government applied this principle of universal service to an unprecedented degree, requiring that all—nobles, townspeople, peasants, and clergy—render service appropriate to their station and rank. Thus the nobility was to provide personnel for staffing the military and civil service; the urban population was to develop trade and manage economic administration; and the common peasantry was to provide the manpower and material support for the state and its servitors. After 1750 the conception of service evolved in new directions, although the essential principle of service held fast. Partly because Peter's coerced service begot more malfeasance and service evaders (the famous *netchiki* of the nobility, though all groups had their equivalent) than effective service, partly because the government realized the need for more initiative and diversity in service, the state significantly altered the Petrine system. It redefined and reordered the service requirements of nobles, townspeople, and clergy; it feared only to tamper with the explosive, integral institution of serfdom.

PETRINE SERVICE

In his zeal to build a dynamic state powered by universal service, Peter eliminated the traditional exemption of the clergy from service. He made the clergy liable to taxes and general civic obligations and also assigned some special service and political duties. At no other period in Imperial Russia would the scope of the clergy's secular service be so sweeping.

That Peter imposed tax obligations upon the parish clergy was hardly surprising. His reign, his reforms, were in large part a desperate search for new revenues, as the tsar tapped every imaginable resource to finance his new administration, imperial grandeur, and especially the gargantuan war machine.[75] Most critical were the early years of the great Northern War, when the tsar repeatedly raided ecclesiastical coffers, violating clerical privilege. This privilege, to be sure, was not unlimited even in the seventeenth century; clerics as individuals were free from state taxes, but they did pay taxes on parish land allotted for their support.[76] In any event, Peter did not ponder precedents but between 1705 and 1710 simply decreed a host of new taxes on the clergy. His officials began to collect taxes on bathhouses, on exemption from military service, for dragoon horses, and for military chaplains.[77]

These new taxes caused severe hardship for the clergy, as for much of the population. In 1713-14 the clerical elders of Moscow petitioned the tsar to lighten the parish clergy's tax burden, claiming that it was ruining them.[78] When the Northern War ended in 1721, most clergy expected an end to the extraordinary taxation and, emboldened by the aggressive clericalism of the new Synod, flooded St. Petersburg with collective petitions asking that the taxes be annulled.[79] Whether from sheer economic exhaustion or in anticipation of Synodal success, the clergy virtually ceased paying the taxes. Colossal arrears quickly accumulated. For the years 1720-23 the parish clergy paid only 7 percent of the levy due for dragoon horses.[80] Urging that the tax be abolished, the Synodal Treasury offered a dreary picture of clerical distress: "Formal replies and petitions have been submitted from many towns and ecclesiastical districts, declaring that [the clergy] have nothing with which to pay the dragoon-horse levies because of their impoverishment and a poor harvest."[81] Even allowing for the stereotyped hyperbole of official reports, it is clear that government taxation had ravaged the clergy as severely as the rest of the population.[82] The foreigner Weber rightly observed that "the white clergy, which usually elicit in Russia less respect than people of other groups, are burdened with a greater tax (for their income) than other citizens."[83]

In addition to economic hardship, the new taxation also exposed the clergy to humiliating abuse by government tax collectors: *pravezh'*, the violence and beatings that zealous officials routinely applied in order to collect unpaid taxes. The bishop of Rostov complained to Peter that "the rural clergy are worse off than beggars, because many are subjected to the beatings of tax collectors and cannot pay."[84] Such reports were ubiquitous in the 1720s and the Synod complained to the state in 1728: "Mercilessly collecting the bathhouse tax in accordance with the registry, the lay commanders detain the clergy in prison and subject them to *pravezh'* and, as a result, not only parish churches but even the cathedrals are left without services and parishioners are dying without last rites."[85] The Synod might have added that such beatings did little to increase public respect for the clergy.

Besides imposing taxation, Peter made the clergy (especially those in the towns) liable for civic duties common to the laity. Above all, this meant that they had to share the onerous burdens of "quartering" and "police duties." Peter had ordered that soldiers be billeted in private residences, with no stipulation of clerical exemption; since many urban clergy owned their own homes, they too had to house soldiers. The city authorities also compelled parish clergy to render common police duties, such as serving as guard at the city jail and working in fire brigades. The clergy protested against the new impositions, arguing that they had to perform daily liturgies and constantly be available to administer such important sacraments as baptism and extreme unction. Despite protests by the clergy and Synod, city authorities summarily seized clerics and forced them to serve.[86]

Most important, Peter introduced a new category of purely secular service obligations, assigning the clergy various administrative, police, and political duties. This was a revolutionary change, emulating Peter's German and Swedish models. Even the Law Code of 1649, which attempted to violate the extra-governmental status of the clergy, gave a purely religious formulation of the priest's role.[87] The clergy in Muscovy owed service only to the Church; Peter's innovation was to draw the clerical *chin* into the service of his secular state. His reasons for doing so were compelling: his bureaucratic machinery was inadequate, especially in the provinces. To bridge the chasm between imperial wish and actual implementation, Peter turned to the clergy, that *chin* closest to the rural population and one that had traditionally handled parish business. Peter deliberately chose not to incorporate the parish as an administrative unit in the secular state, specifically omitting it from the Swedish model he used in his provincial reforms of 1718. Yet he was obliged to use the clergy as an auxiliary to his secular administration, just as in Sweden the priest held major responsibilities for tax collection and recruitment.[88]

Peter thus began to assign the clergy secular duties, the most spectacular of which was the obligation to violate the confidence of confession. According to a decree of 1722, priests were to inform civil authorities of any "ill-intentioned" plots revealed during confession. Peter had first used this device during the Bulavin revolt of 1707-08 but did not develop the idea until the conclusion of the Northern War.[89] The first redaction of the 1722 decree argued that to reveal "evil intentions" was not a sin but a moral obligation for priests, because much harm could result if such intentions were not reported. The draft referred explicitly to the cases of Peter's son and an outspoken critic, Grigorii Talitskii; both had revealed their "evil thoughts" to their confessors and deserved immediate exposure. The decree promised that a priest would be rewarded for a true report, but a cleric who remained silent would suffer "loss of honor, life, and rank." This first redaction was very brief, with few references to the Scriptures or canon law; it was a secular law, designed to satisfy the needs of the state.[90] The final published decree, however, added the necessary scriptural fixtures, which were intended to persuade the clergy that canon law did not forbid them to violate confession. The clergy's duty was explained in prolix detail: "If anyone in confession tells his spiritual father something that is not yet committed, but still planned (thievery, or particularly, treason or revolt against the Autocrat or Government, or evil intentions against the honor or health of the Autocrat or his family)," then the priest must report it immediately or risk merciless punishment.[91] This new duty was incorporated into the "Supplement to the Ecclesiastical Regulation."[92]

The state reinforced the political bonds between cleric and state by requiring the clergy to take a loyalty oath at ordination. The new oath was radically different from the one customarily given to clergy in the seventeenth century. The earlier oath bound a cleric to defend the Church and to pronounce anathema on the Old Belief, but it contained no declaration of political loyalty to the tsar.[93] Peter ordered the appropriate changes. The new oath of 1722 was identical to that given the civil officers (grazhdanskie chiny) and required a priest to swear the following:

What I should and by duty wish, and in every possible way will try to do is: to be a true, good and obedient servant (rab) and subject of my natural and true Autocrat, the most-powerful Peter the Great,

Emperor and Autocrat, etc. . . . . and Her Majesty, Most-Merciful Empress Catherine Alekseevna; to protect, defend, uphold all the rights and prerogatives and privileges belonging to His Majesty's power and authority, and not to spare my life in circumstances requiring it; and, to try to help in all which may concern His Majesty's true service and usefulness to the state and Church, with all possible diligence and zeal.[94]

And, in another prolix passage of the oath, the priest pledged himself to inform the authorities of anything important to the state. This oath was repeated verbatim for subsequent rulers; only the name of the sovereign was changed.[95]

Peter's government also ascribed entirely new administrative duties to the clergy. It obliged them to expose peasants who had evaded the poll-tax registry and who thus deprived the state of badly needed revenues. In May 1721 the Synod ordered priests to inform on poll-tax evaders and warned that if they failed to do so they would be "deprived of their rank, position, and property and be given merciless corporal punishment and enslaved in hard labor." The Synod promised to reward clergy who denounced colleagues for failing to report unregistered peasants: following a policy standard in Petrine Russia, it ordered that the property and position of the guilty cleric be given to the informer.[96] In 1722 Peter ordered the Church to defrock such guilty clerics and to send them to the secular command for punishment.[97] Disturbed by continuing reports that "there are many cases of concealment and failure to inform," the Senate requested the Synod to appoint special deputies to investigate the ubiquitous nonfeasance.[98]

Peter made the clergy responsible for compiling parish registers (*metricheskie knigi*). He first imposed the requirement in 1702 but did not really enforce it until the 1720s.[99] A decree of 1723 ordered priests to collect the data and submit annual reports to diocesan authorities, who were then to send abstracts of the data to the Holy Synod.[100] In the cases of priests who failed to compile the records, authorities meted out severe punishment, sometimes even exceeding that required by law. While the decree prescribed a fine, ecclesiastical authorities in Moscow ordered: "To instill fear in others so that they will not submit late reports, give them a merciless beating with the lash before a gathering of elders and priests of important churches."[101] The Synod, while strictly enforcing the original law, resisted state efforts to expand this administrative burden. It rebuffed, for example, a request by the Office of the Heraldmaster in 1725 for special supplementary reports on the gentry, and even objected to the proposal of the powerful courtier Menshikov in 1726 that the clergy make multiple copies of their reports.[102] Menshikov soon fell from grace and his proposal was forgotten; however, the Synod did not succeed in annulling the basic duty to prepare the records.

Peter's government also required the clergy to compile lists of Old Believers and anyone who missed confession or Communion without good cause. The duty to be on guard against Old Believers was not new; both the seventeenth-century oath for clergy and Patriarch Adrian's "Instructions for Clerical Elders" in 1697 obliged parish clergy to report Old Believers and nonconfessors.[103] Although Peter at first seemed ready to grant limited tolerance for the Old Believers, his views changed as the Old Belief acquired tones of political opposition. Probably the most explosive part of his policy was the "double poll tax on Old Believers," a requirement that they be inscribed in the poll-tax registry and pay twice the poll tax of other subjects. Since the clergy knew best who the schismatics were, Peter obliged them to submit lists of Old Believers in their parishes and threatened harsh punishment for malfeasance: five rubles for the first offense, ten rubles for the second, fifteen for the third, and defrocking for a fourth infraction.[104] No doubt to the government's surprise, this measure provoked fanatical opposition among the Old Believers: believing that inscription of their names in the poll-tax registry meant their personal enlistment in the service of Antichrist, they vigorously opposed demands that they register.[105] The parish clergy were of course caught in the middle of this conflict; many clergy, either fearful of parish retribution or because of a handsome bribe, omitted vast numbers of Old Believers from the lists. Eager to enforce this Petrine decree, the Synod repeatedly admonished priests to obey and, as usual, promised that any churchman who exposed a negligent priest would receive the latter's position.[106]

Peter the Great also utilized the clergy as a communication link to the illiterate population. To publicize new laws, the government often required the clergy to read them aloud to the parishioners during Sunday church services. All were expected to attend church and thus the clergy seemed to be a convenient means for publicizing decrees even in the most remote corners of the empire. But, as Peter later admitted, this practice only tended to encourage absenteeism from church:

Because there are such bad and unreliable people who have no conscience whatsoever and wish not to hear what is decreed to them by God and earthly authority, those places where the word of God and the decrees of the Autocrat are proclaimed are repugnant to them. Therefore, not only on weekdays but also on the Lord's Day, they stay away from church in order not to hear what is read against their consciences. Therefore, catch and investigate all those who, on Sundays and holidays, wander about during Divine Service (unless they do so because of extreme and absolute necessity) or do not go to services to hear the Word of God and Edicts, which are made known in churches on those days.[107]

The absenteeism notwithstanding, the government continued to publicize its decrees through the Church.[108] And, as in the past, the parish clergy still served as local notaries, empowered to compose and sign legal documents on behalf of the illiterate peasants, an authority recognized both by the state and by landlords.[109]

Thus Peter's service state spared none: the clergy, like the tsar himself, were expected to serve the new state.

Service Redefined

After Peter's death in 1725 the government gradually reduced this heavy load of service obligations, and by 1760 had largely freed the clergy from the yoke of Petrine service. To be sure, they still maintained parish registers, reported Old Believers, and took political oaths; yet even these duties had lost most of their former meaning for the state. By 1760 a rural priest old enough to recall Peter's long inventory of duties must have felt virtually emancipated from state service. He now paid no personal taxes, performed no civic duties, and busied himself only in the field and at the altar.

This "emancipation" from service did not derive from a single manifesto but rather was the result of gradual attrition. To some degree it was the consequence of the clergy's poor performance, which indeed caused more problems than it solved. Many tasks they performed so unreliably that the results were worthless; their reports on Old Believers, for instance, were notoriously inaccurate, as bribes and threats caused priests to overlook vast numbers of schismatics.[110] Worse still, from the government's perspective, the clergy used their administrative powers to wreak positive harm, as some clerics composed petitions for peasants rebelling against their landlords and others aided fugitive serfs by forging passports. Such activities by no means implied a desire to combat the evils of serfdom; typical was the case of deacon Mikhail Petrov of Rostov, who admitted composing a false passport for a fugitive serf woman, but explained that he did so while drunk and for ten kopecks.[111] By the 1760s the government deliberately eliminated the clergy from such administrative duties, even explicitly forbidding them to prepare collective peasant petitions against landlords.

The clergy also owed their emancipation to the fact that the government no longer needed their services. For one thing, provincial administration had improved greatly, especially after the provincial reforms of 1775, and regular state officials could discharge duties once assigned to the clergy. For example, even though the clergy still maintained the parish registers of births, marriages, and deaths, the government relied not upon them but upon the poll-tax revisions for information; no longer interested in the ecclesiastical records, the state ceased to threaten the clergy with dire consequences for malfeasance. Moreover, the government found a more reliable alternative to the priest for policing the countryside: the noble landlords, who were released from compulsory service in 1762 in order to assume a greater role on their estates. The government formally institutionalized that new role in 1785 in the Manifesto to the Nobility, an act that established a new corporate organization of the nobility closely integrated with local administration.[112]

The clergy's emancipation also derived in large measure from the efforts of the Synod. Perhaps its most striking success was a gradual restoration of the clergy's tax-exempt status, a freedom from the sundry levies imposed by Peter the Great. The Synod waged a protracted, tenacious struggle against the onerous bathhouse tax, arguing that it was "ruinous" and "unfair" for the clergy, and its view finally prevailed when Anna abolished the levy in 1733. By the mid-1730s the clergy had thus recovered their former privilege and, except for a temporary dragoon-horse tax during the Russo-Turkish War of 1736-39, the parish clergy hereafter remained free from direct personal taxation.[113] In purely economic terms, their victory was a hollow one, as the government increasingly shifted to indirect taxation to raise revenues; yet the exemption did remove the stigma of personal taxation and spared the clergy violent *pravezh'* at the hands of government tax collectors.[114] The Synod also fought to free the town clergy from civic duties, arguing that the parishioners were deprived of liturgies and sacraments as priests were marched off to fight fires and guard the town jail.[115]

These changes in the clergy's secular service, moreover, formed part of the broader shift in state policies toward service. The post-Petrine government sought to elicit better service from all sosloviia, and in the clergy's case it did so by gradually redirecting their duties to the Synodal command. To some degree, the government wanted more effective religious service. Its enlightened skepticism and secularity notwithstanding, the government had compelling reasons for wanting better clergy. One was the crisis in state policy toward the Old Believers: after decades of futile repression and waves of self-immolation by the schismatics, from mid-century the government demanded an end to coercion (which was both costly and an administrative headache); it now insisted that the Church win over the Old Believers through moral suasion, not force.[116] From the 1760s government policy was also colored by a growing concern for social stability, particularly after the Pugachev Rebellion of 1773-75. Catherine's government, like succeeding ones, demanded that the parish clergy exercise a beneficent, calming influence on the peasants and dissuade them from revolt.[117]

Still, once the clergy had shed their secular duties, the government had relatively little interest in their service performance. That had a significant implication: precisely because the clergy performed no essential services for the state, the government had little reason to solve their mounting social and economic problems. To be sure, in the eighteenth and nineteenth centuries the government periodically expressed an interest in the clerical question—usually because of sudden panic over a recent upsurge in peasant disorders or political disaffection among non-Orthodox segments of the population.[118] But in the end the government backed away from fundamental reform: the clergy were too tangential, too superfluous to justify the high economic costs of reform. Rather than solve the clerical question, the state tried to limit the number of "unproductive clerics" and to rechannel their progeny into other social roles.

Serving the Secular State: The Clerical Soslovie

Besides assigning new service roles to the priest, the Petrine state also found ways to redirect the entire clerical soslovie toward state interests and needs. The government felt increasingly free to tap the estate to fill its own manpower needs. The state had threatened such action once in the seventeenth century, but only in the eighteenth did it actually dare to remove the unordained males—churchmen and the clergy's sons. Thus, appropriately enough for a secular state, it satisfied its own needs at the expense of the Church, which fiercely resisted the incursions. The government's utilization of the clerical estate took two forms: the recruitment of educated seminarians into the bureaucracy and professions, and the conscription (razbor) of "excess churchmen and clerical children" as soldiers, peasants, and factory workers.

Recruitment of Educated Youths

The government sought to enlist seminarians because of strong and compelling need: it lacked enough educated personnel to staff the growing civil service and new professions. The government of Muscovy had ruled by custom, not active law; it met its modest needs for administrators by drawing upon the petty gentry and the chancellery estate (prikaznoe soslovie).[119] Peter's dynamic state, by contrast, had an insatiable need for trained personnel. Aspiring to regulate virtually every activity, it needed a large, reliable civil service; the provincial reforms of 1718 failed largely because Peter's empire lacked these human resources, particularly at the lower levels. After 1762 the government faced still more serious problems. It needed replacements for the nobility whose large-scale retirement from state service reduced the pool of qualified personnel, and it had to staff the large administration created by the provincial reforms of 1775.[120] In addition, the state sponsored a new complex of cultural and educational institutions, establishing the Academy of Sciences in 1725 and Moscow University in 1755. Though initially obliged to employ foreigners, the government assembled Russian students at both institutions and proceeded to train its own native staff. Lastly, the government sought to create a medical profession in Russia (largely for military needs), and therefore attempted to imitate European medical services and to train a qualified corps of personnel. Again, students were needed. When no other social group proved capable of satisfying these manpower needs, the state turned to its surest source—the educated progeny of the clergy.

Peter the Great began actively enlisting the clergy's sons into government service. He opened government cipher schools to the clergy's children, hoping to draw them into state service; though the Synod eventually closed this gap, the episode clearly revealed Peter's intentions.[121] The tsar even wanted ecclesiastical schools to serve the state, endorsing a secular seminary curriculum that would prepare both clergy and state servitors. Besides learning such typically Petrine favorites as geometry and arithmetic, the seminarians were "to engage in games which, with amusement, afford some instruction: for example, sailing on water in real vessels, making geometrical measurements, constructing regular forts, etc."[122] Peter allowed the nobility to enroll their children in the Moscow Slavonic-Greek-Latin Academy and recruited its students for his administration; in 1716, for example, he requisitioned students to learn oriental languages and serve in the Chancellery of Foreign Affairs.[123] Peter also supported the demands of the medical chancellery, authorizing it to take students from the clerical schools.[124] He even tried to entice ordained clergy to enter state service. Aware that widowed priests often took monastic vows reluctantly (under pressure from the bishop), in 1724 Peter authorized the widowers to defrock themselves voluntarily and become teachers in government or Church schools.[125]

Over the several decades after Peter's death, the government continued to draw modest numbers from the clerical soslovie. To be sure, the number of transfers was still relatively small; a census of state officials in 1755 showed that officials of clerical origin constituted only 3

percent of the central bureaucracy and 6 percent of the provincial.[126]
But even this number was significant, given the small enrollments of
the seminaries at mid-century. To the Church's dismay, the government tended to recruit the best seminarians, those already in the last
classes of the seminary. Even though the seminaries had gradually increased in size, they still had few students in the uppermost courses,
and it was precisely from this prized group that the government
sought recruits.[127] The government wanted seminarians mainly for the
medical corps, a policy that the Synod stubbornly opposed.[128] Less
commonly the government also requisitioned seminarians for the
Academy of Sciences and Moscow University. In this case, perhaps
because the numbers were fewer and the status higher, the Synod
raised no objections and only insisted that the youths receive "decent
apartments" appropriate to their rank.[129] In general, however, the
Church opposed recruitment; it had its own use for the seminarians.

The state increased its demands after the provincial reforms of 1775,
taking large numbers of the valued seminarians. In 1779 Catherine
gave explicit permission for seminarians to transfer into state service,
opening the door for those eager to leave the overpopulated clerical
estate.[130] One observer in Vladimir wrote that "about 1779 there was a
government raid on the seminary, and many students voluntarily became civil servants."[131] A preliminary investigation by the Synod revealed that 1,565 seminarians from eighteen dioceses had transferred
to the civil service, and later data showed still greater losses.[132] When
volunteers were too few, the government unceremoniously requisitioned seminarians; in 1782, for example, the governor-general of
Moscow ordered the local hierarch to send him 150 youths for government offices.[133] By the end of the century, the proportion of clerical
offspring in the bureaucracy had increased dramatically, constituting
up to 14 percent of officials in central agencies. In provincial administration their proportion was still higher; in Vladimir, for example,
they represented from 34 to 43 percent of the officials in some offices.[134]

Catherine's government also drew heavily upon the seminaries to
staff the new professions. It dispatched many seminarians to the Academy of Sciences and Moscow University, where they constituted a
major proportion of the Russian faculty and student body. At Moscow University, for example, if foreigners (who numbered thirty-three)
are excluded, the professors of clerical origin composed almost two
thirds of the faculty (twenty of thirty-one).[135] Like her predecessors,
Catherine supported the endless demands of the medical college for
seminarians and, however stubbornly the Synod tried to resist, it
could not block the steady exodus of upper-class seminarians into the

medical schools.[136] Catherine's government also found the clergy suitable for teaching in the new public schools; when it founded a new system of schools in the 1780s, it immediately requisitioned a contingent of seminarians for training as teachers.[137] Not without cause could a reform commission in 1808 appeal to the government for greater economic support to seminaries by noting the vast contribution the schools had made to the civil service and professions.[138]

In short, the government drew heavily upon the seminaries, a policy that had serious consequences for the Church and its attempts to modernize. To be sure, the requisitions were not quantitatively great; given the size of the overpopulated clerical estate, the numbers taken were relatively small. But the qualitative effect *was* significant, for the state consistently took the most talented, advanced seminarians—precisely those youths in whom the Church had invested its hopes and its scarce resources.

THE CONSCRIPTION (*Razbor*)

Besides taking educated seminarians, the secular state used the clerical soslovie in a second, more barbarous manner: it conscripted "superfluous churchmen and clerical children" into the army and poll-tax population.[139] As it pruned away the excess through periodic conscription, the government used several arguments to justify its radical violation of clerical privilege. It often claimed that such conscriptions were in the best interests of the clergy themselves. To allow multiple clergy at a single, small parish—sometimes two or three priests held positions where one had sufficed earlier—impoverished the whole clergy, for the fixed resources of a parish could stretch only so far.[140] Moreover, argued the government, overpopulation in the clerical estate was a useless burden to society. Characteristic of his service ethic, Peter denounced the superfluous dependents of the clergy "because one cannot count on usefulness to the state but only an increase in thievery from such people, who wander without service."[141] The secular authorities also complained that numerous sons of the clergy, unable to find clerical positions, turned to crime instead. The notion that idle sons of the clergy often became thieves enjoyed considerable vogue: nobles complained of the problem in their instructions to the Legislative Commission of 1767-68. A provincial governor in Iaroslavl casually told a visitor that "for the most part those involved in crime are of the clerical [estate]." Popular proverb seemed to agree—"a priest's son is a thief and his daughter is a . . ."[142] After several sensational cases of marauding clerical gangs, the War College sent this complaint to the Synod in 1765: "The clergy's children have increased significantly at churches and, because they are idle, pay no poll taxes, and are unfit for the clergy (because of their numbers and illiteracy), they are free to occupy themselves with nothing other than brigandage and robbery."[143] Hence the government, while unable to draft priests or deacons (since they had received sacred ordination), had a number of persuasive reasons to conscript superfluous sacristans and the clergy's children.

Peter was the first to conduct such a conscription. During the Northern War he ordered the removal of excess churchmen and sons, caught some unlucky souls, and doubtless drove many others into hiding.[144] But a systematic conscription was not possible until the 1720s, after Peter had fixed the number of allowable clergy at parish churches and after the first poll-tax census (*reviziia*) of 1719-22 provided comprehensive data on the churchmen and clerical children. While exempting ordained clergy and "necessary" churchmen, Peter ordered that excess churchmen and their children be transferred to the poll-tax population of townspeople and peasantry.[145] In the outlying provinces, where government was less efficient and the clergy sparse, Peter obtained meager results; according to data for Velikii Ustiug and Kazan dioceses, no churchmen and only a handful of clerical children were put on the poll-tax rolls.[146] In the central provinces, however, the catch was much better. Although each diocese showed considerable variation from one district to the next, Peter's conscription took approximately 1.6 individuals per church in Rostov diocese and 2.0 per church in Riazan diocese.[147] Measured against roughly comparable data from 1735, those drafted represented about 20 percent of all churchmen and clerical youths in Rostov and 27 percent in Riazan, a sweep of considerable proportions.[148]

After slightly more than a decade of tranquillity, the government ordered a new conscription in 1736. It had two immediate reasons for doing so: a critical shortage of soldiers at the outbreak of the Russo-Turkish War and very strong suspicions about the political reliability of the clergy. Ordering that 7,000 be drafted from the clergy and lay employees of the Church, Anna sought to leave only enough registered churchmen and youths to fill future vacancies, and consigned the surplus "to staff the army and garrisons."[149] Despite Church attempts to impede the conscription, the government carried out the levy and obtained impressive results, even exceeding the original goal of 7,000.[150] As in Peter's case, the rate of conscription varied considerably: from a mere 6 percent of eligible males in Riazan to a more usual rate of 15 to 20 percent elsewhere.[151]

Although Anna's conscription had statistically less effect than Peter's, hers earned unparalleled notoriety among the clergy. For one thing, her government drafted youths into the army instead of merely inscribing them into the poll-tax registry, as Peter's had done. Such military conscription meant not only personal hardship but also social humiliation for the clerical estate, for it leveled the clergy to the status of the townspeople and peasantry who bore the burden—and stigma —of providing army recruits. Moreover, her government was harvesting where Peter had so recently cut a wide swath; to reach the high numerical goals, it had to conduct the draft with inclement harshness. Some officials so far exceeded their instructions that they even failed to leave enough clergy and youths to staff the churches. A priest in Vladimir uezd, for example, complained in 1737 that his only remaining son was drafted and there was no one left to perform the sacristan's duties.[152] The conscription was particularly merciless in Kaluga province, where it touched off a wave of protests from noble landlords as well as clergy, who claimed that the ranks of the clergy were so depleted that church services had come to a halt.[153] Anna's government even took large numbers of seminarians, ordinarily a privileged status; for example, her conscription took 22 percent of the pupils in the Rostov seminary and 29 percent of those in the Suzdal seminary.[154] No wonder that when Elizabeth came to the throne in 1741 she was greeted with such enthusiasm and relief by the clergy, who filled their sermons with encomia for the new sovereign.[155]

Yet even Elizabeth authorized two conscriptions in her reign. The first came during the poll-tax census of 1743-45, but it differed from Anna's in a significant way: her government did not send draftees to the army or peasantry but permitted them to choose a social position in the poll-tax population.[156] Few voluntarily complied, and in 1748 the Senate gave them three months in which to make a choice—or be automatically registered as state peasants.[157] It was, in some respects, a harsh conscription, as many nobles enserfed unwilling youths and state officials expelled from the clergy any churchman who had ever been registered in the poll-tax rolls.[158] Quantitatively, however, Elizabeth's first conscription had little effect, and the government ordered a new levy in 1754. As in the first conscription, nobles eagerly seized vulnerable churchmen and clerical sons, especially to man the new factories on their estates; although the Synod vehemently protested this policy, the Senate staunchly upheld the nobles' interests.[159] But, as in the earlier attempt, the conscription netted relatively few people, largely because of Church opposition: bishops resisted, consistories procrastinated, and the Synod dexterously manipulated data to show vast numbers of clerical vacancies.[160] Hamstrung by diocesan opposition and the Synod's direful warnings of "a cessation of holy services" in the churches, Elizabeth's conscriptions thus achieved little.

After 1762, however, Catherine's enlightened despotism conducted

far more effective conscriptions. Her first attempt in 1766, largely because of Church opposition, was an utter failure, but in 1769 her government ordered that large numbers of clergy be drafted to fight in the
new Russo-Turkish War.[161] This time the state paid no heed to the
Synod's statistics showing 13,000 vacant clerical positions; it instructed
its officials to draft 25 percent of all youths and 50 percent of the excess churchmen (that is, those exceeding the number allowable for a
parish church). To thwart mass evasion by sudden matriculation into
the seminaries, the government exempted only those seminarians who
had been enrolled prior to the publication of the decree. The results
were impressive: almost 9,000 were taken.[162] When the new poll-tax
revision of 1781-83 revealed large numbers of excess clergy, Catherine
ordered a new conscription in 1784. Notwithstanding the Synod's attempt to deflect and restrict the conscription, it proved the most devastating levy of the century. This time the state gave no refuge, ordering local officials to remove *all* excess churchmen and *all* uneducated
youths over age 15.[163] However, in a typically Catherinian hope that
the superfluous youths would pursue professions of greatest utility to
the state, it allowed them to select their new social position. The levy
netted over 32,000 individuals, catching many who had successfully
eluded past conscriptions and fully removing the "superfluous" clergy,
as subsequent reports verified.[164] Yet, because most chose their new
status, their fate was not all that grim; in Moscow province, for example, 28 percent entered the bureaucracy, 18 percent the merchant
class (*kupechestvo*), 49 percent the townspeople ranks (*meshchanstvo*),
and 5 percent became state peasants; none became field serfs, soldiers,
or factory serfs.[165] After war broke out again with Turkey in 1787,
Catherine ordered a new conscription the following year, drafting the
excess individuals "so that they are not left idle and a burden to society."[166] Even though its conscription of 1784 had been highly effective,
the government still managed to seize over 5,000 individuals in the
new draft.[167] By appointing the idle youths to church positions, drafting the excess into the army, and encouraging still others to transfer
voluntarily, Catherine reduced the number of "unappointed clerical
sons" from 105,798 (in 1784) to 67,361 (in 1793).[168]

The final conscription of the century occurred during the reign of
Catherine's son, Paul. Shortly after ascending the throne in 1796, Paul
received a Synodal report showing a large number of unappointed
clerical children, and he took the customary decision, ordering the
Church to fill all vacancies and then hand over the excess to the army
to serve "in defense of the fatherland." It was a rigorous draft, taking
over 12,000 churchmen and clerical youths; it particularly affected the

central dioceses, where disproportionately large numbers were dispatched to the secular command.[169]

Thus the government, while freeing the clergy themselves from secular service, did not remove the harness from the whole soslovie, which throughout the century served as an important reservoir of manpower. It routinely recruited seminarians to staff the bureaucracy and professions, and even significantly increased such levies in the last quarter of the century. At the same time, it tapped the surplus population of the clerical estate through rigorous conscriptions, often consigning them to the army as mere recruits. Both measures wrought considerable harm for the Church: the removal of educated seminarians deprived the Church of its best talent, while conscription eroded clerical status and caused enormous hardship for families where husbands and sons were sent to the army, peasantry, and factories.[170] Rather than devise a means to stabilize the clerical population and systematically shift excess children into other groups, the government relied on sporadic raids, which often proved very effective, especially toward the end of the century. Indeed, precisely because the conscription yielded such benefits to the state, it obviated any compelling necessity for the state to solve the clergy's demographic imbalance. That problem steadily worsened, reaching catastrophic proportions by the mid-nineteenth century and at last compelling the state to seek some solution.

Political Opposition

Peter the Great certainly created unprecedented hardships for the parish clergy. Priests and churchmen, even in the most isolated hamlets, had cause for complaint: they paid many new taxes, performed onerous new duties, lost their sons in conscriptions, and lived in dread of a visit by bailiffs and tax collectors. Thus it is hardly surprising that Peter generated considerable opposition not only among laymen but also among the white clergy. During the tumultuous early years of his reign, clergy figured prominently in the cases brought before the Preobrazhenskii prikaz, comprising about 20 percent of all cases in the years 1699-1705.[171] Many expressed the popular apocalyptic view that the world was coming to an end and Peter himself was Antichrist. The opposition was intensely personalized; the object of complaint was Peter, rarely his specific reforms. In 1717, for example, a priest in Moscow denied that Peter was even an Orthodox believer: "The Tsar himself is of German confession; I heard that in Moscow from good people." Others prated about the tsar's role in the death of his son Aleksei, and one priest claimed that the "Sovereign is living adulterously with the wife of a landowner."[172] A few, however, did protest specific measures. A priest from Riazan uezd exclaimed: "What kind of sovereign is this? This is a German, not a sovereign. He has upset the entire world, and has even put the *d'iachki* [sacristans] into the poll-tax census."[173]

In the years of the Supreme Privy Council (1726-30), instances of opposition declined, but a few still attracted the attention of authorities. The most interesting was a 1729 case of a priest's son who tried to reverse Peter's conscription of 1722: he forged and disseminated a "decree" abolishing the poll tax for all clerical youths and churchmen who had previously been inscribed in the register. This crime against the exchequer earned him a grim fate: "Torture and use fire on the writer of false decrees, the priest's son Stepanov. If nothing else comes to light, execute him and make a public announcement beforehand [so that spectators will attend]."[174] Two priests in Riazan diocese were arrested in 1729 for cursing the new emperor, Peter II, and refusing to perform a church service for his health; predictably, they were immediately dispatched to the government for appropriate treatment.[175]

After the acute political crisis of 1730, Anna's government suspected widespread opposition not only among the elite but also among the clergy.[176] There was, to be sure, some genuine political opposition. For example, in 1735 a priest in Suzdal diocese complained to his archpriest about the church services required in honor of Anna's coronation anniversary and declared, "You are celebrating the devil." The archpriest tended to agree and asked the local state official for his opinion. He was the wrong person to ask: both clerics were promptly arrested, defrocked, and dispatched to the secular government for further investigation.[177] A priest in Suzdal, who had recently been punished for various misdeeds, began to make "insulting remarks" about the Law Code of 1649 and the secular state as well.[178] The most sensational case involved the cleric, Savva Dugin, who fell into the hands of the Secret Chancellery in 1732 after writing two petitions to the empress. One described his "vision" about the restoration of the patriarchate: he saw the empress in a dream and on her crown was written "patriarchate." His other petition contained a fantastic project to make the clergy into a social and political elite. "Since the clergy brings man close to God," he argued, it is only fitting to raise the status of the ecclesiastical rank. As for the Church hierarchy, Dugin proposed that the number of bishops be increased and that they be selected from men of all ranks, not just the monastic clergy. More important, archpriests should hold power at the lower echelons, and "there should be no elected clerical elders." All men, lay or clerical, must heed the archpriest, who was to oversee not only the clergy but the local state officials as well; in Dugin's scheme the archpriest should even investigate unsolved crimes. If any layman insults a cleric, "then immediately seize him, take away his rank, put him in prison for one month, and at the end of a month give him thirty blows with a knout." Or, "if anyone hits an archpriest or priest with his fist or a rod, or mercilessly beats him, then cut off his left hand just as if he had violated Christ the Lord." Whether because of his "vision" of the patriarchate's restoration or other unspecified remarks, Dugin was interrogated, tortured, and finally executed in March 1732.[179]

Though such political cases were rare, the suspicious government discerned political opposition in two other, common offenses: the failure to take loyalty oaths in 1730-31 and the omission of church services on state holidays. The failure to take the oaths proved particularly disturbing to the government: given the political core of the oath, it concluded that "unsworn clergy" must be disloyal. Its concern redoubled after an investigation showed that 5,000 clergy and their children had not taken the oath.[180] That was a significant figure; in Suzdal diocese, for example, 32 percent of the churchmen missed the oath, and in Kolomna diocese the number reached 38 percent of all churchmen.[181] Specific reports emphasized, however, that the clergy had not missed the oath for political reasons. Some clergy never heard the order, others misunderstood it, and still others took the oath but just forgot to sign the lists.[182] Anna's government, however, believed the worst and made the unsworn clergy pay dearly for their ignorance or carelessness: it forbade the ordination of anyone who had missed the oath, an order that the Synod and diocesan officials closely observed.[183] But the government's main reprisals came in 1736-39, when its conscription specifically focused on unsworn clergy, who were first flogged and then dispatched to the army as recruits.[184] Only in 1739, when the Synod adduced evidence of large-scale clerical vacancies, did Anna's regime modify the conscription rules, eventually exempting from punishment those who missed the oath "not from evil intent or stubbornness or any other evil reason, but just because of their simpleness."[185] After Anna's death the government fully exonerated unsworn clergy and even released many from the army to return to their old positions.[186]

Anna's government also suspected opposition in another offense: the omission of church services on state holidays. Here too suspicion was exaggerated; in most cases the clergy missed services not because of bold political protest, but for more banal reasons—such as drunkenness, forgetfulness, or absence from the parish. A typical case involved a village priest, Fedor Ivanov, of Vladimir uezd. In 1736 his landlord seized him in Moscow and handed him over to the Synodal

Chancellery because the priest "did not serve the liturgy and prayers on February 19, 1735, the day of Her Imperial Majesty's accession to the throne." The priest admitted his offense, but gave this explanation to authorities: "Because he had nothing to eat, he had gone to Moscow to ask his landlord Petr Kologrivov for food." After three years of investigation, the Moscow Synodal Chancellery finally sentenced the priest to a "merciless beating with the lash" but waived the hard labor in a monastery that was often prescribed in such cases.[187] In a similar case involving a Iaroslavl priest, the Secret Chancellery showed no such leniency: "For failing to serve on several state holidays because of drunkenness, the priest Fedor Avraamov is to be beaten mercilessly with the lash instead of the knout, sent to a monastery, and to remain there at hard labor for one-half year."[188] So many priests committed the offense without political intent that the Secret Chancellery amended the rule that all offenders be sent to its chambers: "If the Church investigation reveals no evil intent by the clergy who do not perform these services (because they left their homes without proper releases; because they forgot about them; or because they were drunk), then do not send them to the Secret Chancellery."[189]

After 1740 cases of political opposition among parish clergy virtually disappeared, a stark contrast to the stormy days of Peter the Great and Anna. To be sure, there were still such misdemeanors as the omission of state liturgies, but the state ceased to construe these as political crimes. When several clerical youths missed the loyalty oath, Elizabeth ordered no floggings and merely directed them to make up the oath.[190] The case of a Iaroslavl sacristan in 1761 also reveals the government's new attitude: he was absent-mindedly performing his part of the liturgy and when the service reached a section requiring a chant for the empress's health, he intoned "To Her eternal memory." The offender was hastily dispatched to the Secret Chancellery but was eventually "forgiven" for his carelessness.[191]

The clergy's acquiescence had a number of sources. The shock of the Petrine reforms had passed; most of society had adjusted to the new order, and even the peasants who once groaned under Peter's yoke now hailed him as a folk hero.[192] The calmer climate no doubt helped silence the clergy. Moreover, by mid-century the state had removed some major sources of clerical grievance—Peter's taxes and rigorous enforcement of secular duties. True, state conscriptions bore down mercilessly, but the clergy themselves were secure, and they could protect their sons by enrolling them in the seminary. Thus, if the state failed to solve the clergy's demographic and economic problems, it did at least remove the main grievances and effectively undercut political disaffection.

In conclusion, state policies toward the clergy underwent a significant evolution during the eighteenth century. In a dramatic break with the tradition of clerical privilege, Peter's government for the first time defined a secular service role for the white clergy; like lay social groups, they too became a service soslovie. Thus Peter's government imposed a double set of obligations, one on the clerical *chin*, the other on the clerical soslovie: the priest paid taxes and rendered sundry services to the state; his sons were liable to recruitment and conscription. After Peter, as the state redefined the service of the nobility and townspeople, it also modified the Petrine policy toward the clergy. It altered only half of the Petrine formula, however: the government freed the clerical *chin* from taxation and most secular services but continued to utilize the clerical soslovie for recruitment and conscription. The parish clergy did not experience a full "emancipation from service" like that accorded the nobility; only the priest, not his family, enjoyed an improved status. Government policy on the clerical soslovie, meanwhile, wrought its devastation: conscription threw the clergy into turmoil and dread, recruitment spirited away the Church's best seminarians.

The Hierarchy and
the Parish Clergy

3

The clergy of old Muscovy were not the tsar's subjects, but the bishop's. Because of Church autonomy, the priest was under the exclusive jurisdiction of the Church and rendered service solely in the bishop's domain. And there he was squarely under the broad, almost unlimited authority of the monastic hierarchy. The bishop's formal authority was indeed awesome, resting firmly on canon law and centuries of Church tradition. As Christ's vicar, the bishop endowed the priest with the power "to serve the sacred rites" and exercised responsibility to oversee the priest in his service thereafter. In Muscovy this formal authority was saturated by the prevailing political style, where tsar and *voevoda* ruled like oriental potentates. That an Orthodox bishop imitated secular rulership is understandable. Some hierarchs, like Aleksei and Filipp, came from the aristocratic elite (*boiarstvo*), naturally transferring the social attitudes and values of that group into the hierarchy. More important, perhaps, the bishop adopted the secular style to fortify his worldly power and prestige, especially against state encroachments on Church lands and immunities. The Church was thus a mirror image of lay society: the bishop was an ecclesiastical prince, the clergy his subjects.[1]

Peter's reforms confirmed this traditional relationship. He welded the Church to the state but left the ecclesiastical rank responsible to the Church or Synodal command.[2] The Church sometimes had to withstand state intervention but in general preserved jurisdiction over the clergy throughout the eighteenth century. Even though the state held ultimate authority, the Church exercised a basic operational autonomy. As long as a matter did not concern vital state interests, the hierarchy ruled the Church and clergy free of state interference. The over-procurator exercised only nominal supervision over the Church; government offices, meanwhile, had no time, expertise, or interest in purely ecclesiastical affairs.

Nevertheless, the traditional relationship between priest and bishop gradually disintegrated in the eighteenth century. The government, unintentionally, was partly responsible. By subjecting bishops to arbitrary punishment, by subordinating them to Synodal supervision, the state undermined the bishops' independence and power. The bishops were now vulnerable from below, a fact plainly evident to the parish clergy. The state also changed some basic components of the traditional relationship, however; particularly significant were the reforms of the 1760s that abrogated or restricted the bishops' authority to tax and punish priests. Most important in recasting the traditional relationship was a broad modernization of the hierarchy and Church administration. The bishops, deprived of their former status, became effective administrators intent upon improving the priests' conduct and service. Wielding a more efficient administration than in Muscovy, the eighteenth-century bishop enforced stringent new service demands. The Muscovite bishop could only berate the clergy's foibles and malfeasance; the Petrine hierarch could effectively supervise, reward, and discipline the subordinate clergy. These two changes—government intervention and modernization in the Church—sharpened tensions between the white and black clergy, dormant and rarely articulated in Muscovy.

It is important to reexamine these tensions which subsequently became such a crippling weakness in the Church and, in particular, to reconsider a stark stereotype that prevails in traditional historiography: an impoverished parish clergy, mercilessly oppressed by the monastic hierarchy. Much of the literature on the parish clergy, written in the late nineteenth century, suffers from a liberal bias that idealizes the lower parish clergy and stereotypes the bishops as hopeless reactionaries.[3] That view, first expressed in such illegal publications as I. S. Belliustin's *Description of the Rural Clergy* or D. I. Rostislavov's *On the Black and White Orthodox Clergy*, achieved wide acceptance and popularity in lay society.[4] An anti-hierarchical movement sought —and found—historical legitimacy, especially in the memoirs and source publications of liberal journals. Hence Gavriil Dobrynin's memoir of an atypical bishop captivated the public, winning acceptance as a valid description of the typical bishop in the eighteenth century.[5] Moreover, liberal and populist intellectuals were inclined to sympathize with the truly impoverished priest, who seemed so close to the people and equally worthy of compassion.

This chapter will consider these tensions between bishop and priest against the background of broad institutional development in the Church. After examining "modernization" in the Church, those fundamental changes in the structure and operation of ecclesiastical administration, one can then more fruitfully probe the major areas of interaction between bishop and priest—ordination, taxation, and justice—and see how these gradually evolved in the eighteenth century.

Ecclesiastical Modernization

The Church experienced an organizational revolution in the eighteenth century, making dramatic improvements in its administrative system. It was a natural result of the Church's new relationship to the secular state: because of the formalized interaction between the secular and Synodal commands, the Church gradually internalized the methods and norms of Peter's "regularized government." Thus the bureaucratization that had such profound effects on state and society also caused significant changes in the Church. The impact seemed all the greater because of the Church's relative backwardness in the seventeenth century, when it failed to follow the state's example of creating a more elaborate administration. More important, the Church's new bureaucracy governed a relatively small service group, facilitating a level of control unattainable in the vast empire of the tsar. The parish priest, especially in the central provinces, soon found himself in a vast administrative web unimaginable for his Muscovite predecessors.

Administrative Backwardness: The Church in Muscovy

The Church in Muscovy suffered from grievously inadequate administration. It was a premodern organization lacking all the elements of a formal bureaucracy—specialization, hierarchy, formal rules, fixed and official jurisdiction, and a trained professional class of officials.[6] In the early centuries of Russian Christianity such backwardness already posed important problems; principalities and dioceses were still relatively compact, yet even then the bishops could not assert routine control over them. Administrative backwardness had more telling effects after 1450, as Muscovy rapidly increased its territorial size and population. The Church, though now faced with the task of ruling thousands of churches across vast stretches of broken terrain, did not substantially improve its administration. The hierarchs recognized the acute need for change, and Church councils from 1551 to 1682 complained of poor administration. Because of administrative problems, they declared, the Church was unable to suppress superstitions or stem the spreading Old Belief. Yet they balked at taking the first essential step—the division of dioceses into smaller, more manageable units. Such reform threatened to diminish the power and economic base of individual hierarchs; Church councils repeatedly failed to make even minor changes in territorial organization.[7]

Of these administrative weaknesses, particularly important was the hierarchy itself: most bishops had neither training nor interest in day-to-day administration of their dioceses. All were from the monastic clergy, though that in itself was no guarantee of special knowledge about the diocese or parish clergy. For, until Peter the Great closed access to the monastic clergy from lay social groups, the monastic clergy came from diverse social strata, aristocratic as well as peasant, and consequently those governing a diocese often knew little about the life and service norms of the parish clergy they were supposed to rule. Most bishops indeed preferred to reside in Moscow, where the episcopal residence with hundreds of servitors impressed laymen and foreign observers; visitation, that revolutionary device of control in reformation Europe, was virtually unknown in Russia. Nor did bishops have formal education; the Kiev and Moscow academies had just been founded, and bishops owed their positions not to academy diplomas, but to a reputation for ascetic piety, family connections, ecclesiastical politics, or sheer longevity.[8]

The excessive size of dioceses was another crippling weakness, for Muscovy was divided into a few immense dioceses with vast numbers of parish churches strewn randomly across central Russia. Dioceses were so immense, so undefined, that bishops were unable to describe accurately the territorial composition of their own domains. Sheer size also meant that no hierarch could visit even a fraction of the parish churches to correct abuses and irregularities.[9] Paradoxically, administration was weakest not on the sparsely populated borderlands, but in the very center of Muscovy, where the gigantic patriarchal region provided feeble governance for several thousand churches and hundreds of monasteries.[10] The Synod, inheriting this realm in 1721, declared that the unmanageable size of the region even encouraged clergy to misbehave: "Illegal and repugnant acts are committed by priests . . . in the remorseless hope that, because of the distance from St. Petersburg and Moscow, no one keeps strict supervision over them in matters of sanctity and piety."[11] Bishops faced similar problems in their dioceses, which had fewer churches but were still immense.

Moreover, Church administration was highly disorderly, informal, and irregular. Many bishops, residing in Moscow, did not personally govern the diocese; even those who did reside in the diocese took little interest in routine administration, preferring spiritual duties to dry paper work. In both cases the parish clergy were left to the mercy of the bishop's powerful aides and petty clerks, that large number of lay and clerical servitors who handled informal assignments over finances, ordination, and justice. The bishops maintained this administration at the hierarch's residence (*arkhiereiskii dom*), a traditional term that suggests the utter informality of diocesan administration and its failure to adopt even the terminology of new state offices. Lack of rules, chaotic records, the bishop's disinterest—all this created boundless opportunity for abuse and bribes. Even the patriarch, who had begun to imitate the tsar's administrative *prikazy* (chancelleries), had no orderly administration; indeed, clergy in the vast partriarchal region evidently suffered more abuse than their brethren in other dioceses.[12]

Administrative underdevelopment was even more apparent at the district level. The bishop divided his diocese into several districts (*desiatiny*), each under the supervision of a special appointee, usually a monastery abbot but occasionally an archpriest.[13] Like the tsar's *voevody*, these ecclesiastical intendants ruled in lieu of the bishop and exercised plenipotentiary powers over tax collection, supervision, and justice.[14] Notwithstanding their broad mandates, the intendants did little more than collect taxes and failed to provide general supervision over the parish clergy. Preoccupied with their regular duties as archpriest or abbot, they scrupulously performed only one principal task: ensuring the full and prompt delivery of tax revenues due the bishop.[15]

Ecclesiastical administration was still weaker at the local level. The Muscovite bishop did not appoint local stewards but ruled through the clerical elder (*popovskii starosta*), who was elected by the several score of clergy in a tax district. The elders, mentioned in documents as early as the thirteenth century, became more widespread after 1551, when a Church Council ordered bishops to appoint elders to collect taxes and oversee the parish clergy. The bishops, however, were slow to introduce them until a Church Council of 1675 required that the lay employees (*desiatil'niki*) be replaced by clerical elders.[16] The main impulse for the Council's decision was not a desire to tighten control over the clergy but to improve fiscal administration and curtail abuse of the white clergy by the Church's lay tax collectors. The "right" to elect the elder had transparently fiscal motives, for electors had to stand surety for the elder's performance: if he defaulted or absconded with tax revenues, the electors had to make up the losses. When some clergy stayed away from the elections to avoid this responsibility, in 1697 Patriarch Adrian made attendance mandatory and fined those who did not comply.[17] The hierarchs also emphasized the primacy of the elders' tax duties in their "Instructions to Clerical Elders"; although they vaguely charged the elder to exercise general supervision, these brief guides dwelt mainly upon the procedures for tax collection and delivery.[18] This narrow definition of the elder's role was also given in the electoral petitions signed by clergy; making no mention of ecclesiastical supervision, they simply stated that the elder was selected "for the collection of the fixed assessed taxes [okladnye den'gi] from the churches."[19] As a result, the bishops had no regular control over parish units; they were powerless to contain heresy, superstition, or flagrant violations of Church law. Characteristically, the patriarch could not assert control even in Moscow. Despite constant efforts, he could not disperse the irregular vagrant priests (kresttsovye popy) who gathered in Moscow market places to sell their services, scandalizing laymen and clergy by their outrageous, drunken misconduct.[20]

PETER'S "REGULARIZED GOVERNMENT" IN THE CHURCH

The Church overcame this administrative weakness in the eighteenth century through a fundamental bureaucratization. To some degree, the state fostered this development in the Church; the injunctions of the Ecclesiastical Regulation and ceaseless demands for exact data compelled the Church to enlarge and improve its administration. The over-procurator, a lay bureaucrat overseeing the Synod, speeded the process by transplanting state methods into the Synodal administration. Ia. P. Shakhovskoi, over-procurator in the 1740s, recalled his own role: "I found much to prescribe for better order, as I had seen in the chancellery of the Senate."[21] Significantly, however, such changes occurred not only at state insistence. Whether from a desire to rival the Senate or to defend Church interests, the hierarchs made many improvements in administration on their own initiative. As a result, by the 1760s the Church wielded a much more efficient administration at all three levels—the Synod, the diocese, and the district.

The Synodal reform, even if inspired by political calculations (to eliminate recalcitrant patriarchs), was shaped by Peter's conception of a regularized government, and it therefore brought significant improvements to Church administration. One was institutional centralization; the Synod provided the church with a supreme organ that routinely set standard policies and regulations. In the seventeenth century the patriarch had been symbolic head of the Church, but in administrative practice each bishop followed his own whim and local tradition.[22] The Synod ended such decentralization; its decrees, touching upon every dimension of church and clerical life, swept across central Russia to iron out particularisms and irregularities. The Synod automatically distributed its decrees to each diocese, required an acknowledgment of receipt, and expected observance and implementation. The Synod also functioned as a general supervisory organ over the bishops, ensuring that they performed their duties scrupulously.

Peter also established an auxiliary network of "spiritual fiscals" (*du-khovnye fiskaly*) as a check on bishops; when the government abolished this office in 1727 because of abuses, the Synod resumed principal responsibility for overseeing the bishops and diocesan administration.[23] Now a bishop had to follow the Synod's orders, implement its decrees, and submit reports at its request.[24] Thus the bishop ceased to be an autonomous ruler and became an agent of the Synod. The Synod's scrutiny was especially intense in sensitive areas that concerned the state, such as the new rules on limiting clerical appointment or conducting conscription.[25] Besides overseeing the bishops, the Synod directly intervened in other ways to improve diocesan administration. In order to alleviate the problems caused by a long hiatus between episcopal appointments, it petitioned the emperor to fill vacancies promptly and established ad hoc procedures for the interim period.[26] It standardized administrative practices in dioceses, using the General Regulation (*General'nyi reglament*), a Petrine civil service manual on everything from protocols to archives.[27] The Synod also compelled bishops to establish a uniform diocesan administration, based on the advisory board or consistory (*dikasteriia* or *konsistoriia*), an important new institution for orderly, regular governance.[28]

Administration at the diocesan level improved in several ways. One fundamental step, first taken in the eighteenth century, was to reorganize central Russia into smaller, more manageable dioceses. Most important were the reforms of 1742-44 that divided the Synodal region into several smaller dioceses. Where dioceses were still unwieldy, the Church established special vicariates (*vikariaty*) that functioned like small semi-independent dioceses. For instance, it established such a vicariate in Moscow diocese in 1764 because "there are a great number of churches and towns that are widely separated, and it is difficult for one hierarch to administer them."[29]

Moreover, the emperor selected more effective administrators as bishops. This change was signaled by the Ecclesiastical Regulation, which explicitly prescribed the bishop's numerous duties: he must reside in the diocese, make visitations to parish churches, oversee diocesan administration, open a seminary, and submit annual reports on the condition of his diocese.[30] Under close Synodal scrutiny, bishops gradually began to fulfill Peter's comprehensive prescriptions. Even visitations, the most onerous and difficult of all injunctions, became common after mid-century.[31] More important still, the episcopate experienced a basic change in social composition: it came to consist of men well-educated, ambitious, and born to the clerical estate. Peter began the change by giving preference to Ukrainians, for the monks from Kiev had good formal education and seemed receptive to the tsar's reforms; his successors continued that policy and by 1762 Great Russians constituted only 12 of 26 bishops in the empire.[32] Although some Ukrainian hierarchs (like Metropolitan Platon I of Moscow) zealously sought reforms in the lower clergy and parish life, others earned the government's enmity by their staunch defense of Church interests; foreign hierarchs (like the Georgian Antonii of Vladimir diocese) did not even speak Russian and only nominally ruled their dioceses.[33] After mid-century the sovereign did not abandon the preference for educated hierarchs but began to favor the Great-Russian monks now emerging from the new seminaries in central Russia.[34] Most monastic clergy in Great Russia by this time had been born to the clerical estate, for Peter barred tonsure to other classes in an effort to reduce the number of "parasitic, useless" monks.[35] Because of their clerical origins, the new bishops had a sharp perception of church life and village custom in central Russia. More important, they owed their careers to their superior education, usually acquired at the Moscow Academy; such careers were often meteoric, young men quickly rising to top positions while in their thirties. Those elevated to the episcopate without such formal education were exceedingly rare, and hereafter the Russian Church would be ruled by a new elite, the "learned monks" (uchenoe monashestvo).[36] As a result, the Church acquired competent, scholarly bishops like Simon Lagov of Riazan and Arsenii Vereshchagin of Rostov, bishops who zealously aspired to improve the parish clergy, who earned renown for their urbanity and culture, and who enjoyed popularity and respect among nobles as well as peasants.[37] Some, to be sure, inspired more dread than respect; for example, priests in Vladimir stood in terror before Bishop Ieronim, who had not only churchmen but even priests flogged after corporal punishment had been outlawed.[38] But, whatever their temperament, bishops after mid-century were more efficient administrators exercising new levels of control over the lower clergy.

Not only the bishops but also the diocesan administration became better fit to govern. One new component was the consistory, a collegial board of three to five clerics who were responsible for routine administration of the diocese. They investigated clerical offenses, heard petitions, and prepared resolutions for the bishop to review and confirm. The consistory also had a keen perception of the clergy's problems and foibles, since its members usually included some archpriests and priests; in a typical list of 1756, for example, the white clergy represented 38 percent of active consistory members.[39] At the district level the bishop established a similar body, the ecclesiastical board (dukhovnoe pravlenie), instead of an abbot as district administrator. Consisting of one or two abbots and one archpriest, the boards became effective, fundamental units of diocesan administration. Those in Pereslavl diocese were typical: numbering six in all, they governed a relatively small area (with forty to fifty churches) and had a full staff of clerks and bailiffs.[40] The Church firmly defended their vital importance in the 1760s when the government, for reasons of economy, proposed to eliminate or reduce them; the bishops successfully argued that the boards performed essential tasks—disseminating decrees, making arrests, gathering information, conducting inquiries, and arbitrating minor disputes among parish clergy.[41]

Even more dramatic changes occurred at the local level. Although most bishops formally retained the traditional clerical elder until the 1760s, they substantially expanded the elders' administrative role to embrace more than mere tax collection. The Ecclesiastical Regulation provided a decisive impulse for the change: "Stewards or superintendents—appointed specifically in all towns as a kind of ecclesiastical inspector—are to supervise everything and report to the bishop."[42] The Synod often reiterated that injunction, and in 1738 even prepared model instructions for clerical elders in Moscow.[43] As a result, by mid-century bishops laid increasing emphasis upon the elder's role as general supervisor, and some even established an ancillary set of stewards (*zakazchiki*) specifically to perform the supervisory function.[44] As a harbinger of what lay ahead, the metropolitan of Moscow in 1751 established appointive (not elected) superintendents of good order (*blagochinnye*), who coexisted with the tax-collecting elders and performed a new role as the metropolitan's overseer.[45] The driving motive for such changes was explicitly stated in 1753 by Bishop Amvrosii of Pereslavl, who resolved to appoint such deputies "so that there can be proper sanctity in the Church and reliable supervision over the white clergy."[46] Even bishops who retained the traditional clerical elder gave new emphasis to the supervisory role. Metropolitan Arsenii of Rostov, for example, prepared a new set of "instructions" that significantly enlarged the elder's responsibility as diocesan overseer.[47]

After the 1760s this change acquired hard institutional form as bishops replaced the elected elders with appointed superintendents—*blagochinnye*, who represented not the priests but the bishop. Once the state abolished diocesan taxes on the parish clergy in 1764, bishops no longer had need for elected elders and instead could concentrate administrative and supervisory powers in the hands of appointed deputies. The metropolitan of Moscow abolished the election of elders almost immediately after the 1764 reform and placed full authority in his stewards as "overseers of decency."[48] In 1775 Metropolitan Platon defined the new office in his *Instructions for Ecclesiastical Superintendents*, which portrayed not a tax collector but a plenipotentiary of the bishop—an appointee who would inspect churches, oversee the

clergy, and check religious deviance among parishioners. In 1787
Platon organized the superintendents into small "superintendent districts" (blagochinnye okrugi), each with twelve to fifteen churches.[49]
Bishops elsewhere emulated the Moscow example, and the superintendents became an important new tool for diocesan control over the
parish clergy.[50]

While this new administrative structure allowed unprecedented
control over the parish clergy, the Church's administration still suffered from important deficiencies. One persistent problem was fiscal;
the Church was unable to finance the growing bureaucracy and forced
it to depend heavily upon irregular assessments and bribes. Some dioceses had never possessed significant amounts of landed wealth;[51]
those that did gradually lost control over their land as the Petrine state
began to tap the Church's wealth for its own use. Moreover, the government appropriated some traditional diocesan fees, such as the tax
on marriage licenses (venechye pamiati).[52] The new dioceses established in central Russia in the 1740s were in particularly difficult
straits, for they had no power to expend several traditional diocesan
taxes and instead had to surrender these revenues to the Synod. When
the state secularized Church lands and peasants in 1764, it gave the
Church small budgets that were patently inadequate compensation.[53]
The government divided dioceses into three classes, allotting each category a fixed amount for the bishop, his house, and the consistory.
Although the budget provided a regular income free from the vagaries
of monastery harvests, it reduced the support for the consistory, forcing many dioceses to cut their staffs and functions. Bishop Sil'vestr of
Pereslavl, who had just improved his diocesan administration, was
forced to make sharp reductions in administrative personnel; the Moscow hierarch reluctantly took similar steps.[54] Worse still, inflation
over the next three decades eroded even these modest budgets; not
until the end of the century did a new emperor, Paul, approve significant increases.[55]

Consequently, bishops fought a constant battle against the bribery
and extortion that pervaded state administration but seemed even
more reprehensible in the Church. Platon of Moscow put offenders on
bread and water, threatened to dismiss them, and in 1787 compelled
"consistory employees to sign an oath that they will not take bribes."[56]
The diary of a Rostov priest shows that each visit to the consistory to
deliver reports or bring petitions cost him several rubles in bribes to
miscellaneous employees, from the consistory secretary to the lowliest
bailiff.[57] The district boards were in even worse straits, for the state
allotted them no budget at all, and the bishop perforce had to allow
clerks to assess incidental fees on petitions and paperwork.[58]

The consistory itself suffered from several other problems. Its members sometimes were inattentive to their duties. Earning no salary for consistory work, they still had to perform their regular duties at the monastery or cathedral. In 1758 the bishop of Pereslavl prepared new rules for his consistory and made this complaint about its members:

We have observed many disorders in the affairs of the consistory, for which we have subjected the members to frequent reprimands and fines. Our decrees have frequently demanded a better performance, but hitherto this has not been visible. This is due mainly to the fact that the members (as is evident from the signatures on the reports) are not always present in the consistory . . . As a result, there are procrastination and delays in its affairs.[59]

In the 1750s the Riazan hierarch, Dmitrii, made a similar complaint about his consistory: "Many important and criminal cases are incomplete after ten years; many others are full of errors and disorders; because of this, innocent people suffer unnecessarily from red tape and losses, while the guilty remain without any just punishment."[60] Moreover, the consistory's staff and clerks often came from the families of white clergy in the diocese, and the ecclesiastical superintendent was appointed from the parish clergy in a particular district.[61] As a result, diocesan business often suffered from the influence of family connections, which served either to protect an offender or to persecute some clan enemy.[62]

Nor did the bishop always fulfill his tasks effectively. Sometimes he simply could not: many hierarchs held outside appointments, such as in the Synod or the Moscow Synodal Chancellery, and were unavoidably absent from their diocese for very long periods. For example, the bishops of Pereslavl diocese were routinely gone from their diocese, frequently serving on the board of the Moscow Synodal Chancellery.[63] It was not easy to return to the diocese, and the bishop had to solicit special permission from the Synod or emperor to do so.[64] Such protracted absences invited abuse by the bishops' subordinates, and in the case of Bishop Platon of Vladimir the empress herself intervened, ordering him to return to his diocese and investigate charges against his officials.[65]

Even the most qualified and energetic bishop could not fulfill the tasks ideally prescribed in the Ecclesiastical Regulation of 1721. Though the bishops now governed smaller dioceses, they still had difficulty making visitations. Bishop Platon of Vladimir explained in 1750 that "it was still impossible to travel [to many rural churches] because of the marsh and great mud."[66] Similarly, Bishop Amvrosii of

Pereslavl emphasized the difficulty of inspecting parishes: "Although His Grace, according to the Ecclesiastical Regulation, is to maintain appropriate supervision over the pastoral activities in his diocese, it is not convenient for His Grace to visit the diocese often because of the great distance and because many churches are in the midst of forests, marshes, mud, and many other obstacles."[67] To overcome such obstacles, Moscow hierarchs made elaborate preparations befitting a military campaign; they sent ahead messengers to organize horse relays, provisions, and meetings with parish clergy in the district.[68] And, as the diary of a Riazan bishop from the late eighteenth century shows, even then hierarchs made only irregular, brief visitations to churches in their dioceses.[69] Moreover, the bishop still had to perform not only official functions but also traditional and sacerdotal roles; beyond religious services, he had to attend to such chores as the consecration of new churches just built by proud nobles, who viewed the opening of their church as a great social occasion and demanded the bishop's presence.[70] The bishop was also expected to show charity and mercy, a role he was loath to surrender; thus he was perpetually dispensing alms and trying to show compassion for petitioners, even at the risk of violating Synodal or state law.[71] The Synod, symbolically, forbade bishops to use "most-merciful" in their title (a prerogative of the emperor), and constantly prodded them to implement state decrees conscientiously.[72] But some bishops still could not resist the temptation to demonstrate the traditional compassion, even by obstructing state conscriptions—to the fury and dismay of government officials. One such bishop, Feodosii of Tambov, was condemned to dismissal by a joint Synod-Senate investigation; Catherine eventually issued a pardon, but ordered the Synod "to remind the bishops hereafter to be more reliable in the implementation of decrees."[73]

One fundamental weakness of Church administration stemmed from an intrinsic ambiguity: the Synodal command was both a bureaucratic organization and a "subsociety." Formally, the Church had a clear hierarchical structure; it included the whole clerical organization, from the metropolitan to the lowliest churchman. However, bureaucratization reached only the diocesan level, and the white clergy remained outside its budget and appointment system. Instead, the parish clergy derived both income and appointment from the parish and therefore had strong ties to the lay population wholly outside the "Synodal command." This introduced an important strain of inconsistency: the parish clergy were subject to the rules of the Church organization but remained socially and economically dependent upon the laity. This contradiction magnified the traditional social differentiation in the Church, driving a wedge between bishop and priest, making their antagonism perhaps more intense than that known to the Church in Western Europe.[74]

In conclusion, the Church internalized the state's model of bureaucratization. It acquired the features of a modern organization and expanded its administrative organs even at the local level. Such changes allowed the Church by mid-century to penetrate the parish, exposing the priest for the first time to continuous supervision by the Church authorities. Yet this new bureaucracy was at best only semi-modernized and still suffered from major deficiencies. These defects— from abuse of authority to rampant extortion—were not new to the eighteenth century; what was new was the increased interaction between Church and parish clergy. However oppressive Church administration may have been in Muscovy, its contact with the parish clergy was limited mainly to tax collection. The large, powerful administration of the eighteenth century, by contrast, intruded far more frequently into the lives of priests even in the most remote village, and on a scale impossible for secular bureaucracy in its far larger domain. Thus the parish clergy felt the full effect of ecclesiastical modernization: the sudden expansion of control, the full costs of its incompleteness.

Governing the Clergy

From medieval times the bishop exercised three main lines of jurisdictional authority over the parish clergy. First, he enjoyed the exclusive right to make formal appointments to a church; only he could ordain priests and deacons, or confirm churchmen. The bishop could not delegate this to any subordinate but bore personal responsibility to ensure the installation of individuals worthy of the clerical rank. Second, the bishop held broad tax powers over the clergy and derived a large share of his revenues directly from them. Third, he was the clergy's overseer and judge, meting out punishment to those who violated their service obligations or committed minor crimes. How did these three bonds—ordination, taxation, and justice—change in the eighteenth century?

Ordination and Installation

In Muscovy the lay parishioners had the right to select their clergy, and the bishop only confirmed or ordained their choice. This peculiar system of the "democratic election" of priests arose not from canon law (which had very little to say on the subject)[75] but from the Church's administrative weakness. The bishop simply lacked the means to locate and select worthy candidates for his far-flung diocese, a pattern also found earlier in the history of the Western Church.[76]

Consequently, bishops depended upon the parishioners to elect worthy candidates, and this practice was confirmed by Church law both in Muscovy and in the eighteenth century. Although bishops controlled some appointments (for example, at cathedrals) and could reject an unqualified candidate, they continued to recognize the electoral power of the parish throughout the eighteenth century.

Even though the bishop recognized the power of the parish, he gradually assumed a more active role in regulating and supervising the selection. In the seventeenth century the bishop had merely given an interrogation (*dopros*) to candidates and assumed that the election certificates were valid; even in Moscow the hierarch had no routine system of investigating either candidates or petitions.[77] From the 1720s, however, the authorities began to order the clerical elder to verify the authenticity of the certificates, partly to ensure that the parish really wanted the candidate, partly to determine if there was a real vacancy under the rules of the clerical registry.[78] A still stronger impetus came after 1725: the government issued strict regulations on the ordination of candidates from the poll-tax population—only when formally released by a landlord could such people enter the clergy.[79] As a result, routine and systematic investigations became standard in the central dioceses by the 1740s. For instance, in his "Instructions" to the ecclesiastical stewards, Metropolitan Arsenii of Rostov ordered them to investigate each case and then sign the election certificate, indicating that "it is genuine and not false, and also that the elected person is a good man beyond suspicion, and is being appointed to a vacant position."[80] Bishops made such investigations even more rigorous after 1764 as they improved their system of lower superintendents. In Riazan the bishop issued an order in 1778 for all candidates to come with not only the parish's election certificate but also the superintendent's recommendation. Platon of Moscow even instructed his superintendents to attend the election itself to ensure its propriety and the presence of "respectable" parishioners.[81]

This enhanced supervision had unwanted consequences for the parish clergy. Above all, it meant rigorous enforcement of state laws against "excess clergy." Thus the priest could arrange his son's appointment only if the rules recognized a vacancy; even with parish approval, excess appointments were easily detected and rejected by the bishop. The priest also might find his son disqualified for other reasons: lack of sufficient education, past inscription in the poll tax, or the presence of too many relatives at the same church. The diocesan administration made more careful investigations, kept good records, and became very proficient in detecting such facts about the candidates. In short, even though the parish still selected the candidate, the bishop's greater control and vigilance created new pressures on the parish clergy.

Once the candidate (*stavlennik*) had been elected, he went to the bishop for formal ordination. In the pre-Petrine period this procedure was very simple. The first step was a "hearing" (*slushan'e*), a perfunctory test in reading and singing. If he passed this examination, he was given an interrogation (*dopros*) about his background and the vacancy he claimed to fill. He then made confession, received brief instruction in his duties, and underwent formal rites of ordination. The new priest had to purchase an ordination charter (*stavlennaia gramota*), which attested that he had been formally ordained and authorized him to minister the sacraments in a specific parish. With this written certification to show the clerical elder and parishioners, he could return home and begin service.[82]

In medieval Russia this procedure provided rich opportunities for diocesan officials to extort bribes. At each step of the way the candidate had to pay miscellaneous fees and bribes, and to give a generous sum to the bishop himself for ordination and the ordination charter. The total costs were indeed high, eliciting clerical complaints in the mid-seventeenth century and inspiring a satirical tale about a corrupt Moscow priest, who mercilessly plundered clerical candidates coming to Moscow for ordination. In 1675 Patriarch Ioakim tried to limit the total fee for the ordination of a churchman as priest to only two rubles, which were apportioned into exact shares for each of the diocesan officials who signed documents, heard confession, or otherwise participated in the procedures. But his decree remained a dead letter, and the candidates were still defenseless victims of diocesan extortion.[83]

In the first half of the eighteenth century Church authorities continued to exact the ordination fees and even increased them. To be sure, the Ecclesiastical Regulation admonished bishops against excess levies, and the new Synod hastened to reconfirm the patriarchal limit of two rubles for ordination.[84] These measures never took effect, however, and the costs of ordination steadily increased. In some cases the bishop's subordinates were guilty of extortion; Pososhkov complained in the 1720s that such bribes enabled unfit candidates to be ordained, for a "gift" in the proper quarters would assure them of passing the examination.[85] Some bishops were accused of demanding excess fees in cases that provoked stern warnings from the Synod against exceeding the legal amounts.[86] Such admonitions had little effect, and after 1735 the Synod ceased to apply even this modest pressure.[87] By the 1740s the over-procurator Shakhovskoi vehemently protested against the excess fees and urged a new Synod resolution to stop the practice.[88] All this failed to limit the cost of ordination, however, and to protect themselves some candidates simply disappeared after receiving the ordination rites to avoid purchasing the ordination charter. Because these charters yielded considerable revenue to the bishop and because they were essential for identifying genuine priests from "pretenders," the hierarchs were zealous in compelling clergy to purchase the document and in ferreting out those who lacked it.[89] Despite the mounting pressure, candidates still resisted; a systematic check of documents in the 1740s uncovered priests in almost every district without the proper documents.[90] The cost of ordination steadily rose, far exceeding the Synod's limit of two rubles, and by the 1750s some bishops exacted as much as seven to ten rubles for installation. Feeling the pinch of declining revenues, they used this income to help pay for the increased cost of administration and for such capital expenditures as the repair or construction of cathedrals.[91]

Ordination also became significantly more burdensome for the candidate in still another way: he had to undergo much more rigorous examination and instruction. Unlike the brief formalities in Muscovy, the eighteenth-century ordination required much higher standards of literacy and special training. Peter repeatedly demanded that the bishops install only trained clergy, and in 1722 the Synod specifically instructed bishops to give candidates basic instruction in their profession and the faith.[92] In 1739 Empress Anna went much further: she ordered the bishops to keep the candidates for a special three-month session, where they would receive instruction and close moral scrutiny by the bishop. Although only sporadically implemented, her decree did encourage the bishop to examine candidates much more rigorously than in the past.[93] By mid-century most bishops appointed a special examiner, who taught the candidate and certified his readiness for ordination. This meant that the candidate now had to support himself for a prolonged period in the bishop's center and constantly dole out bribes and "gifts."

After 1760 the bishops made ordination even more rigorous. To ensure regularity, many hierarchs took a more active role; Platon of Moscow, for example, personally administered the "hearing" and wrote down evaluations of the aspirant.[94] Moreover, the candidate now had to pass a stiff examination in the catechism, and after 1780 had to show at least some formal schooling to obtain appointment. The quality and cultural level of the clergy were thus raised, but at the expense of the clergy themselves, who had to bear the full costs of this education.

But the second half of the century brought one major gain for the parish clergy: in 1765 the state abolished all excess fees for ordination, authorizing a specific fee for the rites and charter and categorically forbidding all others. It authorized bishops to collect only two rubles and warned them "not to exact anything beyond that under any pretext."[95] It was an important reform, lifting a major burden from the clergy. There were of course some bishops who sought to evade the decree—Dobrynin's Bishop Kirill of Sevsk was one.[96] He was exceptional, however; most bishops observed the law. The parish clergy were not shy about exposing abuses, but the Synod received few complaints of extortion or violations.

Thus in the eighteenth century the bishop's relationship to the candidate at ordination changed significantly. Most important, the bishop developed a rigorous system of examination and training; whereas Muscovite hierarchs merely complained about the candidates' ignorance, the bishops of the Synodal period imposed demanding new standards. The costs of ordination rose steadily in the first half of the eighteenth century, but the state eliminated this source of tension in 1765, when it fixed low ordination fees. Ordination still generated friction between bishop and priest, but the cause was different: not traditional abuse but higher standards made ordination an onerous burden for aspirants to the clerical rank.

TAXATION

Once installed, the priest in medieval Russia owed a perpetual financial obligation to his bishop. Each year he had to pay the fixed annual fees (*okladnye den'gi*) and miscellaneous irregular ones (*neokladnye den'gi*). By far the most important regular fee was the parish-church tax (*dannye den'gi*), a fixed assessment on each parish church.[97] It varied from one parish to the next, according to the number of parish households and their social category, the land and resources placed at the disposal of the clergy, and the number of clerical households.[98] This levy formed the basic part of the bishop's revenues, and in the patriarchal region it reached a total of 7,000 rubles per year in the 1690s.[99] The bishops also collected a number of minor taxes, such as 30-kopeck levy per church to support their lay employees. And at irregular intervals the bishop could collect some additional taxes—when he reconfirmed old ordination charters upon appointment, issued special licenses permitting widowed clergy to remain in service, and signed permits to transfer to other dioceses.[100] Like the secular government in Muscovy, the Church used the principle of "feeding" (*kormlenie*), a simple, decentralized fiscal system where authorities were "fed" by their subjects.

After 1700 the bishops continued to collect all these traditional taxes, making few modifications in them. The parish-church tax was most important and still brought large sums into the diocesan budget.

It was a considerable sum: while the peasant had to pay 70 kopecks for the poll tax, the clergy of each church collectively had to pay an average of two rubles.[101] Behind this average lay immense variation, for the tax assessment ranged from a few kopecks to several rubles, depending upon the type and size of parish. In addition, the bishops collected special taxes for transfers and widowed clergy, frequently in excess of the legal amounts: while the Synod specified 25 kopecks for transfer licenses, the bishops of Moscow and Pereslavl collected one ruble in the 1750s.[102]

Most onerous for the parish clergy was the new seminary tax. Peter's Ecclesiastical Regulation of 1721 ordered bishops to open church schools and authorized them to support the new institutions by an annual levy on the parish churches (one-thirtieth of harvests) and monasteries (one-twentieth of harvests).[103] By the late 1730s most bishops had established a school and began to collect the levies with increasing regularity. In Pereslavl diocese, for example, the clergy had to pay 5 kopecks for each dessiatine of land and 1.5 kopecks for each household in their parish; an average church had to pay 1.42 rubles a year in seminary taxes.[104] The bishop of Riazan even exceeded the legal tax, collecting three times the permissible amount.[105]

This tax was extremely burdensome for the parish clergy in two respects. First, it was a considerable sum to take from the clergy's meager, irregular income. The average income at most churches was between 15 and 40 rubles per annum at mid-century, and thus a tax load of 4 to 5 rubles represented 15 to 30 percent of their total income. Many impoverished clergy submitted petitions for temporary exemption because of their "complete ruination." Nor did the taxes fall equitably, for often the parish clergy had to pay taxes on resources or households that were once ascribed to them but no longer existed. One indication that the taxes were excessive is the pattern of mounting arrears, which began to increase by mid-century, especially after the addition of the seminary tax. In one district of Vladimir province, for example, unpaid taxes increased from 168 rubles to 363 rubles between 1749 and 1762. Similar arrears piled up in other dioceses, effectively frustrating the bishops' attempts to expand the seminaries.[106] One bishop even admitted that the clergy could not afford to pay the seminary tax and suspended part of it—but only for that year.[107]

Furthermore, the taxes exposed the clergy to rapacious abuse by ecclesiastical tax collectors, who were no less ruthless than state officials in their pursuit of unpaid levies. In 1720 the Church authorities sent this order to their agent in Vladimir: "Have the city and rural priests and deacons who are disobedient and violators of the [tax] law brought to the monastery and detained in submission; beat them mercilessly until they pay all the arrears and this year's dues."[108] Even in the 1750s bishops still resorted to such extraordinary measures. For instance, the clergy of one church pleaded impoverishment but the consistory took no heed: "Arrest one-half of the clergy there [presumably only one-half were arrested so that church services would not be interrupted], bring them to the consistory, and keep them constantly under arrest until they pay in full their arrears on the seminary tax."[109] The authorities detained clergy even for a small sum—one deacon was kept in a consistory jail for a tax debt of 68 kopecks. Some bishops even took personal responsibility for harshness in tax collection; one bishop in Vladimir warned his officials that "if the seminary money is not collected because of your laxness, then you shall receive a most unmerciful beating."[110]

In 1764, as the government secularized Church lands and gave the Church a budget, it abolished the diocesan taxes on parish clergy. A manifesto of 28 February 1764 ordered the Church "to remove the white clergy completely from the collection of the parish-church tax that was previously established by the patriarchs."[111] Noting that the bishops and seminaries now had state budgets, it concluded that such levies were no longer necessary. The state, through its Commission on Church Estates, may have adopted this measure as a sly political gesture, designed to split the parish clergy from the hierarchs, who were more likely to condemn secularization. Catherine plainly feared hierarchical opposition, to judge from her summary treatment of one hierarch who opposed secularization—Metropolitan Arsenii of Rostov; he was tried, deprived of rank, and secretly removed to a distant monastery.[112] Catherine may also have been influenced by European models, by reformist advisers or ecclesiastics, or perhaps by her own Enlightenment rhetoric. But one compelling reason was a desire to complete the administrative regularization of the Church: her reform ended the remnants of a feudal vassal fee and converted the Church into a salaried bureaucratic organization, with a regular table of organization and budget.

Whatever the motivations for the reform, it did not abolish all fees. The diocesan administration still exacted some minor levies and no doubt depended heavily on irregular fees to supplement minuscule budgets. The lower ecclesiastical boards, moreover, were entirely supported by the parish clergy, usually through incidental fees on petitioners. And although the seminary tax was formally abolished, the clergy still carried the actual economic burden of formal education. Few students received seminary stipends; most had to pay their own way.[113] When the Church opened district schools in the late eighteenth century, the clergy had to pay tuition and support their sons; in Vladimir the tuition for a priest's son was three rubles, a large sum for a rural cleric.[114]

The reform of 1764 thus had contradictory consequences. It formally sundered the tax nexus between bishop and priest; the hierarch who violated the new law risked exposure, censure, even removal. Yet the inadequate state budget compelled the Church administration to depend—increasingly—upon irregular exactions. This contradiction between reality and law, Church needs and clerical rights, provoked new tensions unknown to the Church in Muscovy.

Diocesan Justice

The seventeenth-century bishop did not possess an effective apparatus to supervise the parish clergy, but his successors in the next century did. The Muscovite bishop often bewailed the clergy's poor service performance, yet did nothing to improve it. At most he made a few exemplary cases—subjecting an offender to brutal punishment in the hope of terrifying the rest into submission. By contrast, bishops in the eighteenth century were full-time administrators and under close Synodal scrutiny; using their more elaborate administrative apparatus, they raised the Church's service demands on the clergy. As a result, the judicial relationship between priest and bishop assumed an entirely new significance.

The bishops' motivation derived only in part from Synodal pressure. They themselves recognized the new cultural threats to the Church and sought to fortify Orthodoxy by improving the clergy's service and behavior. To a large degree, they justified this pressure in traditional terms: a good priest is an effective one, a bad priest a temptation to evil (soblazn'). Although seventeenth-century ordination charters admonished priests to perform their duties faithfully and to behave well,[115] only the eighteenth-century bishop had the possibility of enforcing even these traditional standards. Bishops also began to define the role of priest more broadly: besides giving the traditional liturgies and sacraments, the priest was now enjoined to preach and to exercise more active spiritual control over his flock.[116]

Moreover, the bishops registered a perceptible note of status anxiety. They repeatedly warned that misbehaving priests were "degrading the ecclesiastical rank," risking not only corruption of the commoners but also humiliation of all the clergy, hierarchs included. For example, in 1723 the Synod complained that numerous clerical vagrants came to Moscow and were guilty of persistent misconduct: "As a result, not only among the Russian people but especially among foreigners, the ecclesiastical rank suffers great scorn and this causes moral harm."[117] When defrocking a priest in 1772 for alcoholism and general misconduct, a bishop in Riazan argued that such behavior "causes a temptation to evil for the parishioners and disgrace for the ecclesiastical rank."[118] In 1780 Platon of Moscow asked the Synod to confirm his decision to defrock a tipsy deacon, for the cleric was guilty of "acts indecent for his rank."[119]

The hierarchs complained about some types of misdeeds that persisted throughout the century. Above all, the bishops sought to eliminate flagrant service violations, especially those related to the sacraments. They occasionally discovered priests who failed to render baptism or extreme unction, either from sloth or drunkenness. The bishops also prosecuted priests who used sour wine for the Eucharist, who collaborated with heretical Old Believers, who violated the Orthodox rules on marriage and kinship, and who encouraged absurd superstitions.[120]

But there were some interesting changes in the bishops' focus of attention after mid-century. Previously, they tended to apply extreme punishments only for errors in service—such as the use of sour wine or the spilling of the Elements.[121] Or, especially in the 1730s, they vigilantly prosecuted priests who failed to perform liturgies on state or imperial holidays. The bishops, however, showed little interest in the clergy's personal behavior; although they swiftly defrocked priests for adultery, they seldom prosecuted clergy for drunkenness or general misconduct. After mid-century the bishops expanded their scope of jurisdiction and control. They began to defrock clergy who violated canon law regarding marriages, even if the priest did so under landlord or peasant compulsion. For the first time, they began to investigate and punish priests for drunkenness, improper dress, brawling, and other conduct "unbecoming the ecclesiastical rank."[122] In short, the bishops subjected the white clergy to ever broadening supervision and accountability.

Whatever the offense, a cleric faced certain hardship during investigation and trial. Once informed of a crime by the superintendent, another cleric, or possibly the parishioners, the consistory usually sent an order to the priest to come voluntarily for an investigation. If he refused or delayed, the consistory dispatched a bailiff to arrest him and bring him by force—at the expense of the accused. With the priest now in its hands, the consistory subjected him to full interrogations, which were written out and then signed by the defendant; if necessary, the consistory interrogated other clergy or lay witnesses. Having gathered the evidence, the consistory prepared an abstract of the case as well as summaries of pertinent laws from the Ecclesiastical Regulation, and any relevant state, Synod, or diocesan decrees. The consistory board then made a recommendation on guilt and proper punishment; the bishop reviewed the case, either confirming or modifying the consistory's recommendations.[123]

Investigation itself was oppressive. It meant months, even years, of confinement while the wheels of diocesan justice turned ever so slowly. During this time the priest not only had to pay for his keep in the consistory jail but also lost his regular income, for his absence deprived him of a right to share in parish income and land. Consequently, the priest and his entire family faced starvation and ruin—long before he was even judged guilty. Some clerics appealed in desperation to the bishop or Synod to speed up the investigation, but most quietly awaited the outcome, fearful of provoking the bishop's wrath.[124] A few quick-witted clergy appealed to the bishop's traditional sense of "mercy and charity" and asked for a temporary release or the right to employ an interim priest so that their "innocent families" would not starve and "wander from house to house in search of alms." The bishop often granted such requests.[125] When clerics could no longer endure the burden of investigation, they frequently broke out of the makeshift diocesan jails.[126]

Time was not the only problem for an accused cleric: the consistory used torture and physical abuse liberally, seeking not so much truth as a full confession. To avoid subsequent appeals and claims of innocence, the consistory insisted upon a signed confession, and used whatever coercion seemed necessary to overcome the "stubbornness" of clergy who denied their guilt. In a complaint to the Moscow Synodal Chancellery, one priest alleged that the officials in Vladimir had extracted his confession by force: "The clerk Ksenofont Golovashkin, who was writing down the testimony, struck [me] on the temple with his fist and said: 'You know what we're talking about.' "[127] If the evidence was inconclusive, the bishop sometimes gave up and left the offense to the priest's conscience; if the priest would swear "on his conscience" that the charges were false, he was permitted to resume service.[128] More often, however, Church authorities persisted in efforts to extract a confession from the accused cleric. Even after the Synod abolished corporal punishment of priests in 1767, consistories still found subtle ways to harass and persecute suspected clerics. In one such case in 1771 the Synod finally intervened on behalf of the cleric and warned the diocesan officials "not to subject any of the involved clergy to special observation or oppression, or, in particular, abuse or undeserved punishment."[129]

Once the cleric was judged guilty, the bishop meted out the punishment, and in the first half of the eighteenth century he did so with great severity. He ordered harsh punishment, as the verdicts frequently declare, not only to chasten the culprit but also "to instill fear in others" (na strakh drugim). The hierarch sometimes only fined the priest (for example, for missing a mandatory icon procession) but often administered a flogging, even in the most trivial cases. In some cases, the law specifically required such punishment, as did Anna's decrees on the failure to give church services on state holidays. Often, however, the bishop had no legal guide, and at his own discretion ordered floggings for clergy who withheld marital fees, filed false reports, or otherwise disgraced themselves. As an added humiliation and lesson to others, the bishop sometimes had the victim flogged "in the presence of the city and nearby rural clergy."[130] For more serious offenses, the bishop prescribed a term of hard labor in a monastery or simply suspended the priest from service; because monastery detention deprived the clergy and their families of a livelihood, it was to be dreaded more than a quick flogging.[131] Finally, for the most serious offenses, the bishops readily defrocked priests and deacons, who were then permanently confined in a monastery or transferred to the secular command.[132]

Besides administering terrifying and brutal punishments, some bishops followed a practice that was hated by the clergy and banned by law: the compulsory tonsure of widowed priests and deacons into monasticism.[133] Bishops in Muscovy had routinely done this until the Church Council of 1667, which strictly prohibited forcible tonsure and allowed widowed clergy to remain in their positions under a special charter renewable each year. Nevertheless, hierarchs still forced widowers to enter the monastery, particularly those guilty of some misdeed. This was originally a preventive measure; hierarchs doubted that a widowed priest could remain above community suspicion. The bishop had another motive after 1723, when Peter and his successors forbade the tonsure of any *except* widowed clergy.[134] Predictably, within a few years the monasteries complained of an acute shortage of monks.[135] The Moscow Synodal Chancellery noted the shortages in 1739 and even made bold to propose the tonsure of widowed priests and deacons; the Synod, however, cautiously rejected the proposal as patently illegal and contrary to previous imperial decrees.[136] But many bishops continued to coerce such widowed clergy to enter monasteries. In 1756 one widowed deacon in Suzdal uezd complained that the diocesan authorities "by force compelled me to sign that I will leave the orphans [of my deceased son] without waiting for further decisions [in my case] and take monastic vows."[137] During the conscription of 1755, Metropolitan Arsenii of Rostov removed numbers of widowed clergy from their positions and dispatched them to the monastery.[138]

The parish clergy, however, could resist diocesan authority by submitting a direct appeal to the Synod. They owed this important privilege to the Ecclesiastical Regulation, which admonished them to respect the bishop but authorized petitions to the Synod in the event of abuse.[139] Disgruntled clerics either sent a petition by mail or traveled personally to Moscow or St. Petersburg to lodge their complaints. Even though petitions often proved false, the Synod examined them conscientiously and sympathetically; it stayed sentences temporarily, ordered a copy of the file sent from the diocesan administration, and ultimately issued a resolution on the case. Although the Synod saved some innocent priests, it usually found the petitioner undeserving and returned him to his diocese.[140] To be sure, priests could not use this device lightly; they were dissuaded both by its costs (for preparing the document, bribing officials, and mailing or delivering it) and especially by fear of later retribution from the bishop. But the right of appeal gave them an important weapon, one that they used with special alacrity against bishops who had just fallen into disgrace. For example, once Riazan's bishop came under investigation in 1729, over thirty of his clergy hastened to file accusations against him.[141] The right of appeal, no doubt, tempered the bishop's vindictiveness and perceptibly diminished the vast authority he once claimed. Predictably, such appeals infuriated the bishops, and inspired the imperious Metropolitan of Rostov, Arsenii Matseevich, to complain that Synodal intercession for petitioners only produced "indulgence for other such scoundrels" and left "us poor hierarchs" without defense.[142]

After mid-century diocesan justice changed significantly, showing a striking new moderation in the treatment and punishment of clergy. In part, this moderation resulted from changes in the hierarchy: unlike such bishops as Arsenii (Rostov) or Platon (Vladimir), who terrorized the clergy with threats of "the most merciless punishment," the new generation of hierarchs was more restrained and cultivated. They reflected the influence of Enlightenment ideas current in lay society and undoubtedly wished to appear no less tolerant and merciful than their counterparts in the secular command. The government, moreover, directly intervened on behalf of the white clergy. In his brief reign Peter III upbraided the Synod in 1762 for failing to protect the lower clergy and to review complaints properly: "For a long time, to our great displeasure and to the general disgrace of all, it is noted that petitioners who come to the Synod about their authorities or the diocesan hierarchy, after a protracted delay here and without any decision whatsoever, are sent back to the very same hierarchs (against whom they petitioned) for resolution."[143] Similarly, when Metropolitan Arsenii denounced plans to secularize Church property, Catherine shrewdly exploited rumors that he abused his parish clergy. She ordered a review of his recent judicial decisions (of which a number were reversed) and published in a Moscow newspaper a declaration (in French and German only) condemning Arsenii for his abuses.[144]

The bishop, furthermore, now faced closer Synodal scrutiny, for after 1765 the Synod reviewed all episcopal decisions to defrock priests.[145] This tightened the Synodal command considerably. Hereafter the bishop had to submit detailed abstracts of the case, the crimes, and the legal basis for the decision to defrock. Consequently, he not only had to pass judgment in fear of a cleric's appeal to the Synod but also had to beware of automatic Synodal review and a formal reprimand for improper investigations and decisions. The Synod discharged its duty punctiliously, often reversing a bishop's decision or punishment.[146] For example, when a churchman of Kolomna complained in 1773 about diocesan injustice, the Synod agreed that the bishop had made an improper investigation and reinstated the churchman.[147] The Synod also defended a priest who had been incarcerated in a monastery solely on the basis of a noble's accusation and without any investigation, and sternly censured the diocesan authorities for their handling of the case.[148] Moreover, the Synod was very lenient in accepting appeals, even when the petitions did not formally comply with regulations. For example, although each petition was to be submitted on expensive official paper (gerbovaia bumaga), the Synod temporarily exempted a Kolomna cleric who claimed that he could not afford it.[149] The Synod was also tolerant of priests who journeyed illegally to Moscow or St. Petersburg to deliver their petitions. One priest, for example, obtained a passport to "see his relatives in Moscow" but actually used it to lodge a petition with the Synod; paying no heed to the ruse, the Synod ordered the priest's bishop to review the case personally.[150] Despite scores of state and Synodal bans on travel without passports, the Synod ignored such offenses and treated the cases on their own merits.

The hierarchs also moderated diocesan justice because of their growing concern about the clergy's waning status. After the emancipation of the nobility in 1762, the hierarchs became perceptibly fearful of a relative status decline for the "ecclesiastical rank," a concern transparently revealed by their demand at the Legislative Commission in 1767-68 that the clergy have equal status with the nobility.[151] Failing that, they tried to raise the clergy's status by initiating changes within the Synodal command, and "enlightened justice" was one way to do this. The most important measure was the exemption of the clergy from corporal punishment, a privilege accorded the nobility in 1762. Four years later the Synod declared in one case that corporal punishment was "indecent for the [clerical] rank"; that comment is all the more interesting because the case involved a cleric guilty of giving a solidarity oath to rebellious peasants, and ordinarily authorities showed little mercy in such cases.[152] Nevertheless, the Synod issued no general decree, and the priests remained liable to corporal punishment. Only in the following year did the Synod abolish such punishment of priests by ecclesiastical authorities in a decree that clearly communicated its acute concern for safeguarding clerical status:

> In many dioceses and monasteries, the ecclesiastical administrators (*dukhovnye komandiry*), as punishment for offenses, give the ordained clergy physical punishment and use torture in the interrogations, just as the secular government does to the common people. Because of this, the clergy—and especially the priests—lose the proper respect due them from society. They become objects of scorn and their flocks are subjected to great temptation to evil.[153]

But this privilege extended only to the rank: once defrocked, a priest suffered corporal punishment in the secular command like any commoner. The Synod, in the last year of Catherine's reign, petitioned to obtain full personal inviolability for the clergy; after some delay, Emperor Paul approved the request in December 1796. Although Paul soon abrogated this permanent inviolability (not only for the clergy but also for the nobility), the privilege was restored in 1801 by Alexander I.[154]

For all these reasons, the bishops now displayed a new moderation in their treatment of parish clergy. Above all, they renounced the intimidating technique of public floggings and abandoned traditional rhetoric, including such cherished phrases as "beat mercilessly in order to instill fear in others."[155] Instead, bishops now ordered rebukes and mandatory prostrations for most offenses and sentenced inveterate offenders to brief terms of monastery confinement. The bishops artfully assessed fines on offenders, both to chastise the guilty and to increase diocesan revenues. The bishops became more reluctant to defrock priests, deciding upon such punishment only after a long history of misdeeds. The detailed abstracts of defrocking cases, which bishops automatically submitted to the Synod after 1771, show that such clergy had usually committed an extraordinary number of crimes before finally exhausting the patience of the bishop.[156] Illustrative was the file on a Kolomna deacon, Ivan Gavrilov. Observing that the deacon "leads a bad life, always drinking and visiting taverns, plays cards, and indulges in other needless acts," the bishop noted that the deacon "had received corporal punishment on many occasions" and even spent one-half year in monastery confinement. Gavrilov had also missed a church service on an imperial holiday in 1770 because (in the deacon's words) "I had drunk myself into an unconscious stupor," and he had even "stolen money from the church."[157] Another typical case involved Boris Ivanov, a priest in Vladimir diocese whose record of crimes past and recent was long and varied: Ivanov had remarried a peasant woman from a village outside his parish without investigating to determine whether her husband (a soldier recruit) was still alive; during one liturgy he grabbed his sacristan by the hair and gave him a severe thrashing inside the church; he had been caught purloining apples and other food products; he had been frequently punished and even flogged for drunkenness; and Ivanov had even tried to steal an icon. Only after all these offenses did the bishop conclude that the priest was unreformable and resolve to defrock him.[158] Even in the case of such incorrigible clergy, bishops often resorted to one final act of clemency: rather than defrock a priest and dispatch him to the army or peasantry, they would permit the offender to assume a position as churchman.

The Synod moderated diocesan justice still further by reducing the punishment recommended by bishops. In exceptional cases the Synod increased punishment, especially if the case had broader implications for the state; usually, however, it softened the bishop's verdict.[159] For example, when one bishop proposed to defrock a priest for horse theft, the Synod amended his verdict to demotion to churchman, since the priest had voluntarily confessed and had no prior offenses.[160] In 1776 it reduced another defrocking verdict to demotion for a priest in Arzamas uezd who had maltreated his churchman and had married an underaged boy to a grown woman.[161] The bishop of Pereslavl recommended life imprisonment in a monastery for a priest who was a drunkard and who had violated the marriage laws; the Synod reduced that sentence to one year in monastery confinement.[162] Another bishop proposed to defrock a priest for violating laws against bigamy and underaged marriages but, "for the sake of supporting his family," the Synod reduced his punishment to demotion to churchman.[163] Thus the Synod's routine review of defrockings frequently brought an amelioration of punishment, even if well deserved.

The reformed system did not, however, eliminate tension between the bishop and subordinate clergy. The most serious problem was the lack of a unified law code: the Church, like the secular government, did not obtain a new law code or even an orderly publication of previous legislation until the reign of Nicholas I in the nineteenth century. In each case the consistory culled what seemed pertinent from canon law, government decrees, and Synodal resolutions; only rarely did it draw upon materials from the Holy Scriptures or from the pre-Petrine Church. Thus the legal guides were profuse and contradictory, often without exact prescription, a legal void that permitted the bishop to set penalties arbitrarily.[164]

Such legal chaos generated not only occasional instances of hierarchical abuse, but also frequent clerical appeals. A priest could calculate on receiving a more sympathetic sentence from the Synod, just by pleading for "charity and mercy" and emphasizing the hardships suffered by his "innocent family." Moreover, the clergy often *felt* themselves wronged; the arbitrariness of the bishop's decision, the lure of a Synodal amelioration encouraged many to file sweeping allegations against the local consistory or even the bishop and thereby find at least temporary refuge from punishment.[165] However justifiable such Synodal reviews, they undermined the bishop's authority and inspired a surprising audacity among the parish clergy. The peak of such insubordination occurred in the 1760s, when rumors of impending secularization and perhaps the summary treatment of Arsenii encouraged many priests to file complaints against diocesan authorities. Indeed it was this flood of complaints that caused the Synod to make reviews of all defrockings: so many clergy appealed that the Synod ordered bishops to file reports on all cases to expedite the reviews.[166] The parish clergy were quick to remind bishops of their right to appeal—a hint often given in the form of a veiled threat. An embittered priest in Suzdal, for example, expressed dissatisfaction with the bishop's decision and threatened him with an appeal to the Synod.[167] Thus the very reforms that aided the parish clergy also undermined the bishop's authority.

From the late 1780s the Synod began to reduce its role in reviewing appeals. Particularly in the case of clergy who had been illegitimately conscripted, the Synod cautiously eschewed any review—regardless of the circumstances or patent injustices. For example, when a churchman protested in 1785 that he had been drafted from the clergy on the basis of an uninvestigated accusation, the Synod declined to review the case; it replied that the conscription was already over (and could not be reopened) and that, after all, there was no shortage of clergy.[168] The Synod showed a new reluctance even toward affairs purely within the ecclesiastical command; waning liberalism, new Synod membership, and increasing secular influence (through "personal decrees" of the sovereign and the over-procurator) account for the change.[169] Thus when one Suzdal cleric accused his consistory of abuses, the Synod refused to consider the appeal because of a mere technicality, the expiration of the three-month limit for lodging appeals.[170] In 1791 a priest accused the Riazan consistory of abuse and family influence, allegations which earlier would have elicited Synodal protection; now the Synod refused the petition on the grounds that it was not written in the "proper legal form" or on official embossed paper and threatened to punish the appellant if he troubled the Synod again.[171] By 1803 a new over-procurator, A. A. Iakovlev, complained that "the majority of the Synod are just the same kind of episcopal despots [as other bishops], and they support the bishops' arbitrariness and avarice."[172] The main safety valve for grievances was thus closed; hereafter grievances accumulated against the hierarchy that would find release only in the ecclesiastical reform movement of the 1860s.

Thus the parish clergy held a relatively privileged legal status in the second half of the eighteenth century. They suffered from abuse and arbitrary justice but, because of the Synod, probably less than other social groups. And by mid-century rule by intimidation finally gave way to more moderate, even lenient treatment of misbehaving clergy. The Church improved judicial administration and moderated punishments, but it also threatened priests with a much broader scope of supervision. Although the clergy now received better justice, they also had to satisfy much higher standards of conduct and service—a requirement that many would find impossible to satisfy.

Disobedience and Rebellion

The obstacles to open rebellion against the hierarchy were formidable indeed. Above all, both state and Church authorities unequivocally commanded that parish clergy obey their bishops. The Ecclesiastical Regulation, though deliberately belittling the bishops' "pride and conceit," nonetheless placed the clergy under their command.[173] An instruction booklet for the clergy made the same point in ecclesiastical terms: "Hold your bishop as you do God; do his will in everything; preserve love and fear for him, as to Christ."[174] The Synod routinely reminded the clergy to obey a new bishop who had just been appointed. In 1748, for instance, when announcing the appointment of Platon to Vladimir diocese, the Synod ordered the parish clergy "to render the proper obedience to His Grace, as your pastor."[175] It also dealt out summary punishment to clergy who dared to insult their bishops. In the case of a priest from Riazan who had made false accusations against his bishop in 1784, the Synod issued this resolution: "Andreev has dared to make a false provocation against his diocesan hierarch, His Grace, Simon, bishop of Riazan, and for that—in accordance with the Ecclesiastical Regulation—he has made himself liable to the most cruel punishment."[176]

Consequently, it was virtually impossible to challenge the bishop's authority directly, even though a disgruntled priest had the right to appeal an abuse of that authority. There was, however, one important exception: Archpriest Petr Alekseev of Moscow. Alekseev was a diligent scholar, the author of several important treatises and translations. He also enjoyed good relations with the court but was constantly at odds with Metropolitan Platon (Levshin) of Moscow.

Drawing upon his vast (if erratic) scholarship, Alekseev challenged the principle of monastic domination in the Church. Alekseev had little use for monks and in 1789 complained that "here [in Moscow] life for the white clergy is impossible because of the monks' avarice."[177] He argued that widowed priests should be able to become bishops without taking monastic vows, a thesis that would flourish among parish clergy in the nineteenth century as well.[178] In a manuscript unpublished until much later, he rummaged through early Church history to prove that monastic power had no historical legitimacy, adduced examples of hierarchs who were not monastic clergy, and even argued that "the monastic rank is not a prerequisite for receiving the hierarchical rank but even forms a hindrance."[179]

The rank-and-file parish clergy did not challenge the principle of episcopal authority, but they certainly were willing to resist and ignore it. Even in the first half of the century, when the bishops retaliated with blunt force, the parish clergy were known to put up armed resistance to their ecclesiastical superiors. The Synod's Economic Chancellery received scattered reports in the 1730s that the rural clergy had used force to drive off ecclesiastical tax collectors.[180] Not only the distant Synod but even the immediate bishop encountered overt disobedience. The parish clergy generally acquiesced in the traditional taxes (such as the parish-church tax) but resented the new seminary tax that the bishops began to collect regularly from the 1730s and 1740s. Few priests saw any need for the "Latinist" education and, as one bishop reported, they simply refused in his diocese "to pay the tax because of their stubbornness and disobedience."[181] The parish clergy also challenged diocesan justice and resisted attempts by the consistory to arrest them. In 1728 one priest in the Moscow district even called out his peasant parishioners to help fight off the diocesan bailiffs who had come to arrest him.[182] A similar battle erupted in Riazan: when the bailiffs came to arrest several clergy for missing the loyalty oaths of 1730-31, the clergy cried out "Thieves!" and "rang the tocsin" to muster support from their parishioners.[183] Faced with frequent cases of such disobedience, the bishop of Pereslavl decreed in 1755 that "if anyone does not obey a district board and ecclesiastical consistory, then do not report this to the consistory but [immediately] seize him and, with the help of witnesses, bring him to the district board and consistory."[184]

Disobedience and open rebellion reached a peak in the 1760s and 1770s, when episcopal authority seemed to be on the verge of dissolving. Exploiting their right to petition, most clergy did not use violence but simply submitted a petition to the Synod. Some petitioners were astonishingly bold in their language, even though such insubordination risked Synodal condemnation.[185] Moreover, some priests flouted diocesan authority openly, especially during the turmoil that accompanied secularization in 1762-64. The state dispatched officers into the countryside to make inventories of church holdings, and the clergy even in the most remote backwaters were thereby alerted to the impending change; they perhaps may also have shared the peasants' wild hopes for emancipation, which the nobles had just received. In any event, the clergy ceased to pay parish-church and seminary taxes even before the state abolished them in 1764; as one priest wrote to the consistory in Vladimir, "We've heard much about the demands [for seminary money] but let it be known that in Iaropol'ch district no one will pay."[186] In Moscow the consistory complained in 1775 that the clergy were frequently heedless of ecclesiastical orders: "Some clerics appear with great slowness not only at the second, but even the third summons, and, having come to the consistory, they go home on their own will without having given the required testimony."[187] Bishops also encountered open expressions of contempt and disrespect, as some clergy cursed their bishops in the coarsest language, notwithstanding the costs of such articulateness.[188] Some hierarchs blamed the problem on the abolition of corporal punishment, which enabled disorderly priests to escape due correction; in 1772 the Synod itself adopted this argument and ordered bishops to defrock such priests.[189]

Some parish priests also went outside the ecclesiastical command for justice, appealing to secular authorities. The Synod severely punished such "insubordination," a serious threat to its own authority. In 1721 the Synod sternly rebuked a Moscow priest who had petitioned the secular command rather than the Synod, and it admonished all clergy to respect its authority.[190] When the Synod encountered such cases subsequently, it defrocked or flogged the offender—as in two cases in 1744.[191] Lower authorities encountered similar cases; the bishop of Pereslavl complained in the 1750s that "many clerics in our diocese are disobedient and insolent . . . and, avoiding their own ecclesiastical authorities, they turn to secular officials for administration and justice."[192] The government formally upheld the integrity of the Synodal command, but in some cases rebuked the Synod for punishing clerics who appealed to the civil government.[193] And of course the Synod did not dare punish clergy who appealed to the emperor. All rulers received petitions in their name and encouraged still more by treating them sympathetically; both Peter III and Catherine personally intervened on behalf of such petitioners, and the many rumors about Paul inspired a torrent of direct petitions in 1797.[194]

Thus the eighteenth century marks a significant turn in internal Church relations: the traditional bonds of hierarchical authority began to dissolve just as the hierarchs made a first systematic attempt to apply their formal authority over the parish clergy. The parish clergy, inspired both by hopes for sympathetic protection and by a sense of the bishop's vulnerability, were surprisingly audacious in their resistance to hierarchical pretensions. In more spectacular cases this meant open defiance of the bishop's rule, from armed resistance to petitions; in more typical cases, it meant a willingness to defy the bishop's demands on service and personal behavior—especially when such demands exceeded the clergy's means or violated their ties to the parish. But throughout it generated a pervasive, explosive tension in the Church. Znamenskii, observing the fruits of this tension in the 1860s, lamented the consequence of this conflict: "The inevitable result of the administrative system we have described was a complete rupture between the authorities and the subordinates, and a paralysis of the spiritual forces of the clergy."[195]

Thus the Church dramatically improved its administrative system between the 1720s and 1760s, experiencing a kind of organizational revolution. The selection of better administrators, the creation of smaller dioceses, Synodal centralization, the reorganization of diocesan administration, the establishment of new district offices—such changes significantly enhanced Church control over popular religious life, even in rural parishes. No longer did the priest receive ordination and disappear into the hinterland, free of episcopal control; he now served under a cloud of regular diocesan supervision. The hierarch could now more strictly enforce traditional obligations of the priest and even significantly expand the clergy's service role, with new demands that formed a principal part of the Church's struggle against paganism, superstition, and the Old Belief.

Ecclesiastical modernization, however, suffered from major deficiencies. The Church's new bureaucracy had an inadequate budget and structural problems; it still suffered from irregularity and knew venality on an even grander scale than before. These defects, though neither new nor unique to the Church, were particularly onerous for the parish clergy because of expanded service roles and greater interaction with diocesan administration. In a word, tensions between priest and hierarch after the mid-eighteenth century were not due to traditional abuse by "ecclesiastical princes"; on the contrary, most bishops shared the enlightened outlook of high society, and significant reforms had been made in ordination, taxation, and ecclesiastical justice. Instead, the new tensions resulted from the uneven process of ecclesiastical modernization. As the Church integrated the parish clergy into the Synodal command, it not only imposed tighter supervision and new service standards but also subjected them to the deficiencies of a semi-reformed administration.

The New World
of the Seminary

4

Before the Petrine reforms, the parish clergy of central Russia received
no formal education at all. Although they were the most literate group
in Muscovite society,[1] their preparation for church service was limited
to informal instruction by the local priest or a lay "master."[2] They had
no seminaries for advanced instruction; even their literacy was rudimentary—they often could "read" only the primer they had memorized
and even more often could only read, not write. Hierarchs deplored
the problem but did nothing beyond issuing decrees for the clergy to
educate their children.[3] By the early eighteenth century laymen had
also begun to criticize clerical ignorance.[4] N. I. Novikov evoked this
stereotype in 1772, when he referred ironically "to those blessed times,
when people became priests without knowing how to read and write."[5]

Such stereotypes, however, lost validity in the decades after the
Petrine reforms, which laid the foundations of a new institution in
Great Russia: the seminary. By the 1780s the new schools flourished in
every diocese and exerted an ever increasing influence over the careers
and culture of the parish clergy. More broadly, the new schools were
essential to the Church's task of modernizing or revitalizing the traditional religious culture. Only a well-trained priest could effectively
counter the challenges of the Old Belief from below, of Westernization
from above.

Successful training, however, depended not only on the mere
founding of schools but on how they developed and functioned. The
task here is to analyze that experiment in formal education—its purposes, patterns of growth, formal curriculum, and impact on the students and clergy.

The Aims of Education

Almost from the beginning, state and Church authorities agreed that the new schools were intended for the clergy's children, who were expected to enter church service. They did not formally exclude outsiders, however, and until mid-century some nonclerical children were occasionally admitted to ecclesiastical schools. Nevertheless, only clerical progeny were obliged to study in them "in hopes of becoming ordained clergy." This policy seemed to imply strictly religious schools, institutions which could give optimal service to the Church. Lay and Church authorities, however, did not consistently adhere to this view; rather, they formulated seminary policies with other—even opposing—considerations in mind.

In theory, the seminary could fulfill three functions. First, it could train candidates to perform the liturgy and services more accurately, more skillfully. Peter wanted the clergy "to learn how to administer the sacraments before being raised to this rank" and the Supplement to the Ecclesiastical Regulation mercilessly catalogued their egregious errors in service.[6] Second, a seminary could prepare a skilled pastor, competent to transmit and teach Orthodoxy, refute Old Believers, subdue the superstitious, and hold the respect of cultured noblemen. Third, formal education could aim to fashion a new ecclesiastical elite by providing the sophisticated learning appropriate for a bishop or archpriest. Specialized education was surely important to the Church; it alone could spawn an ecclesiastical intelligentsia capable of defending and developing "high Church culture." A seminary that performed these functions, combined in proper measure, could render maximum service to the Church. Purely religious aims, however, were not the only motives shaping the educational policy of the state and Church.

The state, at least formally, claimed an interest in ecclesiastical schools that would serve Orthodoxy. Peter declared that only educated priests could overcome superstition, enlighten schismatics, and convert the growing number of non-Orthodox minorities in the empire.[7] In the 1730s Empress Anna proclaimed a desire "to see that the holy churches are provided with learned priests in order to implant Christian law and decency more firmly" among the base commoners.[8] In 1762 Catherine II expressed similar views and blamed popular sinfulness and crime on the clergy's ignorance: "We are grieved to see that our simple people are quite far removed from proper conduct. Many priests, wearing the pastoral robe, not only do not know the true path to the people's enlightenment, but they themselves—often being barely literate—frequently serve as a harmful example for the simple people."[9]

Despite such pious avowals, the government did not vigorously promote an ecclesiastical education but rather pursued two other aims, both nakedly secular and self-serving. One was political stability. State officials shared the rationalist conception that education freed man from political error and forged unswerving loyalty to rightful authority. When priests were apparently involved in rebellion, the authorities unwittingly applied serf psychology, crediting their behavior to "ignorance" or "simplicity."[10] The state also encouraged formal political education in the seminary. Peter approved the study of Pufendorf's works and Paul even prescribed a kind of political surveillance over seminarians.[11] The second state aim was considerably more important: the government utilized the seminary to staff its bureaucracy and cultural institutions. As early as 1700, Peter told Patriarch Adrian that graduates of the Moscow Academy "should be put to various uses: church service, civil service, military service, architecture, and medicine."[12] As we have seen, Peter and his successors did indeed exploit the seminary, taking its best students, and Catherine specifically encouraged secular subjects suitable for lay careers.[13] Consequently, the government's verbal commitment to religious education counted for little.

The Church hierarchs were naturally more committed to a religious education. They wanted to prepare clerics who could proselytize and gave particular attention to homiletics in order to train skilled preachers.[14] The hierarchs, moreover, were keenly interested in high church culture. During the 1760s and 1770s they advanced several proposals to establish an "ecclesiastical university";[15] the Synod also responded eagerly to Catherine's invitation to train seminarians abroad and in 1765 dispatched several to England and Germany.[16] At the same time, the hierarchs resisted state attempts to secularize the seminary curriculum and to divert their students into lay professions.

Their commitment to religious education, however, was eroded by other concerns. Above all, the hierarchs wanted the clergy to be an educated elite, not simply competent pastors; the schools were to provide advanced education, not elementary instruction in reading or writing, or apprenticeship in performing the sacraments. Consequently, students were expected, before arriving at the seminary, to master the traditional primer (*bukvar'*, a reader which usually included a brief catechism).[17] At the seminary the youths were to absorb the education of a Latin grammar school, acquiring the hallmarks of contemporary European erudition—knowledge of Latin and classical culture. The preoccupation with Latin rather than with traditional culture was justified by a seminary reform project of 1766: "This [Latin] language is already studied in our seminaries and, moreover, a great number of useful books are in Latin, which can be regarded as a language of learned people, insofar as all learned people in Europe can converse and communicate in it."[18] That was true; Latin was the language of scholarship, in Protestant as well as Catholic lands, a consideration that caused European critics of the Latin curriculum to favor its retention, though on a lesser scale.[19] It is clear that the "Latin seminary" was designed not merely to train pastors but to mold a cultural elite.

This was surely an inflated ambition, one that exceeded the Church's resources and ignored its primary needs. The hierarchs were sensitive to the clergy's declining status, and presumed that education (and culture more generally) could restore public deference for the clergy, especially among the nobility. This was a transparent motive in Church policy by mid-century and received its most startling expression in a Synod proposal to the Senate in 1743. The Synod complained that, in contrast to European countries, "such learned persons [as the seminarians] are not as respected as they should be." Arguing that this discouraged the clergy from educating their children, the Synod wanted to bestow upon the seminarian the surest guarantee of respect in Imperial Russia, an official rank:

Decree and establish in Russia (as there is in other European states) a reward for students who have completed rhetoric class and entered philosophy class, who have written testaments from the Academy [of Moscow] and seminary teachers, and who have led honest and untarnished lives. [This reward should be] officer's ranks, gentry status, and swords. Upon completion of their schooling, grant them diplomas or patents for this.[20]

The Senate ignored the proposal; its aristocratic members had no enthusiasm for ennobling seminarians.

The linking of education to social aspiration became still more pronounced after mid-century. As the gap widened between aristocratic and ecclesiastical society, the hierarchs' status anxieties became still more acute, and their desire to emulate the nobility even more concrete; some bishops would attempt to transplant aristocratic culture into the seminary, from the social graces to the French and German languages. Such efforts, to say the least, did not answer the pressing religious needs of the Church. For the same reason, the hierarchs continued to defend the study of Latin, believing that it made the clergy more "learned" than the nobility. Metropolitan Platon, who wrote the first theological textbook in Russian, nevertheless defended the Latin curriculum as a valuable status symbol:

I do not advise that we allow lectures at the church schools to be given in Russian. Our clergy are viewed by foreigners as almost uneducated, since they do not know French or German. But, in our defense, is the fact that we speak and write in Latin. If we were to study Latin as we do Greek [that is, poorly], then we would lose our last honor, insofar as we would not speak or correspond in any [foreign] language.

Platon also justified the Latin curriculum by "the lack of learned books in Russian," but as the above statement suggests, the driving concern was clerical status.[21]

Status anxieties inspired still another unworkable policy: an effort to educate the entire clerical estate, not merely to train candidates for church service. In part, this policy resulted from the structure of the Synodal command, which made the hierarchs solely responsible for the clergy and their children's education. The hierarchs wanted a "mass" clerical education because of their concern for clerical status: by educating the whole clerical estate, they hoped to eliminate the traditional stereotype of "ignorant clergy and clerical youths." As a result, bishops measured success not by qualitative improvement but by mere increases in enrollment. Herein lay the contradiction: their fixed, limited resources (especially after Catherine's budgets in 1765) were intended to support elite schools, not mass education for the whole clerical estate.[22] The hierarchy therefore were pursuing contradictory aims—an elite education (with full Latin curriculum) and "mass" clerical education. It would prove an unworkable combination.

The Rise of the Seminary

Even before the Synodal reform of 1721, Peter the Great impatiently demanded that bishops establish formal schools and rebuked them for ordaining unqualified candidates. He admonished the Metropolitan of Rostov in 1705 to "ordain as priests and deacons candidates who are educated people, who are fully literate."[23] In 1708 the tsar decreed that "the priests' and deacons' sons are to study in the Greek and Latin schools" and often reiterated this demand in subsequent years.[24]

Despite Peter's thunder, few bishops opened schools before 1721. Besides the older academies in Kiev and Moscow, new schools were established in only three Great-Russian dioceses—Novgorod, Tobol'sk, and Rostov.[25] The Moscow Academy was a formidable institution, with several hundred pupils and a full course of study; yet it was not really an ecclesiastical school, for both curriculum and student population were decidedly secular.[26] The most promising experiment was the school founded in Rostov diocese in 1702. It reached an enrollment of two hundred pupils and even offered the Latin-Greek curriculum, not merely instruction in elementary Slavonic. This school was the personal creation of Metropolitan Dmitrii, however, and did not long survive his death in 1709.[27]

After the Synod was established in 1721, it goaded the hierarchs into making more serious efforts to open schools and compel the clergy to enroll their sons.[28] Its clamor brought immediate results.[29] Alongside the Moscow Academy, new schools sprang up in several central dioceses—Riazan, Suzdal, Kolomna, Rostov—as well as in outlying regions. The bishop of Riazan attached a church school to the local cipher school in 1722; a fully separate church school opened in 1726, and the following year it reported an enrollment of 269 pupils, some of whom had advanced from Slavonic to Latin.[30] In Suzdal a school lasted four years (1723-26), and 109 pupils matriculated; another school opened in Rostov and by the late 1720s had a significant enrollment.[31] The bishop of Kolomna founded a school in 1723, collecting some thirty pupils; by 1725-27 it had an enrollment of 720 pupils in Slavonic and Latin studies.[32]

These gains, however, were still quite modest. Even where established, the schools had only a slight impact: the 109 pupils in Suzdal mattered little in a diocese with several thousand clerical positions. Since most pupils came from the diocesan capital and adjacent uezd, most of the diocese was totally unaffected by the new institution. The curriculum was primitive; for most pupils, the school just duplicated the primer instruction traditionally taught at home. For instance, only about one third of the pupils in the Suzdal seminary advanced beyond the primer to study Slavonic grammar and some "orthography, etymology, and syntax."[33] Most important, the vast stretches of the Synodal region lacked even these modest beginnings.[34]

The dismal results were due to several problems that would persist throughout the eighteenth century. First, as many bishops complained, the schools had inadequate financial support.[35] The Ecclesiastical Regulation of 1721 authorized collections in kind from monasteries (1/20th of the harvest) and the parish clergy (1/30th of the harvest).[36] Yet bishops found it difficult, if not impossible, to collect the grain. They lacked precise data on landholdings and harvests; it was also unfeasible to transport grain from the distant parts of a diocese.[37] Bishops therefore had to content themselves with periodic threats that delinquent clergy would "lose their rank."[38] Second, bishops could not find competent teachers, and the Synod itself admitted "the dearth of satisfactory teachers."[39] The ambitious Latin curriculum required by the Ecclesiastical Regulation perforce remained a fantasy until trained Latin teachers could become available. Third, the parish clergy resisted the new educational demand as a superfluous, costly burden; most seminaries had great difficulty just finding and keeping enough pupils on the premises.[40] Fourth, some bishops were indifferent, even hostile, to the new schools, and they adroitly invented credible excuses to avoid fulfilling Synodal demands.[41]

In the second period, from Peter's death in 1725 until the 1760s, the schools expanded, but slowly and unevenly. Until the 1740s, in particular, the gains were minimal; a Synodal report of 1739 revealed that most seminaries in the central provinces had few students and only an elementary curriculum (Table 2). From the 1740s, the schools expanded steadily, and the development of Riazan's seminary was fairly typical. It opened as a separate school in 1726, and three years later boasted an enrollment of 359 students in elementary Latin. A newly appointed bishop showed little enthusiasm for the school, however; it rapidly declined and finally closed. Under Synodal pressure, the bishop reopened the school in 1738 but stubbornly refused to offer the Latin curriculum. In 1741 the exasperated Synod sent a decree "with the most severe rebuke for indifference to the implementation of decrees and, under fear of losing [your] hierarchical rank, it is reaffirmed that [you] establish Latin instruction in the school and find suitable teachers."[42] He at last complied, and by the 1750s the seminary claimed a sizable enrollment and fairly complete Latin curriculum.[43] The schools in Suzdal and Rostov followed a similar pattern: initially small, unstable, and often closing, they gradually achieved

Table 2. Seminary enrollments, 1739

Course level	Moscow Academy	Kolomna school	Riazan school	Rostov school	Empire
Latin school					
Theology	11	0	0	0	35
Philosophy	12	0	0	0	76
Rhetoric	16	0	0	0	288
Poesy	21	0	0	0	178
Syntax	39	0	0	0	251
Grammar	34	5	0	0	390
Infima	111	0	0	0	424
Fara	148	6	0	0	1,177
Total	392	11	0	0	2,819
Slavonic school	37	13	153	77	2,296
Greek school	0	0	0	0	93
Total	429	24	153	77	5,208

Source: ODDS, 17:32.

stability, larger student populations, and a fuller curriculum by the late 1750s.[44] Moreover, seminaries struck roots into some areas of central Russia for the first time. Most important was the new school at Trinity-Sergius Monastery, which opened in 1742 and soon became one of the best seminaries.[45] New schools were also founded in Vladimir (1750) and Pereslavl (1753); they too became stable, expanding institutions.[46] By the 1750s a Latin seminary thus existed in every central diocese.

Nevertheless, a real breakthrough was yet to be achieved. The growth was sluggish, and seminary enrollments were small compared to the size of a diocese. A report from Pereslavl in 1756, for example, showed that only 5 percent of the clergy's sons were enrolled in the seminary, a dismal picture even if one discounts the underaged or otherwise unfit.[47] When the bishop of Vladimir surveyed a district recently transferred to his diocese and containing 128 churches, he was dismayed to learn that only 28 clerics there had ever attended a seminary.[48] As before, pupils still came mainly from the diocesan capital and surrounding villages, leaving most of the diocese untouched by the new school.[49] Moreover, the seminar's structure was very pyramidic: most pupils were concentrated in the lower forms of Latin grammar and left before reaching the higher courses—the very pertinent subjects of philosophy and theology.[50] That fact inspired this critical comment by Over-Procurator Shakhovskoi: "As the submitted reports show, in some seminaries—after quite a few years—only a few students are enrolled. Even these are mainly in the lowest grades; from them (especially the obtuse ones, who are very numerous in all seminaries) one can expect little benefit and not very soon either."[51] Notwithstanding the Synod's admonitions and the bishops' efforts, most pupils left the seminary with only a smattering of Latin, having received neither religious training nor elite culture.

The slow, erratic growth in 1725-60 was due to the same problems that had bedeviled Peter's schools. Financial difficulties were particularly crippling. The parish clergy boldly resisted paying the seminary taxes, and monastery abbots and peasants were no less delinquent.[52] To simplify collection, most bishops after 1750 converted the tax in kind to monetary payments, but resistance did not abate.[53] Seminaries were still plagued by an extreme shortage of competent teachers, a fact often stressed by bishops and the Synod.[54] Instructors were available from the Moscow and especially Kiev academies,[55] but they commanded salaries that few seminaries could afford to pay. Some bishops dispatched promising youths to the Trinity-Sergius seminary or the Moscow Academy, which trained youths from other dioceses to teach in their home seminaries.[56] But in most cases the bishops had to use their own seminary graduates to teach, however ineptly.[57]

The bishops also had to contend with opposition by the parish clergy, who refused to surrender their children to the seminary.[58] The added costs, the seminary's legendary brutality, the seeming "superfluousness" of Latin studies, the loss of a son as a field hand and churchman—all these factors cemented the clergy's resolve not to hand over their sons. The priests submitted false reports on their sons, declaring them "illiterate," "underaged," or "overaged" in hopes of disqualifying them from the seminary.[59] Or they made them unacceptable to the seminary by marrying them early and having them installed as churchmen; when the bishop of Vladimir resolved to punish such marriage tricks by requiring the culprit to work in the seminary as a common servant, he soon had enough servants for the next ten years.[60] The bishop sometimes even met with violent resistance. For example, in 1750 a priest and his sons repelled the diocesan bailiffs with force and shouted: "Why did you come to me? What kind of pupil do I have? I never had one, you're a rogue, just coming to ruin us for no reason at all!" A churchman in Riazan diocese showed a similar enthusiasm for his son's schooling; according to the bailiff who tried to "announce the order to him," the churchman "did not comply, drove us from his courtyard with a club, cursed us with every kind of unseemly word, and called us thieves and rogues."[61] More often the clergy simply ignored the bishop's command. For example, when the Vladimir seminary ordered a "draft" (nabor) of new pupils in 1759, it obtained few; of 93 youths ordered to appear for examination, many sent lame excuses, some asserted illiteracy, and others simply never reported at all.[62] To ensure voluntary compliance, one bishop obliged his clergy to sign this oath: "We swear to the office of His Grace that those children selected will be sent without fail by next January, 1750 to study [at the seminary]. If for any reason we do not appear by that date, however, we will subject ourselves to whatever punishment is determined by His Grace."[63] Such oaths mattered little, and bishops had to use more than moral suasion to deal with resisters, dispatching squads to collect truants and making liberal use of fines, floggings, incarcerations, and even defrocking—all to no avail.[64] Indeed, once a bishop had collected pupils, he was loath to release them, even for short vacations. In Vladimir, for example, the bishop refused to allow the pupils to go home until a raging epidemic forced him to close the seminary.[65]

The Church partially compensated for the slow growth in its schools by improving informal education. The clergy opposed sending their sons to the seminary but willingly provided them with better home instruction—partly because the ordination examination had become more rigorous, partly because conscription menaced unlettered youths. To encourage home instruction, the Synod published and distributed new primers and catechisms in the 1740s.[66] A survey from the late 1730s shows that, of sons aged seven to fifteen (and still residing at home), very high proportions were judged literate: 69 percent in Suzdal diocese, 88 percent in Vladimir uezd, and 94 percent in Pereslavl uezd.[67] In addition, the Church established special schools after 1739 at the bishop's residence to provide intensive, brief training for candidates just before their ordination.[68] Some hierarchs even tackled the problem of remedial education for clergy who were already serving. One device was to arrange sessions on Sunday afternoons at the city cathedral, where the clergy and their sons were to hear explanations of the catechism and other religious materials. Those clergy in outlying districts were to study on their own and appear after the fall harvests for an examination.[69] Metropolitan Platon I of Moscow, complaining that his clergy "forget everything after ordination," in 1753 ordered his clergy to "memorize all that concerns their profession in the booklet published by the Synod."[70] Hierarchs occasionally even suspended "ignorant clergy" until they could read more fluently or knew the catechism better; the truly hopeless were dispatched to the secular command as illiterate and unfit for the clerical rank.[71] These measures on informal education were still very modest, however. By no means could they overcome the deficiencies of the seminary.

The breakthrough in seminary education came in the period after the 1760s, when the seminaries began to acquire a larger enrollment and a more complete curriculum. The growth followed a temporary decline in the 1760s, after Catherine had secularized monastery and church estates in 1764 and budgeted niggardly sums for the seminaries.[72] In many seminaries, the revenues were less than their income before secularization. For example, the seminary in Vladimir received about one thousand rubles per year before secularization, but only 653 rubles under the new state budget.[73] The budget had a devastating effect, forcing bishops to reduce seminary staffs and enrollments.[74] The retrenchment took place throughout the empire, not just in the central dioceses, as seminary enrollments decreased 20 percent between 1762 and 1766.[75] Once the seminaries had absorbed this initial shock, however, they began an unprecedented rate of growth, especially after 1780. The growth was indeed dramatic, as data for the whole empire show (Table 3), and seminaries in the central provinces followed this general pattern.[76] By the 1790s each seminary had hundreds of pupils and at least a small class in theology and philosophy (Table 4).

This upsurge in enrollments was due to several developments. One

Table 3. Growth of seminary enrollments, 1766-1808

Year	Enrollment
1766	4,673
1778	6,012
1783	11,329
1784	12,000
1793	13,312
1796	16,951
1797	17,130
1799	20,393
1808	29,000

Sources: TsGIA, f. 796, op. 51, g. 1770, d. 470, ll. 11-12; Titlinov, *Gavriil,* pp. 539, 541, 546, 797; Titlinov, *DSh,* 1:5-6; TsGIA, f. 796, op. 65, g. 1784, d. 443, l. 5 ob.; *PSPRPP,* 38; M. T. Beliavskii, "Shkola i sistema obrazovaniia v Rossii v kontse XVIII veka," *Vestnik MGU,* Istoriko-filologicheskaia seriia, 1959, no. 2, pp. 105-120.

Table 4. Structure of seminary enrollments, 1790s

Course	Suzdal (1793)	Kolomna (1790)	Riazan (1790)	Rostov (1790)	Moscow Academy (1790)	Trinity-Sergius (1790)
Theology	32	21	25	32	52	14
Philosophy	34	38	36	54	60	33
Rhetoric	113	79	72	104	111	65
Poesy	-	-	-	51	72	-
Syntax	125	117	76	217	127	54
Grammar	115	-	-	-	-	-
Infima	114	102	98	170	137	76
Fara (analogiia)	89	156	118	-	412	-
Slavonic	-	132	107	66	-	59
Total	622	645	532	694	971	301

Sources: TsGIA, f. 796, op. 71, g. 1790, d. 417, ll. 87-152, 385-454, 486-519; d. 418, ll. 517-590; op. 74, g. 1793, d. 94, ll. 349-421; Smirnov, *ITS,* pp. 238-240.

was the founding of the district school (*dukhovnoe uchilishche*), which offered elementary Latin courses and made study more accessible to all parts of the diocese. Metropolitan Platon of Moscow established the first district schools in 1775, and by the 1790s all the central dioceses except Riazan had followed suit.[77] These schools were largely responsible for the better geographical balance in the seminaries as well as overall increases in enrollments; by the 1790s the sons of rural clergy represented almost 90 percent of the student population.[78] Moreover, the parish clergy had become more cooperative, if not enthusiastic, about seminary education for their sons, and the problem of flight and resistance sharply diminished after 1770.[79] The change of heart was due to the fact that a youth could now obtain appointment only by attending the seminary, however briefly. The Synod categorically reaffirmed this educational requirement in 1770, and within a decade enrollments were large enough that bishops could strictly enforce the rule.[80] The seminary also protected the youths from government conscription, for by the 1780s even the Synod approved the removal of idle youths not enrolled in the seminary.[81] Although the state did draft "obtuse and corrupt" seminarians, the school still provided the best refuge from Catherine's inclement conscriptions.[82]

This very growth, however, aggravated the seminary's financial problems. Catherine disingenuously called the budget of 1765 "temporary" but actually made only modest increases thereafter.[83] When some importunate hierarchs tried to solicit larger sums, in 1787 the aging empress crossly forbade them to seek further increases in seminary budgets.[84] The schools obtained no significant relief until 1797, when Paul approved large new budgets for the seminaries.[85] Until then, however, the hierarchs had to use a host of ingenious devices for supplementary revenues. Some bishops even dared to collect special levies from the clergy, although this had been outlawed in 1764.[86] The bishop of Vladimir, for instance, made assessments on the diocesan clergy to purchase books for the seminary library, and the bishop of Riazan took similar measures.[87] Metropolitan Platon of Moscow, however, drew a formal reprimand in 1787 for making more general assessments on his clergy.[88] Sometimes, the clergy gave voluntarily; the district schools, in particular, were financed by the local clergy, who preferred to maintain a district school rather than send their children to the distant seminary.[89] Bishops also supported pupils by awarding them reserved positions (*zachislennye mesta*); the seminarian formally held a clerical position, obtaining a share of the parish revenues.[90] This practice, legally condoned by the Synod,[91] was selectively applied in all the central dioceses.[92] The distribution of such awards in Rostov seminary was typical: priest or deacon appointments were rare (and limited to students in the uppermost grades), while the less valuable positions were given to younger pupils, often orphans.[93] Another source of income for the seminary was fines, levied on misbehaving clergy and donated to the seminary.[94] Some seminarians were supported by actual employment, either as teachers in the seminary or as tutors for the local gentry.[95]

All these resources, however, fell far short of seminary expenditures. The bulk of the budget had to cover fixed basic costs—the teachers' salaries, administration, and plant maintenance. Consequently, only a portion of the budget—less than one third—could be used to support the seminarians directly.[96] Thus most pupils had to obtain support from their parents; from 75 to 90 percent of the seminarians studied "at their father's expense" (Table 5). If the pupils in the district schools are added to those in the seminaries, the percentage increases still more.[97]

The seminary, consequently, faced a perpetual problem of penury and hardship. It could not—as the Ecclesiastical Regulation had intended—provide free instruction, enabling every clergyman's son to receive a full education; rather, supported by their fathers, pupils reached the middle courses and simply withdrew after satisfying the demand for some seminary attendance (Table 6). Worse still, the quality of seminary education suffered from financial difficulties. The school could not afford to employ qualified teachers, to maintain adequate dormitories, or to expand the seminary library. In a word, the new institution fell far short of its grand ambitions.

A Seminary Education

Wherever the clergy's sons matriculated, they found a fairly uni-

Table 5. Sources of seminarian support, 1790s

Seminary	Year	Stipend		Reserved position		Father	
		No.	%	No.	%	No.	%
Kolomna	1790	70	10.9	85	13.2	490	75.9
Moscow							
Academy	1790	240	25.6	30	3.2	666	71.2
Riazan	1790	53	10.0	12	2.3	467	87.7
Rostov	1790	58	8.4	102	14.7	534	76.9
Vladimir	1793	46	7.4	34	5.5	542	87.1

Sources: TsGIA, f. 796, op. 71, g. 1790, d. 417, ll. 87-152, 385-454, 486-519; d. 418, ll. 517-590; op. 74, g. 1793, d. 94, ll. 349-421.

Table 6. Grade achieved at departure from school, 1790s

Grade level	Riazan Seminary	Kolomna Seminary	Moscow Academy	Rostov Seminary	Suzdal Seminary
Theology	0	2	19	13	12
Philosophy	2	0	8	14	14
Rhetoric-Poesy	0	1	14	38	38
Upper Grammar	7	5	7	54	42
Lower Grammar	21	7	13	21	35
Preparatory	12	0	10	3	3
Total	42	15	71	143	144

Sources: TsGIA, f. 796, op. 71, g. 1790, d. 417, ll. 87-152, 385-454, 486-519; d. 418, ll. 517-590; op. 74, g. 1793, d. 94, ll. 349-421.

form curriculum of the Latin grammar school. It first appeared in the Ukraine in the seventeenth century, where it was adopted by the Orthodox Kiev Academy in its struggle with the Jesuits.[98] After 1700, when many Ukrainian hierarchs and monks entered church service in Great Russia, they brought the Latin curriculum along with them.[99] Introduced into the Moscow Academy by the Kievan graduate, Stefan Iavorskii, it later became standard in all diocesan schools. This curriculum was similar to that of contemporary European grammar schools, where it provided the foundation for an elite education.[100] The Ecclesiastical Regulation of 1721 proposed significant changes in the Kievan model; to suit Peter's practical interests, it incorporated a full-year course in arithmetic and geometry.[101] However, as the new schools took shape in the 1740s and 1750s, the hierarchs disregarded these instructions and built their seminary curriculum after the Kievan design.

In the period before 1760, a full curriculum consisted of four main divisions—a preparatory school, elementary school, advanced Latin school, and school of philosophy and theology (Table 7).[102] Only the preparatory school offered instruction in Slavonic writing and reading. This was an apparent duplication of traditional home instruction but was justified as necessary for orphans; more important, it was also used to help prepare enough students, since the clergy often claimed that their sons were still unprepared for the seminary. The preparatory school also taught the pupils note singing (notnoe penie) and the catechism.

The elementary school was devoted almost entirely to Latin. The first "form" or grade (variously called fara, analogiia, or elementar') provided an introduction to Latin and required the pupil to begin his

Table 7. Structure of the seminary curriculum

Division	Course	
	1750s	1790s
Preparatory school	Slavenskaia shkola (Pis'mennaia shkola)	Russkaia shkola
Elementary Latin	Fara (analogiia) Infima	Nizshaia shkola
	Grammatika Sintaksima	Vysshaia shkola
Advanced Latin	Piitika Ritorika	Piitika Ritorika
Philosophy and Theology	Filosofiia Bogoslovie	Filosofiia Bogoslovie

first reading and writing in Latin. The pupil then advanced to a formal three-year program of Latin grammar, which was based on Emmanuel Alvarez's three-volume textbook, widely used at the time. It began with the preliminary course (*infima*), where the pupil learned more Latin grammar, brushed against etymology, and attempted his first translations. The next year (*grammatika*) was a systematic study of grammar and a preliminary overview of syntax; here pupils made more extensive translations, practiced conversational Latin, and memorized a Latin lexicon to enrich their vocabularies. The final year was syntax (*sintaksima*); by then the pupil was expected to have full command of Latin. Theoretically, the elementary school was to last four years, with one year for each of the courses. But most youths found the Latin studies an exasperating experience; coming from culturally deprived backgrounds, they found the material totally alien and incomprehensible. Consequently, pupils often remained two or more years in a single course and gladly departed at the first opportunity. A fair share of the blame belongs to Alvarez's textbook, which "is extremely difficult to understand not merely for someone just beginning Latin but even for someone whose knowledge is already fairly extensive."[103]

The few who survived elementary school went on to advanced Latin studies, intended to equip them with polished, literary Latin. Classes were conducted entirely in Latin, and pupils spent most of their time translating or writing Latin compositions. The first year of the advanced course was poesy (*piitika*), a one year course on the rules and forms of versification. Pupils learned to write verse in Latin;

only rarely did they compose Slavonic verse. The next course was rhetoric (*ritorika*), the highest course available in most provincial seminaries before 1760. It was devoted to Latin prose composition, although occasionally students wrote in Russian. During these two years, pupils acquired the adornments of Latin and classical culture and learned to weight down their compositions with cumbersome apostrophes and irrelevant allusions to classical deities. Even essays on Christian faith and tradition were not spared a thorny underbrush of classical allusions that obscured the writer's point—if he bothered to make one.[104]

The uppermost levels, theology and philosophy, were reached by only a minuscule number of students. Before 1760 these courses existed only at Trinity-Sergius seminary and the Moscow Academy; other central schools did not introduce them until the 1760s, sometimes as late as the 1780s. Surprisingly, even here the Church did not steep the seminarian in an Orthodox education: philosophy and theology courses were undisguised imitations of Western scholasticism. In philosophy, the seminarian learned Aristotelian logic; in theology, he absorbed the teachings of Thomas Aquinas. Lacking Russian theological textbooks and too busy to study Orthodox sources, the instructors made only modest changes in their Western guides.[105] As critics have complained, this whole course of instruction was a barren formalism, giving the student a Latin and dialectic form devoid of intellectual and religious content.[106]

The busy schedule of Latin conjugations and declensions left little time for actual religious instruction. Some bishops tried to attend to this essential task. The pupils studied a catechism from their first course, and some bishops arranged special sessions to explain its meaning.[107] Moreover, even though the courses were conducted in Latin, they nonetheless dealt with religious subjects—as did student compositions.[108] And later advanced seminarians were given practical experience in preaching at the seminary church.[109]

The curriculum before 1760 also included some secondary subjects but gave them only nominal attention. The schools, intent on teaching Latin, generally disregarded Greek, despite its obvious importance to the Eastern Church; even Moscow Academy, once a staunch defender of Greek studies, resumed this instruction only in 1738—and had to send to Latin Kiev for a teacher. Other seminaries taught Greek but haphazardly and poorly. Hebrew, it goes without saying, was even more neglected. The secular subjects outlined in the Ecclesiastical Regulation—arithmetic, geometry, geography, and history—received virtually no attention.[110]

The Latin curriculum was firmly rooted in the seminary by 1760, but it suffered from grievous inadequacies. In the words of Catherine's acerbic critique:

> Hitherto the diocesan schools have had very few worthy and reliable pupils, a poor system of study, and inadequate support for students. In some places, they often learn Greek and Latin from incompetent teachers. And they know nothing except the schoolish beginnings of Latin. They do not study philosophy and ethics, ecclesiastical or secular history, or the globe and places where other peoples live.[111]

Her assessment was justified. Instructors were incompetent, overworked, and transient; few stayed long enough to learn their own courses.[112] Moreover, the seminaries had only minuscule libraries, which consisted mainly of textbooks, not more serious literature; even a Bible was rare. The seminary in Riazan had accumulated two hundred volumes by 1741 and almost all were textbooks and lexicons; the Suzdal library recorded only 27 titles by 1763.[113] A petition from the bishop of Vladimir in 1761 reveals the full seriousness of the problem: "In the seminary, due to the lack of books, there exists such a need that, for the rhetoric course, it was necessary to transcribe orations from several books in the Suzdal seminary."[114] Only Trinity-Sergius seminary, with a registry of 2,655 volumes in 1762, could boast of an adequate library.[115]

After 1760 seminary education underwent some change.[116] The Latin curriculum retained its basic structure, with minor reorganizations and modifications in nomenclature,[117] but there were some improvements. In the elementary school, the Alvarez grammar was replaced by a more comprehensible textbook by Lebedev.[118] More significant were the changes at the uppermost level. In philosophy, instructors replaced Aristotle with Friedrich Christian Baumeister's textbook, popular for its direct reply to Enlightenment skepticism.[119] In theology, the seminaries abandoned Aquinas and began to use the writings of Feofan Prokopovich and new theological textbooks written by Russian hierarchs.[120] The bishops also allotted more time for purely religious instruction at all levels of the seminary.[121]

There were also some attempts to supplement the Latin core with other subjects. One was Russian itself. This was partly due to the government, which required the Church to use government textbooks for secular subjects; these books were of course in Russian, not Latin.[122] But it was also due to the bishops themselves, who perhaps were sensitive to the general European reaction against the preoccupation with Latin and who realized that seminarians would be preaching not in

Latin but in Russian. Even a staunch defender of Latin like Metropolitan Platon encouraged the study of Russian: "Exercises should alternately be done in both languages [Russian as well as Latin], for it is foolish to take up the Latin tongue and discard one's native language."[123] In the intermediate courses the students now wrote compositions in Russian, and in the uppermost courses they practiced giving sermons in Russian.[124] The metropolitan of St. Petersburg even argued in 1786 that most students should abandon Latin studies, which would be a "necessary study" only for advanced students.[125] His proposal finally became law in 1803, when the Synod authorized elementary "Russian schools."[126] From the 1760s the seminaries also expanded instruction in languages, offering not only Greek and Hebrew but also French and German.[127] Finally, at the government's behest, the seminary introduced more secular subjects—history, geography, and arithmetic.[128]

Despite these changes, the Latin yoke still lay heavily upon the seminary. Its domination was so pervasive that the Tula seminary even used a Latin translation of Platon's theological textbook, originally written in Russian.[129] Even if the Latin textbooks had improved, most pupils still found Latin grammar incomprehensible. The attrition rate in elementary courses remained devastatingly high; as before, proportionally few reached the essential courses of theology and philosophy.[130] Moreover, because of the Latin domination, serious attention to other subjects was impossible. Even the library holdings were in Latin: 304 of 330 volumes in the Suzdal collection in 1770 were in Latin, only 26 books were in Russian.[131] Few pupils actually learned the modern languages, for the level of instruction in provincial seminaries remained abysmally low.[132] Other secular subjects suffered a still worse fate. Called "extra-ordinary subjects," they were papered over the Latin core and given only nominal attention. A typical attitude was expressed by the hierarch of Riazan, who wanted students to learn only enough mathematics in order to "understand the Holy Scriptures, other sciences, physics [that is, metaphysics], . . . and the general needs of life."[133] A commission on seminary reform observed in 1808 that "exclusive exercises in this [Latin] were the cause of a gradual weakening of the study of Slavonic and Greek, so necessary to the Church."[134]

After 1760 the authorities still failed to solve two major problems that had troubled seminary education throughout the eighteenth century: faculty and libraries. Their teaching staffs were still poorly trained, unspecialized, and unstable.[135] Most seminary teachers were either white clergy or laymen (recent seminary graduates, probably waiting for a choice appointment). This happened in spite of the bishops' preference for monks, which Platon explained in this way: "It is necessary to allow the tonsure of educated people who wish to do so, for the white clergy are not reliable [as teachers]. A year, or at most two, and they ask to be released: they desire to teach only in hopes of a better [clerical] position. Monks, however, are more reliable."[136] But the educated monks were few and expensive; most seminaries had to settle for local priests or former students.[137] Their abilities were so poor that during the seminary reforms of 1808-14 the authorities released many of these instructors as incompetent.[138] Seminary libraries, likewise, improved little. Except for Trinity-Sergius seminary, which had amassed 6,000 volumes by 1782, most libraries still consisted of basic textbooks and chance gifts.[139]

Thus the seminary was of limited usefulness to the Church; it was not an intensive preparatory school for robed cadres. For those few who graduated, it provided an excellent education. Just as defenders of the Latin grammar school argued that it produced many distinguished figures, so too have supporters of the seminary noted the learned prelates and scholars among its alumni.[140] It is arguable, however, whether such figures emerged because of the seminary or in spite of it;[141] in any event it is clear that the seminary brought little return on the Church's crucial investment. Latin studies were valueless to the multitude of pupils who withdrew prematurely to become priests and churchmen: they left the seminary knowing neither Latin nor their pastoral profession. Metropolitan Arsenii, for all his obstinacy and brutality, showed uncommonly good sense on this matter: "No other kind of episcopal schools are needed than Russian ones, for our Church services are not in Latin or in any other foreign language, but in Russian."[142] That led to Arsenii's preference for simple religious instruction in the catechism: "This booklet [Peter Mohila's catechism] is more essential for the priest than philosophy or other academic books, especially in the countryside, where one must toil [in the fields] to support himself."[143] Arsenii, who remained oblivious to the challenges raised by Westernization,[144] was wrong to deny altogether the need for elite schools, but his critique of the contemporary seminary was certainly apt. In addition, the seminary demonstrated a decidedly secular inclination; seminarians often had only the haziest conception of Orthodoxy. And there was even a hint of radical impiety, a characteristic that became pervasive in the nineteenth-century seminary and made it a seedbed of radicalism; Radishchev's *Journey from St. Petersburg to Moscow*, appropriately enough, includes an encounter with a skeptical seminarian, and by the latter decades some hierarchs even took measures to censor and regulate the reading of "dangerous books."[145] The first generation of Chernyshevskiis and Dobroliubovs was not far off.

The Seminary Experience

The seminary, a boarding school for most pupils, was a formative experience. Boys ordinarily matriculated between the ages of ten and fifteen, though sometimes as young as six or seven.[146] For most youths it was a traumatic uprooting, a sudden removal from the carefree abandon of the home to the strict, alien world of the seminary.[147] If they remained long enough, their cultural experience transformed them into a distinctive social type—the seminarian. It was not an enviable status. Nobles resented the seminarian, who aspired to high government service; townsmen identified the seminarian as a thief and a ruffian, and their mutual hostility often erupted into bloody brawls.[148] Scorn for the seminarians persisted in the nineteenth century, when aristocrats treated them with transparent condescension.[149] Even a democratic *raznochinets* like Belinskii used the term "seminarian" as an epithet.[150]

The Ecclesiastical Regulation of 1721 provided a specific model to regulate life at the seminary, which was to be built "in the form of a monastery." Above all, the youth was to be strictly isolated from the outside world, especially his own family: "No seminarian shall be given leave from the seminary into the cities or anywhere else to visit his family until he has become accustomed to living in the seminary." A school official was to accompany him on visits to his kinsmen; or, if they came to the seminary for a visit, the official was to be present at their meeting. These rules were intended partly to frustrate escape plots but also to protect the youth from the corrupting influences of his own family—an interesting commentary, to say the least, on the author's opinion of parish priests. To ensure order and serious study, the seminary authorities had virtually unlimited disciplinary powers over the pupils: "The rector, the highest authority of all, can use any punishment, according to his finding." In true Petrine spirit, the Regulation sought to arrange every detail of life: "Times shall be assigned to the seminarian for every activity and relaxation, when to go to sleep, when to get up, to pray, to study, to go to the refectory, to stroll, etc." It was eminently appropriate for the Regulation to offer a military metaphor: "Each of those hours will be designated by a bell, and all seminarians, like soldiers upon a drumbeat, shall enter upon their work, whatever is scheduled for the set hour, upon the sound of bells." Such regimentation could hardly appeal to the new students, and the Regulation admitted that "such a way of life for young people appears to be irksome and similar to imprisonment." But, it added reassuringly, "for him who becomes accustomed to live thus, if even for a single year, it will be most agreeable."[151]

In the period 1721-60 the seminaries did not implement the Regulation in all its ornate detail, but they accepted its basic spirit. Like the tsar, the bishops identified seminary education as a service obligation of the clerical soslovie; they treated students not as children but as young men officially beginning service.[152] Consequently, they regarded truancy and childish pranks as serious crimes, deserving the most severe and merciless punishment. This was a typical Petrine attitude; similar views prevailed in the civil service and military. Strict service discipline seemed all the more necessary if the bishops were to quash the clergy's and their children's resistance to "educational service." In theory, the seminary was concerned about the youths' moral upbringing, since they were presumably to enter the clergy; accordingly, the Ecclesiastical Regulation and the bishops' decrees explicitly required the seminary authorities to oversee the seminarians' conduct.[153] School reports and the graduation certificate (attestat) included an evaluation of the bearer's conduct at the seminary.[154]

Moral training in the seminary, however, was a clear failure. Since the school was seen as part of "service," most attention was on discipline, not moral upbringing.[155] The seminary administrators and teachers were sometimes even accused of corrupting the seminarians.[156] This reprimand to the teachers in Riazan seminary in 1752 was typical: "Perform your school duties with extreme zeal, and be occupied with the reading of useful books—and not card playing, as previously observed."[157] The rector of the seminary in Vladimir was dismissed in 1759 (in the bishop's words) "because of his sloth in attending to teaching in the seminary and because of his well-known drunken behavior."[158] Yet, even without corruption, the seminary was a brutal disciplinarian, modeled more after Peter's regiments than Prokopovich's monasteries. The teachers indulged their whims, arbitrarily slapping and switching the pupils.[159] Some of the worst abuses stemmed from the institution of komandirstvo—where an elder student was appointed "commander" (komandir) and tyrannized his defenseless "subjects."[160] Students sometimes rebelled in desperation, petitioning the bishop to protect them;[161] most, however, meekly tolerated their hardships, fearful of retribution from the seminary authorities. The maltreatment in the seminary gave rise to this song, popular among seminarians of Vladimir in the 1750s and 1760s:

Living in school is not for us,
They flog us a hundred times a day.
Oh Woe! Oh Grief!
They're always beating us![162]

Each seminary had a few chilling tales of brutality, and it is hardly surprising that the word "seminary" still struck terror into the hearts of clergy even in the nineteenth century.[163] The priest and his son would have derived scant comfort from knowing that such discipline was common to all schools, European as well as Russian; for the clergy the seminary simply represented a great burden and traumatic experience, unknown either to their forefathers or to most of their contemporaries.

The seminary, moreover, was a pedagogical disaster. It rarely expelled pupils, however unfit or incorrigible. Although the Ecclesiastical Regulation instructed the bishops to remove "obtuse students," most hierarchs were reluctant to do so—probably because of the difficulties in finding replacements.[164] Each class therefore accumulated a number of unfit pupils, who were a poor investment of the seminary's meager resources.[165] Furthermore, teaching methods were primitive and insensitive; instructors literally demanded rote memorization. The teacher read out each lesson for the pupils to memorize (textbooks were rare) but did not quiz them on their comprehension; pupils memorized the material, without grasping its meaning. There are, for example, reports of whole classes who could read fluently one book in Latin or Greek—but no other; the youths had simply memorized the one volume.[166] The same thing was true for the catechism, whose abstract terminology conveyed little to the pupils.[167] As Bishop Simon of Riazan aptly remarked, "Pupils often leave the seminary much duller than they entered."[168]

Students also suffered from hardship and deprivation at the seminary. Because of the seminary's small, unreliable income, it often had some very lean years; its only real prospect was for things to get worse. Students who had stipends suffered perpetual deprivation; in the 1740s, for example, Riazan seminarians repeatedly implored the bishop to increase their food allowance, claiming that "we are suffering from great starvation."[169] The seminary of Vladimir reported in the 1750s that "many pupils, deprived of the support due them at the seminary because of insufficient collections, go out and beg food like common beggars."[170] Students without stipends fared worse still. Townspeople fearfully watched hungry seminarians wandering the streets in search of food, ready to steal some unguarded morsel.

Understandably, students fled the seminary in droves—with diocesan bailiffs in hot pursuit. The proportion of pupils in flight at any given time was surprisingly large; in 1750 the seminary of Riazan reported that 31 percent (47 of 153) of its students had vanished; every seminary chronicled similar reports.[171] Most fugitives were recaptured and mercilessly flogged; yet they continued to flee.[172] Some even took the extraordinary step of volunteering for the army or peasantry, as did one desperate seminarian in Vladimir in the 1750s.[173] He had entered the seminary at the ripe age of twenty "to study the Latin dialect" but in a few years began to run away "because of the incomprehensibility of Latin science and because of the intolerable beatings." After repeated failures to escape, he disappeared once more in 1754; this time, however, he went to the government authorities and volunteered to become an army recruit. That he should make such a request is astounding; to be sent as a recruit was regarded by the serfs as one of their master's severest punishments. But the youth lacked a written release from the seminary (as part of the ecclesiastical command), and the army returned him to the school—where, predictably enough, he received another sound thrashing. He last appears in the archival record in one final act of desperation: he filed a false declaration of "word and deed" against seminary authorities. This time his wish was granted: after one last flogging, he was dispatched to the army.[174]

The atmosphere in the seminaries, however, improved significantly after Catherine came to the throne in 1762. The empress broadcast Enlightenment rhetoric about education, and the new state pedagogy gradually reshaped Church as well as secular education. Catherine rejected the narrow Petrine conception of education as advanced, professional training; instead, she professed an interest in learning itself, favoring a broad humanistic curriculum. Catherine also wanted to replace service discipline with attention to the broader tasks of moral upbringing.[175] She also tried to improve pedagogical methods and ordered that the seminaries replace rote memorization with the new question-and-answer techniques of state schools.[176]

The new pedagogy quickly penetrated the seminary, as Church hierarchs hastened to emulate this model of cultivated behavior.[177] To be sure, the new style was slow to reach the provinces—one lad in Suzdal was disabled for two weeks in 1772 after insulting a teacher.[178] And the Petrine love of regimentation died slowly; bishops still issued comprehensive instructions on every aspect of seminary life.[179] But the spirit was different. In his "instructions" for the seminary in Riazan, Bishop Simon used a language of gentle concern and directed teachers to correct pupils through persuasion rather than stark terror.[180] The instruction for Vladimir seminary in 1782 ordered the teacher to "take the place of the student's parents," for the school is responsible for the seminarian's moral upbringing. The teacher must "treat the pupils as if he were their father, that is, with affection and love, [and], taking upon himself the feelings of a loving father, the teacher should be affectionate, and should never be morose, angry, hot-tempered." Hence punishment was not to be administered in anger but only to serve "the goal of correcting pupils."[181] Hierarchs also left corporal punishment to the exclusive discretion of the rector, who was to use it only in extraordinary cases. This new climate helped defuse the clergy's dread of the seminary, and the tasks of gathering and retaining students became considerably easier.[182]

The seminary authorities, however gently, were still supposed to mold the youths into suitable candidates for church service. They used inspectors and "censors" to observe the students' behavior and required the seminarians to attend church regularly.[183] The seminary of Trinity-Sergius monastery even prepared a list of written instructions for the seminarians to observe, especially when away from the school during vacations.[184] In 1784 the hierarch in Vladimir tried to prevent seminarians from frequenting the local taverns: "Do not release them [the seminarians] from the monastery anywhere without a teacher or appropriate bailiff. They are not allowed to go to the banks along Trinity or Ivanov, or other tempting places under any circumstances—for drunkenness is to be noted in many who go there."[185] These measures corresponded to a similar policy being applied to the clergy themselves.

And just as in the case of serving clergy, the bishops tried to instill in seminarians the genteel air of polite society. The hierarchs were sensitive to the clergy's declining status and deliberately tried to transplant gentry manners into the seminary and distinguish students from commoners. Metropolitan Platon, who was especially concerned about the clergy's status problems, made the most dramatic attempts. He appointed an inspector to the seminary, who was "responsible for the seemliness and welfare of the pupils." More specifically, the inspector was "to implant in the students a noble pride [blagorodnoe chestoliubie], which will guide them in their behavior like a spring." The inspector should also try "to teach civility and courteousness" to the seminarians. Platon wanted the youthful seminarians to use the full polite form of address (imia-otchestvo) and even to address each other as "Mr." (gospodin). To eliminate "barbarousness" (dikost'), the seminarians were to receive "materials for conversations and other exercises seemly and appropriate for their rank." Platon gave detailed instructions on table manners; he even ordered that "the seminarians, for natural needs, always go to the place appointed for that [purpose]."[186] His efforts were surprisingly successful; not only did the Moscow seminarians learn to "go to the place appointed for that" but they also acquired a striking gentility that astounded provincial seminarians coming to Moscow.[187]

Other seminaries likewise attempted to imitate aristocratic gentility. Pupils were encouraged to study French and German in order to gain access to the homes of the nobility; as one cleric noted, "those who know Greek and Hebrew are never hired to teach as tutors at nobles' houses, whereas those who know French and German are constantly invited."[188] Provincial bishops even tried to make the annual (or bi-annual) theological debate (*disput*) into a public event. The debates were ostensibly designed to display the seminarians' knowledge of philosophy and theology; the youths treated such questions as the unity of the Trinity or the inadequacy of reason alone.[189] But in fact the debate became a great social occasion. The bishop invited local nobles to attend the festivities, which included not only theological debates but also recitations of poetry, music, and refreshments.[190] Seminarians were also called upon to perform a similar role in various public ceremonies; the opening of the new guberniias in 1778, for example, was celebrated by public assemblies, where seminarians recited adulatory verse about the empress and local dignitaries.[191]

Beneath this genteel veneer, however, the provincial school was still an utter nightmare for most seminarians. Their living standards sharply declined in the 1780s and 1790s, when the frozen seminary budgets could not support the growing enrollments. The students received negligible support;[192] they lived in crowded dormitories,[193] or took lodging in the squalid hovel of some local townspeople.[194] Nor did Catherine's enlightened rhetoric always dissolve the disciplinarian instincts of the rector and teachers; only a determined bishop could enforce his gentle "instructions."[195] Ironically, these hard conditions produced the very opposite of what the hierarchs had wanted. Instead of cultivated and refined seminarians, the typical provincial seminary produced youths hardened to the sins and foibles of townspeople; they left the seminary with neither an elite Latin education nor the polite gentility of the nobility.

The Impact of the Seminary on the Clergy

The seminary inevitably reshaped the basic contours of the social and cultural profile of the parish clergy. One significant effect of this institution was discernible almost from the very beginning: it set the clergy apart from the rest of society. This was partly a cultural process; the Latin culture of the seminary clashed violently with Russian culture—old and new, peasant and noble. The seminary was also socially significant: it enrolled only the clergy's children and rarely matriculated the children of other social groups. Once the seminary became a prerequisite for clerical appointment (as it did toward the end of the century), its exclusion of outsiders helped transform the clergy into a closed social group.

The seminary also sharpened the lines of stratification within the clergy. In the first place, it widened the gap between priest and churchman, for educational level soon became a basic determinant of an individual's rank—especially toward the end of the century, as bishops consistently began to choose advanced seminarians for the best clerical positions. State and Church law authorized "priority" for the learned candidates, and as the number of philosophy and theology graduates increased, education became a more significant factor in clerical appointments. The Synod ordered in 1770 that bishops advise upper-class seminarians of clerical vacancies,[196] and such listings had appeared by the 1780s.[197] Bishop Viktor no doubt expressed a widespread view when he declared that "it is inappropriate and humiliating for a graduate to become a churchman."[198] To be sure, the seminarian still needed the approval and consent of the parish; but, with the firm support of the bishop, with the cultivated landlord's preference for a learned and sober priest, such confirmation was not difficult to obtain. The seminary, moreover, deepened priest-churchman differences in another way; those who left the seminary in the lower grades were doomed to remain in the lowly status of sacristan. Poor students were released from the seminary with the notation that they were to remain permanently in the rank of churchman, a policy that became more and more common by the end of the century.[199] There were even hereditary overtones; churchmen sent disproportionately fewer children to the seminary and could ill afford to maintain them in the more advanced courses.[200] Thus the seminary helped lay the foundations for the priest-churchman gap that became so salient in the nineteenth century.

The seminary also intensified regional differences within the parish clergy. Though differences had existed earlier between urban and rural (and, especially, Moscow and provincial) clergy, they now became much sharper. The elite were graduates of the Moscow Academy or the Trinity-Sergius seminary, where a sophisticated education promised them excellent clerical positions, preferably in Moscow itself. The cultural impact of the seminary was thus particularly strong on the Moscow clergy. Reports on "learned priests" show a remarkable increase in Moscow: from a mere 12 (in 1734) to 116 (in 1781).[201] Although such learned priests were still a minority, even among the clergy in Moscow,[202] the improvement was nevertheless vast. The phenomenal growth of the seminary after 1780 would complete this cultural transformation by the early nineteenth century.

The cultural level of provincial clergy was considerably lower. Those in provincial towns occupied an intermediate level; especially in the diocesan capital or certain district towns, the bishop helped secure ideal positions for the advanced seminarians—often so that they could continue teaching in the seminary or district school.[203] The rural clergy, however, rarely had advanced seminary education: few parishes sought such expensive priests, few seminary graduates sought rural parishes. Most educated clergy shared the popular view that rural life barbarized the seminarian, forced him to toil like a serf in the fields, and made him vulnerable to the noble landlord's caprice and cruelty.[204] They were sensitive to the aristocrats' disdain for the village clergy, neatly summarized in the 1780s by Tooke: "The worthiest clergymen run great hazard of becoming boorish themselves from the total want of any social intercourse that might supply food to their minds, and keep up a dignity of manners: they are commonly obliged to work in the fields, the barn, and the stable with their own hands."[205] To spare the clergy such a fate, the bishop of Pereslavl in the 1750s toyed with a special project to support "learned clergy" so that they would not "forget their learning" while serving in rural parishes; ultimately, however, he took no specific measures.[206] The bishop of Rostov sent a proposal to the Synod in 1767, arguing that the clergy should receive a salary rather than have to farm parish land: "It is impossible to appoint those who have studied at the seminary into the priestly or churchman rank at rural churches; they themselves do not desire appointment to such churches, because from youth to adulthood they have studied at the seminary and, because of their ignorance [of agriculture], they cannot at all become accustomed to farming."[207] As we shall see, the Synod and state both considered reform proposals to free the clergy from manual labor or at least give special support to "learned" clergy.

A further peculiarity of the seminary was its "over-success"— quantitatively. By the 1780s the seminaries were already quite large, and the bishops concluded that the schools could supply any candidates needed for the white clergy.[208] Yet this was only the beginning of rapid increases in enrollments, and by the 1790s the seminary had far too many youths for the available clerical positions. The bishops, however, refused to restrict enrollments and to concentrate on the best seminarians, a policy the state favored as early as the 1760s. They refused to do so because they wanted to have the largest possible pool of candidates and to envelop the whole clerical estate in superior education and culture. But this only squandered the scant resources of the seminary. By the mid-nineteenth century the problem had reached catastrophic dimensions, each diocese reporting hundreds of unplaced seminary graduates; this critical situation impelled one bishop even to propose a blanket exclusion of churchmen's children from the seminary.[209]

Yet the seminary did not provide students with an education specifically useful for a clerical career. To be sure, the cultivated learning of the elite student was socially useful; if nothing else, it at least made the priest acceptable in some circles of provincial gentry. The nobleman

Bolotov, for example, wrote warmly of the cathedral priest in Bogoro-ditsk: "In a short time, he became for me and my son not only our best conversationalist, but also a colleague in our scholarly work."[210] More important, however, the seminary did not impart knowledge useful for pastoral service; its secular curriculum meant that the seminary was not a professional ecclesiastical school. The seminarian did not learn how to proselytize against Old Believers and probably knew less about the religious texts than the self-taught dissenters. Nor did the smattering of Latin impress the laity, to judge from the occasional derisive remarks about the *latinniki*. Even the rhetoric of the advanced seminarians probably had little value, only ballasting their sermons with formalistic classicism. One startled priest in Zvenigorod was shoved from the pulpit by an exasperated townsman, who began to preach—"to show the priest" how it should be done.[211] In the last two decades authorities tried to supplement the priest's education with practical knowledge, such as mastery of the civil script and even some expertise in medicine, but these efforts brought scant results and in any event did nothing to improve pastoral preparation.[212]

For all its inadequacies, seminary education cost the clergy dearly. In economic terms alone, it was an onerous burden, as fathers supported sons at the seminary and paid various taxes and tuitions for the schools. Even those who did not have sons had to subsidize education through fines, levies, or the scholarship of a "reserved position." Given the small resources of most parish clergy, the costs of seminary education were indeed high. It has been argued that most nobles could ill afford "Westernization"; that argument bears even greater validity for the white clergy and their "Latinization."[213]

Finally, the seminary generated additional frictions between the bishop and the lower clergy. Particularly before 1780, the bishop had to wage virtual war on his own clergy in order to collect taxes and the clergy's sons for the seminary. The history of every seminary is a melancholy chronicle of fruitless punishment, hopeless evasion. The incidence of open resistance declined after the 1770s, when the seminary became more tolerable and essential for appointment; that did not, however, efface the clergy's dread of the seminary even into the nineteenth century.

The seminary thus came to play a major role in the lives of the eighteenth-century clergy. Its growth, so uneven before mid-century, finally became steady after the 1760s; by the end of the century, the enrollments tallied into numbers that far exceeded the personnel needs of the Church. Yet, for all that, the seminary provided instruction of limited usefulness for the clergy and Church. It did train a scholarly elite, the "learned monks" and erudite archpriests like Petr Alekseev of Moscow, but only at the cost of disregarding the essential needs of rank-and-file parish clergy. Moreover, although the elite seminaries equipped their students with a superior culture and social graces, most provincial seminaries subjected the youths to a harrowing experience of deprivation, hardship, and intellectual abuse. Brutal discipline and rote memorization, to be sure, marred education in Western Europe as well as Russia; for the Russian seminarian, however, such learning promised scant reward, entailed physical privation, and bore little relevance to past or future experience. The seminary's impact upon the whole clerical soslovie was no less disastrous. Except for the elite of the Moscow clergy and diocesan cathedrals, the seminary did not eradicate clerical boorishness, give them professional training, or raise their social status. Instead, it sealed off the clergy from other social groups and made them alien to Russian culture, traditional and modern; it ravaged clerical finances, aggravating further the tensions between priest and bishop. Thus the seminary, potentially an instrument of ecclesiastical modernization, had profoundly disturbing consequences for the clergy and the Church.

The Structure and Economics of Clerical Service

5

In theory, the clerical estate was a unitary social group—its members shared a common juridical status and served within the single institutional framework of the Church. Yet the clergy were stratified into a miniature society, marked by kaleidoscopic differences in economic and social position. At the top was the archpriest of a Moscow cathedral, receiving an income of several hundred rubles per year and enjoying all the accoutrements of a rich nobleman; at the bottom was a village churchman, earning a meager five or ten rubles per year and fitting the classic stereotype of the destitute clergyman. And between these two extremes lay most of the white clergy.

This social diversity resulted directly from the complex structure of church finances: each church had a unique economy, varying widely in the amounts and kinds of support it could provide the local clergy. Some churches were extremely rich, others extremely poor. Some churches traced their roots back centuries and prospered; others rose and fell in a single generation. In a word, the churches, different in size and economic viability, reflected the amorphous particularism in medieval Russia, where institutions sprang up and grew in an unregulated, spontaneous fashion. This traditional economy of clerical service was preserved in all its premodern purity into the eighteenth century; the essential question for the "regularized" Petrine state was how to bring order and rationality to the structure of local churches and their respective finances.

Formally, there were several specific categories of churches, the numbers of which are indicated in a Synodal report of 1779 (Table 8). The elite category was the cathedral (*sobor*), which constituted 2

Table 8. Types of churches, 1779

Diocese	Cathedrals	Endowed and convent churches	Private chapels	Parish churches	Total
Kolomna	10	7	4	910	931
Moscow	7	43	82	777	909
Pereslavl	8	4	3	594	609
Riazan	14	9	1	955	979
Rostov	5	40	11	787	843
Suzdal	5	4	0	628	637
Vladimir	8	5	1	709	723
Empire	407	488	157	20,019	21,071

Source: TsGIA, f. 796, op. 60, g. 1779, d. 162, ll. 1-10.

percent of all churches in the empire. Theoretically, it had no parishioners but obtained support from other fixed sources of income—populated estates, government stipends, and diocesan revenues. The second type was the endowed church (ruzhnaia tserkov'), one that
received a benefice or fixed grant from the tsar. The number of
endowed churches gradually declined in the eighteenth century and by
1779 constituted about 2 percent of all churches in the empire. The
third type of church was the private chapel (domovaia tserkov'); intended for the personal use of important aristocrats, the chapels represented about 1 percent of all churches in the empire. A fourth category
was the parish church (prikhodskaia tserkov'), which constituted 95
percent of all churches. Finally, there were several other minor categories—convent churches, special cemetery churches, and military
churches; these, however, were very few in number and statistically
insignificant.[1] Together, these churches composed a common net of
service opportunities: the cleric could aspire to serve in any type of
church, for all were manned by members of the white clergy.
    More important than the formal category was the real economic
condition of a church. The glittering title of "cathedral" could be
attached to a poor church with peasant parishioners; it did not indicate the economic condition of the church's clergy. The income of an
individual cleric, at any church, depended upon the resources of the
church, the number of clergy on hand, and the cleric's own rank. The
church's resources were possibly many: the number and prosperity of
parishioners, the amount and fertility of lands, and (rarely) auxiliary
revenues, such as populated estates or government subsidies. The
number of clergy at a church varied significantly, depending upon the

size of a parish and the type of church; under Peter's rules, a staff could have as few as two clerics or as many as ten or more. A cleric's income varied inversely with the number of colleagues: overstaffing or understaffing thus directly affected his earnings. A cleric's income was also determined by his formal rank; priests usually received two to three times the income of churchmen at the same church.

It is important to examine closely the complex structure and economy of clerical service, a system that profoundly affected the clergy and their relationship to parishioners. The first task is to consider the "semi-reform" begun by Peter, an attempt to regulate the structure of service through new controls on churches and appointments, but without changing the traditional economics of clerical service. The second task is to examine the amorphous structure of clerical economics to determine what changes took place in basic support, staffing, and differences in rank. Such an analysis can suggest how the structure and economics of service contributed to the instability and internal strife so characteristic and so debilitating for the parish clergy.

The Structure of Clerical Service

One prominent refrain throughout the sixteenth and seventeenth centuries was the denunciation of "excess" churches and clergy that surpassed "actual" needs. Both state and Church officials complained that parishioners built too many churches and employed too many priests and churchmen. The Church Council of 1551 (*Stoglav*), for example, reproved parishioners who senselessly constructed parish churches out of "a false sense of piety," even though they could not afford to maintain them afterwards.[2] No means of enforcement were adopted, however, and the problem persisted. Indeed, the Church had no rules for determining how many clergy should serve at a particular church. Some parishes indulgently maintained several priests and deacons, while others made do with just a priest and his son as churchman. Clerical staffing varied according to lay resources; the number of clergy, very simply, depended upon the parish's economic resources and generosity. In any event, the bishop had no administrative means to regulate the size of parish staffs.

In the absence of external control, the number of churches and clergy steadily proliferated. Although comprehensive statistical data are lacking, the available evidence confirms the hierarchs' complaints about "excess churches and clergy." In Moscow itself the number of churches increased from 194 to 242 between 1628 and 1658.[3] In Ruzskaia desiatina of Moscow province the number of churches increased markedly, from 8 (in 1600) to 35 (in 1700).[4] Kolomna diocese reported a similarly rapid growth of churches from 500 to 636 between 1674 and

1700—an increase of 27 percent.[5] Simultaneously, many churches maintained such large parish staffs that the government threatened several times in the seventeenth century to draft the excess.[6] In the more spectacular cases, the number of clerical households almost equalled the number of parishioner households.[7] Such overstaffing, quite clearly, meant impoverishment for the clergy and an intolerable burden for the laity. The hierarchs' indulgence toward overappointment prompted Peter to complain in 1705 to the metropolitan of Rostov: "You ordain to parish churches in excess—two or three priests or more, as well as many deacons, where previously there was only one priest."[8]

The authorities therefore faced the difficult task of controlling and regulating two variables—the number of churches and the number of clergy. Both the state and Church authorities had a strong interest in such control, but their motives and goals were different. The government, for its part, generally regarded excess clergy as an unproductive drain on society and in proper mercantilist spirit hoped to rechannel them into more useful occupations. It also wanted to reduce expenditures on the endowed churches; burdened with chronic tax and fiscal problems, the state could ill afford the large subsidies to churches that sometimes did not even serve a parish. However disingenuously, the state also argued that strict controls were necessary in order to solve the problem of clerical poverty: the sparse resources of a parish church could not support swollen staffs.[9] Significantly, such a policy contradicted the government's interest in using the clergy to control unruly peasants and convert people of other confessions; a similar desire to use priests for state purposes led Habsburg Emperor Joseph II to increase, not decrease, parishes and clergy in the 1780s.[10] But the Russian government had to regulate a social estate, not a celibate service order; in its estimation, the costs of support outweighed the anticipated gains. Thus the government's goal was to reduce or at least freeze the number of churches and clergy.

The Church hierarchs of course had a quite different perspective on the problem. They shared the government's view that clerical overpopulation aggravated the problem of poverty, but they had other concerns as well. The bishop tended to shield the subordinate parish clergy, seeking to find all a secure place and shelter them from state conscription. He found it difficult to resist the traditional plea for episcopal mercy and granted appointments beyond the permissible limits. Even in the late eighteenth century, when state control became more intense, he still responded to such pressure from below. Many bishops also felt obliged to honor petitions from the laity, especially nobles, who frequently requested permission to open a new parish or appoint additional clergy (especially deacons, who were highly prized for their singing abilities). As long as the parish promised to provide adequate support, the bishop was inclined to grant their wishes.

To curtail such arbitrariness (or "episcopal mercy"), it was essential for the state to fashion a fixed system to regulate the number of churches and clergy.

CONTROLS ON CHURCHES

The state had little difficulty in restricting the number of cathedrals and endowed churches. The cathedrals already existed in most major cities but were not increasing. More troublesome were the endowed churches, which by the late seventeenth century constituted perhaps 15 to 20 percent of all churches.[11] Receiving full or partial stipends (*ruga*) from the state, such churches symbolically expressed the tsar's personal bond to the Church in medieval Muscovy. But Peter saw little reason for such expenditures and from 1698 began to reduce their stipends. His successors generally followed this policy, and the number of endowed churches steadily dwindled. Consequently, where in the mid-seventeenth century there had been 1,500 such churches, by 1782 only 202 remained.[12]

More challenging, however, was the task of limiting the two types of churches supported by the laity—the nobles' personal chapels and regular parish churches. Private chapels had begun to proliferate in Russia in the seventeenth century and by Peter's reign aroused opposition from both the state and the Church.[13] Just as in the Western Church, a private chapel was an impressive symbol of status, a visible mark of wealth and power.[14] To Peter's mind, such chapels were very wasteful, requiring a priest to serve just one family; nor did the tsar overlook the implied social pretensions—chapels once were the exclusive prerogative of the tsar. Church hierarchs also opposed the chapels, which removed wealthy aristocrats from parish churches and thus undermined the economic viability of local parishes. Magnates also tended to select priests indiscriminately, giving refuge to vagrants and even clerical fugitives.[15] Bishops also feared the social implications of a chapel, where the dependent priest could easily sink to the status of a house servant.[16] Although sometimes swayed by influential nobles, the bishops were generally hostile to requests for chapels.

Moreover, the authorities made repeated efforts to close the existing chapels. In 1718 Peter ordered all chapels closed, except those belonging to members of the Imperial family.[17] This decree brought no results, and in 1722 the tsar categorically reiterated his order; this time all were sealed shut.[18] After howls of protest, Peter relented slightly, allowing select magnates to reopen a chapel if they were physically unable to attend a parish church.[19] But he did not ease the restrictions further and succeeded in sharply reducing the number of chapels. After Peter's death in 1725, Catherine I acceded to aristocratic pressure, allowing nobles to open a chapel if they demonstrated real need and if they employed local parish clergy for the services.[20] For instance, one Moscow noble (with the rank of colonel) obtained authorization to open a chapel "because of the distant location from the parish Church of Peter and Paul (in the village of Kolontaev), because of the problems of access (due to the forests, low-lying places, and especially the flooding in spring and fall), and because of Tolstoi's illness, which do not permit him to travel to that church and attend holy services."[21] This tolerant policy was briefly rescinded in 1762 by Peter III, who closed the chapels and only increased the nobles' disgruntlement with the emperor.[22] Immediately after her coup d'état in 1762, Catherine allowed nobles to reopen the chapels, hoping no doubt to win favor among the aristocracy.[23] Although the empress remained rather tolerant of the chapels, the Synod steadfastly resisted their growth. Mainly because of its opposition and pressure, the number of chapels remained fairly static from the 1760s until the end of the eighteenth century.[24]

The authorities also tried to regulate the number of parish churches. Early in his reign Peter had complained about the proliferation of churches, and in 1716 required bishops to take an oath that they would not "build (or allow others to do so) churches beyond actual need, just for the sake of caprice."[25] Two years later, the tsar ordered that each church have a definite number of households, without, however, troubling to specify that definite number.[26] The turning point came in 1722, with the promulgation of new and precise rules: a parish should have at least one hundred households, and new parishes could be opened only if access to another existing church was physically impossible. Shortly afterwards, the Synod temporarily prohibited further church construction without the special permission of the Synod itself.[27] To be sure, the authorities did not abolish "undersized" parishes that already existed. The decision not to do so came in a Synod decree of 1723, which responded to a query whether all small churches (less than fifty households) should be eliminated. The Synod ruled that such parishes should be preserved, slyly using a Petrine rationale: to abolish them would deprive the Church of the parish-church tax.[28] In 1726 the bishops again acquired the authority to consecrate new churches but were cautioned to exercise that authority with discretion.[29] They carefully scrutinized applications to determine if the parish was large enough, if it was truly isolated, and if it could adequately support the local clergy.[30] They made the necessary investigations through the clerical elder and rejected petitions where the claims were unfounded.[31] In 1770 the Synod also ended the ambiguity on minimum size: city parishes had to have at least twenty households, rural parishes at least forty.[32] This was still a far cry from the theoretical norm (100 households), but the gap was closing.

These new controls enabled the authorities to limit the number of churches and even achieve reductions in some areas. The cities, despite the general increases in population, now acquired a fairly stable number of parishes and some (especially Moscow) even made notable reductions (Table 9). Only in a few cases did the number of urban churches increase, and everywhere the average city parish exceeded the norm of 20 households.[33] Because of the territorial reorganizations of 1775, it is impossible to make valid statistical comparisons of rural areas, but indirect evidence here too suggests that the bishops managed to restrict the proliferation of churches. For the period of 1744-84 (that is, between the second and fourth census revisions), the total population for the central zone increased by 26 percent; during the same period, the average parish increased in households by 50 to 85 percent, and in per capita membership by 21 to 38 percent (Table 10).[34] For the central dioceses, at least, the rapid, uncontrolled pro-

Table 9. Number of urban churches, 1747 and 1783

Type of city	1747	1783	Change
Major economic cities			
Moscow	327	300	-27
Iaroslavl	46	45	-1
Kaluga	28	28	0
Tula	24	24	0
Traditional religious cities			
Suzdal	26	24	-2
Murom	20	20	0
Pereslavl-Zalesskii	29	24	-5
Riazan	21	19	-2
Rostov	37	30	-7
Administrative cities			
Shui	4	5	+1
Zaraisk	6	8	+2
Zvenigorod	3	3	0

Source: TsGIA, f. 796, op. 28, g. 1747, d. 216, ll. 124 ob.-125, 140 ob.-143, 173 ob.-175, 180 ob.-182, 346 ob.-353, 482 ob.-486; op. 64, g. 1783, d. 580, ll. 1-284.

Table 10. Changes in average size of parishes, 1740-83

| Diocese | Average size of parish | | | | | |
| | Households | | | Individuals | | |
	1740	1783	%	1740	1783	%
Kolomna	53.5	85.5	60	343	415	21
Riazan	65.3	99.4	52	333	438	32
Rostov	68.4	105.8	55	309	384	24
Suzdal	61.3	113.7	85	274	379	38

Source: ODDS, 20:Prilozhenie 10; TsGIA, f. 796, op. 64, g. 1783, d. 580, ll. 58 ob.-65, 84 ob.-96, 145 ob.-151, 155 ob.-162.

liferation of churches that had been so characteristic of old Muscovy had finally come to an end.

CONTROLS ON THE CLERGY

Peter the Great routinely admonished bishops against ordaining superfluous clergy, but to no avail.[35] The Synod observed in 1722 that, since Patriarch Adrian's death in 1700, bishops had ordained priests in excess of the "number of clergy recorded in the old census books and ancient records."[36] Verbal threats were meaningless, however, until a numerical standard was established. As early as 1711 the tsar broached the idea, when he suggested fixing a proportion between priests and deacons. A few years later, in 1718, Peter announced his intention to fix the proportion between clergy and parish households but did not actually adopt any specific measures.[37] He finally took the crucial step in 1722, adopting a clerical registry (*dukhovnyi shtat*)— a kind of table of organization. It was actually the Synod itself that drew up the registry, after receiving a memorandum from the Senate asking for a suitable *shtat.*[38] To end the traditional ambiguity on the proper size of church staffs, the Synod's registry established a fixed proportion between clergy and parish size.[39] The parish norm was to be 100 households, and it would have a three-man clerical staff—one priest and two churchmen. For larger parishes (which required more clergy to administer rites and which, theoretically, could afford to support them), the registry allowed proportionately larger staffs (Table 11). According to this system, only registered (*shtatnye*) clerics would be legally recognized; those appointed outside the table of organization were considered unregistered (*zashtatnye*), therefore legally "idle" and subject to removal or government conscription. The registry therefore provided a precise instrument to identify needed and excess clergy.

Table 11. *Dukhovnyi shtat*, the clerical registry of 1722

Clerical rank	Number of clergy per church type				
	Episcopal cathedral	City cathedral	"Triple parish" (over 300 households)	"Double parish" (200 households)	"Single parish" (100 households)
Archpriest	1	1	0	0	0
Kliuchar'	2	0	0	0	0
Priest	5	2	3	2	1
Archdeacon	1	0	0	0	0
Deacon	4	2	2	0	0
Psalomshchik	2	0	0	0	0
D'iachok	0	2	3	2	1
Ponomar'	2	2	3	2	1
Total staff	17	9	11	6	3

Source: ODDS, 2, pt. 1:756.

The *shtat* suggestively indicates the new relationship between Church and state in Imperial Russia. Its very creation revealed the powerful regularizing influence of the state and, superficially, implied the clergy's absorption into the state structure, for the clerical registry was an ecclesiastical counterpart to the new *grazhdanskii shtat,* the table of organization for civil administration. At the same time, the *dukhovnyi shtat* of the Church reveals to what degree the clergy were not integrated into the state: unlike the civil service registry, the clerical *shtat* did not provide for salaries, and the clergy were still to depend upon the traditional forms of parish support. Herein lay the great contradiction: the *shtat* descended from above without a meaningful economic relationship between the table of organization and parish resources. The Muscovite parish, at least, had borne a crude relationship to economic reality; a parish retained as many clerics as it could afford, and others were starved out. The Petrine registry made appointments correspond to raw numbers of parish households; yet the "household" was an economically meaningless unit, revealing neither the number of individual males (the usual Petrine tax unit) nor their social-economic status. Thus the new *shtat* was essentially a bureaucratic formalism, heedless of economic realities in the parish.[40]

The state and Church did not rigorously enforce the registry system in the initial period of 1725-62. They upheld, to be sure, the formal structure of the *shtat* and introduced no basic modifications.[41] Nevertheless, they did not disturb the small parishes, where 50 or fewer households might still have a full single staff (one priest and two sacristans). These undersized churches, which often could not be combined and which were quite common, were in a semi-legal status, for the 1722 *shtat* did not specify their acceptable staff size. The Synod attempted in 1743 to legalize their right to a full single staff but obtained no agreement from the Senate; the question thus remained unresolved.[42] Nor did diocesan authorities rigorously enforce the registry. In 1727 the Moscow consistory ordered all "unregistered" clergy (those appointed in excess of the registry) to remain in their positions until they could find new appointments. In Moscow itself, the registry was virtually ignored until Metropolitan Platon I began to enforce its requirements in the 1750s.[43] Similarly, the hierarchs in Suzdal tolerated surplus clergy and their reports gave no explanation for irregularities.[44] Such "unregistered churchmen" were caught during the government conscriptions, but in the meantime bishops did not unduly fret over violations in the registry. Still, the 1722 *shtat* did curtail the more extreme excesses reported in the seventeenth century.

This registry system was significantly tightened by Catherine's government in the 1760s and 1770s. In 1768 the Synod clarified an important ambiguity in the 1722 *shtat* regarding deacons. The original registry had not specified rules for their appointment, and many small parishes abused this loophole to obtain deacons, chosen for their strong bass voices. The new regulation forbade such appointments: only large village parishes (with two staffs) or rich city parishes ("where the clergy can receive satisfactory support") had the right to employ a deacon; absolutely no rural parish with fewer than 100 households could have a deacon even if the parishioners asked for one.[45] More important was the new registry of 1778, which sought a major reduction in the numbers of clergy. Now churches could have a second priest only if there were more than 150 (not 100) households, if "in ancient times" there had been two priests, and if one priest could not perform all the ministerial tasks.[46]

The new decrees were not dead letters. Central authorities insistently and repeatedly admonished bishops not to appoint excess clergy and enforced those decrees by close scrutiny of diocesan administration.[47] In 1781, for example, the Synod discovered that Bishop Tikhon of Suzdal had appointed priests and sacristans in excess of the *shtat*, opened an investigation, and in the end sternly reprimanded him for the violations.[48] That vigilance caused others to be more cautious, and typical was the report by the bishop of Kolomna in 1797: it listed all irregularities, both excess appointments and new churches, and provided a legal rationale for each decision.[49] Bishops refused to appoint deacons unless a full one hundred households were in the parish and even rejected requests when a village was within a few households of this bureaucratic norm.[50]

Thus the authorities imposed a two-part system of controls—both on churches and on clerical appointments. They hoped thereby to regularize clerical service and to eradicate the serious, uneconomic imbalances of the traditional Church. The result was a new bureaucratic structure of service that took effect between the 1720s and 1770s, gradually descending upon the myriad particularism of the Muscovite parishes.

FAILURE OF REFORM

Both state and Church authorities demonstrated genuine interest in reforming the system of economic support for the clergy. They deplored the spectacle of dilapidated churches and vagrant priests and also knew that impoverished clergy were all the more susceptible to bribes and parish pressure—and hence evasion of their service duties. Consequently, they considered various plans and projects for converting the spontaneous, irregular support of an individual parish into a more reliable and fixed income.

The authorities first approached the problem in 1721 in the Ecclesiastical Regulation, which proposed to establish a fixed salary for the clergy. The Regulation declared an intention "to determine the number of households for one parish, from which everyone will pay a specific tax to the priests and other churchmen of his church so that, as far as possible, they will have complete self-sufficiency and will not henceforth solicit fees for baptism, burial, marriage, etc."[51] Although concerned about clerical impoverishment, Peter was especially critical of the clergy's solicitation (domogatel'stvo), as priests badgered their parishioners for ever larger fees when performing various rites and sacraments. In a marginal notation to a draft of the Ecclesiastical Regulation, Peter showed that his goal was not only clerical self-sufficiency but also a proper distinction between sacraments and payment; the priest, wrote Peter, should be paid "not at the time when he performs some rite but several weeks later."[52] The Synod did prepare a clerical registry to regulate clergy-parishioner ratios; not until 1724, however, did it investigate the question of reforming the system of economic support for the clergy. Significantly, it looked to the West; just as the Petrine government did for its military and administrative reforms,[53] the Synod ordered its chancellery to prepare a summary of Swedish and Danish legal documents on the problem. The translations were prepared, but the Synod subsequently failed to pursue the question—perhaps because of the political turmoil inside the Synod after Peter's death in 1725.[54]

Several laymen also advanced reform projects, all proposing a fixed parish (not government) salary for the clergy. The general aim of each proposal was to free the clergy from agricultural labor, which distracted them from pastoral duties and which seemed "inappropriate to the clerical rank." The merchant writer Pososhkov devoted the first chapter of his *On Wealth and Poverty* to the clergy, giving particular attention to the parish clergy's economic problems. So that the priest might tend his parishioners rather than his garden, Pososhkov proposed that the clergy receive 10 percent of the parishioners' annual harvests and income.[55] A. P. Volynskii, a prominent statesman of the 1730s, proposed a fixed levy for the clergy from the parishioners and wanted to ban agricultural labor by the clergy altogether.[56] V.N. Tatishchev, historian and government official, made a similar suggestion: "Reward him [the priest] with comfortable support and money, not land—so that he will not smell of manure. . . . For money he will attend to the church rather than his own land, ploughed fields, and hayland—which is unbecoming his rank."[57] But these proposals appeared only sporadically and did not inspire serious reform projects, either in the government or in the Synod.

Not until the Legislative Commission of 1767-68 were new attempts made. As the Synod prepared instructions for its deputy to the Commission, Bishop Arsenii of Rostov raised the question of clerical support. Noting that seminarians shunned appointment to rural parishes for fear of becoming mere field hands, Arsenii took up the proposal of a standard tax on parishioners as a suitable replacement for clerical farming. The Synod moderated his proposal in the final instruction to its deputy: "Request that some appropriate means be sought to provide them [the parish clergy] with support and to free them from work inappropriate to their ranks."[58] At the Legislative Commission, the Committee for Civil Affairs took up the question of clerical support, perhaps under the influence of the Synodal deputy, Metropolitan Gavriil. It proposed to increase the average size of parishes (thereby raising available resources), and it even broached the idea of a central fund for supporting the clergy. Similar schemes were devised in 1771 by the Commission on Church Estates, the joint Church-state organ that carried through secularization.[59] Neither proposal, however, led to concrete results.

Behind this persistent stalling was Catherine's own indifference to the question in the first years of her reign. Her attitude at the time is revealed in an ill-humored reply to Governor Sievers, who inquired about rumors of a salary and land grant for the parish clergy: "I do not know who told you that the rural clergy are to get land grants. They will remain just as before. No doubt this rumor is being spread by sanctimonious bigots (khanzhi)."[60] But the Pugachev Rebellion of 1773-75 sharpened Catherine's interest in the clergy, when she realized their value as an instrument of social control. Responding to reports of clerical involvement in the rebellion, Catherine wrote one adviser of her plans for reform: "One of my first concerns after the termination of the present troubles [the Pugachev Rebellion] is to establish ecclesiastical schools wherever possible. But then another question is raised—that of providing support for the clergy in accordance with their education."[61] A few years later Catherine scribbled out a proposal to establish a network of educated priests in all dioceses, allotting them a state budget of 22,000 rubles per year; interesting as it is, the proposal did not go beyond her own records.[62]

The most important attempt at reform came in the 1780s, when the state began serious study of the problem. Catherine initiated this effort in May 1784, when her emissary sent this message to the over-procurator of the Synod: "For the general welfare it is necessary to order the churches so that their number corresponds to the parishioners attached to them, and so that those serving at them can have adequate support free from popular control."[63] The Commission on Church Estates began a full investigation of the question. St. Petersburg Metropolitan Gavriil quickly advanced an idea he had developed earlier: to give the clergy a large allotment of land, which would be leased to the parishioners for a proportional share of the harvest. The Synod supported his proposal, and it was approved by the Commission at its third session (29 May 1784). When government members asked for comprehensive data on clerical income, the Synod replied that no data were presently available and it was impossible to compile full data, for each church was unique. As a compromise, Gavriil prepared full data on two districts in his own diocese to serve as a working model. But General-Procurator A. A. Viazemskii still insisted on data for the entire empire, and the Synod began slowly to comply. Gavriil, meanwhile, made a systematic study of European systems of support. Despite all this effort, no concrete proposals emerged; frustrated by the complexity of the task, the Commission abandoned the attempt and sent its materials to the archive in 1796.[64]

With Paul's accession to the throne in 1796, the Synod made haste to revive Gavriil's proposal of parish-cultivated church land. A joint conference of the Senate and Synod agreed on the general terms, and in December 1797 Paul approved the proposal. The plan was, however, very complicated and difficult to implement: parishes varied in size and population (thus creating inequities in the labor requirements); some local officials would not enforce the law; the parishioners frequently refused to comply; and some clergy demanded excessive rent for land given the laity. The initial conflicts abated, and the law seemed to be working smoothly by 1800. But the whole scheme was scuttled after Paul's assassination in March 1801: the new emperor, Alexander I, hurriedly repealed the law, perhaps under the influence of the nobility.[65]

The many projects to reform clerical economy thus failed. In Peter's reign the government built a stable, bureaucratic structure of clerical service, imposing from above a fixed table of organization—the *shtat*. But the state failed to reform the underlying economic system of clerical service, and the clergy still depended upon their particular church for economic support. This half-reform left an important discrepancy in the system of service: appointments were determined not by the parish "market," but by arbitrary regulations blind to economic reality.

The Economics of Clerical Service

Thus the clergy, throughout the eighteenth century, still depended upon the immediate parish for their livelihood. Since each church had its own combination of resources that varied in form and value, the support available to clergy was wildly heterogeneous. It is important to map out the general patterns of this clerical economy, examining each category of church, its customary sources of revenue, and the general range of economic potential. Such an analysis can suggest the complex picture of wealth and poverty in the white clergy.

To put this analysis in perspective, it is important to recall some benchmarks on money values and incomes in the eighteenth century. Although the clergy, like nobles, also received goods in kind (both from their parishioners and their own farmlands), monetary income was particularly important in their relationship with the outside, be it the diocese, state, or new secular culture. Priests in the central provinces received 20 to 50 rubles per year in the 1750s to 1780s; others received as little as 10 rubles, some more than 100 rubles. How did this compare with other monetary incomes? State officials received considerably more. According to the state budget of 1762-63, a governor received 1,875 rubles per year, a city *voevoda* 375 rubles, a chancellery secretary 225 rubles, and a *kantseliarist* 100 rubles.[66] Noble landlords, however, received much less. According to data on peasant quitrent (*obrok*), in 1775 most nobles had relatively modest monetary incomes from their estates: 32 percent received less than 35 rubles per year (placing them together with many priests), another 31 percent had incomes of 35 to 105 rubles, and the remaining 37 percent had higher incomes from the quitrent.[67] With these reference points in mind, we can now turn to the parish clergy's economy.

CATHEDRALS

The cathedrals, which theoretically had no parishioners but sometimes did, were divided into three main ranks—the Moscow Kremlin
Cathedrals, the episcopal cathedrals, and the district cathedrals in
provincial towns. Despite their impressive pasts and and formal title,
the term cathedral actually said little about their economic condition,
for they fell along a broad economic spectrum, from the immensely
wealthy cathedrals of the Kremlin to the bankrupt cathedrals in some
provincial towns.

The Kremlin cathedrals—(Bol'shoi) Uspenskii, Arkhangel'skii, and
Blagoveshchenskii—provided lavish support for their clergy. They
were under the special jurisdiction of the Synod, which made all appointments and exercised supervision over the cathedrals, even after
the Moscow diocese opened in 1742.[68] The most important resource of
the Kremlin cathedrals was their populated estates: by 1763 these
three cathedrals owned 40 percent of all serfs belonging to cathedrals
and churches (but not including monastic or episcopal serfs). Arkhangel'skii Cathedral possessed 7,051 peasants, Blagoveshchenskii Cathedral 5,304 peasants, and Uspenskii Cathedral 1,476 peasants.[69] These
estates yielded immense revenues; for example, from one estate in
Vladimir district, Uspenskii Cathedral received 883.32 rubles per
year.[70] Because of these resources, Kremlin Cathedrals could maintain
impressively large staffs; Uspenskii, for example, reported 37 clerics
on its staff in 1744.[71] And these clergy were extraordinarily wealthy.
According to one report in the mid-eighteenth century, the clergy of
Arkhangel'skii Cathedral had personal serfs, house servants, and fash-
ionable carriages—a description equally suitable for many nobles in
the capital.[72]

When Church peasants were secularized in 1764, all three cathedrals
received a state budget. Though smaller than earlier revenues, the
budgets were still relatively generous: archpriests received 300 to 600
rubles, priests 150 to 200 rubles (depending upon the cathedral). Such
incomes made them the highest paid clergy in Russia; not a few nobles
could envy their salaries. Although these incomes suffered from later
inflation, they provided more than ample support for the most vener-
able cathedrals in the land. These large incomes still allowed some
clergy in the Kremlin cathedrals to accumulate considerable personal
wealth, as the occasional wills attest.[73]

A middle-range cathedral was the bishopric cathedral (katedral'nyi
sobor). Serving as the bishop's church, this cathedral was the foremost
church in a diocese, with a large staff and adequate resources. It derived most of its support from the diocesan budget; in some dioceses,
the bishopric cathedral made regular collections from the laity and

parish clergy.[74] The cathedral clergy often supplemented their income by serving in diocesan administration, where they sold marriage licenses or examined candidates for ordination.[75] Such administrative work provided a salary and the inevitable "gifts" from parish clergy. Some episcopal cathedrals also owned populated estates, though on a much more modest scale than the Kremlin cathedrals. Dmitrovskii Cathedral of Vladimir, for example, owned two large villages where the peasants paid an annual quitrent of 100 rubles. Much poorer was Uspenskii Cathedral in Vladimir, which had one small estate with 15 peasants who paid no quitrent at all.[76] In short, each cathedral had its own combination of resources and thus the economic support of the cathedral clergy varied from one diocese to the next. In the better cathedrals like Rostov, the archpriest probably earned 80 to 100 rubles per year before secularization, while those in other cathedrals were considerably poorer. The archpriest in Pereslavl, for example, reported only 27 rubles per year, perhaps a deliberate underestimation, yet roughly indicative of his unenviable plight.[77]

After secularization in 1764, the clergy of diocesan cathedrals received annual salaries from the government.[78] The cathedrals, like the dioceses themselves, were divided into three "ranks" with appropriate distinctions in salaries and the size of the cathedral staff. In the central provinces, Rostov and Riazan belonged to the second rank; all others (Suzdal, Vladimir, Pereslavl, and Kolomna) were relegated to rank three. The new budgets, which presumed that the clergy had additional income, were meager indeed: in second class cathedrals the archpriest received only 80 rubles and the priest 40 rubles, and in third class cathedrals the archpriest received 60 rubles, the priest 30 rubles.[79] Even if some cathedral clergy lost income, others (such as those in Pereslavl) profited from the change. Moreover, the clergy now enjoyed fixed, regular incomes, free from the vagaries of harvest and famine. The clergy of such cathedrals also obtained sizable revenues from other sources, such as diocesan administration and seminary instruction; the archpriest of Uspenskii Cathedral in Vladimir, for example, received an additional 125 rubles per year for teaching in the local seminary.[80] In short, the clergy of a diocesan cathedral still enjoyed substantial incomes after seculariztion.

Much poorer were the district cathedrals, located in the administrative towns of each uezd. Such churches often had small resources, few parishioners, and rarely a stipend from the bishop or state. But there were some exceptions, and a comparison of three such cathedrals in Vladimir province suggests the range in economic level. A cathedral in Viazniki reported in 1744 a gross income of only 65 rubles for the entire staff, giving the archpriest only 13 rubles per annum and his subordinates far less. The clergy at this cathedral forlornly complained that they were "driven into starvation" and that religious services at the cathedral had in fact ceased.[81] A second cathedral in Iur'ev-Pol'skii (a small town in Suzdal diocese) had no parishioners and a state stipend of a mere 17 rubles per year; its clergy too, predictably, complained of acute hardship. To increase their support, the bishop abolished two parishes in the city and transferred their households and church land to the cathedral.[82] By contrast, the cathedral in Murom possessed a sizable population of peasants, who owed large quitrent and labor dues each year. Although the cathedral clergy had difficulty collecting these dues, during the more tranquil interludes they had a generous income.[83] The Murom cathedral was not unique; of similar stature was a cathedral in Iaroslavl, which obtained 300 rubles annually in quitrent and which maintained a staff far exceeding the formal *shtat*.[84] The data are fragmentary and perhaps somewhat distorted by clerical attempts to underestimate incomes; yet they do suggest that most (but not all) district cathedrals had at least adequate support before 1764. Such sufficiency is also indicated by the fact that most were stable, in constant operation, and rarely with vacant positions.[85]

Unlike other types, the district cathedral did not receive a state budget after secularization in 1764. The only exceptions were those possessing relatively large populated estates (with 20 or more male peasants), and there were only 32 such cathedrals in the whole empire. In most cases, the compensation they received was far less than their former revenues; archpriests received 30 rubles, priests 20 rubles, and the rest of the staff proportionately less.[86] Most district cathedrals, however, were unaffected by secularization, holding on to their modest but adequate income. The cathedral in Dmitrov was probably typical; in 1786 it had 14 parish households and received land rents of 70 to 100 rubles per year for the entire parish staff.[87] To aid poorer cathedrals, the bishops continued to reassign them parish households.[88] Thus in most cases the district cathedrals were just glorified parish churches, differing little from a parish church in economic condition and even in staffing.

The cathedral economies thus varied significantly, from the opulence of a Uspenskii cathedral to the squalor of a district cathedral in Klin. The rank of cathedral clergy was no symbol of status and wealth; like most formal categories, it embraced clergy of very different economic status. Still, most cathedrals were at least economically viable, if not prosperous. The bishops gave them special protection, the local voevoda himself was a parishioner, and as a last resort more townspeople could be assigned as parishioners to bolster a sagging income. The cathedral, especially in the upper categories, provided an enticing economic opportunity; the archpriest's or priest's income could have appealed to many a rural nobleman, not to mention village clergy.

ENDOWED CHURCHES

Endowed churches received a regular stipend in kind or money (*ruga*) from the tsar, for whom the church gave special religious services.[89] The stipends provided either full or supplementary support, from salaries at some churches to small donations for the cost of candles and the like at others. In most cases, the stipends were a substantial part of the endowed church's income, although it often had land and parishioners in addition. But such royal generosity ended with Peter the Great. In 1698 the tsar abolished payments for those churches that owned land and in the following year extended the decree to include churches with parish households and other incomes.[90] Peter and his heirs also placed a low priority on prompt payment of the stipend, and the clergy of endowed churches suffered acutely from such delays.[91] In 1736 the government directed the Synod to compile a list of endowed churches, with the clear intention of regularizing and probably further reducing the expenditures for endowed churches. The Synod did not complete the task until 1740, however, and Elizabeth's government did not pursue the matter.[92] The reprieve was but a temporary one, for secularization in the 1760s inspired new reductions, as the government eliminated stipends for many churches.[93] In 1768 endowed churches still cost the government 27,703 rubles per year,[94] a sum Catherine reduced to 22,606 rubles by 1782.[95] Catherine also toyed with the idea of a new system of benefices for "educated clergy" costing 22,000 rubles; the coincidence of sums suggests that she may have intended to divert the endowments for this new purpose. She did not pursue the scheme, however, and the endowments remained.[96]

This general policy had its greatest impact upon the central provinces, where endowed churches were once so thickly concentrated. Moscow, as capital of medieval Muscovy, naturally had many endowed churches, reporting 30 in 1747.[97] Few of these were abolished, but their incomes were relatively small—only 47 rubles (plus quantities of grain) in 1781-82.[98] Because of this, Metropolitan Platon began to convert endowed churches into regular parish churches, reallocating their stipends to other exclusively endowed churches.[99] Outside Moscow, endowed churches fared still worse. In 1747 Suzdal diocese reported that only 3 of the 5 churches were functioning; 2 were closed because no candidate desired the vacant priestly position.[100] Similarly, in Rostov diocese the endowed churches were reduced from 6 to 1 (1766-81); the remaining church received 25.50 rubles per year for its three hungry clerics.[101] In Pereslavl diocese, the number of endowed churches shrank from 21 to 4 during the period 1747-79. In Pereslavl uezd itself, there were 7 endowed churches in 1747; twenty years later, only 2 remained (and one was closed for lack of a priest). By 1782 both churches still existed, but they received a paltry stipend of 5 rubles per year.[102] In short, a traditional source of clerical support had dried up; few churches still received subsidies, once a vital supplement to the economy of many churches in central Russia.

PRIVATE CHAPELS

An impressive symbol of power and influence for the eighteenth-century Russian nobleman was the private chapel (domovaia tserkov'). It was separate from the local parish, usually staffed by a full-time priest, and served only that particular nobleman. Because of fairly strict controls by the state and especially the Church, permission to open a chapel was granted only to high-ranking, powerful nobles.[103] Men of influence ordinarily lived near the two capitals, and hence most chapels were naturally located in Moscow and St. Petersburg dioceses. According to a list compiled in 1771, there were 156 private chapels in the Empire; 96 were in Moscow diocese (62 percent) and 19 in St. Petersburg (12 percent). Fifteen dioceses, including Suzdal, had none at all; elsewhere in the central provinces they were rare, from 1 to 6 chapels per diocese.[104]

Such churches provided adequate but uncertain support. Although a chapel was not supposed to have a separate, full-time priest, the noble nevertheless preferred to hire his own priest on the grounds that the local cleric was too busy or inaccessible.[105] The nobles often maintained the priest in high style. A private chapel belonged to a rich aristocrat in Kolomna, Prince Cherkasskii, "who did not want to pray together with his 'slaves' but wanted his own church and priest." He paid the priest a salary, obliged him "to wear shoes [not peasant lapti] and stockings" and rewarded the priest with such items as a silver-headed walking stick.[106] But a chapel appointment was very unreliable. Though some magnates managed to keep a chapel (regardless of health), other chapels unexpectedly closed, leaving the clergy displaced.[107] The private chapels were therefore sharply restricted in numbers and had negligible impact upon the clerical economy.

PARISH CHURCHES

Most white clergy served in the parish churches, which were owned and supported by the lay community. Unlike cathedrals or endowed churches, the parish church received no outside assistance from the state or the Church and depended entirely upon the parish for support. Each parish church was a unique economy, combining several

potential resources: landed estates or other real estate; land for culti-
vation or leasing; special stipends from landlords or other patrons;
and payments in kind or money from parishioners for services like
marriage or baptism.

Few parish churches owned church peasants or other real estate.[108]
The officers' surveys, conducted on the eve of secularization, graphi-
cally show the limited value of such holdings. In Vladimir district,
only 6 percent of the parishes (twelve churches) had populated estates.
Nor were these holdings large: they had only a small number of peasants, who paid a few rubles in quitrent each year—and irregularly at
that. The only exception was the parish of Uspenskii pogost, which received 120 rubles annually in quitrent.[109] In Iaroslavl uezd only eight
churches possessed holdings, and they collected an average of just
15.50 rubles per year.[110] This pattern was typical throughout central
Russia; similar reports were submitted on the districts of Moscow,
Murom, Romanov, and others.[111] In addition, some city parishes derived rental income from other kinds of real estate—idle land or buildings. Especially in booming commercial cities, some churches owned
shops that yielded regular and substantial revenues for the church. For
example, in Iaroslavl a 1781 report showed that of 43 churches, 3
owned land and 10 others owned shops (lavki), which returned an
average income of 30 to 40 rubles (in one case, 100 rubles). The shops,
gifts from merchant parishioners in remembrance of kin, provided
generous supplements to parish revenues.[112] Such resources, however,
were very uncommon.

The second major resource was a stipend or salary (ruga), usually
given by a landlord to compensate for the lack of land or sufficient parishioners.[113] For example, a parish in Moscow uezd had only 12
households, too few to provide adequately for the clergy, and the
landlord promised to supplement regular parish incomes with an annual stipend of 15 rubles.[114] Stipends were most common in Moscow
uezd, for here resided the wealthy nobles most inclined to grant such
salaries. A great landowner like Sheremetev, with vast holdings of
serfs, paid salaries to 78 clergy.[115] On most estates the stipend itself
was quite small in the 1730s and 1740s: from 5 to 20 rubles, plus some
provisions.[116] By the 1770s, however, the stipend had increased
slightly; one priest in Moscow uezd received 25 rubles and provisions,
and a priest in Suzdal was given a salary of 20 rubles and some land.[117]
One priest received the enormous sum of 100 rubles, but a stipend
rarely exceeded 40 or 50 rubles even in the Moscow area. Evidently
desiring a more genteel priest, some landlords also specified good
cloth for a cassock as part of the stipend.[118]

These salaries, however, were very unreliable: nobles often broke their promises of money or provisions. A priest in Moscow uezd complained in 1739 that "the landlord does not give the promised salary (as the contract stipulates), and there are only four households in the parish."[119] Another cleric in Moscow uezd filed a similar petition, claiming that he "had no sustenance" because the landlord "refused to give the promised support."[120] It was by no means a simple matter for the bishop to intercede and defend the clergy. Metropolitan Platon I of Moscow, for example, was able to obtain the salary promised two priests in his diocese only by threatening to close the nobles' churches.[121] Moreover, the priest had no guarantee that a new landlord (whether heir or purchaser) would honor an old agreement. Such difficulties made the Synod insist in 1753 that all parish churches receive a full land allotment regardless of any promises, so that the clergy would always have some way to support themselves if their stipends were subsequently terminated.[122] In any event, the stipend was relatively uncommon; especially outside the large gentry estates, few nobles had the desire or means to pay salaries to the local priest.

More important was a third resource—parish-church land, which belonged to the parish church and which the clergy could cultivate or lease to laymen. The parishioners were supposed to allot land to a new church in perpetuity, but they often did so begrudgingly, especially as the shortage of land became more marked in the central provinces. As a result, the Church had to wage a constant battle to obtain allotments of adequate size and quality.

Church authorities first attempted to secure a minimum land allotment in the early seventeenth century. They did so, no doubt, partly out of concern for the parish clergy's well-being, but their own interests were also at stake: the bishops' main revenues—the parish-church tax—included an assessment on the landholdings of a parish church.[123] When cadastres were compiled in the 1620s, each parish church was supposed to receive a minimum allotment of 15 to 30 dessiatines, depending upon the size of the parish.[124] The decree was not strictly enforced, however, and many churches failed to receive the allotment. In the 1680s Patriarch Ioakim took advantage of a new state land survey to press for full allotments. He divided parishes into three categories (according to size, land, and social composition), which allotted the churches from 15 to 30 dessiatines of land. The land was to be in a single piece and near the parish church—partly to simplify access for the clergy, partly to prevent gradual reabsorption by the peasants. The patriarch hoped that hereafter "the priest and churchmen at these churches will have sustenance."[125] But Ioakim's effort also failed, and most churches remained without sufficient land.[126]

The Church continued its demands for sufficient parish land in the eighteenth century. The bishop's main weapon was his control over ordination and establishment of new churches: before approving a parish petition, he insisted that sufficient land be apportioned to the clergy. Both the Ecclesiastical Regulation and Synodal decrees made this procedure automatic and mandatory, and bishops scrupulously followed it.[127] They required their local agents (clerical elder or steward) to confirm by personal visit parish claims about resources available to the clergy. Parish communities and landlords were also required to promise that "the priest and church serviceman who are to be at this church will be apportioned arable land for their support, namely, 5 dessiatines per field [that is, 15 dessiatines in the three-field agrarian system]."[128] The consistory in Vladimir reported in 1763 that it routinely investigated petitions for ordination to determine whether the clergy had sufficient land.[129] Until a parish agreed, the bishops ignored their petitions. In a case in Pereslavl diocese, the bishop decided that insufficient land had been promised a candidate for priesthood, and he delayed ordination until the parish granted additional land.[130]

How much land did the clergy actually have before mid-century? According to data on church landholding in the 1730s, some parishes had no land at all: in Kolomna diocese 12 percent of the churches had no land, in Suzdal diocese 10 percent, and in Riazan diocese 23 percent.[131] Presumably, landless churches had other resources—rich parishioners, a state subsidy, or a landlord stipend; whatever the substitute, these churches left their clergy totally dependent upon the laity. Further, if a church owned land, it usually had just the bare minimum of 15 dessiatines; only in Riazan diocese were the holdings significantly higher (Table 12). Since large parishes with two or three priests had to allot more land according to Church regulations, they no doubt artificially raised the diocesan average to minimum levels; most small parishes probably fell below the 15 dessiatine norm. Parish landholdings also varied enormously within a single diocese. In Riazan diocese, for example, the average landholding ranged from a mere 11 dessiatines in Murom uezd to well over 20 dessiatines in other areas.

The data on formal land claims, moreover, yield too optimistic a picture. They indicate only total amount of landholding, not the quality or accessibility of the land; parishioners could satisfy the land requirement with poor land as well as good. One village church in Iaroslavl uezd, for example, had formal ownership of 33 dessiatines, but the land, marshy and overgrown, was actually worthless.[132] The parishioners also were known to seize land they had given the church "in perpetuity." A 1723 report on the central Synodal region complained that "the landowners, having taken church land and hayland from

Table 12. Average size of parish church landholdings, 1735-40

Diocese or district	Number of churches[a]	Total area of landholding (dessiatines)[b]	Average allotment (dessiatines)
Kolomna	691	10,911	15.79
Riazan	935	19,926	21.31
Rostov	826	12,358	14.96
Suzdal	449	6,070	13.52
Vladimir *uezd* and Gusskaia *desiatina*	212	3,588	16.92

Source: ODDS, 18:288; 18:Prilozhenie 16.
[a]For Kolomna, Riazan, Suzdal, and the Vladimir area data on the number of churches include only those actually claiming land; for Rostov the only available data were for all churches, including those without land.
[b]The data include all three fields.

them [the priests and churchmen], use it arbitrarily and do not let them take possession of it."[133] If the priest lodged a protest, the bishop could try to recover the property; Bishop Varlaam of Suzdal, for example, excommunicated a landlord and his peasants for seizing church land.[134] Metropolitan Arsenii of Rostov dealt summarily with similar offenders in 1746:

Major Shishkov actually seized church land, and his wife Shishkova ignores archpastoral appeals communicated to her by the diocesan superintendents. She wrongly claims the land as her own and does not want to return the land to the priest and churchmen. It is evident from this that the holy church is not necessary or required by the Major or his wife—it is just as if it were burned down. So inform the Major and his wife that divine and archpastoral blessing is withdrawn. And order both the Ilovaiskii priest and all other priests absolutely not to visit the Shishkov residence to administer church sacraments or to give blessings.[135]

If this ploy failed the bishop was powerless to do more. Many clergy, moreover, were reluctant even to seek the bishop's aid, fearing such reprisals from the parishioners as false reports of misconduct or drastically reduced gratuities. As a result, clerical landholding was insufficient and irregular. When diocesan authorities began to collect seminary taxes in the 1740s and 1750s (based on landholdings), they were dismayed to discover how often the clergy did not possess land formally attributed to them.[136]

Aware of the clergy's lack of land, the Synod deftly seized an opportunity to obtain a systematic allotment in the 1750s, when the state announced plans for a general land survey. The Synod proposed that surveyors assign standard allotments to parish churches; land shares were necessary, it argued, because the landlords so often broke their promises of land or annual stipends.[137] The government approved the proposal, perhaps hoping to eliminate clerical vagrancy (the result of impoverished churches or suspended stipends) and to make the white clergy self-sufficient. The General Surveying Instructions of 1754 therefore ordered land grants for parish churches. As a first step, churches were to repossess parish land which had slipped into lay control; surveyors were to honor claims based on the seventeenth-century cadastres. If a church still fell short of a minimum allotment, surveyors were to measure off additional land from the parishioners. They were also to observe certain rules, designed to protect the clergy: the church land must be qualitatively similar to land elsewhere in the parish, and not useless or poor; it must be located near the church; and it must be in a single piece to thwart gradual reabsorption by the laity.[138] But Elizabeth's general survey proved a failure because of technical problems and the gentry's opposition.[139] The Synod's efforts, temporarily, came to nought.

Catherine undertook a new survey in 1765, and this time the government was successful. Unlike the earlier attempt, the new survey recognized the nobility's present landholdings (and thus legalized their past seizure of state lands) and discouraged court disputes by making litigation prohibitively costly and risky. The provisions for Church lands show a similar realism and concern for workable compromise.[140] Like Elizabeth, Catherine ordered a minimum allotment (15 to 30 dessiatines of arable land, depending upon the parish). The surveyor was to measure off the land even if the local clergy did not request it. This automatic allotment would protect them in the future: they might surrender their right of usage for a salary but could later reclaim the land if necessary. The priest was also granted access to common forestland for his own use (but not for sale). To balance these losses to the parish church, Catherine gave the parishioners legal ownership over the land of defunct churches, puncturing ecclesiastical fantasies of a great land recovery. If an operating church had historic claims to land in excess of the norm, it was to be settled just like any other land claim, preferably through private compromise. But unlike Elizabeth, Catherine refused to support the historical claims of parish churches; under the terms of the survey, they could not risk litigation, and outside the courts they were sure to lose in "compromise settlements" with the laity. In short, Catherine promised the parish clergy a minimum allotment but made important concessions to the parishioners as well. As for the entire survey, her aim was to achieve a speedy, uncomplicated settlement—even at the expense of Church or state land claims.

Nevertheless, the survey provoked strong resistance from the laity, who were already beginning to feel the pinch of land shortage in the central provinces. Almost immediately, the Senate received reports that landlords refused to allot land for the local church or used their influence with state surveyors to sabotage the provisions for church land.[141] The bishop of Pereslavl complained to the Synod in 1775 that government surveyors abused the clergy and, disregarding state instructions, refused to give sufficient land to the churches. Indeed, he complained, churches received useless plots of infertile soil and sometimes even lost land.[142] A similar complaint was submitted in 1785 by the bishop of Vladimir. He reported that the clergy in one parish had received only half the minimum allotment, even though the local peasantry had ample land. He had protested to provincial officials, to no avail. The Synod supported the bishop, demanding additional land for the church "so that the clergy will not suffer want and poverty." It obtained a proclamation from the Senate ordering the governor-general to take appropriate steps "so that these clergy are afforded satisfaction without delay, in accordance with the laws."[143] Because of this and similar incidents, the Senate had to reaffirm the survey instructions several times—in 1767, 1775, and 1778.[144]

Catherine's survey was completed by the 1780s in central Russia, but, as the repeated Senate decrees suggest, it did not solve the problem of parish land shortage. Although we have no comprehensive data on the question, it is clear that the clergy gained little from the survey. The survey's failure became evident in 1798-1801, after Paul ordered parishioners to till parish land for the clergy. As Church authorities tried to implement the decree, they discovered significant variations in parish landholding—some parishes had far more than 30 dessiatines, others considerably less.[145] The reform commission of Alexander I, which also considered the problem of support for the white clergy, reported in 1808 that clerical lands were very irregular in value.[146] Nor indeed did the situation change in the next several decades, and in the clerical *cahiers* of 1863 the clergy still complained that their land was insufficient and of poor quality.[147]

This lack of land magnified the importance of the clergy's fourth kind of support: emoluments from parishioners for sacraments and prayer services. These fees were not considered a tax, but a voluntary gift that varied according to the parishioner's wealth and good will. Paid in money, kind (eggs, produce, and the like), even labor, the emoluments constituted an essential part of the clergy's income. Their importance was emphasized in the petitions of suspended priests, who could not give rites and thereby earn gratuities. Pleading that it was impossible to survive without emoluments and claiming that their families "wander from house to house like beggars,"[148] they implored the bishop to reinstate them.

Like landholdings, emoluments varied from one parish to the next. The amount for a service depended upon the parishioner's social and economic status; nobles and merchants gave more than peasants, rich peasants gave more than poorer brethren. The emoluments also followed regional patterns, as the local social structure and economy set general limits on customary amounts. For example, a marriage ceremony brought 25 to 50 kopecks to a priest in Moscow, 20 to 25 kopecks for a priest in Iaroslavl, and in many other areas "the fees for service were of course considerably lower and made mainly in kind, not money."[149] Bishops recognized the importance of social differences, noting whether a parish had richer laity (merchants, nobles, officials) or consisted mainly of peasants.[150]

The income from emoluments was also determined by the number of parishioners. Since the authorities failed to recarve parishes into roughly equal units, the range in parish size was still enormous. Some were small parishes of ten households; others were mammoth congregations with several hundred households. The Synod frequently took note of this diversity in its legislation, and the available data give an interesting picture of the variations.[151] In 1767, for example, Pereslavl uezd reported a few parishes with 200 and even 300 households; most, however, had fewer than 100 (Table 13). The diversity was also evident in the parish-church taxes, which were determined by the size of landholdings and economic value of parish households. In Vladimir, for example, the assessments varied from 50 kopecks to 3 rubles in city parishes, from 29 kopecks to 6 rubles in rural parishes.[152]

Because of this diversity, the clergy's economic status varied significantly. At one extreme was a tiny corps of clerical elite—in Moscow, selected provincial towns, and even a few rural parishes. The clergy in Moscow served churches which generally had fewer parishioners but which often included generous nobles, officials, and merchants. Even a stagnant town like Rostov had a few prosperous churches; of its 45 churches, 5 paid quite substantial parish-church taxes.[153] Some exceptionally rich parishes were also to be found in the countryside, such as those located in Sheremetev's "factory villages" in Vladimir province.[154]

Rich parishes were exceptional, however, and the priest of a middling parish in the 1770s had a more modest income, perhaps 25 to 40 rubles per year. One priest in Iaroslavl, for example, meticulously re-

Table 13. Size of parishes in Pereslavl and Pereslavl uezd, 1767

Type of parish	Pereslavl (city)		Pereslavl (uezd)	
	No.	%	No.	%
"Triple parish" (300 households)	0	0	4	1.6
"Double parish" (200 households)	1	4.3	14	6.0
"Single parish" (100 households)	22	95.7	217	92.3

Source: TsGIA, f. 796, op. 48, g. 1767, d. 547, ll. 444-498.

corded all his revenues in a diary, and his yearly income amounted to no more than 40 rubles.[155] In 1780 Bishop Tikhon of Suzdal appraised the value of a d'iachok income at 12 rubles per year; since the priest received twice that amount, his income was only 24 rubles per year under the bishop's estimate.[156] At best, such incomes permitted the priest to accumulate only modest possessions. One priest in Riazan, for example, gave a dowry for his daughter that was valued at 60 rubles and included a bay gelding, a sheepskin winter coat, various kinds of cloth, and a few other goods.[157] Also revealing was the inventory submitted by a Kolomna priest, listing his meager and tattered possessions that had been stolen.[158]

Some churches fell below the poverty line and had difficulty even maintaining a staff. In 1737 the bishops of Suzdal, Riazan, and Rostov dioceses reported a number of such churches, which simply lacked sufficient resources to support churchmen or even a priest.[159] One was a village church in Suzdal diocese, Khoriatina: it had 9 households and very little parish land.[160] The fate of another village, in Pereslavl uezd, was similar: "No volunteers from other churches have appeared for appointment and this is because of the small amount of support apportioned for the clergy at this church."[161] City parishes too floundered. In 1754 the bishop of Pereslavl observed that many city parishes were quite small, and "as a result the city clergy have become impoverished." He pointedly added that "it would be better to be in the peasantry than a churchman at such small parish churches."[162] The clergy naturally seized the first opportunity to leave these churches and cited the need "for sustenance" to justify petitions to transfer to another parish.[163] But even this safety valve was gradually closing; because of the tight controls against "excess appointments" and the constant threat of a new government conscription, many clergy could not transfer and sank ever more deeply into poverty. The diocesan consistory of Vladimir received a number of petitions from clergy declaring that "we have come into such total ruin that we do not even have our daily sustenance." Even allowing for the petitioners' flair for exaggeration such claims ring true.[164] The testimony of outsiders confirms the pattern of endemic poverty, as do the recurrent reports on clerical vagrants wandering in search of "food and sustenance."[165]

The economic stratification of the white clergy—amorphous, undefined, irregular—did not change throughout the eighteenth century. The only visible difference by the end of the century was the elimination of some uneconomic parishes; those which could not maintain a clerical staff were gradually weeded out. But this did not overcome the great heterogeneity in parish size, for the bishops eliminated only tiny parishes and did not regroup the larger ones. As shown by the data for Suzdal diocese in 1781 (Table 14), gigantic par-

Table 14. Size of parishes in Suzdal Diocese, 1781

| Number of parish households | Number of churches per category | | | | | |
| | Suzdal | | Iur'ev-Pol'skii | | Shui | |
	City	Uezd	City	Uezd	City	Uezd
0-20	2	5	1	9	0	1
21-40	10	17	0	22	1	4
41-60	5	34	2	36	2	6
61-80	3	17	1	16	0	5
81-100	1	25	0	16	0	8
101-120	0	19	0	13	0	10
121-140	0	3	0	1	1	4
141-160	0	1	0	0	0	3
161-180	0	2	1	2	0	5
181-200	0	1	0	1	1	0
201-220	0	2	0	2	0	1
221-240	0	0	0	0	0	2
241-260	0	0	0	1	0	2
261-280	0	1	0	1	0	0
281-300	0	0	0	0	0	1
301-320	0	0	0	0	0	1
321-340	0	0	0	0	0	2
341-360	0	0	0	0	0	0
361-380	0	0	0	0	0	0
381-400	0	0	0	0	0	0
401-500	0	0	0	0	0	4

Source: TsGIA, f. 796, op. 62, g. 1781, d. 195, ll. 67-140 ob.

ishes still coexisted with very small ones and some were still below the legal minimum of 20 households (city parishes) or 40 households (rural parishes). This picture changed but little by 1808, when a reform commission investigated the clergy's economic problems. Only a small fraction of parishes could provide large incomes: "All others, from this amount [1000 rubles] and gradually descending downward in income, are in the most impoverished condition; in some, the income is 5 to 10 rubles per year, in most cases it constitutes 50 to 150 rubles [for an entire staff]."[166] Hence the average priest's income was 25 to 75 rubles in 1808—small indeed after the runaway inflation of the late 1790s.

The economics of clerical service thus created a diverse social group, as varied in economic status as the nobility, townspeople, and peasantry. However unified by their separate, peculiar legal status, the clergy were divided by profound economic differences. These differences invited upward social mobility; provincial clergy eagerly aspired to the prized positions in a diocese, or better yet, Moscow itself. The career of Vasilii Fedorov in Pereslavl reflected such mobility. Sometime in the late 1690s Fedorov became *d'iachok* at his father's church, and in 1703 was promoted to deacon in the same parish. His big opportunity came in 1713, when townsmen in Pereslavl selected him as priest in the city's cathedral, and in 1735 he reached the pinnacle of a provincial career, becoming archpriest in the same cathedral.[167] After mid-century education became the key to such mobility and made possible meteoric careers like that of Aleksandr Levshin. His studies at the Moscow Academy (1748-60) earned him the prize appointment as deacon in a Moscow church in 1760, and three years later he became priest in the same parish. In 1767 Levshin transferred to a priestly position in another Moscow parish, and the same year reached the apex of a white cleric's career when he was named archpriest of Uspenskii Cathedral in the Kremlin.[168] Such mobility, to be sure, was constrained by the lack of new openings, poor communications, property obligations, and various legal commitments. But for the talented and ambitious, upward mobility was a tantalizing possibility and a cogent reason for the priest and his son to remain in the clerical estate. The Church explicitly defended differences in support, arguing that they permitted the bishop to reward honorable, responsible priests and to punish bad ones.[169]

This unreformed system of clerical economies, however, bred serious disorders. One was intense conflict within the parish clergy, who competed, fought, and sued for the better positions. Moreover, the system impeded the bishops' attempts to improve the clergy's education and status; though it lavishly provided for the elite, it sentenced many others to unrelieved penury and privation. And, of particular moment, it made the clergy dependent upon their parishioners; land reform had failed and other resources were negligible, making the parishioners' "voluntary" emoluments the key component of a priest's budget.

Income Distribution and Rank

Besides the economic resources of an individual parish, a second factor in determining the income of a cleric was his rank—priest, deacon, or churchman. Each parish staff shared land and income according to rank, with the priest ordinarily receiving two to four times the share of the churchman. Hierarchs made no attempt to regulate this sharing before the 1730s; as in most questions, the bishops had neither the means nor the desire to meddle in internal parish matters. Nor was there any compelling need to do so; since the priest and churchman often were father and son, episcopal rules were superfluous. Although disputes over land and income arose that required arbitration or judgment by the diocesan administration,[170] in general the share due each rank remained an internal parish matter.

After the 1730s, however, as bishops began to regulate parish life with greater zeal, they also tried to set standard schedules for the sharing of income and land in their dioceses. In 1732 the bishop of Suzdal ordered that a priest receive twice the share of a churchman, whatever the size and structure of the parish staff.[171] In 1747 Bishop Arsenii of Pereslavl promulgated a much less equitable system: a priest was to receive four times the share of a churchman.[172] Authorities in Vladimir diocese accorded the priest three times a churchman's share, according to a schedule established in 1767.[173] In Iaroslavl, during the same period, a priest received only twice a churchman's share.[174] More complex was the sliding schedule adopted in 1776 by Metropolitan Platon of Moscow. Rather than a fixed proportion, the churchman's share varied from 25 to 43 percent of that given the priest—depending upon the size of the parish staff.[175] Whatever the system, it confirmed significant differences of income within a parish staff.

Thus, however inadequate the priest's income, a sacristan always fared much worse: 10 to 20 rubles per year was perhaps a common figure in the 1770s and 1780s.[176] A miserly sum by contemporary standards, it left the churchman with marginal chances for survival; as one sacristan of Murom uezd complained, bad harvests so dimmed parishioner generosity that his income fell from the usual 15 rubles to a mere 6 rubles.[177] To ease their lot, churchmen sometimes accepted second jobs. Though church law forbade clergy to hold secular positions, some clerics nevertheless worked as chancellery scribes and others became hired laborers.[178] In utter despair some sacristans quit the clerical estate; two churchmen in Vladimir, for example, even volunteered to become serfs and received land and aid in settlement from the landowner.[179] Bishop Viktor observed in 1789 that "the ordained clergy live in satisfaction, but the deacons and churchmen, who receive only their share [of parish revenues], have fallen into extreme poverty and hardship, and they suffer from great wants in their support."[180] The laity also recognized this difference, and one popular eighteenth-century proverb used the *ponomar'* as a standard for poverty: "There are some nobles [even] worse off than a *ponomar'*."[181]

At least some bishops tried to narrow the gap between the ordained clergy and churchmen. In 1754 the bishop of Pereslavl reduced the deacon's share in order to enlarge that of the churchman. But he met with stout resistance from the priests and deacons, and within a few years the former schedule was restored.[182] The bishops of Suzdal and Vladimir attempted similar reforms to aid the churchmen several times in the 1770s and 1780s. In 1775 the bishop of Suzdal prepared a new scale of sharing, giving a much larger portion to the churchmen. The disgruntled priests complained to the Synod, which—for the sake of tranquility—upheld the priests and ordered restoration of the traditional schedule. After the creation of a single Vladimir-Suzdal diocese in 1788, Bishop Viktor noted that various parts of his diocese used different scales. Interested in ameliorating the churchmen's economic distress and establishing uniformity throughout his diocese, he proposed a new schedule that greatly diminished the priest's share in Vladimir diocese. When the bishop first explained his intentions to the Synod and asked for approval of the plan, the Synod declined to pass judgment and instructed the bishop to resolve the question on his own. The priests, who suffered from the change, protested to Viktor in collective petitions in 1789 and 1791. When these brought no results, they appealed to the Synod to reestablish the old system. The petitioners (12 city and 29 rural priests and deacons) claimed that the old system had not caused disputes and, "for the sake of harmony," asked that it be reinstated. The dispute simmered for another three years before the Synod in 1794 acceded to the priests' request. To end the quarreling and litigation, it ordered Bishop Viktor to rescind his decree and to restore the old system of sharing.[183]

Sharp economic differences between priest and churchman thus remained the norm throughout the eighteenth century; the few attempts to narrow the gap failed. Economic differences, in turn, generated a broader pattern of social and cultural stratification between the two levels of white clergy. This made little difference if the churchman was just the priest's son; if he were not (and this was increasingly the case), the economic inequality was socially significant. It tended, moreover, to become self-perpetuating and hereditary, since churchmen could less easily afford to educate their children in the seminary or send them to the more advanced courses.

The economic difference between priest and churchman was important because it coincided with a sharpening distinction between their statuses and rights. The state assigned the churchman a markedly inferior status, subjecting him to corporal punishment and conscription from which the priest was free. The Church too elevated the priest above the churchman, formalizing and expanding his supervisory powers. Metropolitan Platon of Moscow, for example, ordered "deacons and churchmen to show respect to their priest as head of their church and not to insult him by word or deed."[184] Typical too was an order by the bishop of Vladimir in 1779 for the priest "to observe and oversee closely that the clergy in his parish perform their duties carefully and correctly, lead a good orderly life, do not get drunk, and do not visit taverns."[185] Similarly, the churchman's installation charter admonished him to be "obedient to your priest in everything which is not contrary to divine law and which is appropriate to your rank and profession."[186] A churchman's disobedience, in fact, could even be grounds for removal. Thus in 1773 the bishop of Kolomna proposed to defrock a *ponomar'* for "disobedience toward his priest" (among other misdeeds), and in 1796 the bishop of Vladimir removed a *d'iachok* "for drunkenness and disobedience toward his priest."[187]

The cumulative result was evident by the nineteenth century: a basic split within the parish clergy, where ordained clerics and churchmen represented distinct, separate strata. Mobility from churchman to priest, to be sure, remained; those who persevered in the seminary had equal rights, whether sons of a *ponomar'* or priest. But usually sheer economics prevailed, making such upward mobility difficult and unlikely. To conserve church resources and to rid the clergy of its "proletariat," by the mid-nineteenth century many proposed to expel churchmen from the clerical estate—a long step from the days when a churchman was the priest's own son.[188]

Staffing Problems

Once the registry or *shtat* had been confirmed, the Church and government began a long dispute about "excess clergy" and "vacant positions." Paradoxically, the evidence at any given time showed both superfluous clergy and many vacant clerical positions. Such contradictory data could be used to support opposite policies—a new conscription (to remove the overpopulated estate of "superfluous, excess" members), or the appointment of many more clergy (if need be, from the poll-tax classes and nobility). The government, predictably, emphasized the data on "idle churchmen and clerical children," who failed to find a registered position or voluntarily leave the clerical estate. The Synod opposed conscriptions and wanted to admit outsiders; therefore it compiled impressive data on clerical vacancies and the acute need for more clergy. The bureaucratic skirmishes thus left behind very contradictory pictures—one of stifling overpopulation, another of severe and chronic shortages of clergy.[189]

Statistical data from the mid-eighteenth century reveal several patterns in clerical staffing. First, numerous shortages were reported in almost every diocese of the empire. Evidence of this was first compiled in 1736-39, as the Synod tried to blunt the thrust of Anna's conscription. It concluded that "there is a great shortage and insufficiency of clergy at churches," and many bishops even claimed disruptions in services because churches could not find priests.[190] The number of vacancies varied significantly among the central dioceses; as data from 1747 show (Table 15), the shortage of clergy ranged from 8 percent in Kolomna diocese to 29 percent in Rostov. Second, the problem of vacancies was chronic, not a temporary dislocation caused by government conscription. The data for 1747 came eight years after Anna's conscription; since then many sacristans had been reappointed and others had had ample time to fill the vacancies. Data on Suzdal diocese for 1738-52 show hundreds of vacancies, year after year, quite independent of state policy.[191] Likewise, Pereslavl diocese reported that 17 percent of all positions were vacant in 1747 and 23 percent in 1767, years remote from effective conscriptions.[192] Third, vacancies coexisted in the same town or district with "surplus clergy" (zashtat-

Table 15. Staffing shortages in central dioceses, 1747

Diocese	Number of churches	Number of allowable clergy (per shtat)	Actual clergy		Vacant positions	
			No.	%	No.	%
Kolomna	805	3,099	2,835	91.5	264	8.5
Moscow	1,838	7,374	6,526	88.5	848	11.5
Pereslavl	583	2,171	1,793	82.6	378	17.4
Riazan	1,220	5,161	4,663	90.4	498	9.6
Rostov	834	3,159	2,230	70.6	929	29.4
Suzdal	476	1,915	1,611	84.1	304	15.9

Sources: TsGIA, f. 796, op. 28, g. 1747, d. 216, ll. 124 ob.-125, 140 ob.-143, 173 ob.-175, 180 ob.-182, 346 ob.-353, 482 ob.-486.

nye, that is, those in excess of the *shtat).* A report on Suzdal in 1741, for example, maps out this paradoxical arrangement of surplus and shortages in each city and district of the diocese; in the city of Suzdal, for example, there were 5 surplus clergy and 38 vacancies, and in Suzdal uezd there were 64 surplus clergy amidst 377 vacancies. In almost every area, for almost every rank, there were both shortages and excess clergy.[193] Bishop Afanasii of Suzdal had noted this pattern in 1737: "At many churches there are no churchmen, but at many others there is an excess of unappointed [churchmen] who live with their parents."[194] Over-Procurator Shakhovskoi made a similar observation in in 1743 and urged the Synod to order a redistribution of clergy.[195] Fourth, the pattern of surplus and vacancies generally coincided with rank: most surplus clergy were priests, most vacancies were in the churchman ranks (Table 16). Yet the correlation was not iron-clad or axiomatic; a report on Suzdal in 1741 shows some surplus churchmen as well as a few vacant priestly positions.[196] Finally, staffing irregularities appeared in city as well as rural parishes. Some cities like Suzdal and Moscow had fairly complete staffing, with few vacancies (5 and 6 percent respectively). Usually, however, the staffing shortages affected urban parishes no less severely; these numbered, for example, 16 percent of all positions in Iaroslavl and 34 percent in Rostov.[197]

The main reason for this simultaneous surplus and shortage was the vast economic diversity among parishes. Each parish had its own combination of resources and thus different capacities for supporting clergy—sometimes above the number permitted by the registry, sometimes fewer. Contenders naturally sought appointments in viable parishes, while shunning small, landless churches. This consideration was particularly compelling for churchmen, who received one half to one third the priest's share. The hierarchs were well aware of the economic

Table 16. Staffing patterns according to rank, 1747

Diocese	Percentage of allowable positions filled		
	Priest	Deacon	Churchman
Kolomna	115	88	80
Moscow	108	55	91
Pereslavl	95	107	71
Riazan	108	96	80
Rostov	98	51	62
Suzdal	103	93	71

Source: TsGIA, f. 796, op. 28, g. 1747, d. 216, ll. 124 ob.-125, 140 ob.-143, 173 ob.-175, 180 ob.-182, 346 ob.-353, 482 ob.-486.

cause of uneven staffing, but as long as the parish economy was particularistic and not regularized, they could not redistribute the clergy to fit the neat symmetry of the registry.

The uneven distribution was also due to the fact that the parish and local priest did not welcome outside candidates. The local clergy lost income when an outsider joined the staff, for the inelastic resources—land allotments and gratuities—were simply sliced into smaller shares. Metropolitan Platon regarded this as a major cause of vacancies, complaining that the priest deliberately kept sacristan positions vacant, hired temporary outsiders at cheap rates to perform the churchman's duties, and thereby increased his own income.[198] Sometimes the parishioners too opposed a full staff for economic reasons. For example, in 1729 the parish of a church in Vladimir uezd asked not to have an additional priest, declaring that "no support is available due to our poverty and the poor harvests."[199] A priest also wanted to keep a vacant position for his own son; the son's appointment kept that share of parish income in the family, prepared a candidate for his father's priestly position, and meanwhile protected the youth from state conscriptions. Because of minimum age limits (30 for priest, 25 for deacon, 15 for churchman), positions often had to be left vacant until the heir came of age. Moreover, the parishioners and clergy looked askance at the appointment of an alien cleric to their church, rightly suspecting that he would hasten to denounce any irregularities—such as concealed fugitives, Old Believers, superstitions, or hidden distilleries. A local clerical clan depended upon parish good will for income and the selection of kinsmen as future clergy and hence was not disposed to betray parishioners. An outsider knew no such loyalties; on the contrary, he was promised rich rewards for informing on parish irregularities or on clergy remiss in their duties.[200] Whatever the reason, parishes willfully left positions unoccupied and refused to select new candidates. To surmount such resistance, in 1743 the Synod proposed to set a timetable for filling vacancies and to fine parishes that procrastinated; although the Senate approved the scheme, it was never enforced.[201] In 1755 the Synod prohibited the practice of reserving positions for "underaged sons" but this measure too was never enforced.[202]

The pattern of clerical staffing changed dramatically by the 1780s. Most important, numerous vacancies disappeared in the central provinces; except for Moscow, all central dioceses had virtually full staffing by 1784 (Table 17). The change was striking, as a comparison of 1747 and 1784 shows: the proportion of full staffing rose from 71 to 95 percent in Rostov, from 84 to 100 percent in Suzdal, from 92 to 99 percent in Kolomna, from 83 to 95 percent in Pereslavl, and from 90 to

Table 17. Staffing patterns in central dioceses, 1784

Diocese	Number of churches	Number of allowable clergy (per shtat)	Actual clergy		Vacant positions	
			No.	%	No.	%
Kolomna	925	3,709	3,655	98.5	54	1.5
Moscow	814	2,947	2,649	95.2	298	10.1
Pereslavl	608	2,564	2,442	95.2	122	4.8
Riazan	981	4,629	4,618	99.8	11	0.2
Rostov	834	3,575	3,379	94.5	196	5.5
Suzdal	637	3,239	3,255	100.1	0	0
Vladimir	730	3,524	3,544	100.6	0	0

Source: TsGIA, f. 796, op. 65, g. 1784, d. 443, ll. 71-85.

100 percent in Riazan. Only in Moscow had the change been negligible, increasing from 89 to 90 percent; yet here too the bishop eliminated all vacancies after the 1784 conscription.[203] In this respect, the central dioceses were quite different from the outlying provinces of the empire, which still reported significant numbers of unoccupied positions and, in some cases, would still do so in the nineteenth century. As before, the remaining vacancies were concentrated in the sacristan ranks: Moscow lacked 30 priests, but 286 churchmen; Kolomna diocese had 2 excess priests, but lacked 150 churchmen.[204]

This dramatic change in staffing was due to several factors. One was the impact of church controls, which gradually eliminated or reformed uneconomic parishes and generally increased their size, and by the 1780s these controls had achieved noticeable results. Full staffing was also caused by Catherine's more ruthless conscriptions, which encouraged clerical youths to accept any available position. Another factor was the effort of Church authorities, who relocated and transferred clergy in order to erase vacancies or surpluses. The bishops assumed an unprecedented role during the conscription of 1784 when, at government insistence, they redistributed clergy in strict conformity with the registry. In Moscow, for example, the bishop reported 10 percent vacancies before the conscription; in 1784 he made sufficient transfers to eliminate virtually all vacancies (Table 18). Churchmen's numerous appeals to the Synod after the conscription attest to the punctiliousness of the bishops, whom they accused of "merciless" and even illegal measures; the Synod rejected such appeals, declaring that the conscription was already over and denying any need for recovering the churchmen.[205] Finally, the seminary had some impact through

Table 18. Moscow staffing before and after redistribution, 1782 and 1784

| | Number of allowable clergy (per | Number of actual clergy | |
Rank	shtat)	1782	1784
Priest	859	854	856
Deacon	382	382	382
Churchman	1,693	1,387	1,693
Total	2,934	2,623	2,931

Source: TsGIA, f. 796, op. 62, g. 1781, d. 588, ll. 117-124, 127-131.

the "reserved positions" which bishops increasingly awarded to seminarians as a kind of scholarship.

The achievement of full staffing in the central dioceses had important consequences for the clergy. It meant, in the first place, that candidates—even seminarians—had difficulty finding positions after the 1780s. All positions were filled in 1784; new vacancies opened but slowly. This occurred just as the seminaries burst into rapid growth and left the Church with its first bumper harvest of "excess" seminarians. Thus began a vicious cycle; difficulties in obtaining appointment persuaded more youths to enroll and that in turn produced more and more excess candidates. The results were evident by 1800: a glut of clerical youths who could not find a church position, yet who lacked sufficient education in the seminary to qualify for state service. The Church dramatically shifted from complaints about too few qualified candidates to complaints about a multitude of unneeded seminarians. Moreover, the new situation of the 1780s—when staffing was full and youths genuinely expendable—explains why Catherine's conscriptions were so much more effective than earlier ones. Anna and Elizabeth had been stymied by Synodal claims of clerical shortages and warnings that churches are "idle and without divine services"; Catherine could draft massive numbers and achieve full staffing. In addition, the new data on staffing persuaded even the bishops to modify their views about the proper social policy on the clergy's offspring: many now agreed with state officials that the Church had no need to ordain individuals from other social estates. Besides, the bishops preferred the "educated candidates," and the supply of seminarians already exceeded Church needs.[206] As a result, the bishops ceased to contest state policies (such as the poll-tax rules) that excluded outsiders from entering the clergy and turned the clergy into a closed, hereditary group.

The Strains of Clerical Service

Beginning with Peter, the authorities made substantial changes in the structure of clerical service. They placed tight controls on churches and established a precise registry (*shtat*) to regulate possible appointments. They drew short, however, of making fundamental changes in the economics of clerical service. Except for a very small segment, most clergy still depended upon the traditional forms of parish support. The result was an incomplete reform: a bureaucratic structure of service was imposed on a traditional parish economy. This partial reform had devastating effects on the clergy.

First, it intensified the problem of clerical impoverishment. The clergy, to be sure, had known poverty before these changes, but the Petrine system was an aggravation, not a solution. The registry was an artificial system of appointment, determined by raw numbers of households and not parish revenues. Peter intended to reconstitute parishes into viable units, but neither he nor his successors completed the reform. Clerical appointment now became separated from "market demand": whereas staffing in pre-Petrine Russia had adjusted to the parish economy, it now followed the arbitrary rules of the registry. In the 1740s and 1750s the clergy still refused to occupy marginal positions (especially that of churchman), and they often managed to keep positions vacant to increase their income or even to overload the staff in violation of the registry. By the 1780s such illegality, which had cushioned the bureaucratic rigor of the registry, was eliminated. Bishops no longer tolerated vacancies, and the clergy accepted a "registered position," however poor the church. Furthermore, the Church for the first time actually acquired large numbers of churchmen, whose meagre income guaranteed certain poverty and hardship. Until mid-century the sacristan function had been performed by a son or not at all; now a separate group of servitors was emerging within the white clergy that would become a kind of clerical proletariat in the nineteenth century.

Moreover, the service structure was a major cause of intense strife in the white clergy. The clergy feuded and brawled, sued and slandered, and even committed an occasional homicide.[207] Untangling these conflicts became the major burden of diocesan administration; harried bishops devoted much of their time trying to reconcile or arbitrate the ubiquitous disputes.[208] The service structure, to be sure, was not the only cause. Often the priest simply abused his authority in the parish, punching or kicking his churchman.[209] But most disputes involved problems that arose directly from the system of service.

One frequent point of dispute was land and income. Even though the hierarchs promulgated explicit rules on sharing in order to reduce the conflict that had become so common, the clergy of a parish still fought over the spoils. The usual complaint was illegal sharing of the emoluments; predictably, some clerics tried to defraud their colleagues. A typical dispute arose in a Suzdal village in the 1770s, when the sacristans complained that the parish priest withheld some emoluments for his own use and refused to share them. The bishop made no attempt to amend past injustices but, to prevent future conflict, ordered that "the income be collected and put into an urn, and then divided into appropriate shares each week or month."[210] A more general solution to the problem was sought by Metropolitan Platon, who had to judge frequent disputes over income. He specifically ordered the ecclesiastical superintendents to ensure that priests do "not offend the deacon and churchman or withhold their income."[211] Nevertheless, the scramble for parishioner emoluments persisted, breeding ill will and mutual suspicion among parish clergy.[212]

A second point of dispute concerned clerical positions. Because of the fixed regulations of the registry, a priest or sacristan could obtain promotion—or a position for a son—only by eliminating a competitor. Even marginal slots were filled by the 1780s, and the competition for positions became particularly acrimonious and desperate. One priest in Pereslavl, for example, filed a false accusation against the churchman in his parish in order to make room for his son.[213] In another case in Vladimir diocese, the bishop received a petition from a priest who asked that a colleague be removed as "superfluous" because there were too few households in the parish.[214] A priest who sought a position for his son played a most unkind trick: he left his churchman's name off the census report (skazka), causing him to be drafted in the next government conscription as "unregistered."[215] Some clergy resorted to even more desperate measures. A cleric in Riazan diocese was appointed to a parish in the 1790s that proved to be the hereditary enclave of a single family. The clan deeply resented the newcomer, who met with harassment, threats, and abuse; even an occasional musket shot came in his direction before the bishop finally interceded.[216]

This internal strife not only caused individuals great hardship but also seriously weakened the whole group. At one level, it invited public scorn and derision for the clergy. The spectacle of two clerics, literally brawling and cursing at the altar (with the eventual victor dragging his foe "by the beard"), cost the clergy dearly needed social respect. The feuds, moreover, were often financially ruinous. Bolotov recounts that his local priest, whose feud with a peer lasted for decades, would have been a wealthy man had he not squandered his income on perpetual litigation.[217] Finally, internal conflict weakened the clergy against external society. Divided by strife, they did not form a cohesive group with a broader consciousness of their common interests; the vicious struggle for income and positions emphasized their mutual animosities, not interests. Internal weakness only made them still more vulnerable to abuse and manipulation by the surrounding lay society.

The Clergy and
the Parish Community

6

The parish community was the nuclear unit of the Church, forming the primary bond between Church and society. The parish was complex and unique, each different in size, geographic unity, and social composition. But whatever its structure, the parish was not a mere administrative-religious unit; it was also a fundamental social organization, governing the community as well as its church. From the earliest period of Russian history, the parish had been founded and ruled not by a hierarch, but rather by the laity. It functioned as an autonomous unit of self-rule, fusing together secular society and religious organization into a single unit—the parish commune (*prikhodskaia obshchina*). This traditional parish lasted into the eighteenth century, when it underwent significant changes in its structure and function. These changes inevitably affected the parish clergy, their relationship to the parish, and the ability of the Church to adapt to a modern secular society.

What were the changes recasting the parish? This development has been construed in the traditional historiography as a simple disappearance of the parish. According to this view, the parish lost its traditional autonomy and power to the new state and Church bureaucracy, which expanded rapidly after Peter's reforms and simply displaced the parish. The parish's demise is allegedly revealed by the loss of an important right—the prerogative to select candidates for the bishop to ordain. Consequently, the clergy supposedly became appointees of the bishop rather than elected representatives of the parish.[1] This view of the parish derived from a broader conception that pervasive bureaucratization was crushing the "vital forces" of the nation. A leading church historian, for example, drew this melancholy picture of the process:[2]

The eighteenth century was not a time of the development but of the decline of social forces in all spheres of popular life, a time of the intensified development of government regulation and tutelage—by every kind of authority, great or small—over popular life, a time of the final establishment and rapid extension of serfdom. Social life died off in all its functions.

Falling victim to this bureaucratization, the parish allegedly surrendered its traditional powers and functions to Church hierarchs and ceased to exist as a self-governing autonomous community.

Yet this conception, while generally accepted, is not drawn from a broad and systematic study of the primary sources. In contrast to the immense (if uneven) literature on the Church hierarchy and administrative institutions, there has been no comparable research on the parish.[3] Nor does the parish elicit much attention even in the rich literature on individual social groups (nobility, peasantry, and townspeople).[4] To a large degree, this neglect can be explained by the problem of sources: no institutional archive has comprehensive material on the parish, and pertinent materials are scattered and not easily reconstituted. This paucity of materials was a direct result of the peculiar structure of Church-state relations, where jurisdiction over society was divided into a Synodal command and a secular command. The Church governed only the clergy, not the parishioners; hence it ordinarily collected data on the clerical estate but not the whole parish. The state, which had used the parish as an administrative tool in the seventeenth century, dropped this unit during the provincial reforms of 1718; hence it too failed to collect data on the parish. In the absence of social information on parish communities, historians have relied upon the printed collections of state laws, which project legislative wish rather than a picture of the parish's actual development.

This chapter will investigate the changes in the parish and its relationship to the white clergy. The first task is to reconsider the parish's development. This traditional institution was not simply crushed but underwent complex changes; the aim here is to analyze the evolution of the parish as a social and religious organization. The second task is to assess the impact of these changes on the parish's relationship to the clergy and to determine whether the parish lost its authority over the priest and churchman. In order to chart the pattern of clergy-parish relations, it is necessary to examine the four main areas of their interaction—the selection of clergy, their forcible removal by the parish, economic relations, and the clergy's personal inviolability. An analysis of social relations inside the parish can also provide some insight into the clergy's social and religious roles. And that in turn can suggest some broader generalizations about the parish's impact upon the stability, cohesion and influence of the clergy.

The Transformation of the Parish

Before the eighteenth century, the Russian parish had one very striking characteristic: it was identical to the commune; the parish and community (*obshchina* or *mir*) were the same. While the type of parish—state peasant, landlord, monastery, or urban—varied considerably as a social environment, all nevertheless showed the same identity of parish and community. As Znamenskii has pointed out, "the old Russian *obshchina* was defined by the church parish, so that the parish and social community were identical, both in fact as well as in the language of the documents."[5] This overlap of community and parish was also once true of Europe; it endured longer in Russia, where the parish performed functions that central authorities could not fulfill because of administrative backwardness.[6] As a church administrative unit, the parish was of course primarily a religious organization, designed to serve the spiritual needs of the laity. What makes the parish as a unit of social organization so fascinating, however, was its broad set of extra-religious functions for the community.

The parish performed essentially three such functions for the laity of old Muscovy. First, it was the administrative center of the community. Because the state had only a skeletal administration in the provinces, the community assumed routine functions of self-government and made the parish church its administrative center. The laity convened at the church to make collective decisions, to hold court in minor matters, and to draw up legal documents.[7] This explains why many vital dates in medieval law—such as St. George's Day in serf relations—coincided with religious holidays. The administrative function of the church even affected the clergy's role: one sacristan acted as village clerk and the term for his clerical rank (*d'iachok*) was derived from the word for clerk (*d'iak*).[8] Second, the parish church held much economic importance for its members. It was the commercial center of the community, which used the occasion of Sunday services to conduct a lively trade.[9] The great trade fairs of medieval Russia, likewise, were held on the chief religious holidays.[10] The parish church itself sometimes became an enterprise: it acquired land and valuables, operated businesses, and extended loans to parishioners.[11] Third, the parish was the cultural center for the community. While secular tastes and interests became increasingly evident in the

seventeenth century, religious celebration still provided the main
focus of the parishioners' cultural experience. The church and clergy
usually provided such education as there was, through the informal
parish schools; some churches could even boast of sizable libraries.[12]
The simple parishioners also used the church for entertainment and
merry-making. A parish church usually had a small annex (*trapeza*)
for assemblies and especially for feasts and celebrations; where
annexes were lacking, the parishioners even held these festivities
inside the church.[13] As one group of parishioners complained, irrever-
ent parishioners gathered outside the church to "play games of chance,
sing the devil's songs, . . . and indulge in every imaginable kind of
unseemly act next to the Church of Nicholas the Miracle-Worker."[14]

The parishioners wielded complete control over their local church.
This broad local autonomy resulted primarily from the administrative
weakness of the Church: because of the vast size of each diocese and
poor communications, close hierarchical control was impossible in
medieval Russia.[15] The laity alone built and maintained the parish
church; they provided the land and revenues to support the resident
clergy. Probably the most impressive display of their power was the
right to select clergy: the parish (either community or landlord) chose
candidates, who were then routinely ordained by the bishop.[16] And to
oversee "their" church, the parishioners elected a layman as church
elder (*tserkovnyi starosta*), a kind of churchwarden who managed
church revenues and enjoyed considerable esteem, even official recognition.[17] This broad parochial authority and independence provoked
one frustrated bishop in the late seventeenth century to complain that
"not the hierarchs but the peasants are running the churches."[18] Indeed
they were.

This traditional integrity and cohesion of parish and community
began to disappear in the eighteenth century. While rate and form
varied, depending upon the surrounding social environment, the
parish everywhere experienced basic changes in its structure and functions. Two processes were at work: the parish underwent basic structural changes and, more important, it gave up the traditional extra-
religious functions.

One primary structural change was a bureaucratic reorganization of
parishes. As we have seen, Peter placed controls on the establishment
of new churches and encouraged bishops to recast small parishes into
larger, economically viable units. Church administrators heeded his
general regulations, and although not a systematic reorganization
(like that in the Habsburg realm in 1782 or in Russia in the 1870s),[19]
the new policy brought some regrouping of parishes. This had profound social consequences: the arbitrary redrawing of boundaries de-

stroyed the traditional identity of parish and community. Now the bishop, not the lay community, began to determine whether a parish should continue to exist or whether a new one could be established. Notwithstanding parish appeals and sometimes even against his own desire, the bishop had to enforce regulations against small parishes, especially after mid-century.

In the eighteenth century such parish reorganization was most effective in the towns, and Moscow was the most important case. It was particularly in need of parish reorganization; a list of 100 churches, compiled in 1771-72, shows that many had fewer than 10 households —far below the legal minimum of 20.[20] The plague of 1771 provided a convenient opportunity to reorganize parishes; the authorities did not allow decimated parishes to reopen and arbitrarily transferred remaining households to neighboring parishes.[21] After his appointment in 1775, Metropolitan Platon resumed the policy of eliminating and merging parishes. In his *Instructions to Ecclesiastical Superintendents*, Platon directed his deputies to report any churches which were underpopulated or which lacked adequate financial support.[22] The results of his effort became clear by the 1780s, when Moscow reported the largest decrease in total number of churches.[23] Platon was actually too zealous for many laymen; he aroused considerable public discontent, even ominous threats of a government investigation.[24]

Bishops outside Moscow took similar measures against city parishes. In 1754, for example, Bishop Amvrosii found that "most of the churches in Pereslavl are underpopulated, with 2 to 5 households and at others none at all." He then ordered a systematic redistribution so that each parish had at least 30 households.[25] Diocesan authorities similarly divided a large parish of *iamshchiki* (coachmen) in Klin, reassigning part of them to help support the city cathedral.[26] Not all bishops, however, attempted a full reordering of parish households; Rostov and Suzdal, for instance, still had undersized parishes in 1781 and the range in parish size was indeed very great.[27] But most hierarchs attended their duties punctiliously; throughout most of central Russia the average size of city parishes increased steadily, and by the 1780s it far exceeded the minimum size of 20 households. The hierarchs had thus gone far toward the elimination of uneconomic parishes. One indicator that urban parishes were more economically viable was the appearance of expensive stone churches, even in provincial towns: by the late eighteenth century most city churches were no longer built of wood but of stone—and they were virtually the only stone structures in most towns. In Riazan, a traveler reported, the buildings and houses were uniformly wooden and ugly, but 23 of the 25 churches were of stone.[28] The state further disrupted city parishes in the 1780s, when it began to reconstruct and reorder provincial cities, often requiring a relocation of parish churches and general regrouping of parish units. Once again old bonds were sundered.[29]

In rural areas, however, the bishop found parish reorganization much more difficult. Above all, he faced almost insurmountable obstacles of nature—forests, marsh, rivers, and spring flooding. Rural Russia was broken down into many scattered villages, hamlets, and tiny settlements that were combined to support the parish churches in the countryside.[30] Yet a bishop could not heedlessly merge units without regard to natural barriers, for he would deprive parishioners of sacred rites—in particular, baptism and extreme unction. For such vital services, the parishioners required immediate and sure access to the church and priest.[31] The interests of lay authorities (whether state or landlord) also impeded reorganization, for they preferred to limit parishes to a single social category—state, crown, economic, or landlord peasant.[32] Data on Suzdal diocese in 1781, for example, show that mixed parishes (with multiple types of peasants) were exceedingly rare.[33] Virtually all the parishes remained under a distinctly separate category of jurisdiction (*vedomstvo*)—landlord, crown, or economic peasantry. The only exception was to be found among landlord parishes, where the serfs of several petty landlords were often united into a single parish. Most districts of central Russia had more gentry residences than parish churches; for instance, Riazan district had 471 noble families for 184 parishes, and Tula district had 199 families for 88 churches.[34] Hence parishes with landlord serfs (unless on the estate of a great magnate) were often multiple-landlord parishes.[35] But in general the juridical separation was observed, imposing an important barrier to parish reorganization.

Bishops nevertheless managed to force through many reorganizations, disrupting the cohesion of parish communities. If circumstances permitted, they closed and divided parishes. Metropolitan Platon reordered rural parishes in his diocese as zealously as he did those in Moscow.[36] The bishop of Kolomna, similarly, gave this instruction to ecclesiastical superintendents: "If your inspection shows churches to be very small in parish population or land, or to have poor utensils, and the parish staff to have very poor support, and in the proximity to such churches there are other parishes, report about these (with details) immediately."[37] In 1793 the bishop of Vladimir transferred 36 households from one parish to another, solely in order to increase support for the latter.[38] In another case a bishop reassigned 67 households from a rich parish to an underpopulated church nearby.[39] Such measures inevitably caused new divisions between parish and community, church and society.

A second structural change was the internal disintegration of the parish community, a process that inevitably accompanied the quickening pace of social and economic development. This pattern was most pronounced in the cities. Under the impact of the Petrine reforms, the city collective (*obshchina*) began to disintegrate; a merchant oligarchy emerged to rule the city, its economy, and its churches.[40] Moreover, the cities were inundated with peasants and other migrants, despite legal obstacles and the townsmen's opposition.[41] A revealing picture of this new diversity is conveyed by the confessional lists of all 23 parishes in Pereslavl-Zalesskii in the late eighteenth century: each recorded a broad variety of social groups.[42] As a result, the parish ceased to be identical to a unified social group; the parish church was no longer the center of a secular collective with a single juridical status, common service obligations, and sense of community.

Equally important changes were occurring in the countryside. Social stratification increased markedly among the peasantry, with a more prosperous segment coming to dominate the village and its church. Furthermore, many older peasant communities were uprooted, either by forced relocation to virgin lands in the east or by voluntary movement due to land shortages.[43] Especially in the central provinces, the land-hungry or enterprising peasant turned to nonagricultural labor; rural communities, once tightly knit and insular, began to dissolve as persons departed, seasonally or permanently.[44] Landlord parishes experienced a dramatic turn of events after 1762: the noble master, now freed from obligatory state service, came home to rule his estate and the local church, thus putting an end to collective self-rule organized around the parish church.[45] Together, these changes seriously weakened the cohesiveness of the parish and its viability as an autonomous social organization.

The functions of the parish as an administrative, cultural, and economic unit also eroded in the eighteenth century. Its administrative role, once so important, declined as the state administration expanded and gradually took over parochial responsibilities. It was, however, a gradual process. Although Peter the Great refused to incorporate the parish into the structure of provincial administration, he could not resist using the parish as an auxiliary link to rural communities. He required priests to collect vital statistics, to inform authorities of "evil-intentioned thoughts" revealed in confession, to read state laws aloud in church, and to perform a host of other services for the state. After mid-century, however, even this recognition of parish authority receded. In part, the change was due to the increased responsibility of the noble landlord, whom the state entrusted with full police powers in the countryside. As the state made it easier for nobles to leave state service and reside on their home estates, they had greater possibility for personally using this administrative power.[46] The government, in addition, improved its administrative controls over the other categories of peasantry—state, crown, and economic.[47] A particularly important change was the provincial reform of 1775, which significantly increased effective government authority at lower levels.[48] The parish also fell victim to the government's increased fear of peasant rebellion; Catherine forbade the peasantry to submit collective petitions and curtailed the use of local clergy as parish clerks and lawyers.

The parish lost some of its economic importance as well. Instead of taking place on Sundays around the parish church, most trade was conducted on regular market days in the city square. Provincial towns had two or three days a week specifically designated for trade, when the merchants opened their shops and peasants came in with foodstuffs, firewood, and handicrafts.[49] The economic value of the church further declined when the laity were forbidden to store valuables (even icons) in the church for safekeeping, a rule that was intended to protect the clergy from unwanted responsibilities, but one that also eliminated a vital function of the medieval church.[50] Urban parishioners, moreover, even came into economic conflict with the local church. Peter gave the parish church the exclusive right to sell church candles, a new monopoly bitterly resented by merchants and shopkeepers.[51] They stubbornly refused to abandon this lucrative trade, however, and continued to sell the candles. The bishop of Kolomna complained to the Synod in 1733 that, "scorning the previous decree of 1721 [granting the candle monopoly to the church], the townspeople of Kolomna keep large quantities of candles in their shops and are constantly selling them."[52] Further decrees were also ignored, and in 1744 the over-procurator of the Synod complained that "instead of the church elder selling the candles and thereby bringing the church large profits, they are sold by people of various ranks, who are indecently hawking them along the streets."[53] Exasperated by the laity's obduracy, Metropolitan Arsenii of Rostov ordered his consistory bailiffs to raid the townsmen's shops in 1762 and seize the contraband.[54] Even in the 1780s, hierarchs were still struggling—unsuccessfully—to stop the townspeople's illegal trade in candles.[55] In the rural parishes, serious economic conflict erupted after 1754, when the state ordered each parish to allot the local church a sizable share of land. The nobles and peasants resisted the order, and multiple government decrees failed to smooth away the parishioners' discontent. Thus the parish church not only lost its economic usefulness but even became a burden and a threat.

Finally, the parish church lost its monopoly over the social and cultural life of the community. It ceased to provide education, for the parish schools virtually disappeared in the eighteenth century. Informal parish instruction survived in a few towns, but in general it gave way to special education for each estate and later to formal state schools.[56] There were some contrary currents; proposals for parish schools under the local clergy were advanced by the Commission on Church Estates, by delegates to the Legislative Commission of 1767-68, and by various Church hierarchs.[57] But their proposals were not enacted, and the state even deliberately undermined the Church's role in education. Revealingly, when the state school was opened in Suzdal, the local clergy had to forswear any teaching, presumably in order to eliminate competition: "There must absolutely be no teaching of children in their homes, as has hitherto been the past custom."[58] Furthermore, the laity turned from the church to other sources of culture and entertainment: nobles had a secular theater and literature, townsmen and peasantry had more vulgar diversions. To preserve the church's sanctity, hierarchs deliberately sought to separate the church from the laity's secular culture. In the 1740s the Synod demanded that taverns (which traditionally crowded around a parish church) be relocated a respectable distance away, for the shouting and merriment in the tavern disgraced the church and interfered with the worship services. The Senate at first demurred, fearing a loss in state liquor revenues. Eventually the two bodies reached a compromise: existing taverns could remain, but no new ones were to be built within a specific distance of parish churches.[59] In a word, the parish church, once so intricately fused with the community, was "desecularized," gradually separated from the cultural and social life of the laity.

Such changes affected the laity's interest in the parish church, and one index of that new attitude was the declining status of the church elder. This position, which had once elicited respect, fell into disuse, as many parishes simply ceased to elect church elders. Complaints that the parish lacked an elder appeared as early as 1705 and multiplied rapidly thereafter.[60] Although parishioners never explained why they refused to elect an elder, evidently they had come to disdain the position as a burdensome responsibility—overseeing the church and safeguarding parish valuables and funds. The parish treasury was often a modest amount, saved for the purchase of candles and minor repairs of the church; sometimes, however, it involved considerable sums—up to several hundred rubles.[61] When the parish forced the local clergy to perform the elder's functions, the clergy sometimes pilfered parish savings or sold parish icons to pay off debts.[62] Even if most clerics were honest, suspicion of peculation nevertheless lingered. To prevent such temptation or suspicion, the authorities insisted that the parish elect a lay elder to keep a written account of parish revenues and expenditures.[63] But many parishes disregarded these injunctions. Even in Moscow, only 5 parishes were reported to have an elder in 1743, and only with great difficulty did the authorities compel most Moscow churches to elect elders by the 1760s.[64] Bishops of provincial dioceses were less successful, and at the end of the century were still struggling to have elders elected.[65] Yet the compulsory election of elders, even when successful, could not compensate for the social disorganization of the parish. Instead of the priest, now the church elder embezzled parish funds, while the unconcerned laity looked away.

The parish thus underwent a fundamental change. It ceased to be a "parish commune"; even if it was not a landlord parish, it ceased to coincide with basic social, administrative, and cultural units. This resulted from changes in territorial organization and internal composition; it was also due to the loss of vital functions that bound the laity to the parish church. Parish and community had thus diverged, and their traditional integrity was fast disappearing.

Clergy and Parish

The parish in the eighteenth century changed as a social organization, but this does not mean that it also vanished as a religious organization, humbly surrendering its authority to the diocesan administration. For, even though the parish changed, its lay members were still outside the Synodal command and had, like virtually any individual social group, sufficient power to repudiate the pretensions of the Church. Both on aristocratic estates and elsewhere, the parish continued to claim and exercise its traditional right to manage and rule the local parish church. By extension, this meant the power to govern and control the local clergy. Priests and sacristans were not only responsible to the Synodal command; they also felt the even more compelling influence of the parishioners. The laity's domination of the clergy, as in the past, rested on four main powers: appointment, removal, economic support, and direct punishment or mistreatment.

APPOINTMENT OF CLERGY

The traditional historiography generally holds that the parish lost the right to select candidates for ordination in the first half of the eighteenth century or shortly thereafter. Znamenskii, for example, declares that "in Great Russia by this time there remained barely noticeable traces of the old parish elections. Clerical positions, for both ordained clergy and churchmen, were under the control of diocesan authorities."[66] His view has considerable logic, especially when tested against eighteenth-century legislation. Bishops had long complained about parish selection, arguing that it produced ignorant, immoral candidates and that it made the clergy dependent upon the parish.[67] Though medieval bishops willy-nilly had to rely upon the parish to select "honest candidates," this was less true in the eighteenth century. Now the new seminaries placed a number of choice candidates at the bishop's disposal, and both state and Church law required that priority in appointment go to them. Peter presented this demand as early as 1718, and it was reaffirmed many times thereafter.[68] This implied that the bishop could overturn a parish election; the bishop was later specifically enjoined to appoint educated candidates to good positions, even if the parish had not requested them.[69] Often, of course, there was no reason for the bishop to expect resistance; an educated nobleman like Bolotov gladly accepted the learned seminarian sent to him by the bishop.[70] And even if the parish disliked the appointee, how could it resist the force of law? In Znamenskii's words, "Open protest against diocesan authority could have no success whatsoever, because the latter, in support of its decrees, always had the possibility of presenting firm legal ground and could persecute those who resisted as clear rebels against Imperial decrees."[71]

For all its initial cogency, this view disintegrates upon contact with the sources: the parish clearly retained the authority to select candidates. In the first place, the parish did not lose the legal right to select candidates, a right firmly grounded in medieval Church law. Thus the Church Council of 1551 (*Stoglav*) declared: "Parishioners are to elect priests, deacons, and churchmen who are skilled, literate, and of irreproachable behavior to serve in the holy churches."[72] More important, the Ecclesiastical Regulation of 1721 confirmed the parish's right:

> When the parishioners or landlords who live on their estates elect an individual as priest on their estates, then they must certify in their petitions to the bishop requesting installation that the candidate is a person of good behavior and above suspicion of misdeeds. And if a landlord does not reside on his estate, then his subordinates and peasants should make the certification on such [candidates].[73]

This principle was reconfirmed many times in Synodal and state laws throughout the eighteenth century.[74]

More important, there is abundant evidence that the electoral right was indeed exercised as late as the 1780s and 1790s. Parish petitions were the routine first step in most appointments, and the central archives contain many such petitions declaring, "We the parishioners, having come to love [the candidate], have elected him" for ordination.[75] The petitions follow the traditional formula, testifying to the candidate's worthiness for ordination; they are signed by the parishioners (or landlord alone, if he is in residence).[76] Parish petitions carried considerable weight in all matters, and a cleric seeking reinstatement (after removal or suspension for an offense) wisely appended a parish request on his behalf.[77] Furthermore, inventories of diocesan archives suggest that parish selection was still the norm.[78] Local diocesan histories, drawing upon diocesan archives, also confirm the survival of the parish election to the end of the eighteenth century.[79]

Further evidence of parish authority was the laity's ability to repudiate episcopal pretensions. Few bishops dared to violate parish electoral rights, and even fewer succeeded in imposing their candidates upon a parish. One of the first bishops to ignore parish prerogatives was Metropolitan Arsenii Matseevich of Rostov. Arsenii ordinarily did not attempt to impose seminarians, since his school was in fact one of the smallest. Yet he claimed the right to appoint clergy and occasionally tried to do so. But to his boundless consternation and fury, he learned that the parishioners abused, starved, and unceremoniously evicted candidates ordained without their permission.[80] His successor, Afanasii, complained in 1767 that "many landlords and parishioners do not accept seminarians appointed to the clerical rank from the seminary to churches, objecting to the fact that they were not installed by [parish] selection."[81] The bishop of Suzdal reported a similar experience in 1781. He had attempted to redistribute the clergy in accordance with the registry and frequently had to violate parish requests. But he finally abandoned the venture because "the parishioners will not accept" and support such unwanted clergy.[82]

The only significant exception was Moscow, where the practice of election seems to have atrophied early. According to a diocesan historian, the authorities began to appoint educated candidates as early as the 1720s, without regard to parish desire. Moscow parishes were most vulnerable to such an invasion, for only the Moscow Academy produced numerous candidates before the 1780s. Moscow parishes were also most affected by parishioner mobility and hierarchical reorganization, and they were not screened off from the bishop by vast, impassable distances. Yet even here it appears that the bishop could not easily impose his will. When the Moscow hierarch dispatched a seminarian to one parish in the 1750s, a merchant objected to the appointment, refused to allow the appointee to give services, and declared that the parish had no need for latinniki with their "superfluous" knowledge of theology. In another case from the same period, a seminarian declined a prosperous position offered by the bishop because he feared abuse and mistreatment by a hostile parish.[83] Metro-

politan Platon of Moscow explicitly recognized the right of parish
election in 1775.[84] Thus even in Moscow, where parish authority
seems to have been weakest, the laity still could lay formal claim to
the selection of candidates.

Why indeed should a parish resist the bishop's appointment? It had a
number of good reasons to do so. First, it opposed the presence of an
"alien" cleric who was not a member of the local clergy. Such outsiders were likely to feud with the original clergy and expose irregularities to the authorities. Moreover, parishes shunned the *latinniki* or
seminarians. Even if not offended by the Latin education that perhaps
reminded some of Catholicism, commoners had good economic reason to oppose an expensive "educated priest," for whom bishops insisted upon larger stipends and support. The local clergy too had their
own reasons for opposing the appointment, as they coveted parish
revenues and positions for their own families. Finally, the nobility
jealously guarded their sovereign authority to rule the parish church
and warned stewards to accept no clergy without their consent.[85] The
bishop was most unlikely to flout a noble's will; even in Bolotov's case
the bishop sent the seminarian "on approval" and did not try to ordain
him without Bolotov's prior consent.

The parish, despite internal changes, maintained its traditional
authority over the local church, for it had several weapons at its disposal to repulse episcopal encroachments. As laymen, parishioners
belonged to the "secular command" and were beyond Church jurisdiction; even an imperious hierarch like Arsenii Matseevich was at a loss
to deal with them.[86] In extraordinary cases, a bishop could excommunicate a stubborn layman or appeal to the civil authorities, but
neither device provided effective, sure means for regular control over
the parishioners. Furthermore, parishioners still held the power of the
purse. Since they provided voluntary economic support to the clergy
through incidental fees, a hostile parish could easily—and legally—
drive off an unwanted cleric by simply withholding emoluments. If
the cleric still insisted upon his fees or refused to give services without
proper remuneration, he was liable to charges of extortion, which
guaranteed swift and permanent removal.[87] Even when a priest in
Pereslavl was proven innocent of such accusations in 1753, the bishop
forced him to move to another parish. Finally, the noble reigned
supreme on his estate, feeling free to punish and even beat his clergy.
Aware of their powerlessness, most hierarchs had the good sense not
to violate a landlord's right to select candidates. Although bishops
could compel an elected candidate "voluntarily" to renounce his election by the parish, most accepted the inviolability of the laity's authority.[88]

It is therefore not surprising that, to the very end of the eighteenth century, bishops continued to recognize the right of parish or landlord selection of candidates. Since there were few pupils in the upper seminary classes (even in the 1790s), bishops had few favored candidates and still relied upon the parish. Metropolitan Arsenii of Rostov ordinarily expected aspirants to find their own positions and return with a parish election certificate; his confrontations with parishioners were exceptional and not imitated by successors.[89] In Vladimir diocese, according to a consistory report of 1763, all appointments began first with a parish election and each candidate had to appear with a duly signed certificate.[90] The bishop of Kolomna similarly confirmed this practice in an instruction of the 1780s.[91] Bishop Simon of Riazan diocese declared in 1794 that only seminarians of the upper grades (a small proportion of the school) could request an appointment without first receiving parish approval; all others still had to present the customary election certificate signed by the parishioners.[92] Metropolitan Platon of Moscow, however, was more disdainful of parish rights, and in his autobiography boasted that he "did not greatly respect the parish election of priests and churchmen." But Platon routinely approved candidates chosen by parishes if they were educated (and most were), and he even explicitly recognized the right of parish election in his *Instructions to Ecclesiastical Superintendents* in 1775.[93] In short, though a candidate still had to pass the bishop's moral and educational examination, his selection by the parish was crucial in obtaining the appointment.

The parish retained its customary right to select candidates and to manage the church, but the deterioration of the parish as a social community had very important consequences: serious problems and disorders became increasingly evident as the parish performed its traditional religious functions. This held true even in the vital issue of electing candidates for the clergy; by mid-century, complaints were common about improprieties and deceptions in the naming of candidates. Some aspirants presented forged petitions or, at most, enjoyed the support of only a fraction of the parish. Bishop Serapion of Pereslavl diocese complained that "the candidates appear before me with signed petitions and declarations, but investigations show that some of them were improperly composed [omitting essential information], while others were forged, with the signatures affixed without the parishioners' knowledge."[94] Even multiple candidates for the same position appeared before the dumbfounded bishop, each bearing a duly signed and certified parish petition for his appointment.[95]

To surmount these difficulties, the bishops began to order routine checks on the authenticity of a candidate's claim. As early as the 1720s, the Moscow authorities required clerical elders (*popovskie starosty*) to investigate whether all the parishioners really wanted the candidate. Such inquiries became a routine step thereafter in the ordination procedure in Moscow.[96] The hierarch of Moscow instructed his ecclesiastical superintendents in 1775 to be present at parish elections; they could thus guarantee validity and regularity in the election, after first opening the assembly with due invocations of divine blessing.[97] Similar measures were adopted by hierarchs in the provincial dioceses of central Russia. In Rostov, the bishop ordered his superintendents to certify that each parish election certificate "was really written and signed with the general consent of all [the parishioners]."[98] In the 1750s the bishop of Pereslavl diocese likewise ordered routine checks and even distributed a standard form for the election certificates.[99] The bishop of Kolomna diocese ordered his superintendents in 1782 to check "whether all the parishioners desire the appointment [of the candidate] to the parish" and in 1787 added the stipulation that all parishioners must sign the election certificate or explain their refusal.[100]

In the absence of a cohesive parish community, bishops came to rely increasingly upon the "better parishioners" when dealing with the parish. Whereas the entire parish had once participated in decision making,[101] authority tended to gravitate into the hands of the more prosperous, respectable parishioners. This development was partly spontaneous; parish petitions usually carried the signatures of literate parishioners and sometimes included the self-description of "the better parishioners."[102] It also stemmed from the special privileges long accorded church patrons (*vkladchiki*), who bore primary responsibility for constructing or maintaining the church.[103] But the dominance of "better parishioners" was also deliberately encouraged by the hierarchy. In Moscow, for example, Metropolitan Timofei decreed that the clergy could construct personal houses on parish-owned land only with the consent of the "main parishioners."[104] Similarly, in his *Instructions to Ecclesiastical Superintendents* in 1775, Metropolitan Platon specifically ordered them to make certain that the "better parishioners" were present at the election of clerical candidates."[105] The bishop of Rostov issued a decree in 1773 that instructed his superintendents to examine parish financial records jointly with the better parishioners.[106] Disputes over clerical appointments were resolved in favor of this same element. For instance, in a 1785 case involving simultaneous claims by two candidates, the bishop finally ordained the one who had the support of "the best people and the nobility."[107]

However necessary or inescapable this policy may have been, it reflected and probably promoted the dissolution of the parish as a community.

The survival of parish appointment, even if malfunctioning, had several implications for the clergy. First, it gave the parish a very effective weapon for controlling the clergy. Appointment was vitally important for the clergy, who sought advancement in rank or placement of sons; to arouse parish animosity and to trust in the bishop was unthinkable. Moreover, the instability of parish elections was a further incitement to clerical conflict and disputes. The custom of parish election, where the laity gathered and literally elected a candidate, was fast disappearing; instead, parish electoral authority now became a powerful tool that persistent clergy could sometimes exploit, seeking out the key signatures to endorse a petition on their behalf. Such disorders only reinforced the bishops' long-standing animosity toward parish selection; it also accounts for the alacrity with which they supported Paul's attack on parish rights in 1797, when peasant disorders first cast a shadow over parish authority.[108]

Expulsion of Clergy

Related to the question of appointment is that of removal: did the parish have the right to expel an unwanted cleric? The legal answer to this question was a categorical no. The Synod addressed this problem in 1722, after receiving reports that many landlords were mistreating and removing priests on their own authority. The Synod circulated a decree that "innocent clergy who are slandered by landlords are not to be removed," and the bishops should remove a cleric only for good cause.[109] In a protracted case involving a priest in Novgorod, the Synod reaffirmed that a landlord (or administrator on government estates) could not expel the clergy ordained to his church; if a cleric really deserved removal, the landlord had to go through regular diocesan channels and secure a legal, forced transfer.[110] The Synod reacted to another case of forcible expulsion in 1735, reiterating that only a bishop could remove an ordained cleric and even ordering punishment for the landlord.[111] The Synod prepared a general resolution for the Senate's approval in 1743:

Henceforth, without having petitioned or filed a written report at the ecclesiastical administration (wherever appropriate) and without having awaited a ruling on the case from ecclesiastical authorities, no landlord should dare, on his own arbitrary will, to remove a priest from a church and expel him from his estate, whether for good cause or because of a private quarrel with the priest. Anyone who dares to violate this rule shall unfailingly be fined like a criminal, regardless of who he is or what his rank is.[112]

A joint Synod and Senate decree endorsed this resolution in its entirety in 1746.[113] The Synod actively tried to apply this rule in actual cases, even to the very end of the century when its power waned. In 1794 it rejected the claim of a landlord in Suzdal to have the right to expel an unwanted priest: "Landlords themselves do not have the right to ask for the removal of clergy until there has been a judgment on the accusations against the priest."[114] In theory, then, a parish or landlord could not evict a cleric; only a bishop could do so.

In fact, however, a parish could force out an unwanted cleric. The simplest way was to file accusations against the cleric for misbehavior, demanding removal on the grounds that his conduct was "an insult to the clergy and a harmful example for the parishioners."[115] Laity who were hostile to a cleric could provide lively—and probably inflated—descriptions of this misconduct: "Both in the past and now, he causes disputes and curses the churchmen and parishioners in the divine church. Moreover, he sometimes gets into fights with the sacristans. Hence he cannot be a good example to the parishioners (and, particularly, the peasants) of good honest living and fear of God. Instead, by his dissolute living he leads the peasants astray."[116] Even when the accusation was false or unproven, the hierarchs often acceded to the laity's demands for the cleric's removal. In the 1750s a priest in Vladimir diocese quarreled with his parishioners, who later filed various accusations against him; although evidence of his guilt was inconclusive, the local consistory ordered him to transfer elsewhere so that peace could be restored in the parish.[117] This consideration weighed heavily in the 1767 decision of a Rostov bishop, who ordered the transfer of a cleric for relatively minor offenses.[118] A case of 1765 in Moscow diocese is particularly revealing. The parishioners falsely accused a deacon of adultery, and a thorough investigation eventually established his innocence. Nevertheless, the Moscow Synodal Chancellery concluded that the deacon was tainted by slander and so detested in the village that he could no longer serve there; it therefore ordered him to find another position.[119] This policy of removing innocent or "suspected" clergy found formal acknowledgment in the *Charter of Ecclesiastical Consistories* in 1841: "When these complaints are not proven with legal clarity, yet a large part of the parishioners nevertheless request that the accused be removed from their church, the latter are to be transferred to other positions."[120]

The parish or landlord did not always bother with such legal niceties but simply drove the priest out by economic pressure or physical violence. Such cases, to judge by the central archives, were particularly common in the first part of the eighteenth century. The bishop of Suzdal reported in 1722 that "many landlords, after committing unjustified slander, expel innocent priests from their churches and demand new ones."[121] One Suzdal landlord later proved especially cavalier about expelling clergy. He compelled one sacristan to leave in 1734 "because of certain manifestations of insolence."[122] A few years later, in 1741, the landlord's priest sent an urgent appeal to the Synod for protection, claiming that the nobleman had prevented him from giving services and had even threatened his life.[123] Complaints of physical expulsion, though rarer, still appeared in the second half of the century. A deacon in Vladimir province appealed to his bishop in 1776 for protection from the local steward, who had driven him from the village and forbade the peasants to admit him to their homes. The bishop evidently took no action, and the deacon was compelled to leave the parish.[124] Most bishops, however, actively supported their clergy against such mistreatment and reported that their administrative offices were preoccupied with defending priests against landlords' abuse.[125] Sometimes, they were successful. But ordinarily the bishop lacked the power to force parishioners to comply and could offer little real protection to a priest. One cleric realized the hopelessness of resistance and voluntarily asked for release from a hostile parish.[126]

In short, the formal rules against forcible expulsion were a dead letter: whatever the law, the parish or landlord could and did remove unwanted clergy. This significantly extended the parish's power and deepened the clergy's fundamental dependence on the laity. Even though forcible removal was also possible before the eighteenth century, it was now fraught with graver consequences—given the threat of conscription and the difficulty of finding a suitable vacancy.

ECONOMIC RELATIONS

With few exceptions, the clergy depended directly on the parish for economic support—whether land or emoluments. There was an attempt to allot the clergy a sizable share of parish land, but this encountered much opposition among the laity and proved unsuccessful. Even when the clergy did receive the allotment, they still depended heavily upon emoluments for their support. Herein lay a fundamental source of tension and conflict.

Gratuities for performing sacraments were supposed to be voluntary gifts from grateful parishioners, not a tax or fee. Precisely because the emolument was a "gift," there was no fixed amount for any rite; the priest received a gratuity according to the parishioner's generosity and means. In any event, the priest was strictly forbidden to solicit a larger sum. The Supplement to the Ecclesiastical Regulation repeated a standing admonition: "For services (e.g., baptism, marriage, burial, etc.), the priest is not to bargain but be satisfied with the reward voluntarily given."[127] Metropolitan Arsenii reiterated this rule verbatim in his instructions to clerical elders.[128] In 1775 Metropolitan Platon reaffirmed the warning: "[Priests and deacons] are not to be greedy and insolent, but to be satisfied with their payments, and hence they are not to solicit fees from their parishioners for any services but to be satisfied with voluntary gratuities."[129] If strictly observed, the rule would have placed the clergy at the complete mercy of parishioners.

The priest, however, was not defenseless: parishioners had to obtain religious services and sacraments, and they could do so only from the priest in their parish. The state issued decrees for compulsory church attendance, confession, and communion; violators were suspected as Old Believers and fined.[130] The Synod added its own decrees, requiring the clergy to record absenteeism and report the guilty for fines and investigation. Bishops took similar measures; for example, the bishop of Pereslavl in 1746 ordered the clergy to "inform parishioners of every rank (and obtain their signatures in assent) that they will unfailingly go to the divine church in their parish on Sunday."[131] Abbots who managed Church estates also required the peasantry to attend church, and landlords issued similar instructions.[132] Parishioners, moreover, had to obtain services in their own parish, while the clergy were ordered to serve only their own parishioners. This rule derived originally from canon law, which held that a priest was ordained to serve a particular parish. But its immediate mainspring was a desire for social control—to assure that parishioners fulfilled their obligations, that priests adhered to Church law. Thus the clergy had an implicit monopoly over the parishioners; though clergy (especially in cities) served immigrants and visitors, only the local priest was to serve the parishioners in his village.

This monopoly enabled the priest to extort higher fees. At the most innocent level, he could refuse to give his blessing—an omen of ill fortune for superstitious parishioners. More obdurate parishioners could be reported as Old Believers if they missed confession or communion. The priest might even withhold services until he was promised adequate remuneration. This risked provoking accusations of solicitation (domogatel'stvo), but such pressure could be very effective. In short, the emoluments were a very ambiguous system of parish support, providing no clear definition of mutual obligations; they engendered constant tension between the clergy and parish.

The Commission on Church Estates sought to end disputes and solicitation by proposing a schedule of fixed rates. Confirmed by Catherine in 1765, the reform established a specific fee for each rite, prohibited any fee at all for confession and communion, and strictly admonished clergy not to solicit additional sums. It permitted the parishioners, however, to make "voluntary gifts" beyond the fixed amount.[133] The reform thus sought to regularize clergy-parish relations; the clergy could anticipate a definite fee, and those who demanded more were easily detected and identified. The Synod, in the following years, strictly enforced the new regulation and punished violators severely. In a case in 1772, it decreed that "the priest Vasilii Ivanov is to be defrocked for his crime [of solicitation] and turned over to the secular government for assignment to wherever he is fit; so that the clergy of other dioceses learn of this and refrain from such misbehavior, send . . . a decree to Synod members and diocesan hierarchs [for distribution among their subordinate clergy]."[134]

Despite its intent, the reform was a failure and indeed even aggravated the problems concerning emoluments. The new schedule certainly failed to eradicate the clergy's hopes for larger fees: it did not regulate many important services, and, even for those that were regulated, it allowed parishioners "voluntarily" to give larger amounts. Thus the clergy could still seek larger fees by applying traditional forms of pressure. More important, the legal rates were so abysmally low that clerical solicitation actually became automatic and unavoidable; if parishioners had observed the legal rates, the clergy would have been destitute. As Table 19 shows, the customary fee significantly exceeded the legal amount. The data on Moscow also reveal that the actual fees increased steadily (with inflation) and thus the gap between the legal and norm widened even more. When the Synod made an unsuccessful bid in 1784 to reform the clerical economy, it used vital statistics to show just how little income a priest and staff could legally expect. The "legal" income was astonishingly small—only 1 to 4 rubles per year for the entire staff in average parishes (Table 20).[135] That was a far cry from the income of a typical priest—20 to 40 rubles.

Table 19. Legal and actual fees for church rites (in rubles and kopecks)

Rite	Legal fees (1765 law)	Actual fees		
		Iaroslavl 1770s	Moscow 1774	Moscow 1786
Baptism	3 k.	8 k.	25-50 k.	50 k.-1 rub.
Marriage	10 k.	20-25 k.	1-2 rub.	1-2 rub.
Confession	0	2-3 k.	n.d.	n.d.
Communion	0	2-3 k.	n.d.	n.d.

Sources: PSPREA, 1:225; Semevskii, "Sel'skii sviashchennik," pp. 507-510; Rozanov, Istoriia, 2, pt. 2:337; 3, pt. 1:148.

Table 20. "Legal" income from rites (in rubles)

Diocese	Average income for entire staff from baptism, marriage, burial	Average additional income for priest (for prayers for women giving birth)
Kolomna	2.61	0.43
Moscow	2.73	0.46
Pereslavl	3.01	0.43
Riazan	2.96	0.44
Rostov	2.50	0.31
Suzdal	1.79	0.17
Vladimir	2.33	0.31

Source: TsGIA, f. 796, op. 64, g. 1783, d. 580, ll. 1-284.

The reform of 1765 therefore could not solve the problem of solicitation and parish complaints. It aroused much dissatisfaction among the clergy, perhaps predisposing some to join the Pugachev Rebellion a few years later. One priest bluntly expressed their resentment: "If a priest proves good in everything, he deserves a good reward for his services." But, he continued, the law of 1765 violated that right and deserved the utmost scorn.[136] The Synod surely realized the absurdity of the low rates but did not succeed in having them increased until 1801.[137]

Since the reform compelled every priest to seek additional "voluntary gifts," the complaints of solicitation did not abate. In 1784 the parish of Zatish'e in Riazan accused the local priest of extortion, and the cleric complained that "for two years they did not permit me to give church services or perform rites."[138] A priest in Moscow was also found guilty of simony: military officers asked him to swear in new army recruits, but he refused to do so without a fee. The officers complained, and the priest was promptly arrested, tried, and defrocked.[139] The parishioners of a rural church in Vladimir diocese complained that their priest refused to give burial services until paid three rubles.[140] The peasants in another village claimed that their priest "Semenov does not charge for services according to the ability to pay or according to the provisions of the law [of 1765] but instead Semenov took one ruble . . . for marriages."[141]

The system of voluntary gratuities had several significant consequences. First, because the fees were so indefinite (even after 1765), the parish wielded vital economic power over the clergy. It could even remove the cleric for solicitation, if it so desired; the priest needed additional amounts and was therefore vulnerable to charges of demanding excess sums. Thus the parish held the clergy in virtual economic bondage; few clerics could dare violate parish interests to obey episcopal or state demands.

A second important consequence was the stereotype of the greedy cleric, interested only in his fee. Popular proverb often lashed at this avarice: "Birth, baptism, marriage, death—you give the priest money for everything!" Likewise: "Who collects money from both the living and the dead?"[142] An anonymous writer from the early eighteenth century divided the parish clergy into two types—the spiritual and the greedy: "There are few of those [priests] who work for Jesus; most of them work for a piece of bread."[143] The image of clerical cupidity was also etched into a popular woodcut: "A sermon on how the devil unmasked the priest."[144] A writing of popular origin satirized the people's enemies—rich merchants, whores, and the like—and found an honored place for corrupt simoniac clergy. According to the story, Satan was greeting each of his workers; when the foul priest appeared, he "lost his senses" from joy. He recovered to deliver this paean of praise to the priest: "You loved sweet food, banged your nose on the tavern door, drank wine and beer as if water were poured down your throat, drank yourself into an unconscious stupor, and carried on like swine. You have endeavored to save the soul neither of yourself nor your flock; you just took their offerings and had a good time."[145] The aristocratic Fonvizin struck the same note:

The humble pastors of our souls and hearts,
Are pleased to collect fees from their sheep.
The sheep marry, give birth, die.
Meanwhile the pastor fills his pockets.
For money they forgive every sin.[146]

The clergy of course had little choice; they had to badger the parishioners for support. Nevertheless, this seriously impaired the clergy's claim to spiritual leadership and deeply alienated the laity. As a reform commission aptly noted in 1808, "The collection of fees for services places the priest in constant conflict with the very same people whose love and respect are most necessary to him."[147]

Personal Inviolability

The clergy formally belonged to the jurisdiction of the Church, or Synodal command. This meant that they were beyond the control not only of state officials but also of the local landlord or parish. Whatever their grievances, the laity were to obtain satisfaction by appealing to diocesan authorities; they themselves could not arrest, incarcerate, punish, or expropriate the parish clergy.

This status was reinforced by various legal and religious powers. The state established legal protection for the parish clergy in the mid-seventeenth century, when an ukase of 1648 warned parishioners not to abuse them.[148] More comprehensive was the Law Code of 1649 (Sobornoe ulozhenie), which included the clergy in the system of fines for injured honor (bezchest'e). The amount varied according to the priest's status—from 100 rubles for the archpriest of Blagoveshchenskii Cathedral to a mere 5 rubles for a rural or idle priest.[149] The Law Code also set severe penalities for "church rebellion," which was loosely interpreted to cover any disruption of church services; it gave the clergy a useful weapon against obdurate, hostile parishioners.[150] The legal guarantees around the clergy were reaffirmed in the eighteenth century, at Synodal insistence. In 1769 the Synod complained that "some landlords not only abuse the clergy but even administer corporal punishments to them," and demanded a Senate proclamation to stop such humiliating treatment. The Senate immediately complied and ordered state officials to enforce the decree.[151]

The Church exercised certain religious powers to tame unruly parishioners. A primer urged readers to "respect with every honor and obey affectionately their priest," and another church publication appealed to parishioners to defend their clergy from "the many ill-intentioned people who despise the pastor for exposing [their sins] and dream up many slanders against the priest."[152] The bishop, moreover, could punish offending laymen in various ways—by pronouncing anathema, closing the parish, or asking state officials for police action. The bishop of Suzdal, for instance, excommunicated three nobles who had insulted a priest and firmly rejected their appeals to rescind the order.[153] The priest himself had the power to punish disrespectful and recalcitrant parishioners. An instruction manual for clergy published in 1705 upheld his power to exclude parishioners from communion and warned laymen not to take communion if they were "under prohibition from this by their hierarch or priest."[154] In 1734 the Synod observed that "priests are expelling their spiritual children and parishioners from the church without the knowledge of the bishop" and complained that they did so "not for legitimate reasons but because of their private disputes [with the parishioners]."[155]

This wall of protection, however, gradually crumbled during the eighteenth century. Above all, diocesan authorities lost the power to deal with obstinate laymen. The bishop could still pronounce anathema, but his prerogative became very narrow. The Ecclesiastical Regulation contained a prolix section that denounced the abuse of this power and warned bishops to use it cautiously and sparingly.[156] When Metropolitan Arsenii of Rostov acted otherwise, summarily banishing landlords and serfs from the church, he was sharply reprimanded by the Synod.[157] The Synod presented its modest definition of episcopal power to the Legislative Commission in 1767: a bishop absolutely could not incarcerate or excommunicate laity but could only temporarily exclude them from church services.[158] It complained in 1780 that bishops abused this power and ordered them to be more cautious in its application.[159] Nor could the bishop count on cooperation from state officials to punish those who offended the clergy. The bishop's rank was equal to that of a provincial governor; therefore, he could not send an order (*ukaz*) requiring compliance but only a memorandum (*promemoriia*) requesting action.[160] Frequently, the lay officials disregarded the bishop's requests, especially if the local nobility were involved. As a final resort, the bishop could appeal to the Synod and demand satisfaction (*satisfaktsiia*) from the Senate, but that was a slow and unreliable device, rarely used by the bishops.

The priest himself lost the power to impose sanctions on parishioners. He risked severe punishment if he withheld services, especially the sacraments; guilty clergy were routinely defrocked for the offense. A typical case occurred in Vladimir diocese in 1785, when a priest was defrocked for excluding a peasant from needed sacraments: "In the [peasant's] petition it is claimed that the priest of his parish in the village Cherevatov, Ivan Gavrilov, abused him and did not give his wife, who had given birth, prayer services for five days."[161] The Synod, moreover, now forbade the priest to exclude parishioners except with the bishop's approval. It decreed in 1734 that "without the knowledge of the local bishop, priests are not to exclude their spiritual children and parishioners from the church on their own will."[162] The hierarchs seriously enforced this law: a priest who banned some parishioners from church services in Vladimir was beaten and sentenced to three years' confinement in a monastery in 1767.[163]

By mid-century, therefore, the clergy were vulnerable to uncontrolled parish pressure or abuse. Peasants regarded the priest as part of the commune and liable to its rules and discipline; when he "committed acts inappropriate for his rank," they arrested and punished the offender themselves.[164] To prevent such illegality, a magnate like Sheremetev instructed his people "not to commit needless abuse of the clergy" and, if they "commit some carelessness in the church, steal parish property, or abuse my peasants, petition the bishop about them."[165] More serious and common was abuse by the landlords themselves. The noble "punished" clergy for various reasons—failure to show respect, informing against Old Believers among his serfs, cutting wood from his forests, or sometimes for no apparent reason at all. To get additional field labor, some landlords even enserfed the "excess" churchmen and clerical sons, despite furious objections from the bishop.[166]

The hierarchs sought to shelter the clergy from such abuse and to protect the dignity of the whole clerical rank. Few had the sly temerity of Arsenii Matseevich: having learned that a local noble abused a priest, Arsenii invited him to visit as a guest—and had him beaten on the spot for insulting the clergy.[167] Yet most bishops displayed remarkable perseverance in protecting the clergy. For example, a deacon in Pereslavl diocese complained in 1759 that a local landlord had flogged him, and the bishop excluded the noble from church services until he made satisfactory amends to the deacon. But this failed to achieve any results; the landlord refused to bow to the bishop's demands. Then the bishop ordered the deacon to petition the local state officials for immediate civil action. The deacon, however, was exhausted from the struggle and asked to drop the case, declaring that he was too poor to purchase the embossed paper required for official petitions. The bishop refused to give up and ordered his consistory to purchase the paper "so that thereby other landlords shall not dare abuse the clergy."[168]

Despite such efforts, the bishops were rarely successful, as the Synod's and bishops' complaints attest. The only exceptions were cases where a landlord insulted not merely a priest but the faith as well. Most sensational were several cases where a landlord attacked a priest bearing the Communion Elements and caused him to spill them on the ground. A Moscow nobleman who struck a priest holding the Elements and caused him to drop them was arrested and tried; a chapel was built on the spot of the mishap and the noble eventually died in monastic incarceration.[169] For committing a similar offense in the 1750s, a noble in Riazan diocese was sentenced to pass six times through a gauntlet of 100 soldiers and then remain ten years in hard labor.[170] To prevent such incidents, the Synod in 1777 directed priests to carry the Elements visibly in front of them in order to forewarn the laity from attacking; this very proposal suggests how vulnerable indeed the parish clergy had become.[171]

The bishops showed growing concern over landlord abuse after mid-century but found themselves powerless to contain it. As the Synod prepared its *nakaz* (instruction) for the Legislative Commission in 1767, local bishops emphasized the problem of landlord abuse, and the Synod then instructed its delegate to raise the problem at the Commission.[172] In a report in 1773 the bishop of Rostov argued that a major function of district boards (lower diocesan administrative organs) was to provide immediate defense of the clergy from lay abuse.[173] The bishop of Suzdal similarly complained in 1783 of widespread abuse: "As cases in our consistory clearly show, many landlords in our diocese mistreat and oppress the clergy, and some even give them beatings."[174] Metropolitan Platon summed up this problem at the end of the eighteenth century, when he explained why seminarians declined to become rural priests: "They do not wish to work in the fields, to live on inadequate salaries, and in almost everything to depend mainly upon the power of the landlord, against whom complaints are ceaselessly being submitted."[175]

This analysis of parish relationships suggests how thoroughly dependent the clergy were upon the parish—for appointment, tenure, economic support, and even personal security. The central authorities attempted to mediate this relationship and even sunder the chains of clerical dependence, but they clearly failed; regardless of legal prescription, the clergy still depended upon the parish. This failure suggests an important consequence of the Church's declining political power and particularly the inherent limits of a "Synodal command": the Church lacked the power to control parishioners, the state had no compelling interest to do so. Inevitably, such dependence made the clergy weak, vulnerable, and complaisant; it was precisely this dependence that priests vehemently decried in the clerical *cahiers* of 1863.[176] Only individual moral authority could protect the cleric from summary treatment by parishioners, whether commoners or nobles. The clergy, consequently, were almost powerless to oppose parish demands, even when these violated their duties to episcopal or state authorities. This dependence effectively frustrated attempts by the Church and state to use the clergy as "official agents" for social and religious control.

Religious and Social Roles

Medieval hierarchs railed against the parish clergy for neglecting their religious duties and eagerly blamed the "ignorant priest" for the ills afflicting the Church—superstition, paganism, heresy, schism. Such malfeasance, whether real or imagined, became a sure target of eighteenth-century authorities, as state and Church attempted to reconstruct society by positive, prescriptive orders from above. For different reasons, both the Church and state expanded the clergy's service obligations; both sought to use the priest to penetrate the insular village and to establish new controls over life and religious practice. The Church, desperately seeking to preserve its power and influence, demanded a more exacting performance of traditional duties—and invented many new ones as well. The government added to this burden.

The state duties, primarily administrative at first, shifted after mid-century to social control: the clergy were to pacify peasants and dissuade them from rebellion. These duties, in effect, defined a new role, one which had not been formally prescribed and enforced before the eighteenth century. Most important, the new role was prescribed without changing the basic structure of social relationships in the parish, where the clergy were so profoundly dependent upon the laity. The crisis broke when the clergy were caught between the two contradictory demands.

NEW PASTORAL RESPONSIBILITIES

In its own peculiar fashion, the eighteenth-century Church in Russia attempted a fundamental "reformation," a dynamic assault on the chronic ills of Russian Orthodoxy, from paganism to the schismatic Old Belief. It was a reformation from "above," a systematic attempt by Church authorities to reorder religious life in the parish, to retailor belief and practice to fit Orthodox canon and conviction. Such reform implied an unprecedented invasion of parish custom and tradition—a rich web of pagan heritage, superstitious wonder, and Christian precept formed during the centuries of anarchic freedom from episcopal control. Armed with its new "regularized government," the Church at last stood ready to intrude into the parish and eliminate deficiencies of faith and mores.

What was the source of this reformation? One was Europe, where Protestant and Catholic governments provided a model of attempts to excoriate religious deviance and to purify the people.[177] The shock waves of the reformation and counter-reformation at last reverberated in Russia, as Peter's Ecclesiastical Regulation borrowed from Swedish and German *Kirchenordnungen*, as Ukrainian bishops brought their experience in Catholic lands to Great Russia.[178] After mid-century this external impulse for reform drew upon a different *Geist*, the Enlightenment skepticism and distaste for popular "superstition," which were partly responsible for the most rationalist reformation of all—Joseph II's religious reforms in the Habsburg Empire in the 1780s.[179]

But the desire for reform was also a response to the Church's domestic crisis. The decline in the Church's political and economic power, the loss of its cultural monopoly, the corrosive effects of the Old Belief and acculturation from the West—all these developments palpably challenged the Church's place in society. One response to that crisis was reform in parish religious life, measures that sought to bolster the Synodal command, save the Church from ridicule among educated strata, and eliminate the "ignorant" Old Belief. This desire to strengthen the church's moral authority through religious reform determined the special character of this "reformation": it was "anti-pop-ular," directed mainly against lower-class simpleness, not noble im-piety—which only later would elicit frustrated criticism from bishops. Anxious to establish bonds between priest and noble, bishops paid little heed to Freemasonry, deism, and the occasional agnosticism of Rus-sian aristocrats. On the contrary, they encouraged seminaries and subordinate clergy to subscribe to the new secular publications of Rus-sia's "Enlightenment"; Metropolitan Platon of Moscow professed to discern no irregularities even in the Masonic writings of Novikov.[180] There were, to be sure, occasional complaints about gentry secularity; in 1743 the Synod proposed that all nobles learn the catechism as a precondition for entering government service, and in 1765 Platon complained that "studies in secular subjects are preferred to the saving knowledge of Divine law."[181] But bishops expressed most concern about the common people—their ignorance of precept and prayers, their foibles, and especially their "paganism." Whether from concern for their own diminished status or a desire to buttress the Church's waning influence, bishops sought to excoriate those elements of reli-gious deviance that provoked mirthful ridicule from foreigners and noblemen. The instrumentality of this reformation from above was not joint lay-ecclesiastical consistories (as in Lutheran countries), not salaried priests (as in Joseph's Austria), but the rank-and-file parish clergy, the Church's only wedge into the Russian hinterland. Herein lay the great contradiction, the crucial flaw of the Russian reformation: this parish clergy, still fundamentally dependent upon the parish, was a fragile wedge indeed.

Not all aspects of this reformation gave cause for parish discontent. The laity did not, for example, oppose the Church's attempt to pro-vide religious education through catechism instruction and sermons by "learned priests." The Synod first attempted to prepare and dissem-inate a catechism for popular consumption in the 1720s, and by the 1740s aggressively demanded that clergy provide religious instruction at least in the major cities.[182] Bishops took similar steps, focusing pri-marily on urban parishes; Platon of Moscow established seven centers for catechism instruction in Moscow in the 1770s.[183] For more sophis-ticated parishioners, the Church after mid-century demanded that "learned priests" provide original sermons.[184] The clergy themselves resisted the obligation, protesting that they lacked the time or libraries to compose such sermons; even in Moscow sermons were a rarity at mid-century—one report for 1749 lists only 40 sermons for the entire year in all of Moscow.[185] To obtain compliance, bishops levied fines and threatened to exile offenders to poor parishes, and by 1800 ser-mons had become a more common element in urban parishes.[186]

Nor did parishioners object to changes in the parish that affected primarily the clergy. Bishops began to enforce a strict protocol on bell ringing in cities, according priority to the city cathedral and fining parish clergy who violated this rule.[187] For the sake of propriety, bishops also ordered the clergy to keep "the altar free from dust and cobwebs," a measure unlikely to disturb parishioners.[188] Prelates also sought to regulate visitations and icon processions by the priest, a traditional feature of Orthodox life but one that gave rise to serious disorders: the clergy zealously solicited gifts and drink, and the cumulative effect of the latter had a predictable result midway through the procession.[189] The new controls aroused little protest from parishioners, though there were some exceptions. In Moscow diocese, for example, peasant complaints finally impelled Metropolitan Platon to permit processions at Easter: "As the peasants of many villages incessantly ask us to permit the former custom [of Easter processions], we take mercy on their request and simple weaknesses and permit them to march with holy icons at Easter." At the same time, the superintendent was to be vigilant against unseemly conduct by the clergy.[190] But the general curtailment of icon processions and visitations caused little sorrow for most parishioners; indeed some had sought to regulate the custom on their own, restricting the number of such visitations by the local clergy.[191]

Once the bishops' reforms extended beyond the clergy and affected the parish itself, their measures did provoke parish resentment and opposition. One such measure was the campaign to rid the church of sacrilegious behavior by the laity, who viewed the parish church as a social center, punctuating a church service with shouts, laughter, even an occasional "Hurrah!"[192] Bishops first attempted to silence parishioners in the seventeenth century, but parishioners blithely ignored their indignant epistles and sermons.[193] Peter the Great renewed the attempt in 1718 and in a characteristically Petrine fashion set fines for offenders to raise revenues. His proclamation had no effect; according to data compiled in 1723, virtually no fines had been collected.[194] The Synod tried again in the 1740s, reaffirming the Petrine rule and commanding bishops to enforce it.[195] Some at least tried. In 1747 the Pereslavl consistory ordered its clergy to collect fines for misbehavior in church, and the Metropolitan of Rostov took similar measures.[196] To deal with well-born offenders, Metropolitan Timofei of Moscow even proposed that noncommissioned officers be assigned to churches to arrest "the magnates" (*znatnye liudi*), whom the clergy feared to offend.[197] Bishop Pavel of Vladimir took more drastic action in the 1770s to deal with violators in his diocese:

Guards, armed with chains, are to stand inside the church near the entrance so that those entering will see them and refrain from conversations in church. If anyone, in spite of that, from temerity dares to speak in church, then, in accordance with His Imperial Majesty's and the Synod's decrees, take the required fine from all such people, regardless of their rank or status.[198]

The clergy, however, complained to the bishop in 1779 that the parishioners were still rowdy in church: "Young men and women, on holidays and Sundays during church services, conduct idle conversations and, standing inside the church, laugh indecently, and say shameful words." The clerics added, however, that they were afraid to arrest the offenders and fine them, for they feared "not only abuse and oppression from the parishioners but even beatings."[199] This episode revealed the whole tenor of parish relations and particularly the clergy's fundamental dependence upon the parishioners.

Another hierarchical reform, begun in the 1740s, proved equally unpopular: the attempt to restrain parishioners from profane use of the parish church. Even while the Synod badgered the Senate to close taverns during church services (because the dancing, horse racing, and general uproar at the tavern disrupted church services), diocesan authorities tried to ban drinking from the church itself.[200] The Metropolitan of Moscow was aghast to learn in 1759 that carousals took place on church premises: "At many churches in important parishes, during the summer holidays, eating tents are set up and wine and beer are sold. This is very indecent. For, having been drinking in the tent, the common people are a source of much noise and shouting during the vespers and matins, and even liturgy; because of this, the singing in the church cannot be heard." The Metropolitan thereupon categorically banned such festivities in the future.[201] Other bishops found that the parishioners held celebrations inside the church, especially after a wedding. The bishop of Pereslavl complained in 1750 that "the parishioners of churches in Pereslavl and the surrounding countryside, during weddings in those churches, bring into the churches from home wine and beer (as an unseemly habit of commoners), which they drink inside the divine church after services." The bishop reprimanded priests "who do not stop their parishioners from indulging in such indecent acts" and threatened with dire punishment those who continued to tolerate the custom. Bishops in Suzdal and Vladimir struggled against the same practice.[202] The local clergy faced an unenviable choice: to ignore the bishop's order or to risk provoking the parishioners' animosity.

The bishop also rigorously demanded that priests expose Old Believers, placing the clergy in some areas under great strain. Especially in the first half of the century, when the secular penalties for schismatics were most severe, the clergy were understandably afraid to inform on them. State and Church authorities frequently complained that some priests concealed Old Believers by falsely affirming that they took communion.[203] Some clergy concealed schismatics for a bribe, as in the case of a Vladimir priest in 1752.[204] More often, no doubt, they feared retribution from angry parishioners, such as this priest reported in 1720:

The priest is afraid to go [and point out] those peasants [Old Believers] because the steward and peasants would complain to Prince Ivan F. Romodanovskii [the landlord] that the priest is ruining his peasants [by causing them to pay the special tax on Old Believers]. And one evening the peasant elder and peasants (six persons altogether) came to the priest and spent the night at his house; for what purpose he does not know; and the elder and peasants let no one leave his house.[205]

Similarly, when the Rostov authorities began to collect the tax with a priest's aid, the villagers bitterly attacked the priest, cursing him and calling him a thief.[206] Much rarer were cases of actual complicity with Old Believers, but a few clerics did perform services according to Old-Believer ritual.[207] There were also some spectacular cases of fugitive priests, who moved from one Old Belief settlement to another before the authorities finally captured them.[208] After 1762, when the state softened its policy toward the Old Believers, many returned to Moscow, raising new suspicions that the local clergy were aiding the schismatics.[209]

The sacrament of marriage caused even greater difficulties for the parish clergy. It was governed by definite canon law; because of the nature of the sacrament, reports of violations could be easily investigated and judged. The priest, moreover, bore full responsibility for observing Church law; he was to make an investigation (obysk), keep records, and marry only his own parishioners.[210] Thus he was particularly vulnerable if he committed any crimes. The parish, however, frequently compelled him to ignore canon law: landlords dictated serf marriages for more labor,[211] and peasant families sometimes arranged marriages that violated Church law. One common violation was the remarriage of soldatki, the wives of peasant recruits, who were most unlikely to return from the army. Orthodox law forbade their remarriage without proof of their husbands' death. Frequently, however, under landlord duress or the influence of bribes, the clergy nevertheless did remarry the soldatki. The guilty priest usually claimed that he had been misinformed, but such a lame excuse was not credible and it was not respected by the bishop.[212] A second crime was to violate kinship laws and marry parishioners who were closely related; again, landlord pressure or a bribe usually account for the clergy's acquiescence in the parishioners' demands.[213] A third crime was to marry youths under the minimum age—thirteen for girls, fifteen for boys. Little attention was given to this rule until 1774, when the Synod declared war on the peasant custom of snokhachestvo—the marriage of young boys to grown women, "with whom their fathers-in-law commit incest."[214] Bishops vigorously enforced the rule, and the number of accused priests mushroomed in the 1770s and 1780s. A typical case arose in Suzdal in 1775, when a priest married an eleven-year-old boy to a young woman.[215] Often, however, snokhachestvo was not involved, and in 1781 the Synod modified its order that guilty clergy be summarily defrocked: if both the girl and boy were underaged, the priest was not to be punished quite so harshly.[216] Marital disorders persisted into the nineteenth century, causing constant difficulties and divided loyalties for the parish priest.

The hierarchs also invaded another precious refuge of village culture—its rich lore of miracles, dreams, wonder-working icons, and superstitions. Peter's Ecclesiastical Regulation ridiculed the more common superstitions, and the Church steadfastly prosecuted clergy who inspired or tolerated such phenomena.[217] A priest in Suzdal diocese, together with several others, found a body in a field, allegedly free from decomposition. The priest pronounced the find to be holy relics (sviatye moshchi) and had the body placed in a crypt. A small chapel was erected over it, and rumors of its miraculous properties quickly spread. The Synod noted that "not only the native peasants but also the landlords and their wives came and heard requiems, evidently hoping for benefits from those remains." For perpetrating a fraud, the local clergy were defrocked and sent to the secular government for disposition.[218] Even the more cultivated clergy of Moscow were guilty of such misdeeds. One priest was defrocked in 1765 because he claimed to have a miracle-working icon that healed.[219] Another priest was reprimanded in 1770, after he had allegedly exorcised "an unclean spirit" from a peasant's house, where it had been the cause of "whistling and pounding."[220] Other clergy were punished for similar misdeeds, especially the possession of magical writings (volshebnye pis'ma).[221] And many clergy probably shared the rich imagination of popular superstition, as Bolotov attests in the account about his own educated priest.[222] The most explosive incident involving an attempt to crush popular superstition occurred in Moscow in 1771, in the midst of a plague that was devastating the city. To control the plague, authorities forbade assemblies of all kinds—including services by free-lance priests. Consequently, when the townspeople flocked to a "miracle-working icon,"

Metropolitan Amvrosii ordered that it be immediately removed, touching off a mob riot among the desperate townspeople. The crowd tracked down the hierarch himself at a local monastery, where he was brutally murdered.[223] That sensational episode dramatized a popular resistance to reform felt throughout the rural parishes as well. In some cases, to be sure, the hierarchs acceded to parishioner wishes: for example, they allowed the clergy to give special services to start—or stop—rain.[224] But in most matters the Church vigorously attacked for the first time many traditional mainstays of popular belief and custom. Whether successful or not, this campaign generated new tensions for the parish clergy.

In sum, the Church reforms struck directly at local tradition and folkways and depended upon the local clergy for implementation. Some reforms concerned only the clergy, and the hierarchy encountered little resistance to them from the laity. More difficult were those reforms that violated local tradition, vital economic interests, or collective beliefs. In such cases—from socializing in church to miraculous icons—the parish firmly resisted episcopal authority and had ample means for compelling the local priest and sacristans to acquiesce. Here the hierarchs could anticipate little success as long as the clergy remained socially and economically dependent upon the parish.

The Clergy's Social Role

Like the Church, the state attempted to make use of the clergy's proximity to the populace by utilizing them as instruments of social control. Peter the Great assigned the clergy a host of administrative and political tasks, but after his death the state gradually eliminated most forms of secular service. From the 1750s it focused upon one particular duty—that of dissuading unruly peasants from "disobedience" or open rebellion. This new emphasis resulted from the government's increasing concern about rural instability; serious disorders began to mount before the Pugachev Rebellion (1773-75), and once that earthquake had subsided, the state and nobility lived in perpetual dread of an imminent *jacquerie*. Catherine took many measures to control the peasantry, and one of them was the requirement that priests urge peasant parishioners to submit to their landlords' will.[225]

In normal times, when calm reigned on the estate, the clergy fulfilled her expectations, helping to reinforce the landowner's authority. How he did this could vary considerably. In some places, the priest might even help manage the estate or assist the steward. The nobleman V. I. Suvorov (father of the famous general) utilized the local priest extensively, giving him broad authority and responsibilities. According to an instruction from Suvorov, the priest was "to resolve disputes among the peasants, who are to be obedient and not to commit any offenses against him."[226] But even if the priest had no administrative role, he served to reinforce the noble's moral authority over the peasants.[227] Tatishchev spoke frankly (if crudely) of the priest's usefulness and stressed the importance of "good" educated priests: "Peasants who have lived a dissipated life, not having a good pastor, become disobedient and then come to hate their masters. . . . But when there is an educated priest and a man of good behavior (especially if he is not in want of money), then of course he will lead the peasants to a prosperous and peaceful life."[228] Perhaps most revealing of estate relations was an illustration in an agricultural journal in the late eighteenth century: a landlord had assembled his serfs and was addressing them—in the pious presence of his priest.[229]

Furthermore, the priest was usually a passive witness to the injustices of serfdom. He did not, it seems, seek to protect and aid individual peasants, at least publicly. Though he *may* have sought to use moral suasion on brutal landlords (we have no evidence either way), priests never seem to have intervened actively in landlord-serf relations. Nor did they do so when the landlord violated serf women or committed other atrocities; no church records indicate complaints or even mistreatment of clergy as a result of such action. Moreover, the clergy did not bring their superior education to bear on the revolutionary shortcomings of the peasantry by providing leadership and cohesion so often lacking in peasant uprisings. Unlike Moslem clergy in the empire who sometimes did sanctify rebellion as a "holy duty," the Russian clergy never articulated revolutionary roles for themselves, much less for the serfs.[230]

Once a revolt erupted, however, the clergy's apparent reliability vanished. There were relatively few peasant disorders before 1760, and the clergy's role was modest—perhaps writing a petition or giving an oath of unity to the unruly peasants.[231] The great test came in 1773-75, when the Pugachev Rebellion ignited peasant uprisings throughout the eastern regions. To the government's dismay, the parish clergy frequently supported the insurgents.[232] Unlike the monastic clergy (who, almost without exception, remained loyal to the government), many parish clergy recognized Pugachev as Peter III and inserted his name into the liturgy.[233] Although in a few sensational instances they joined armed detachments, the clergy's main role consisted in giving formal recognition and pious prayer for Peter III. Hysterical government authorities exaggerated the clergy's role, one governor even declaring that "the cause of all this is our drunken priests."[234] The Synod's assessment, if less colorful, struck closer to the truth: "Clerics, paying no heed to the horrors of their future condemnation, utter Pugachev's name in the divine services, and wherever the scoundrel goes, they meet and accept him."[235] Since Pugachev failed to reach the central provinces, the clergy there were generally untouched by the turbulence to the east, but there were a few incidents in the border areas. The bishop of Vladimir reported cases in his own diocese in 1774: "The clergy, in vestments and with icons, crosses, and ringing of church bells, met three parties of the known state rebel and miscreant Pugachev."[236] Throughout the Pugachev disorders, the clergy's role was generally passive—neither to oppose nor to lead the peasantry. Their impact on the rebellion was nonetheless important, for they legitimized Pugachev's claim to power as the "true Tsar Peter III." Whether from fear or secret hatred for the landlords, clergy mutely acceded to parish will.

After the Pugachev Rebellion was crushed in 1775, the peasantry lapsed into apparent submission for the next two decades.[237] In the interim, there were occasional cases of clerical involvement in disorders—for instance, one priest "incited the peasants to disobedience against their landlord," wrote a petition, and led his parishioners on a march to St. Petersburg.[238] The authorities encountered few such cases, however, and in this period of tranquillity elaborated the clergy's duty to pacify the peasantry:

If any of the peasants rebel against their owners, the clergy are not only to avoid any collaboration with them, but when learning of this revolt, they are immediately to do everything possible to dissuade their parishioners from joining, to remind them of the above decree [of 1767 ordering peasant obedience to their landlords] by reading it to them once again.[239]

Just as Catherine utilized "learned priests" against criminals,[240] so too did she want the rank-and-file clergy to control the peasantry.

Paul's accession to the throne in 1796 touched off a new wave of peasant disorders, which struck with particular force in the central provinces. They often began with rumors that the new emperor would accept written petitions against oppressive landlords, and Paul carelessly took some measures that seemed to confirm the peasants' wildest dreams.[241] The materials on disorders in Vladimir province are unusually rich and provide a clear picture of the clergy's role. In a typical case, the "village priest participated in this [disturbance], wrote the rough draft [of the parishioners' petition], and gave them an oath of unity."[242] The priest did not figure as a leader in the disorder but simply acceded to the parishioners' demands. When one priest refused to heed the peasants' request, they took an icon from the church "and began to swear before it to stand united and never to submit." Some priests were more culpable, however. According to a government report, in one village the priest "appeared with an icon and read [a decree forged by a fugitive peasant] to a group assembled at the church for mass—the deacon, *d'iachok, ponomar'* and peasants." He announced that "the decree declares that the master's forests are to be cut, peasants are not to be moved from one village to another, that they are to pay only three rubles in quitrent, and that factories and enterprises are not to be established." Eventually, the provincial authorities suppressed the disturbances, arresting "ringleaders" and dispersing the rest. Eager to find a scapegoat, the provincial governor of Vladimir went so far as to claim that "the clergy are the primary cause in all the cases of peasant disobedience to their landlords."[243] Actually, the clergy's role was considerably more modest, as the government's own records indicate, limited to writing petitions or administering oaths of unity.

Nevertheless, the disorders of 1796-97 convinced the government of the need to eliminate unreliable clerics. Paul had in vain commanded priests to oppose peasant disorders: "Clergy—above all, parish priests —have an obligation to protect their parishioners from false and harmful rumors, and to establish good morals and obedience towards their masters."[244] In May 1797 Paul issued a broader decree intended to solve the problem once and for all. He ordered bishops to supervise seminarians "so that they are alien to any violent disorder and are irreproachable in their conduct in order that, having entered the clerical rank, they will lead their [spiritual] children into peacefulness, obedience, and good behavior by teaching and their own example." In the event of peasant disturbances, the bishop was to replace immediately those priests who proved unreliable. Loyal priests were to be properly rewarded: "The hierarch shall give appropriate rewards or transfers to a better position to those priests who (by the unique means of the pastor) restrain the peasants from such [disobedience] and bring them into obedience to the established authority." Paul specifically wanted to ban the priest's main activity in disturbances, declaring that "the clergy must not sign any kind of peasant petition or passport." Finally, he sought to sever the parish's firm hold over the clergy: bishops were to make clerical appointments without regard to parish requests.[245] Shortly afterwards, Paul also tried to eliminate the clergy's economic dependence, promulgating his order for the parishioners to till the clergy's land and give them a fixed share of the harvest.[246] Though both these measures were partly or wholly reversed, they reflected a desire to use the parish clergy for social control, a policy that would change little in the next century.

Thus the clergy's role in peasant disorders was far from impressive. It bore little resemblance to that attributed to them by aristocrats and officials, who claimed that priests were indistinguishable from peasants and "naturally" supported disorders. In general, the clergy obeyed the will of their superiors in times of tranquillity; they neither incited the peasants to a *jacquerie* nor ameliorated the abuses of serfdom. Once rebellion erupted, however, the clergy acquiesced in the peasants' demands and played an important, if passive, role. This mixed record was a direct result of the clergy's contradictory status: agents of external authority, but servitors of the local community.

In retrospect, the eighteenth century witnessed important changes in parish relations that profoundly affected priests and churchmen. The parish itself changed significantly as a social institution; it lost its traditional structure and functions and became separate from the new institutions of secular society—developments that implicitly diminished the role and significance of the parish priest. The parish nevertheless remained a powerful religious organization, controlling appointment, tenure, economic support, and even personal security of the clergy. Disregarding the priest's fundamental dependence upon the community, central authorities attempted to enlarge dramatically the priest's role and to make him an agent of religious reform, an officer of social stability. The clergy, torn by the contradictory strains, were unable to perform effectively either of the new charges from above.

A Separate Society
and Culture

7

Nineteenth-century writers frequently described the clergy as a caste, emphasizing thereby its exceptional degree of hereditariness and cultural separateness.[1] Whatever his ecclesiastical rank and status, the clergyman almost invariably sprang from clerical origins and bore the tell-tale imprints of the clergy's unique way of life; as one sensitive memoirist noted, the huge cultural gulf that divided the clergy from the laity was similar to caste barriers.[2] This image of a hereditary caste impelled some to call the parish clergy "Levites," after the hereditary caste of priests in the Old Testament, an analogy that appeared frequently in the press and even in formal state law.[3] Most observers condemned this casteness, blaming it for the clergy's lack of moral influence over the peasantry, and supported reform proposals in the 1860s to dismantle the caste structure of the white clergy.

But, properly speaking, the parish clergy did not form a caste like those in India. It was too diverse internally, with kaleidoscopic variations in social-economic condition and cultural level. It included, at one extreme, the urbane, wealthy priest of an aristocratic parish in Moscow, and at the other extreme, a superstitious sacristan living hand-to-mouth in some isolated hamlet buried deep in the Russian woods. A caste, by strict sociological definition, must not only be hereditary and closed, but its members must possess a common social and economic status—which the parish clergy surely did not.[4] The European model of "estate" seems more appropriate, for it conveys both the juridical separateness and internal differentiation of the group. Still, "estate" is too weak to describe adequately the clergy. For, notwithstanding variations, it was a distinctly separate group, unique in Russian society. Its social and cultural separateness, which crystallized in the eighteenth century, gave outsiders the impression that the clergy were indeed a caste—something unique, almost alien, in imperial society and culture.

Here we shall examine the process that transformed the clergy into a "caste-estate"—the *dukhovnoe soslovie.* Hints of change first appeared in the seventeenth and even sixteenth centuries, but the transformation was completed only in the eighteenth. Its active agents were two: the termination of social mobility (both into and out of the clerical estate) and the formation of a distinct clerical subculture.

The Termination of Social Mobility

Prior to the eighteenth century the clergy was still an open social group: individuals from other social categories entered Church service and the clergy's offspring transferred to other ranks in society. To be sure, there was a natural tendency for sons to take up their fathers' trade, and seventeenth-century hierarchs were already condemning certain manifestations of hereditariness.[5] But as yet there were no firm barriers to impede mobility into or out of the clergy. As Znamenskii rightly points out: "For appointment to the clergy it was not necessary that an individual have a clergyman as a father, but only that he have a high moral character and be literate, that is, know how to read and sing. A priest's son, if he did not know how to read, was removed from the clerical estate, whereas a bonded person (*smerd'*) who was literate freely entered the clergy."[6] Though there is some disagreement on just how easy access was for outsiders, it is generally accepted that the clergy was still an open social group.[7]

Several factors help account for this continuing openness in a traditional medieval society. First, even though some legal barriers existed (for example, bonded persons were not supposed to be ordained), ecclesiastical administration was simply too inefficient and underdeveloped to enforce such prescriptions. Even in Moscow, where the ordination procedure sought to establish that a candidate was a free person, the authorities lacked lower administrative organs for conducting routine investigations and relied upon the testimony of a single witness.[8] And in the sprawling rural dioceses, where hundreds of parishes were dispersed across vast spaces, even this feeble measure was omitted.[9] Second, there was a striking quality of uprootedness to this traditional society: clergy frequently moved about, churches rose and fell suddenly, and youths usually did not succeed their fathers at a given parish.[10] With all this movement, the rudiments of a firmly crystallized hereditary order were simply lacking. Third, entry into the clergy was not barred by special education available only to the clergy's children: standards were low, episcopal testing was perfunctory, and informal instruction at the parish church (or under a local "master") was open to commoners as well as clerical youths. Finally, vast numbers of new churches were constructed throughout this period; hence unencumbered positions constantly opened, creating fresh opportunities for nonclerical youths. In short, outsiders easily gained access to the clergy, while clerical progeny were free to leave the group. This picture was to change dramatically in the eighteenth century.

THE EXCLUSION OF OUTSIDERS

The closing of the clergy was not due to any changes in the formal process of selection, for the methods of choosing candidates were virtually unchanged in the eighteenth century. Appointment still consisted of two discrete stages—formal selection by parishioners, then holy ordination by the bishop. As diocesan administration improved and the seminaries expanded, hierarchs favored "educated candidates," but they still lacked effective control over parishes to the end of the eighteenth century. In any event, bishops actually preferred the appointment of outsiders; they opposed the hereditary claims of clergy and desired the largest possible pool of qualified candidates, regardless of origin or status.

Even though the formal process of selection did not change, would outsiders still *want* to enter the clergy in the eighteenth century? The Russian nobility surely did not, and they rarely entered the clergy in Great Russia.[11] They had the legal right to do so, however: Peter authorized younger sons of the nobility to enter the clergy in 1714 and never formally revoked the law.[12] The Church welcomed such candidates, and in 1742 the Synod sought to reconfirm their right to enter.[13] Nevertheless, in actual practice the state did not expect nobles to become priests; it charted a rigorous career of military service for young noblemen and the Church did not dare ordain them.[14] Nor did gentry family interests favor clerical service: family wealth depended upon state service (with attendant rewards of land and peasants), and a noble entering the clergy lost his noble privileges and serfs. The nobility also regarded the clergy as an inferior social status, and expected the priest to tip his hat, submit to corporal punishment, and do the landlord's bidding.[15] Even enlightened nobles like Bolotov, who wrote favorably of the local priest, hastily added the phrase "notwithstanding his origin."[16] A career in the white clergy could not even promise eventual rise into the hierarchy, which was open exclusively to monastic clergy. Thus, despite some proposals "to place the nobility into the clergy . . . after the manner of European states,"[17] the gentry certainly had no intention of going voluntarily. Unlike the Ukrainian noble (who attended seminaries and willingly entered the white clergy), the

Russian noble gravitated away from the clergy.[18] In Tooke's words, "few nobles feel any violent inclination to become clergymen."[19]

To townspeople and peasants, however, the clergy offered more attractive prospects.[20] The priest enjoyed a superior juridical status and came to share some privileges in common with the nobility—such as exemption from the poll tax, quartering, recruit levies, and even corporal punishment. Furthermore, as contemporaries often noted, the impoverished townspeople and land-hungry peasantry needed an outlet; though many parish churches were indeed poor, others were prosperous, and elsewhere the clergy had an adequate land allotment and income. Thus, for the mass of the poll-tax population, the clerical career promised upward social mobility. Nevertheless, entrance by outsiders declined sharply in the eighteenth century, primarily as a result of three processes: the clergy's efforts to reserve positions for relatives; the new restrictions of the poll-tax registry; and the establishment of formal educational requirements which only clerical children could satisfy.

The clergy themselves were an important force in closing the group, as they sought to reserve church positions for their relatives and to exclude outsiders, whether of lay or clerical origin. The precondition for this development was the clerical family, the result of a Russian Church custom that required marriage before ordination into the priesthood. Hence in law and in fact, the clerical estate consisted not only of clergy but of their clans and families as well. It was a sizable population—in Vladimir diocese, for example, the clerics themselves composed only 22 percent of the entire estate in the 1780s.[21] This created a special group, with a powerful vested interest in monopolizing parishes and positions.

Some of the group's motives were quite traditional, existing long before the Petrine reforms. One motive was simple economics—the appointment of a son or kinsman increased the family share of fixed parish land and income; depending upon the parish and diocese, this represented an additional 25 percent (or more) for the clerical family. That share would be forfeited, of course, if an outsider received the appointment. Thus the sacristan of a church was frequently a priest's son or nephew, even if the youth was below the legal age of fifteen.[22] A second traditional motive was to secure support for the priest when he retired. Since income came from service, a retired priest had no means to support himself or his family. Nor could he always avoid retirement, for the bishop removed aged and infirm clergy who read poorly or seemed likely to drop sacred objects.[23] The number of retired clerics was significant, usually constituting about 6 to 9 percent of the clergy in a diocese.[24] Although elderly priests could enter a monastery, few did so willingly; the only alternative was to find an heir who promised to share parish income until the priest died. The clergy often expressed this concern quite candidly, as in this petition from a priest of Vladimir diocese in 1781: "To take care of me and my impoverished family and wife, order a student at Suzdal seminary to marry my daughter and then appoint this son-in-law to my position."[25]

Some motives, however, were new to the eighteenth century. One was the urgent need to find vacant positions for their sons, who stood in constant peril of a new government conscription. As the number of vacant positions dwindled, the clergy jealously protected their own parish nests. The same concern, moreover, inspired many premature retirements, as priests claimed infirmity in order to create a vacancy for a son who had come of age. The government vehemently condemned such fraud (since it increased the number of idle clerics); nevertheless, violations persisted and partly account for the large proportion of "retired clergy" in each diocese.[26] A further motive for constructing hereditary walls around a parish was the desire to conceal offenses. The clergy were torn by a cruel dilemma—to obey the parish or the bishop's demands. The ideal solution was to keep the parish free of outsiders, who were more likely than kinsmen to report offenses or malfeasance. The Supplement to the Ecclesiastical Regulation in 1722 perceptively noted the dangerous insularity of hereditary parishes: "It is easier [in such parishes] to act unrestrainedly, to be unconcerned with church ritual and order, and to conceal schismatics."[27] The same assessment was given in 1781 by the bishop of Suzdal, who directly attributed the hereditary pattern to the clergy's desire to conceal misconduct.[28] A deacon in Murom, who had exposed the offenses of a local clerical clan, also emphasized this as a reason for hereditary insularity: "Wanting to continue their disorderly conduct more easily in the future and to remain at the church alone with their relatives, the other clergy [at this church] are doing everything possible to encourage the parishioners to expel me."[29]

Even law-abiding clergy had good cause to loathe outsiders, for their mere presence tended to breed conflict. At a minimum, such conflict invoked disgrace and dishonor upon the clergy, a humiliation that invited still greater erosion of the priest's social influence and power. But feuding clergy risked still other hazards. They were frequently dragged into interminable litigation and thereby exposed to the rapacious extortion of the local consistory.[30] If a formal investigation was begun, the "suspected" clerics were suspended from service and thus deprived of a regular income.[31] Given the vagaries of diocesan justice, even patently false accusations could end in disaster for suspected clergy, who were sometimes drafted during state conscriptions on the basis of unproven charges. Several churchmen protested to the Synod in 1784 that they had been drafted because of unproven, even uninvestigated, accusations; nonetheless, the Synod declined to review the cases because the conscription was already completed.[32]

To exclude outsiders from appointment at his parish, the cleric had several devices at his disposal. One was to solicit a regular parish or landlord appointment for his son, a request the cleric could usually expect a parish to honor. Bolotov recounts such an episode on his estate in the 1790s, when a priest's relatives came with a proposal to ordain a kinsman; Bolotov signed the ordination request without objection.[33] The parish was likely to approve such requests precisely because their petition had to affirm the "worthiness" of the candidate; since they knew the cleric's son, they could easily confirm his worthiness. Parishes had little use for tainted clergy. In 1767 a parish in Iaroslavl diocese rejected the efforts of a deacon (who had been removed from his previous post for misconduct) to transfer to their parish, declaring, "We do not need a person unknown to us and we will give an election certificate only to someone we have selected."[34] In 1777 a parish in Kolomna uezd spurned the entreaties of a deacon for appointment "because of his disorderly life, drunkenness, and brawling."[35] It was, moreover, in the parish's interest to select a kinsman of the local clergy, since a hereditary staff was more tranquil and heedful of parish wish than a mixed staff. Once the priest secured his son's appointment as sacristan, obtaining his promotion to priest was simple. The Synod even legalized the right to promotion in 1772, ordering that priority in priestly appointment be given to lower-ranking clergy in the same parish.[36]

Another device was to encumber a parish with property claims. The clergy often constructed their private homes on parish land, and newcomers were expected to purchase them. The value of the house, moreover, was usually inflated, for it reflected the economic value of the clerical position; the same building was naturally worth much more in a rich parish than in a poor one. As a result, the value of such property reached considerable sums, which few outsiders could pay; a son, naturally, would silently inherit the position and the property.[37] The property barrier was not of particular importance in rural parishes; small plots for a peasant hut were readily available and the positions usually had little value. But such property claims were important in the cities, especially in Moscow, where land was valuable and church positions were worth hundreds of rubles by mid-century.[38] The will of a Moscow priest in 1771 reveals the extraordinary value of such positions and how the clergy regarded them as inheritable: "Grant as an inheritance to my nephew, deacon Fedor Afanas'ev, that parish position for which we paid 700 rubles."[39] Such investments discouraged most aspirants, whatever their qualifications.

A third device was an appeal to the bishop to award a position to a kinsman out of "mercy and compassion." A typical appeal asked the bishop to ordain a kinsman who had agreed to support the retired priest or his family; if no close kinsman was of age, then the appellant asked the bishop to reserve the position for his family, who would hire a "temporary priest" until the heir came of age. Even if the clerical family had general support in the parish, the appeal to the bishop was extremely useful for discouraging competitors and for overcoming an heir's educational deficiencies. More important, as hierarchs began to fill vacant positions after mid-century (for example, during the 1784 conscription), it was vitally important to obtain the hierarch's permission to leave a position nominally vacant. Consequently, both retired priests and widows pleaded for the bishop's "mercy," asking him to grant a position to a kinsman or future heir.[40]

Both the Church and the state opposed the formation of hereditary ties to a parish. The bishops regarded hereditary claims to a parish as an insult to the sacred nature of the Church, a view candidly expressed by a clerical instruction manual of the late eighteenth century: "The priest, deacon, or churchman cannot put his son or relative in his own place, for these [positions] are sacred; it is wrong to treat them in accordance with human passions or to subject the divine church to hereditary ownership."[41] Hierarchs, moreover, perceived hereditary claims as a barrier to the placement of educated seminarians. A Moscow seminarian, for example, complained in 1770 to the metropolitan: "As Your Grace knows, clerical positions in Moscow are purchased for the most part, but I am a person of no means for buying a position. Thus I am compelled to remain idle and to suffer great poverty."[42] For this reason, government and Church authorities repeatedly directed that priority in appointments go to a learned candidate, not an heir.[43] Finally, the authorities were dismayed at the special protection afforded clergy in hereditary parishes, where they could safely ignore episcopal orders without fear of exposure. The Supplement to the Ecclesiastical Regulation specifically cited this as a reason for bishops not to permit hereditary appointments.[44] The Synod tersely expressed the same view: "At many churches the priest does not permit the appointment of outsiders as churchmen, but his sons or relatives occupy these positions of service (sometimes beyond necessity), regardless of whether they are satisfactory and literate. And this, besides other faults, is especially harmful because it is more convenient for the priest to conceal Old Believers, not to be investigated, not to be zealous about service and order."[45]

Church authorities, consequently, tried to sever hereditary ties to a parish. By mid-century, bishops regularly questioned candidates about clan relationships in their parishes.[46] The bishop of Kolomna ordered his superintendents in 1782 to investigate candidates and specifically to "check whether the nominee is in kinship with other members of the staff."[47] Moreover, the Synod and bishops often rejected clerical appeals based on crude hereditary claims. In a case in 1748, the Synod rejected a cleric's claim to the position of his father-in-law as a rightful inheritance: "We cannot approve Leontii's petition . . . for under no circumstances will a claim as heir be recognized, not only [for a position] in such a distinguished church but for one in any church."[48] It also repudiated the demand by a priest's widow that she be supplied with a son-in-law, who would assume her husband's position: "There is not the slightest pastoral obligation [for the bishop] to find a sacristan to be the husband for the daughters of deceased clergy."[49] In some instances, the bishop even attacked hereditary enclaves —especially if some outrageous misconduct had come to light. For example, the Suzdal consistory ordered a misbehaving priest to relocate in 1758 because his colleagues were all relatives and likely to conceal future crimes.[50] Another bishop took similar measures in 1788 and gave this explanation: "The clergy at the church are closely related, in violation of the Ecclesiastical Regulation; therefore, I have ordered the priest Florentii to move to another village, because even then his father and two sons will remain at the church."[51]

Authorities also opposed property claims to a position. The Moscow Church Council of 1666-67 righteously deplored the practice: "It is wrong and illegal to sell Christ's churches and clerical positions like patrimony."[52] Peter made the first practical attempt to solve the problem by decreeing in 1718 that parishioners must provide free homes for their clergy: "Priests are not to have their own homes at churches and must sell them; their property is to be purchased with money collected from their parish, which is to have a church elder for this purpose. If a priest now at the church owns his home, the parish must purchase it; when the priest dies or is removed, give these homes to the new appointee."[53] The Synod reaffirmed this rule in 1722, and the following year extended it to cover churchmen's homes as well as priests'.[54] The Synod also tried to solve the problem of "landlessness" in the cities by protecting and even recovering household plots, which were to be church—not clerical—property.[55] After more reports of trading in clerical positions, in 1767 the Synod decried its pernicious effects upon the clergy: "Not only educated but also uneducated—yet honest—candidates have great difficulty and bitterness in finding a position; the best positions are purchased mainly by those who just have enough money, though completely uneducated and not very worthy of their rank." It then strictly prohibited the sale of clerical positions, established rules for the assessment and automatic depreciation of property values, and reaffirmed the parish's obligation to provide housing if church funds permitted.[56] The Moscow authorities, who faced the most serious problems, began a vigorous attack on the sale of clerical positions and systematically applied the Synodal rules of 1767. Metropolitan Platon tightened this policy even further after 1775 and tried to recover former parish land and to make it freely available to new clergy.[57] Platon also dealt harshly with the worst offenders; in 1783 he approved the defrocking of a priest who sold his position "without the knowledge of the Ecclesiastical Consistory" (and hence without a regulated, devalued sale price)—and who then had the temerity to ask the bishop for a new position![58]

For all their persistence, the authorities failed to eliminate family claims to an individual parish. In the first place, the parish or landlord still had the right to determine candidates; as long as a candidate met the prevailing educational standards (if only by a brief sojourn at the seminary), the bishop could not violate parish prerogative. Moreover, even for the bishop, educational claims far outweighed hereditary considerations. Indeed, the authorities even exploited hereditary ambitions to encourage pupils to study. The Moscow Church Council of 1666-67, for example, encouraged the clergy to educate their sons by promising that an educated son would become "heir to his [father's] church and church position."[59] Similarly, the Synod warned that only by acquiring seminary education could a youth hope to succeed his father.[60] The decision of a Riazan hierarch in the 1790s revealed a bishop's preference. A seminarian brought a parish request for ordination in his home parish, but the bishop was reluctant to grant it: "Because of hereditary ties, he should be given a rejection in that village." Nevertheless, educational claims prevailed—the bishop approved the appointment.[61]

Nor were the authorities able to stifle the trade in clerical positions, despite the abundance of threats and warnings. The Synod in 1721-23 made a vigorous attempt to compel parishes to provide free homes for the clergy but eventually gave up; the laity simply would not comply, claiming that they were too poor to assume such a burden. The Synod was powerless to make them obey.[62] That impotence was evident in a case in 1730, when a priest in Moscow refused to purchase his predecessor's house and asked that the Synod compel parishioners to provide him with a home; the Synod lamely advised him to purchase the property or find housing elsewhere.[63] It repeated this resolution in 1741 in another case, silently ignoring stated policy.[64] Not until 1767 did the Synod renew the attack on property ties, in the wake of complaints from seminarians about the difficulties in finding suitable positions. Yet even then it did not categorically ban the sales; instead, it provided a mechanism to depreciate property automatically so that the sale price reflected actual property value, not the value of the clerical position.[65] The Synod, in some instances, disregarded even the sale of clerical positions. The bishop of Suzdal removed two clerics in 1728 because they had purchased their positions (for 40 and 50 rubles each). When the two clerics appealed to the Synod, it reversed the bishop's decision and ordered him to reinstate the two priests in their old positions, because in its view the offense was not sufficiently serious to merit removal.[66] Another case in Pereslavl-Zalesskii during the 1750s showed that it was impossible to prevent the sale of clerical positions as long as the sale of property was tolerated. In this case, the bishop investigated accusations that a rural priest had sold his position for 180 rubles. But nothing could be proven: there was no written contract to disprove the priest's claim that the sale price covered only the value of the property and that no monetary value was attached to the position. Eventually, after a prolonged and fruitless investigation, the diocesan administration dropped the inquiry and permitted the priest to return to his new position.[67]

The third—and most important—reason for the bishops' tolerance of hereditary claims was the social problem created by a clerical estate. When a cleric died or retired, how was his family to be provided for? All these people were under the sole jurisdiction and responsibility of the Church. Since there was no pension system and bishops were expected to be "compassionate," a hierarch had little choice but to allow the family to share the income from clerical positions. The Synod itself recognized this practice. For instance, when a widow petitioned in 1738 for permission to hire a priest temporarily (until her young son was old enough to assume her husband's position) and meanwhile to share the income with the hired priest, the Synod consented and made no remonstrance against the implicit hereditary claim.[68] In 1741 the Moscow Synodal Chancellery recognized the claims of the family of a deceased cleric, overruling the well-established right of the parish to dispose of clerical positions as it saw fit. The Chancellery justified its decision by arguing that "the request of a widow with five small children deserves respect." It added that "although clerical positions are not subject to inheritance, it is nevertheless proper to appoint a son-in-law who will support the orphans."[69] In 1767 the Synod formally recognized the duty to provide for orphans and widows, and approved the hereditary claims of a priest's daughter: "If there remain daughters and nieces after a deceased ordained cleric, and if the widows desire to accept someone for their daughters and nieces [to take] the position of their deceased husbands, appoint such worthy people according to their desire, if no legal obstacles exist."[70] Such requests were routinely honored by the Synod.[71]

Diocesan authorities, like the Synod, yielded to the pressure of family claims. In Moscow, the bishops allowed widows to share the income of a new priest and recognized their claims to a position for a son or son-in-law.[72] Petr Alekseev, who later became the learned and irascible archpriest of Blagoveshchenskii Cathedral, had to give one half of his income in the 1750s to the relatives of his predecessor.[73] Such ties were common, appearing often in diocesan records and files.[74] The bishop of Suzdal explained that it was often impossible to observe strictly the regulations against "superfluous, excess appointments" because of his duty to provide for the clergy's families:

Before me appear the children and relatives of deceased, disabled, and infirm registered clergy (including some sons who attended or graduated from the seminary) . . . [and] they all request appointment to some position, arguing that these old and infirm clergy, or the families of deceased clergy with young children, cannot be left without adequate support or charity.

Thus in one case the bishop appointed a son as deacon in a small parish (in flagrant violation of the *shtat*) "out of pity for his father, the priest of the church, in order to occupy in the future his father's position."[75]

Episcopal compassion for clerical families held fast even when a priest had been removed from his position for some misdeed. When wrongdoers were suspended or sent to a monastery, they often appealed to the bishop to provide for their "innocent families" in the interim, and the bishop usually granted such requests. They authorized the family to hire a temporary substitute, who was to share the income with the family of the punished cleric.[76] The Synod formally approved this policy, issuing similar resolutions itself. For example, when one cleric of Vladimir diocese had been suspended in a case involving uncanonical marriages, his family obtained this favorable ruling from the Synod: "Until the bishop of Vladimir has concluded this case, the priest Mikhail Vasil'ev is to receive one half of the land at the church and any other revenues from the Pokrovskaia Church, and the other half is to be given to whoever performs the services and sacraments."[77] Family circumstances even affected the punishment of misbehaving priests and sacristans: bishops often ameliorated harsh sentences (even when richly deserved), because the priest's "innocent family" would suffer along with the cleric. The Synod itself instructed bishops to indicate the "family circumstances" of clergy whom they proposed to defrock.[78] Even the severity of Metropolitan Platon melted before such considerations; in 1775, for example, he proposed not to defrock a scandalously misbehaving priest but merely to demote him to churchman—only because of his "large family."[79] Significantly, even after the hereditary order had been legally dismantled in 1867-69, bishops still acceded to family needs; they opposed hereditariness, yet found family claims too compelling to spurn.[80]

The clergy were thus an important factor in excluding outsiders. As they struggled to encumber a parish or individual position with hereditary claims, they left little room for individuals from other social groups. The government and Church formally condemned the new hereditary order but failed to enforce their own categorical prescriptions. Though hints of the hereditary bonds had appeared earlier, they became considerably more important in the eighteenth century, when the service structure became stable and the rapid turnover in positions and churches had come to an end.

A second important obstacle to townspeople and peasants was entirely new to the eighteenth century: the poll-tax registry (*podushnyi oklad*) introduced by Peter the Great in 1719-22. After some initial confusion, all of the clergy—churchmen as well as priests—were finally exempted from the poll-tax registry and thus acquired one important privilege in common with the nobility. This concession, however, raised a fundamental question: was it possible to select as clergy the hereditary poll-tax registrants (that is, peasants and townspeople)? The issue first broke into the open in 1725, in an exchange between the Synod and Senate.[81]

The Synod asked the Senate to authorize the ordination of poll-tax registrants, who were in the secular command and thus needed government permission to transfer to the ecclesiastical command. The Synod favored "the ordination of needed people into the clergy from various ranks, from serfs, and from the peasantry." It also proposed to fill vacancies by reappointing those churchmen who had been deemed "superfluous" and inscribed as peasants in the poll-tax registry during Peter's census of 1719-22.[82] The Senate flatly rejected the proposal. It argued that such a policy would cause losses in the poll-tax revenues and feared that to tamper with the registries now would needlessly complicate and impede the collection of the poll tax, already a difficult matter. The Senate complained that bishops had illegally ordained poll-tax registrants without permission and ordered them to desist at once: "In the future, hierarchs are not to ordain such poll-tax registrants into the clergy, thereby causing disruptions in the poll-tax collections."[83] The Synod meekly accepted the decision and distributed it to subordinate diocesan authorities.[84]

But even this categorical ruling did not end such ordinations, and by 1727 the Synod had received numerous petitions to revise the policy on poll-tax candidates. The bishop of Pskov argued that he could not find enough qualified candidates if poll-tax registrants were disqualified. Even though parishioners agreed to pay the poll tax for such people, the bishop refused to ordain them without prior authorization from the Synod.[85] The Moscow Ecclesiastical Consistory also reported that several noble landlords requested the installation of poll-tax registrants as clergy on their estates. The landlords promised "to free these former churchmen from their estates and, together with their peasants, pay the poll tax for them eternally." The Consistory did not explain the landlord's apparent generosity; to judge from later cases, it was probably inspired by bribes from the candidates or perhaps by difficulties in staffing the parish church. The consistory justified the request with appropriate citations from the *Kormchaia kniga* (a codex of church law).[86] The Synod, however, did not dare trespass on the domain of the "secular command" and referred these proposals to the government for consideration.[87] Surprisingly, the Senate approved the petitions: "For the purpose of their appointment to the ranks of priest, deacon, and churchman, former churchmen who were put in the poll-tax rolls under landlords are to be freed from the poll tax at the landlord's request, if the landlords pay the poll tax for them eternally."[88] The Synod wanted a guarantee that the landlord and not the clergy would pay the poll tax (to avoid compromising the clergy's privileged tax status); it obtained a Senate decree in April 1728 that obliged landlords to sign a written release swearing that they, not the released cleric, would pay the poll tax.[89] It should be noted that the law applied only to the landlord's serfs—not the mass of poll-tax registrants (church peasants, state peasants, townspeople, and other miscellaneous groups).

Church authorities nevertheless interpreted the law liberally in the 1730s and 1740s, permitting all categories of poll-tax registrants to enter the clergy. According to data compiled in the 1730s, outsiders had penetrated the clergy in substantial numbers: there were 80 former poll-tax registrants among the clergy in Rostov, 105 in Suzdal, and 182 in Riazan. In relative terms, such outsiders represented 4 percent of the clergy in Moscow, but higher rates in provincial dioceses— for example, about 8 percent in Suzdal diocese. Since many clergy were ordained before the poll-tax system came into existence, the proportion of poll-tax registrants among *new* appointees (since 1722) must have been sizable. In addition, the data on Suzdal diocese show that poll-tax registrants became not only priests but even churchmen, a position of considerably lesser importance. Although precise data are unavailable, many of the poll-tax registrants probably were former churchmen who had been placed in the poll-tax roll in 1722. Finally, the influx of poll-tax registrants shows no geographical pattern; they were distributed throughout the diocese, in towns as well as in the countryside.[90]

The Synod was still dissatisfied even with this moderate poll-tax policy and in September 1742 asked the Senate to authorize unhindered appointments from all social groups. Claiming that there was an acute shortage of clergy, the Synod complained that parish churches "have fallen silent" and parishioners were dying without benefit of last rites. The Synod, as a preliminary step, wanted blanket permission to ordain the clergy who had been drafted into the poll-tax rolls in 1722; if these did not suffice, then the parish should be allowed to select the landlord's servants and serfs—even against their owner's will. The Synod also wanted formal acknowledgment of the right to ordain candidates from the nobility and townspeople, who "are more qualified than landlord's servants to become clergy."[91] The Senate implicitly accepted this proposal in September 1743, but within a year—as a new poll-tax census began—it had completely reversed itself.[92] In an uncompromising decree of 7 July 1744, the Senate not only forbade further appointments from the poll-tax population but even ordered the conscription of churchmen whom the bishop had already installed: "With the exception of those eternally freed by their landlord and given the mandatory written release, inscribe the *d'iachki* and *ponomari* [sacristan ranks] together with their children at their former residence during the current poll-tax registration." It added that only noble landlords could release poll-tax registrants, denying this right to administrators and peasant elders on crown, state, and monastery estates.[93] The Senate continued receiving complaints from local state officials about the appointment of poll-tax registrants and in 1746 categorically banned further appointments from the poll-tax population: "In accordance with the decree of 12 November 1725, henceforth people who were previously in the poll-tax registry and are in the present poll-tax census are absolutely not to be ordained and appointed as priests and deacons or as churchmen without a general Senate-Synod decree, so that there will be no disruptions and arrears in the collection of the poll tax."[94] This did not settle the question, however; for the next two decades a seesaw battle raged between the Synod and Senate: the former demanded an open policy in order to fill vacancies, while the latter cited fiscal and administrative reasons for opposing the ordination of poll-tax registrants. The Synod periodically reopened the question, each time meeting with a firm rebuff from the Senate.[95]

The Senate's tighter policy inexorably took effect, as data from the 1760s demonstrate. For the whole empire, only 1.3 percent of the clergy had come from the poll-tax rolls, and no doubt many of these had entered before the 1740s.[96] This marked a significant decrease from data submitted in the 1730s. In some central dioceses, the proportion was slightly higher; the bishops of Vladimir and Pereslavl, for example, reported 87 and 73 clerics of poll-tax origin—approximately 3 to 4 percent of the total clergy in each diocese.[97] Senate pressure, furthermore, compelled the diocesan authorities to check carefully the poll-tax status of candidates, and by mid-century such investigations were routine.[98] As a result, virtually all poll-tax registrants who were ordained to the clergy had some kind of written release. Beyond this, however, bishops violated Senate law in several important respects. They ordained not merely serfs but other types of poll-tax registrants as well—especially monastery peasants; in Pereslavl diocese, for example, only 38 percent of the poll-tax candidates were former serfs— most were former monastery peasants and lay church employees. Nor did the landlord often pay the poll tax; rather, it was usually the responsibility of the parish in which the clergy were to serve, and sometimes the cleric himself paid the tax.[99] Nevertheless, the Senate's will prevailed: the number of poll-tax registrants had declined sharply, and most were in fact former churchmen who had been drafted earlier into the poll-tax population.[100]

The remaining loopholes were closed during Catherine II's reign, as Senate policy became stricter and the Synod's power waned. In 1764 the Senate compelled the Synod to withdraw a liberal resolution of 1761, and it prohibited further installation of poll-tax registrants. The Synod complied fully, directing bishops to remove churchmen formerly in the poll-tax registry and not to appoint others in the future.[101] In particular cases, however, the Synod still permitted bishops to ordain poll-tax registrants who had been properly released. For example, the consistory in Vladimir cautiously declined to ordain such a candidate; when he appealed to the Synod, it ordered his immediate ordination as one "properly released."[102] It also tried to reopen the question at the Legislative Commission in 1767-68, submitting this proposal: "Permit laymen of any rank, who desire (and who are worthy) to enter the ecclesiastical rank; not only do not scorn them for this, but order that this be considered an honor. If worthy people from the merchant class or poll-tax population (possessing the necessary releases) wish to enter the ecclesiastical rank, permit them to be installed." To placate state fiscal interests, the Synod pointed out that "the exclusion of the illiterate or those suspected [of crimes] from church staffs would compensate for any lost poll-tax revenues."[103]

These efforts came to nought, however, and the state gradually obliged the Synod to abandon its policy of admitting outsiders to the clergy.

An important turning point came in 1774: at the insistence of the Senate, the Synod ordered bishops to expel churchmen who had come from the poll-tax population and categorically forbade them to install anyone from this group.[104] This time the bishops dutifully obeyed, dispatching many churchmen to the secular command—a blow that provoked a new wave of tearful petitions from distraught clergy. The most important was a collective petition from sixteen churchmen submitted not to the Synod (which clearly would have been futile) but to the empress, pleading for reinstatement and decrying their exclusion as unjust. Catherine elected to display her "maternal compassion" and on 16 March 1775 ordered the Synod "to try to appoint these poor people to vacant clerical positions."[105] With bureaucratic shrewdness, the Synod tried to extend this act of imperial grace and apply the manifesto to several other cases—a device to which it frequently had recourse in defending Church interests.[106] But on this occasion a vigilant Senate rebuffed the attempt:

> The Senate cannot agree to permit the appointment of poll-tax registrants to church positions. . . . The Synod knows that, apart from such clerical children in the poll-tax registry, there is a very ample number of people available for staffing clerical vacancies; if they are not appointed and given support and land, the clergy's children not in the poll tax will wander idly. When they are passed up in favor of poll-tax registrants, then even more children of serving clergy will remain a burden to the people and themselves.[107]

The Synod meekly acquiesced and enforced the law scrupulously, rejecting petitions of those who sought installation and for whom peasants volunteered to pay the poll tax.[108] Just how scrupulously was revealed in another case in 1775: because a churchman in Vladimir diocese had been released by the steward (and not the landlord himself), the Synod rejected his release document as invalid—even though the local state officials had willingly accepted it. It refused even to consider a petition from a sacristan in Riazan diocese because he was already listed in the poll-tax registry and thus in the secular, not the Synodal, command.[109]

By the 1780s the former poll-tax registrants had all but vanished from the clerical ranks. The fourth census *reviziia* (1781-83) showed that throughout the empire few churchmen of poll-tax origins remained in the clergy; in the central dioceses too, except for Rostov and Riazan, the number of such clergy was negligible (Table 21).[110] More important, their biographical sketches show that nearly all were ap-

Table 21. Former poll-tax registrants in the clergy, 1784

Diocese	Number of actual clergy (priests, deacons, and churchmen)	Number of poll-tax churchmen	Percent of entire clergy
Kolomna	3,655	39	1.1
Moscow	2,649	26	1.0
Pereslavl	2,442	21	0.9
Riazan	4,618	61	1.3
Rostov	3,379	93	2.8
Suzdal	3,255	24	0.7
Vladimir	3,544	21	0.6
Empire	85,671	667	0.8

Source: TsGIA, f. 796, op. 65, g. 1784, d. 443, ll. 71-85.

pointed before 1762; for nearly two decades the clergy had been virtually closed to outsiders.[111] The coup de grâce came in 1784, when the new conscription devastated the remaining contingent of poll-tax clergy; most were forcibly transferred into the army or back to the poll-tax population.[112] Significantly, as the state struck this final blow, most bishops had lost interest in the recruitment of poll-tax candidates. As Metropolitan Platon wrote in February 1783: "From the reports submitted during the current census of Moscow diocese, it is evident that there is a large number of unappointed clerical children and seminarians. . . . There is no need whatsoever to accept and install those coming from the poll-tax registry."[113] While most bishops opposed the forcible removal of churchmen already installed, they concluded that in the future their dioceses would not need candidates from the poll-tax groups.[114] Restrictions remained ironclad; the fifth census *reviziia* (1795-97) was conducted without even raising the issue of poll-tax clergy.[115] By the late eighteenth century, the clergy had thus become firmly, definitely separated from the poll-tax groups of peasants and townspeople.

A third barrier to outsiders was formal clerical education, a requirement that tended to isolate the clergy not only in Russia but in other countries as well.[116] In old Muscovy candidates needed to satisfy only the most rudimentary requirements and hierarchs ritualistically bewailed the "ignorance" of parish clergy. The low educational standards, which made access possible for outsiders as well as the priest's son, ceased to apply in the eighteenth century. Once Peter began to raise educational qualifications and the seminaries began to function effectively, access became increasingly difficult for outsiders, because the new specialized training was available only to the clergy's progeny. By the end of the century, seminary attendance had become an essential precondition for clerical appointment, a development that effectively closed the door to men born outside the clerical estate.

The legal foundations of educational exclusion were laid in the first half of the eighteenth century. Authorities emphasized the obligation of the clergy to educate their children, and admonished bishops to ordain only educated candidates. Significantly, this legislation focused exclusively on the clergy's offspring as the natural group for clerical careers. In the usual phrase of such legislation, the clergy's children were obliged to study "in hopes of entering the clergy."[117] One of the rare comments about outsiders appeared in the Ecclesiastical Regulation, which nevertheless gave clear priority to the clergy's children: "All archpriests and wealthy priests, as well as those who are not wealthy, *must* send their children to the [Moscow] Academy. This *can* also be ordered for the better urban people and chancellery officials, while for the gentry it will be according to the personal decree of His Tsarist Majesty."[118] This suggestion of potential openness, hesitant and vague, was soon forgotten. The Church showed a single-minded desire to train the clergy's children, while the state had little interest in permitting individuals from other social groups to enter the seminary.[119]

Consequently, the new church schools and informal training were restricted to the clergy's sons. As data from the 1720s and 1740s demonstrate, students in Great Russian seminaries were almost entirely from the clerical estate (Table 22). To be sure, there were occasional outsiders; in 1736, for instance, Suzdal seminary reported that two of its 76 pupils were of peasant origin.[120] Such outsiders, however, were exceedingly rare, and other seminary reports—Kolomna for 1738, Rostov for 1730-38, Riazan for 1738-40, Nizhnii-Novgorod for 1730-38—show that the entire student body came from clerical families.[121] The only exceptions to this pattern in central Russia were the elite schools—Trinity-Sergius Seminary and the Moscow Academy. Trinity-Sergius had a low proportion of clerical progeny (only 47 percent in 1744) because its school was intended not only to train future priests but also to prepare administrative staff for its immense landholdings (over 200 clerks worked in its chancellery).[122] A still greater anomaly was the Moscow Slavonic-Greek-Latin Academy, which from its founding had been more a university than an ecclesiastical school, and which continued to have a significant proportion of its pupils from nonclerical origin. In 1728, for example, the clergy's children composed only 34 percent of the student population, while

Table 22. Social origins of pupils in seminaries and church schools, 1720s-40s

School	Year	Total enroll-ment	Number of clerical children	Number of nonclerical children
Kolomna	1733	45	45	0
	1741	38	37	1
Moscow Academy	1728	474	114	360
	1744	383	333	50
Riazan	1738-40	140	138	2
	1744	133	133	0
Rostov	1730-38	123	123	0
	1744	28	28	0
Suzdal	1723-26	109	109	0
	1736	76	74	2
Trinity-Sergius	1744	139	66	73

Sources: TsGIA, f. 796, op. 14, g. 1733, d. 386, l. 22; op. 18, g. 1737, d. 32, chast' 3, ll. 69-72 ob.; *ODDS,* 9:571; TsGIA, f. 796, op. 24, g. 1743, d. 496, chast' 1, ll. 124-134 ob.; op. 18, g. 1737, d. 32, chast' 3, ll. 73-84; op. 25, g. 1744, d. 134, ll. 64-81 ob.; op. 18, g. 1737, d. 32, chast' 2, ll. 641-650 ob.; op. 25, g. 1744, d. 134, ll. 82-88; op. 18, g. 1737, d. 32, chast' 2, ll. 148-151 ob.; op. 25, g. 1744, d. 134, ll. 107-121.

the majority were the sons of nobles, townspeople, soldiers, and other miscellaneous groups.[123] The Senate, in a memorandum to the Synod, correctly noted that "not only clerical children but the children of every rank" studied at the Academy.[124] But the number of such outsiders steadily dwindled, and by 1744 they constituted only 12 percent of the enrollment.[125]

This closed enrollment was due to several barriers. As the Petrine service state acquired clearer, sharper definition, youths of other estates had little chance to matriculate: the state required sons to enter early the service assigned to their father's rank and to acquire the appropriate apprenticeship or training for their soslovie obligation.[126] Moreover, given the limits of the "ecclesiastical command," the Church lacked the authority to seize the children of lay groups and forcibly enroll them in the seminaries. Even when Bishop Feodosii of Novgorod proposed in 1723 to educate nonclerical youths, the Church was unable to compel the laity to comply.[127] Actually, the Church had little interest even in trying to recruit pupils from the laity. In part, this was due to seminary finances: the Ecclesiastical Regulation authorized taxation only from monasteries and parish clergy, not from the fathers of lay children. Given the straitened finances of most seminaries, the bishop could scarcely be enthusiastic about providing free education for lay children.[128] The Church also feared that the presence of outsiders would produce a curriculum wholly secular, directed toward lay rather than ecclesiastical needs. The state did try to merge church schools with cipher schools in the 1720s and place both under Church control; the Synod vigorously opposed the scheme. Although partly appalled by the added financial responsibility this entailed, the Synod also argued that the ecclesiastical curriculum was designed to prepare priests, not to train youths for state service.[129] The seminary curriculum was not in fact narrowly religious; it was different, however, from the technical education required of civil and military officers.

The bishops had good reason to focus exclusively on the clergy's sons: as members of the ecclesiastical command, they could be mobilized to fill the new schools. Such youths were, moreover, less vulnerable to forcible removal to secular occupations: when the government raided the seminaries for trained manpower, it automatically seized first the children of nonclerical origin and only as a last resort took the children of priests and churchmen. That fact weighed heavily with a prelate seeking to improve the priests' educational level and dreading the loss of his best seminarians. The Synod first realized this fact in 1724, when military authorities removed a soldier's son from the Moscow Academy; the Synod hastily ordered the Academy to review the laws on admitting outsiders, for the first time openly raising the issue.[130] Although outsiders remained a majority in the Academy until the 1730s, authorities showed increasing caution. The Academy's rector, for example, rejected a contingent of nonclerical youths sent by the Herald-Master in 1725: "This Slavonic-Russian school educates only the children of ecclesiastical persons, who can be appointed to the clerical ranks."[131] The Synod confirmed this policy in a decree of 1728, sent again to the Academy:

The soldiers' children in the Moscow Slavonic-Greek-Latin Academy are to be sent to the regiments for service. Henceforth, accept for study those for whom is sent a written release from the regiments in which they serve, [confirming] that now and in the future they will not be needed in the regiments. Expel from the school and henceforth do not enroll peasants' children and people belonging to landlords.[132]

Similar considerations impelled the Riazan seminary in 1741 to refuse admission to two noble youths because they were laymen.[133]

The effects of this educational barrier were evident by mid-century.

The formal schools, to be sure, were still small and unstable, but by the 1750s seminaries existed in every diocese and steadily increased their enrollments. Specialized education outside the seminary also tended to exclude outsiders; informal education, through the distribution of the catechism or special ordination schools, was specifically intended for the clergy's children. As bishops began to examine candidates rigorously with their improved administrative apparatus, youths from other social estates found access difficult if not impossible. The decline of the traditional "parish school" increased still more their educational disqualification.

The educational barrier became decisive in the last quarter of the eighteenth century. Seminary enrollments increased sharply, and by the 1780s and 1790s even churchmen were expected to have attended a seminary, however briefly. Simultaneously, seminary populations were now even more exclusively clerical in social composition. Schools in Vladimir, Rostov, and Kolomna reported no outsiders; Riazan diocese had only 4 outsiders in a total of 532 pupils.[134] Moscow Academy, which once enrolled large numbers of nonclerical children, had a homogeneous clerical population: only 3 of 903 pupils in 1790 were the sons of laymen.[135] The bishops realized the new social significance of the seminary, and in the 1780s argued that the rapidly expanding seminaries easily provided sufficient candidates for their dioceses and thus there was no need to admit youths from other estates.[136] That signified an important change: even if a vacancy appeared and even if a landlord freed a serf to claim it, the outsider lacked the essential educational qualification.

By the last decades of the eighteenth century, then, even potential mobility into the clergy had disappeared. A clerical clan often struck its roots deeply into a parish, producing generation after generation of clergy, sometimes even in the same village; this effectively excluded outsiders, even those of clerical origin. Hereditary tendencies, though evident in Muscovy, became hard-and-fast bonds only in Imperial Russia, as the clergy struggled to achieve economic security, protect their privileged status, and ward off service demands from the Church and state. Added to this were two obstacles wholly new to the eighteenth century—the poll tax and specialized education. Even in a parish where a clerical family was not firmly entrenched (such as a newly opened parish, or one where a cleric was defrocked or died without male issue), aspirants from other social groups found their way blocked by the poll-tax regulations and education. Hence the clergy, which had too little to offer the well-born, had become socially, legally, and culturally inaccessible to the lower status groups most likely to seek entry.

SOCIAL MOBILITY OUT OF THE CLERICAL ESTATE

What was the rate of mobility out of the clerical estate? Those already ordained or installed as clergy certainly had ample cause for leaving. They often endured economic privation, abuse by Church or state authorities, and conflict with fellow clergymen and their parishioners. Canon law permitted voluntary defrocking, and the state raised no objections.[137] Even more likely to leave were the widowed priests and deacons; despite the laws, they still were often forced to take monastic vows. Finally, the clergy's children had still more reason to abandon the clerical estate. Although formally in the Synodal command, they were neither ordained to church service nor inscribed in the poll-tax registry. They were usually literate, thus holding a distinct advantage over other social elements. Above all, they found it increasingly difficult to find a "registered clerical position"; by the 1770s and 1780s, clerical youths far exceeded available positions, and bishops strictly observed the registry rules. Worse still, the threat of a new conscription hung permanently over their heads; procrastination in voluntary transfer invited compulsory inscription into the least desirable poll-tax status—serfdom.

Surprisingly, however, social mobility was exceedingly low in all central dioceses save one—Moscow. Statistical data are not comprehensive, and doubtless many clergy and clerical children simply disappeared.[138] Nevertheless, a remarkably low rate of voluntary transfer is evident in several kinds of data. First, the records on state conscriptions show, invariably, massive numbers of unemployed, "idle" offspring; these data, so large and impressive, served as the routine justification for the government's recurrent conscriptions. Second, diocesan reports on the clergy indicate a low rate of transfer. Data compiled on Suzdal diocese in the period 1722-39 reveal that only a minute percentage of the clergy or their children voluntarily left the clergy.[139] Comprehensive data on Pereslavl diocese for 1744-56 show that only 2 percent of the clergy and their sons transferred to the secular command, and approximately the same rate was recorded for the following decade, 1756-66.[140] A third set of data is provided by the seminary lists, which similarly indicate a low rate of transfer among the students. Except in Moscow diocese, nearly all the departing pupils assumed clerical positions; few entered secular professions.[141] Fourth, information on lay social groups also reveals little seepage from the clergy. Kizevetter's study of the urban population (a relatively desirable status) shows very few recruits from the clerical estate.[142] Likewise, the new, free state schools that opened in the late eighteenth century attracted few clerical children—less than even 1 percent of the number enrolled in the seminaries.[143] The bureaucracy too included few clerical youths, especially at mid-century; even when the raw numbers of such transfers increased at the century's end, they were relatively negligible as measured against the whole clerical estate.[144]

What was the cause of this low rate of mobility? One factor was the lack of attractive outlets in the central provinces (with the important exception of Moscow). Although a youth occasionally chose to become a townsman or serf, such cases were understandably rare; few willingly entered an inferior status that entailed the stigma and burden of inscription into the poll-tax registry. Nor could the priest's son easily enter the merchant guilds. As four churchmen explained in 1784, "We cannot transfer into some other form of service because we lack not only capital but also even the most essential sustenance."[145] The most inviting outlets were the bureaucracy and new professions (such as teaching or medicine), both surely in need of educated personnel. But here too access was tightly limited. The provincial bureaucracy recruited mainly from the progeny of chancellery employees (sometimes called the bureaucratic estate). In any event, it could absorb only a fraction of the clergy's children; the number of clerical youths in each province numbered several thousand, while the provincial administration employed only a few hundred.[146] Especially after the initial staffing that followed the 1775 provincial reforms, new vacancies opened but slowly for the remainder of the century. Similarly, the demand for professional people was negligible in the provinces; even where shortages existed (such as in medicine), only pupils in the uppermost classes of the seminary could qualify.[147] In all these respects, Moscow was radically different; a teeming city of several hundred thousand, it offered a wealth of opportunities in typography, medicine, and civil service. Not surprisingly, the rate of transfer was significantly higher here than elsewhere in central Russia.[148]

A second obstacle to social mobility was the strict control placed by the Church on geographical movement, preventing the clergy from discovering other opportunities in Moscow or even in their own province. The travel restrictions derived from multiple sources—a concern that parishioners not be left without essential sacraments,[149] a desire to eradicate clerical vagrancy (often associated with notorious misconduct),[150] and the general state policy of binding all social elements (save the nobility) to a locality to simplify the tasks of law and order. Consequently, the Synod strictly prohibited clerical movement without a formal travel permit (pashport), and bishops added further rules against movement with their own dioceses.[151] The clergy's children, similarly, could not wander at will; those arrested without a legal travel permit were forcibly returned to their home diocese.[152]

A third and very formidable obstacle was the Church's implacable opposition to transfers out of the clerical estate. In the case of those already ordained or installed, the priests and churchmen, Church authorities were especially adamant in withholding permission to transfer. Priests had a legal right to ask for defrocking, and Peter even encouraged widowed priests to do so, but hierarchs nevertheless sought to quash such requests.[153] Two typical cases arose in 1783 in Kolomna diocese, where the bishop rejected two churchmen's petition to transfer, and they eventually were obliged to appeal to the Synod.[154] A sacristan in Vladimir diocese suffered a worse fate for his untimely request in 1767: Bishop Pavel had the petitioner placed in chains for a week and then thrashed before an assembly of local clergy.[155] To convince the bishop, some petitioners sought to document their unworthiness, as in this petition of 1786 from a widowed deacon in Vladimir diocese: "I have seen that because of my youth I can no longer endure the clerical rank, in view of certain of my habits which are contrary to my rank: I go to taverns and drinking houses, play billiards, and find in myself a great inclination toward what is worldly. Therefore I do not wish to remain in the clerical rank in the future."[156] As a rule, the Synod first ordered the bishop to use moral suasion on the petitioner; only if this failed was he to be released for transfer to the secular command.[157]

Hierarchs were equally opposed to transfer by the clergy's children, notwithstanding government complaints about "excess clerical youths." The bishops dwelt upon the numerous vacancies in their dioceses and even after 1780, when this argument admittedly was no longer valid, they still wished to have the largest possible pool of potential candidates. As one might expect, the Church tenaciously resisted the loss of advanced seminarians, the very group most likely to transfer. The Synod waged its first battle over clerical youths in the 1720s, when it fought to keep them in church schools and exempt from cipher schools.[158] When it received reports in 1731 that Moscow youths were entering government service to avoid matriculation in Moscow Academy, it categorically forbade them to do so:

Priests, deacons, and churchmen of Moscow cathedrals and parish churches are to deliver their children for study, in hopes of serving the Church, as provided for in the Imperial decrees and Ecclesiastical Regulation, without any procrastination and excuses. They are absolutely forbidden to give [their children] to the Colleges [government ministries] and chancelleries as clerks, under penalty of defrocking and merciless punishment.[159]

The Synod then persuaded the Senate to uphold this rule in 1732.[160] Nevertheless, state officials continued taking the prized seminarians into civil service and lay professions; an Imperial decree of 1737 even authorized the practice.[161] The Synod opposed these incursions, especially the incessant demands of the Medical College, and at least during Elizabeth's reign it managed to restrict the drain of advanced seminarians.[162]

Even after 1762, when Church influence declined, the Synod still resisted state demands for seminarians.[163] Alarmed by a report from Moscow in 1767 that "in Moscow diocese not only the clergy's children but churchmen themselves request to be released into government service," the Synod decreed that churchmen and clerical children could transfer to the army or poll-tax population but not to the bureaucracy:

> If these clerical children or churchmen, who are idle and lack support, wish to enter military service or to be inscribed in the poll-tax registry, then exclude such people from the clerical lists and make the appropriate notification of release to the state officials. However, under no circumstances are they to be permitted at their request and desire to enter other services until this has been reviewed.[164]

The conscription of 1769 revealed that some clerical youths nevertheless continued to enter the civil service; at Synodal insistence, the Senate ordered state officials to report any such illegally placed employees, who were to be dispatched to the army as due punishment.[165] In 1770 the Synod rejected the petition of a Moscow pupil to transfer to the University: "Do not release the student Zelentsev from the Academy to the University, because according to the Ecclesiastical Regulation and decrees, children of the clergy shall study in the Academy in hopes of entering the clergy."[166] The Synod reaffirmed in 1775 that individuals could transfer from the clerical estate only with "a release from the Holy Synod."[167] Catherine, however, severed these restrictive bonds, inviting seminarians to enter the bureaucracy or choose some other "role in life." The Synod steadfastly resisted such raids whenever possible, and in 1792 tried to compile data on the problem.[168] It was more successful after Paul came to the throne in 1796, obtaining new controls against transfers by seminarians. According to a decree of 1799, students in theology and philosophy could transfer only with the Synod's approval; pupils in lower classes required the approval of the local bishop.[169]

Bishops energetically pursued a similar policy in their own dioceses. Platon of Moscow was especially hostile to requests for transfer, and for good reason: his diocese suffered most from the loss of advanced seminarians. In 1771, when one student requested permission to transfer to Moscow University, Platon (who was then rector of Trinity-Sergius Seminary) refused: "He is to study in the seminary in hopes of entering the clergy; otherwise, the money spent on him by the school will have been wasted."[170] To impress upon its pupils the duty to remain in the clerical estate, in the 1770s the seminary staged a debate (*disput*) between two seminarians on "what career one should choose." The "good" seminarian warned against seeking a government position: "To receive a rank quickly, it is necessary to have a patron, or a large sum of money, or a good inheritance." When warned against entering the chancellery, the wavering student asked: "Well, why do so many students enter these ranks?" The good seminarian replied darkly: "Don't chase after the wind in the field. Whoever is wise will never enter the chancellery." He then identified the best profession of all: "There is none better than the clerical [rank]."[171] Provincial bishops, who faced less acute problems of transfer, did not always act so energetically as Platon; some, such as the bishop of Rostov, even cooperated enthusiastically when Catherine demanded seminarians for the new provincial bureaucracy.[172] But most hierarchs, probably less intent on winning favor at court, were jealously protective of seminarians. The bishop of Riazan, for example, inserted this command in his general "Instructions" for the management of the seminary: "It is necessary to impress upon the students that as clerical children they have the right to be in the service of the Church. It must be shameful for them to leave for other ranks and give clerical positions to laymen."[173] He was, naturally, most concerned about seminarians in the upper classes and made them promise that they would "never request permission to enter the lay ranks, under fear of being subjected to legal punishment."[174]

Finally, the clergy themselves opposed their sons' transfer. The clerical family needed an heir—someone to monopolize parish revenues, to support the priest in his old age, to care for the family after his death. To be sure, a priest in an elite parish of Moscow would welcome the prospects of a secular career for his son. Elsewhere, however, the clerical family desperately needed an heir and even opposed a son's tonsure into monasticism for the very same reason.[175] Family interests were starkly revealed in the frequent petitions to recover a drafted son, bluntly declaring that the family needed an heir to provide for the priest or his family.[176] Under these circumstances, as long as a position (even potentially) was vacant, clerical youths were induced to linger in hopes of appointment.

The clergy thus became bound to their status, tethered to a closed, hereditary estate. In contrast to pre-Petrine times, when inbred clergy were not uncommon but far from axiomatic, the clergy had become an encapsulated social population by the late eighteenth century. Insurmountable barriers were raised against entry; few individuals of nonclerical origin could penetrate the estate by the 1780s in the central dioceses. Voluntary exit into lay professions was more feasible but was limited mainly to the advanced seminarians. The result was the hereditary, castelike group that became the focus of reform in the mid-nineteenth century.

The Clerical Subculture

Besides hereditary enclosure, another force began to separate the clergy from lay society in the eighteenth century: the formation of a distinctive clerical subculture. In old Muscovy the priest had lived much like his parishioners: he dressed in an ordinary *kaftan* (peasant tunic), wore crude *lapti* (bast sandals), drank bountifully, and worked the fields to support himself. Pososhkov and contemporaries commented critically about the undue similarity between priest and peasant; even later observers professed to discern no difference between them.[177] The priest's material culture had indeed changed little from that of a middling peasant. Even into the early nineteenth century, his two-roomed hut might be whitewashed, but it was nonetheless built and furnished in the traditional peasant manner—so unlike the nobles' two-story homes.[178] Though his material culture changed little, in other respects the priest became dramatically different from the laity: by the end of the eighteenth century he had acquired a distinctive life style, code of behavior, even self-image.

The clergy's separateness resulted partly from the general developments in secular society, where autonomous and distinctive subcultures emerged in the nobility and townspeople. The nobility, in particular, acquired from the West a radically different way of life and cultural identity; their education, homes, consumption patterns, art, and literature were all profoundly affected by the intrusion of European models. Reports of "dandies" began to circulate in the capitals by the mid-eighteenth century, and in the ensuing decades even the country squire mimicked the new cultural fashions.[179] To lesser degrees, the townspeople and peasantry also absorbed new cultural styles—from more secular "manuscript miscellanies" (*rukopisnye sborniki*) to newer forms of home furnishings.[180] To become culturally alien in this secularizing society, the parish clergy had but to remain unchanged. Moreover, since these new consumption patterns were exceedingly expensive (indeed most nobles could ill afford them), it was all the more likely that the parish clergy would remain "boorish and crude" in the eyes of fastidious noblemen.

The clergy's cultural apartness, however, was not only a by-product of the ripening of secular subcultures; it was also the result of a dynamic attempt by the Church to create a clerical life style, at once respectable and pure of secular failings. This campaign to purify the clergy was not narrowly religious, but also social in purpose. Here, as in many other dimensions of Church policy, ecclesiastical authorities were responding to the crisis in the Church: the waning of its influence, the loss of its wealth, the breakdown of its cultural control were changes that eroded the priest's—and the bishop's—status and authority. The bishops' status anxiety fused with traditional religious concerns; the most urbane episcopal bureaucrat and the most God-fearing bishop could both rationalize that respect for the clerical rank was vital to preserving Church authority and defeating the Old Belief. Thus, to rescue the clergy's declining status, bishops tried to improve not only the clergy's education and service performance, but also to change their culture, social ties, and public demeanor. Unable to alter the clergy's underlying social and economic weaknesses, which would have required resources and power the Church no longer possessed, bishops tended to focus upon the clergy's culture and way of life.

These social underpinnings of the bishops' efforts were most clearly revealed by their specific focus upon *public* demeanor and image; relatively little attention was given to the priest's personal morality unless it involved a cardinal sin like adultery. To be sure, ordination charters and decrees recited traditional formulae—a priest should "teach himself (after the example of the Apostles) to be honorable, sober, wise, decent, honest" and so forth.[181] The hierarchs, however, were most concerned about clerical status, and the driving thrust of their campaign was public behavior or mere deportment. This had, to some degree, a traditional rationale: the priest should provide a model of behavior for the parishioners. Yet the bishops actually intended for the priest to become socially distinguishable from low-born parishioners. To secure his necessary "honor," a priest was to "preserve decency in everything toward his rank, that is, in deeds, speech, walk, dress, construction of homes, etc."[182] Like Latin education, such behavior was supposed to shore up the clergy's declining status.

One natural target of the bishops' efforts was drunkenness. Hierarchs had complained of clerical drunkenness for centuries, but until the 1740s they rarely defrocked or severely punished offenders. It is significant that, as the hierarchs attacked the vice, they concentrated on public drinking. Themselves fond of spirits,[183] they were horrified only by the spectacle of inebriated priests staggering along the streets, and consequently, their legislation struck at public inebriation and drinking in village alehouses or taverns. The hierarch of Pereslavl warned in 1748 that "anyone who appears drunk will be cruelly punished," and he hired a soldier to arrest violators.[184] Metropolitan Amvrosii of Moscow, ever impatient with parish clergy, inveighed against public drunkenness of clergy in 1771: "His Grace has learned that many Moscow clergy wander drunk along the streets in the most disgusting way, heedless of repeated directives; [this] causes an extreme temptation for the laity and invokes shame upon honorable clergy." Amvrosii set fines for those who were apprehended in taverns —one ruble for priests, fifty kopecks for churchmen.[185] The bishops of provincial dioceses also attacked the problem vigorously, and this decree by a Vladimir hierarch in 1771 was typical:

> His Grace has learned that some city and rural clergy enter the taverns and leave drunk. This brings upon them and others of their rank open derision and poses a great temptation for the simple people. Therefore, His Grace orders that the consistory strictly reconfirm to all clergy that they are to avoid such behavior and that supervision be established over them in this regard. If anyone henceforth enters taverns and wanders drunk along the streets, seize him and bring him to the consistory, where the mandatory fine will be exacted from him.

The consistory, as a prophylactic measure, required all the diocesan clergy to swear in writing that they would obey the bishop's decree.[186] The Synod showed a similar impatience with drunkenness. In 1771 it defrocked a Suzdal cleric and ordered the bishop to publicize its decision as a warning to others, and the following year it formally made drunkenness a sufficient cause for defrocking.[187]

The hierarchs also sought to improve the clergy's personal appearance so that they would look like priests, not peasants. Until the mid-eighteenth century, bishops showed no interest in the problem; at most, they vainly urged the priest to wear proper dress during the liturgy.[188] Except in Moscow (where the cassock was generally worn by the 1720s or 1730s),[189] the clergy still dressed like peasants. Metropolitan Iosif of Moscow registered this complaint in 1744 about the provincial clergy of his diocese: "From all towns and districts, clerics come before His Grace with petitions for appointment as priests or deacons, dressed in peasant clothes and bast sandals—which is very indecent for the clerical rank."[190] By mid-century, the bishops began to punish clergy for wearing peasant garb and insist that they wear cassocks and shoes not only at Mass but in public as well. Bishop Antonii of Vladimir (a recent arrival from Georgia) was appalled by the Russian clergy's improper attire, and in 1757 strictly forbade them to wear peasant clothing.[191] The resolution of a successor, in 1774, was more comprehensive: "At home (except when working [in the fields]), in the parish, and in the towns—and, especially, at His

Grace's residence—they [the clergy] are to wear shoes and cassocks; they are absolutely forbidden to appear in the clothes of common people and thereby make themselves look indecent."[192] Metropolitan Platon of Moscow issued a similar resolution, and fined priests 25 kopecks for appearing in public without a cassock.[193] Bishop Simon of Riazan displayed uncommon sensibility in a decree of 1779: "Cut the mustaches of those clergy who have let them grow too long, and have them sign a sworn statement that they will hereafter keep themselves neat and have a decent appearance, befitting their rank, in their clothing and in their hair and beards." Violators, he warned, would be fined a ruble each.[194] A Vladimir prelate showed special impatience: in 1795 when one priest appeared in public without a cassock, the bishop had him arrested and placed on a regimen of bread and water for three days as punishment.[195]

The bishops also tried to isolate the clergy from the commoners' secular diversions. The parish church, as we have seen, was traditionally as much a social center as a religious chapel, and the local clergy shared in their parishioners' pastimes. In 1742 the over-procurator of the Synod observed that "many people of the clerical rank, together with laity, watch horse-racing and partake in drunken feasts, which brings disgrace upon the clerical rank."[196] After mid-century the bishops tried to eliminate such "unseemly conduct." A clerical instruction manual of 1776 warned the clergy "not to have a lavish dining table, not to arrange feasts or attend readily those of others, not to commit sacrilege, not to play cards, not to dance, nor to watch these things."[197] The city *gul'bishche*—a popular haven for such entertainment—was declared off-limits for the clergy by diocesan authorities.[198] The bishops' distaste for lower-class activities was evident in the report by the bishop of Vladimir, who summarized the "indecent conduct" of a local deacon:

In violation of the decency proper to his rank, the deacon wears indecent clothing (namely, a ragged smock tied at the waist), ties up his hair in a bun, and strolls about the town square on trading days. He frequently goes to taverns, where he becomes drunk and plays billiards with the *raznochintsy* [common townspeople]. Moreover, he stirs up a fuss and gets in trouble.[199]

Unlike a Muscovite hierarch, the eighteenth-century bishop could detect and punish easily those guilty of "unseemly conduct," as the Synodal files attest.

While the bishop frowned upon lower-class diversions, he encouraged social intercourse with more respectable circles. In the past, hierarchs admonished the clergy to shun "suspicious people" but did not try to regulate their social relations in the parish. By the 1770s, however, some hierarchs sought to encourage the clergy to seek social ties with the upper classes. Metropolitan Platon of Moscow, in his *Instructions to Ecclesiastical Superintendents*, candidly expressed this social ambition:

> The clergy are to have relations and friendships with other clergy; and also with the well-born—landowners, honored merchants, and townspeople; they are not to consort with (and be friends of) just any-one, in an unseemly way. The priest, especially, having been honored with the sacred rank, must deport himself with dignity and thereby bring others to respect him.[200]

The bishop of Kolomna repeated this injunction verbatim in 1779, and other hierarchs similarly tried to foster clerical ties to the more re-spectable classes.[201]

The hierarchs' efforts to separate the clergy from the low-born groups struck a responsive chord in the parish clergy, who nurtured their own pretensions to "honor" and respect. At the cleric's ordina-tion, the bishop's inflated rhetoric taught him that his profession was exceptionally important; the staged "debate" in Trinity-Sergius Semi-nary on "what career to choose" fitted neatly into this attitude of cleri-cal pride and honor. Especially if the cleric had completed the semi-nary, he could lay claim to cultural achievement that few gentry could match. Expressions of this pride, however, surfaced rarely. The priest was, after all, dependent upon the parish and vulnerable to abuse. Most had the discretion to avoid open provocation, but, to judge from later materials, "seminarian pride" did inflate the clergy's sense of self-importance and their proper place in society.[202] Society, at least, per-ceived such pride. It is revealing that in the mid-nineteenth century, when the government tried to determine why the clergy's sons so rarely left the clerical estate, it raised the question whether this was not due to the clergy's "soslovie prejudice."[203]

Such pride was most explicitly expressed in the eighteenth century by archpriests. Their zeal to defend their honor stemmed partly from their relative independence (as cathedral clergy, their income depended little or not at all on parishioners) and partly from their constant en-counters with pretentious state officials. One such cleric was Savva Dugin, the ill-fated clergyman who proposed in 1732 that the arch-priests replace the *voevody* in local administration and become a new local elite, holding secular as well as ecclesiastical power.[204] Also revealing was an incident in Suzdal diocese in 1769, when an arch-priest defended his "honor" against the local *voevoda*. During a state holiday in July, a drum roll had respectfully resounded before the residence of the town's *voevoda*. The archpriest apprehended the drummer and exploded in anger: "Why didn't you, drummer, beat the drum in front of the cathedral—in the archpriest's presence?" In retaliation, the archpriest refused to permit the church bells to be rung in honor of the *voevoda*, and declared, "I am superior [in rank] to a brigadier." The archpriest struck his last blow during mass, driving the *voevoda* from his favorite position in church by a well-aimed swing of the censer.[205] Refusal to tip their hats,[206] use of the title *ierei* instead of the vulgar *pop* for "priest,"[207] requests for government medals and ranks[208]—such acts reveal a conscious desire to defend and uplift the ecclesiastical status that was threatened by a glossy Westernization and pretentious nobility.

Such attempts rarely met with success and only deepened the clergy's separateness. Secularization, episcopal pressure, claims to "honor"—all interacted to drive a wedge between priest and parish. This left the clergy virtually in social isolation, fit for neither gentry nor lower-class society. The profound social and psychological distance between clergy and laity is suggestively drawn in Giliarov-Platonov's memoir on the life of a clerical family in Kolomna in the early nineteenth century. His father had little social intercourse outside the clergy; their speech, culture, dress belonged to a cultural "ring" a century older than that of laymen in the same town.[209] It is significant that the clergy ordinarily married within their own estate, often in "deals" involving clerical positions. They could rarely aspire to marry into the nobility and shunned ties to the poll-tax population below.[210] To be sure, isolation was not ironclad; there were no religious taboos or ritual punishments for those who crossed estate lines. Especially in Moscow, the more urbane clergy mixed in high society, their wives (after mid-century) imitated the latest aristocratic fashion, and their progeny married into respectable circles.[211] But the more general pattern, especially in the provincial dioceses (whether town or village), was toward clerical isolation. Writing of the clergy in the middle of the nineteenth century, one observer drew this striking portrait of a caste-like exclusion: "The clergy [by this time] managed to form itself into an integrated and complete caste-type, to construct itself into a completely isolated society, a special breed with which the other sosloviia have neither blood nor social ties, even being rather hostile toward the clergy."[212]

The Costs of Soslovnost'

The eighteenth century thus signaled the crystallization of a rigid hereditary estate in the clergy, both socially and culturally. Because of

vested interests, the poll tax, and special education, the clergy had become tightly closed to outsiders; most dramatically, the hereditary
order appeared even in the individual parish, where a single clan
sometimes claimed all positions for generations. At the same time,
voluntary exit from the clerical estate was rare; apart from those forcibly removed by government conscription (and pleading to return),
most clergy and their children refused to transfer to other social
groups. The Church hierarchs, who had defended proposals to admit
outsiders and as late as 1767 denied that the clergy formed a hereditary
order, finally accepted the government view in the 1780s: the clergy's
children sufficed to staff the church and outsiders were not needed. At
the same time, the clergy acquired a distinctive subculture, which increasingly differed from the rising new secular culture of the nobility,
townspeople, and even peasantry. The result was the *dukhovnoe soslovie*—the closed clerical estate, hereditary and culturally separate
from lay society. This all-encompassing *soslovnost'* had momentous
consequences for the clergy.

One was serious demographic imbalance: with the service structure
rigid and precisely defined, the growing clerical population simply
could not place its numerous sons in church service. Overpopulation,
in turn, was a constant drain on the meager resources of the clerical
estate, intensifying the problem of clerical impoverishment. More serious still, it inspired the state to conduct massive conscriptions
among "superfluous churchmen and clerical children." These occasional raids were too sporadic and episodic to relieve the congestion;
they served only to denigrate the status of the clergy and their progeny
—who were unceremoniously consigned to the army, peasantry, and
factories. Overpopulation was also a crucial source of the ubiquitous
brawls and feuds among the clergy, who demeaned themselves—and
their rank—in the struggle for promotions or positions for their sons.

Furthermore, the formation of a hereditary estate impaired the religious effectiveness of the clergy, for it meant a "functionary" role-con-
ception of the clergy. It meant that the priest was not so much a religious or spiritual figure as a mere functionary performing rites and
duties for a fee; he reached his position through hereditary ties rather
than a "calling." It is revealing that in their appeals for the bishop's
mercy, the clergy did not rely upon spiritual or religious claims.
Rather, to acquire or regain their positions, they founded their claims
on family genealogy ("by birth I am from the clerical estate"),[213] family residence at a particular church (alluding to their "father's and
forefather's position"),[214] or they simply pleaded for episcopal mercy.
Because of hereditary estate barriers, outsiders claiming religious in-

spiration could not enter the parish clergy had they wanted; they had but two alternatives—monasticism (itself a constricted opportunity) and the heretical Old Belief. Consequently, as the Church faced the rigorous trial of secular modernization, it failed to recruit devout new priests committed to restoring and revitalizing Orthodoxy.

Conclusion

By the late eighteenth century the white clergy had been molded into a clerical estate-caste, the *dukhovnoe soslovie*. Most striking was the rigid hereditary order; virtually all new clergy came from within the estate, few offspring willingly left its fold. The soslovie also acquired a peculiar juridical status; it formed a special *chin* or rank outside secular society but within the state's "Synodal command." Set apart from the lower poll-tax population (peasants and townspeople), the clergy became a special service class with specific obligations to the superior government and Church. Culture further reinforced the clergy's social identity. New secular subcultures had taken root and developed, while the parish clergy stood apart, defending a subculture that was curiously old-fashioned and embalmed with Latin "science." With their special garb, old norms of conduct, archaic church-script and literature, and alien Latinism, the clergy formed an identifiable group distinctly separate from lay society.

The formation of the clergy into a closed soslovie was not a unique process—other ranks and groups of medieval Muscovy had similarly been regrouped into bulky social aggregates or estates. Social amalgamation was one part of the broader process of Russian modernization; as the state authority was centralized, as the economy became nationally integrated, so too were the medieval social categories merged into larger juridical sosloviia. It was a process that was unique to Imperial Russia; while other European countries were beginning to break apart the traditional estate structure, Russia began to build just such an order of closed social estates. The nobility was created from the various service people (*sluzhilye liudi*) of Muscovy and acquired a collective name (*shliakhetstvo*, later *dvorianstvo*) and common juridical status.

The manifold categories of urban dwellers were similarly redefined, fixed, and glued together to form the new Petrine *obshchina* in the city. The state also ground away the fine distinctions between still lower status groups, sorting them into the general categories of state, church, and landlord peasants. These social estates, whether called *zvaniia* or *sostoianiia* in the late eighteenth century, were largely defined by their service obligations and juridical status.

By far the most cohesive of these estates (or sosloviia as they came to be called) was the clergy. To be sure, it had the internal differentiation in social and economic status characteristic of all sosloviia. But the clergy's *soslovnost'* was much more complete. It was the most hereditary group in society; even the nobility (to their dismay) admitted newcomers through Peter's Table of Ranks. It was also the most juridically separate; even the nobility did not have the unique status conferred by the Synodal command. And cultural distinctiveness raised a final important barrier that divided the clergy from lay society.

This new soslovie structure, however, had devastating consequences for the clergy (and in turn the Church). First, the clergy alone formed a single, definable profession; nobles, townsmen, and peasants could work at many different occupations, but the clergy did not have an economic function and served only at the altar. Thus they could easily be identified as "supernumerary" in a secular society—which was precisely the function of the new government *shtat*. This registry was an inelastic structure, a tight-fitting garment that simply could not contain the demographic growth of the clergy. The clergy were frozen into a status; upward mobility into the gentry was almost impossible, downward mobility into the townspeople or peasantry was undesirable. The consequence was an accumulative "overpopulation" that became especially acute after the 1780s. The government's only solution was not an easing of mobility but more exacting conscriptions—the *razbor* that hung ominously over the clergy and grievously degraded their social and juridical status.

The bureaucratic *shtat* also caused new economic hardships for the clergy. The registry was totally disconnected from economic reality; it provided no salary and established only a crude—and virtually meaningless—ratio between the clergy and parish size. Indeed it even legitimized "excessive" staffing in small parishes: two churchmen were permissible at every church, even though it was uncommon to fill both positions in earlier times (and even as late as the mid-eighteenth century). The pressure between the *shtat* and social reality worked like a vise on the clergy, forcing them into a desperate struggle for income and positions. Such endemic strife took a heavy toll in social respect, consistory bribes, and the group's internal cohesiveness.

Finally, the clergy suffered from a devastating role conflict, as it was caught between modernization from above, resistance from below. The clergy were exploited by the central authorities (state and Church), which had streamlined their administration and aspired to new levels of control over society, even at the lowest levels. Whether the task was informing on political criminals or exposing the superstitious, the clergy were obliged to execute the commands of central authorities. Yet the clergy were still firmly tied to the local community, which resisted such encroachments from above and held the parish clergy in complete dependence. The priest, facing the cruel dilemma of heeding the authorities or the laity, risked almost certain reprisals or punishments, whatever his choice.

A comparison with the nobility can underscore the seriousness of the clergy's predicament. In some respects, the two groups were similar: both were free from the poll tax, both exhibited internal differentiation, and both were compelled to absorb an alien culture. But the clergy's position was considerably worse. Unlike the nobility, they had to squeeze into the rigid *shtat* or face expulsion into the army and peasantry; nobles could freely enter service (indeed, they *had* to do so before 1762) and later could rot away on their beloved estates. Moreover, acculturation was probably a less traumatic experience for the nobleman. It came through tutors, service, and foreign travel; it was constantly reinforced by social recognition; it fitted the new "cultural definition" of a true nobleman. Not so for the clergy. Their alien Latin education was tortuously learned at the seminary; it had no relationship to subsequent service, did not elicit public respect, and was quickly forgotten. And the clergy suffered no less than the nobility from the high costs of their respective forms of "modernization." Virtually all the clergy were poorer than the bottom third of the nobility, yet they had to support a prolonged formal education and adopt a living standard that would raise them above the lowly serf.

The authorities, to be sure, were aware of the clergy's problems—the throng of vagrants in Moscow, brigand *popovichi*, and service blunders were constant reminders. Yet all the attempts to reform the clergy failed. The Church and government, curiously, envisioned a cultural solution to the clergy's social problems: as law after law droned out, "education" would improve the clergy's religious service and raise his status as well. That was a fundamental misconception—in the state's case, a convenient error, since education (on miserly budgets) was cheaper than state subsidies or more basic changes. In any event, even seminary education proved abortive: it was misdirected, functioned poorly, and brought marginal returns to the Church. There were, however, some attempts to alleviate the clergy's economic problems—from Peter's promises to Catherine's land surveys. Yet none of these measures solved the clergy's problems, and some—such as Catherine's schedule on gratuities in 1765—even aggravated them. The failure to reform left a major discrepancy: the authorities had integrated the clergy into their machinery for "modernizing" and regulating society but stopped short of "modernizing" the clergy themselves.

That failure was partly due to the Church. It was now powerless to act, for the Synodal command neatly circumscribed a narrow sphere of authority. The Church's jurisdiction reached only to the clergy; it had no control over the parishioners, especially the obstreperous nobility. Hence it could not sever the clergy's social and economic dependence upon the lay parish; it could not establish a tithe or land fund for clerical support; it could not even assert effective control over appointment and removal. In addition, the hierarchy's policy was distorted by transparent status anxieties. They clumsily tried to segregate the clergy from the "commoners" and to link them with the more respectable circles of society. This status alarm had a profoundly dysfunctional effect on education, culture, and even the "religious reformation" begun from above.

Real power lay with the state, and here the clergy could anticipate little sympathy. True, the government liked pretentious hierarchs even less, and it occasionally interceded (as in 1765) on behalf of the lower white clergy. Increasingly, however, the state's policies were guided by a crude *raison d'état* that afforded no compassion for priests and sacristans. Plagued by financial insolvency, obsessed with Great-Power ambitions, the government steadfastly sought to reduce the cost of supporting the unproductive clergy. The state desperately squeezed its marginal economy for every kopeck; after sequestering the Church's immense wealth in 1764, it had no intention of sharing the spoils even with the nobility, much less the parish clergy.

This wrenching process of social change culminated by the end of the century, after an irregular flow of development. The first period came in Peter's prime, when he dismantled the Muscovite Church and left its administration in chaos; apart from new taxes and some frightening decrees, the parish clergy discerned no great revolution in their lives or service. But after 1720 Peter welded together the elements of a new system—the Synodal command, church schools, the *shtat*, and tighter supervision from above. Yet the new system stalled after Peter's death; it began to function effectively only after mid-century, when the Synodal command enforced the *shtat*, expanded education, excluded poll-tax registrants, and ceased to resist state conscriptions. By the 1780s the results were clear: ubiquitous impoverishment, full staffing, uncontrolled growth in seminary enrollments, and a soslovie that was socially inferior and culturally isolated. Here was a population ready to supply more than enough clergy; here too was a reservoir for new bureaucrats and (in the nineteenth century) their dedicated enemies, the *raznochintsy* intelligentsia.

These social and cultural disorders in the clergy contributed significantly to the weakness of the Church in Imperial Russia. Despite vigorous attempts at reform from above, the Church gradually lost its grip on the emerging society and culture. It made but little headway against the abiding problems of superstition and pagan custom; it likewise failed to stem the seepage of the Old Belief throughout the urban and peasant populations. And, in elite culture, the Church lost the battle almost by default. It produced few intellectual figures of note and lost its former cultural primacy to a Westernized intelligentsia. The clergy also disappeared as a social force at the lowest levels of society. They could no longer depend upon the princely bishop or the customary deference of an Orthodox society for protection and support; in the secular Empire they emerged a weak, tangential group lacking in influence and power. The parish clergy thus did not assume a leadership role, perhaps reshaping or moderating the strained social relations; they could not check the whims of landlords, soften the crunch of serfdom, or even hold the stormy peasants in pious submission. The pervasive social crisis in the white clergy thus had far-reaching implications. It was a principal reason for the ideological and popular weakness of the Church in post-medieval Russia; it deprived the polity of a strong conservative class with a firm hold on the peasantry; and it later produced many disaffected members of the revolutionary intelligentsia that would eventually help destroy Imperial Russia.

Notes, Bibliography,
Abbreviations, Index

Abbreviations

AAE	*Akty, sobrannye v bibliotekakh i arkhivakh Rossiiskoi Imperii Arkheograficheskoiu ekspeditsieiu.* 4 vols. St. Petersburg, 1836.
Agntsev, *IRS*	D. Agntsev. *Istoriia Riazanskoi dukhovnoi seminarii, 1724-1840 gg.* Riazan, 1889.
AI	*Akty istoricheskie.* 5 vols. St. Petersburg, 1841.
Chteniia OIDR	*Chteniia v Imperatorskom obshchestve istorii drevnostei rossiiskikh.* Moscow, 1845-1918.
Chteniia OLDP	*Chteniia v Moskovskom obshchestve liubitelei dukhovnogo prosveshcheniia.* Moscow, 1863-1916.
DRV	*Drevniaia Rossiisskaia vivliofika.* 20 pts. 2nd. ed. Moscow, 1788-91.
GBL	Gosudarstvennaia biblioteka im. V. I. Lenina.
GPB	Gosudarstvennaia publichnaia biblioteka im. M. E. Saltykova-Shchedrina.
IaEV	*Iaroslavskie eparkhial'nye vedomosti.* Iaroslavl, 1861-1917.
IM	G. Kholmogorov and V. Kholmogorov. *Istoricheskie materialy o tserkvakh i selakh XVI-XVIII st.* 11 vols. Moscow, 1881-1911.
IRAN	*Izvestiia Rossisskoi akademii nauk.* St. Petersburg, 1894-1935.
ISOVE	G. V. Dobronravov and V. Berezin. *Istoriko-statisticheskoe opisanie tserkvei i prikhodov Vladimirskoi eparkhii.* 4 vols. Vladimir, 1893-1897.

IZ	*Istoricheskie zapiski.* Moscow, 1937-
KEV	*Kaluzhskie eparkhial'nye vedomosti.* Kaluga, 1862-1917.
Khr. Cht.	*Khristianskoe chtenie.* St. Petersburg, 1821-1918.
Malitskii, *IPE*	N. Malitskii. *Istoriia Pereiaslavskoi eparkhii.* 2 vols. Vladimir, 1905.
Malitskii, *ISS*	N. Malitskii. *Istoriia Suzdal'skoi seminarii.* Vladimir, 1905.
Malitskii, *IVS*	N. Malitskii. *Istoriia Vladimirskoi dukhovnoi seminarii.* 3 vols. Vladimir, 1900-02.
MEV	*Moskovskie eparkhial'nye vedomosti.* Moscow, 1869-1900.
ODBMIu	*Opisanie dokumentov i bumag v arkhive Ministerstva iustitsii.* 21 vols. Moscow, 1869-1916.
ODDS	*Opisanie dokumentov i del, khraniashchikhsia v arkhive Sviateishego Sinoda.* 31 vols. St. Petersburg, 1869-1916.
Opis' DKU	*Opis' dokumentov i del, khraniashchikhsia v arkhive Sviateishego Prav. Sinoda. Dela Komissii dukhovnykh uchilishch.* St. Petersburg, 1910.
PBE	*Pravoslavnaia bogoslovskaia entsiklopediia.* 12 vols. St. Petersburg, 1900-11.
PO	*Pravoslavnoe obozrenie.* Moscow, 1860-91.
PS	*Pravoslavnyi sobesednik.* Kazan, 1855-1917.
PSPR	*Polnoe sobranie postanovlenii i rasporiazhenii po vedomstvu pravoslavnogo ispovedaniia.* 10 vols. St. Petersburg, 1869-1916. Vol. 1 (2nd. ed.); St. Petersburg, 1879.
PSPREA	*Polnoe sobranie postanovlenii i rasporiazhenii po vedomstvu pravoslavnogo ispovedaniia. Tsarstvovanie Imperatritsy Ekateriny Alekseevny.* 3 vols. St. Petersburg, 1910-15.
PSPREP	*Polnoe sobranie postanovlenii i rasporiazhenii po vedomstvu pravoslavnogo ispovedaniia. Tsarstvovanie Elizavety Petrovny.* 4 vols. St. Petersburg, 1899-1911.
PSPRPP	*Polnoe sobranie postanovlenii i rasporiazhenii po vedomstvu pravoslavnogo ispovedaniia. Tsarstvovanie Pavla Petrovicha.* St. Petersburg, 1915.
PSZ	*Polnoe sobranie zakonov Rossiiskoi imperii.* 1st series. 45 vols. St. Petersburg, 1830.

RA	*Russkii arkhiv.* Moscow, 1863-1917.
REV	*Riazanskie eparkhial'nye vedomosti.* Riazan, 1865-1918.
RS	*Russkaia starina.* St. Petersburg, 1870-1918.
RSP	*Rukovodstvo dlia sel'skikh pastyrei.* Kiev, 1860-1917.
SIRIO	*Sbornik Imperatorskogo russkogo istoricheskogo obshchestva.* 148 vols. Moscow, 1867-1916.
Smirnov, *IMA*	S. K. Smirnov. *Istoriia Moskovskoi slavianogreko-latinskoi akademii.* Moscow, 1855.
Smirnov, *ITS*	S. K. Smirnov. *Istoriia Troitskoi lavrskoi seminarii.* Moscow, 1867.
TEV	*Tul'skie eparkhial'nye vedomosti.* Tula, 1862-1917.
TKDA	*Trudy Kievskoi dukhovnoi akademii.* Kiev, 1860-1917.
TIaUAK	*Trudy Iaroslavskoi uchenoi arkhivnoi komissii.* 7 kn. Iaroslavl, 1890-1918.
TRUAK	*Trudy Riazanskoi uchenoi arkhivnoi komissii.* 27 vyp. Riazan, 1885-1916.
TsGADA	Tsentral'nyi gosudarstvennyi arkhiv drevnikh aktov.
TsGIA	Tsentral'nyi gosudarstvennyi istoricheskii arkhiv SSSR.
TsV	*Tserkovnye vedomosti.* St. Petersburg, 1888-1918.
TVEO	*Trudy Vol'nogo ekonomicheskogo obshchestva.* St. Petersburg, 1765-1915.
TVUAK	*Trudy Vladimirskoi uchenoi arkhivnoi komissii.* 18 vols. Vladimir, 1899-1918.
UI	*Universitetskie izvestiia.* Kiev, 1861-1917.
Vremennik OIDR	*Vremennik Obshchestva istorii i drevnostei rossiiskikh.* Moscow, 1845-57.
VEV	*Vladimirskie eparkhial'nye vedomosti.* Vladimir, 1865-1917.
ZhMNP	*Zhurnal Ministerstva narodnogo prosveshcheniia.* St. Petersburg, 1834-1917.
Znamenskii, *DSh*	P. V. Znamenskii. *Dukhovnye shkoly v Rossii do reformy 1808 g.* Kazan, 1881.
Znamenskii, *PDPV*	P. V. Znamenskii. *Prikhodskoe dukhovenstvo v Rossii so vremeni reformy Petra Velikogo.* Kazan, 1873.
Znamenskii, *PDR*	P. V. Znamenskii. *Prikhodskoe dukhovenstvo na Rusi.* Kazan, 1867.

Notes

1. The Parish Clergy

1. On the broader problem of secularization and its meaning, see L. Shiner, "The Concept of Secularization in Empirical Research," *Journal for the Scientific Study of Religion,* 6 (1967):207-220, and K. W. Bolle, "Secularization as a Problem for the History of Religions," *Comparative Studies in Society and History,* 12 (1970):242-259.

2. On the ecclesiastical Great Reforms of the 1860s, see the introductory overviews by A. A. Papkov, *Tserkovno-obshchestvennye voprosy v epokhu Tsaria-Osvoboditelia, 1855-1870 gg.* (St. Petersburg, 1902), and N. Runovskii, *Tserkovno-grazhdanskie zakonopolozheniia otnositel'no pravoslavnogo dukhovenstva v tsarstvovanie Aleksandra II* (Kazan, 1898).

3. *Prikhodskoe dukhovenstvo v Rossii so vremeni reformy Petra Velikogo* (Kazan, 1873); hereafter *PDPV*. In addition to numerous articles, Znamenskii also published a useful study of the clergy in Muscovy: *Prikhodskoe dukhovenstvo na Rusi* (Kazan, 1867); hereafter *PDR*.

4. Ioann Znamenskii's *Polozhenie dukhovenstva v tsarstvovanie Ekateriny II i Pavla* (Kazan, 1880) is a mere summary of legislative materials. More solid research was completed on the Ukraine; see E. Kryzhanovskii, "Ocherki byta malorossiiskogo sel'skogo dukhovenstva v XVIII v.," *Rukovodstvo dlia sel'skikh pastyrei* [hereafter *RSP*], 1861-64.

5. Most important is V. E. Den, "Podatnye elementy sredi dukhovenstva XVIII v.," *Izvestiia Rossiiskoi akademii nauk* [hereafter *IRAN*], 1918, nos. 5-7, 13-14.

6. O. F. Kozlov, "Tserkovnaia reforma pervoi chetverti XVIII v." (Kandidatskaia dissertatsiia, Moscow State University, 1970); for published portions, see his "Reforma tserkvi Petra I i otkliki na nee v russkom obshchestve v pervoi polovine XVIII v.," *Vestnik MGU,* Seriia IX (Istoriia), 1968, no. 5:86-92, and "Dva neizvestnykh sochinenii XVIII v. o Sinode i monastyrskikh dokhodakh," *Sovetskie arkhivy,* 1972, no. 3:76-82.

7. I. Z. Kadson, "Krest'ianskaia voina 1773-1775 gg. v Rossii i tserkov'," (Kandidatskaia dissertatsiia, Leningradskoe otdelenie Instituta istorii, 1963); see idem, "Tserkov'—aktivnyi uchastnik podavleniia krest'ianskogo vosstaniia pod rukovodstvom E. Pugacheva," *Ezhegodnik muzeia istorii religii i ateizma*, 6 (Leningrad, 1962):291-304, and idem, "Vosstanie Pugacheva i raskol," ibid., 4 (Leningrad, 1960):222-238.

8. Leiden, 1964. Znamenskii's work has also been followed in A. A. Kartashev, *Ocherki istorii russkoi tserkvi*, 2 vols. (Paris, 1959), 2:501-542. Other works which touch upon the clergy include Christopher Becker, "The Church School in Tsarist Social and Educational Policy from Peter to the Great Reforms" (Ph.D. diss., Harvard University, 1965); James Cracraft, *The Church Reforms of Peter the Great* (London, 1971).

9. The Synodal archive is in Tsentral'nyi gosudarstvennyi istoricheskii arkhiv SSSR [hereafter TsGIA], *fond* 796; for other pertinent collections in TsGIA, see the bibliography. The decrees of the Synod are available for 1721-41 (*Polnoe sobranie postanovlenii i rasporiazhenii po vedomstvu pravoslavnogo ispovedaniia*, 10 vols. [St. Petersburg, 1869-1916]; hereafter *PSPR*), for 1741-62 (*PSPR. Tsarstvovanie Elizavety Petrovny*, 4 vols. [St. Petersburg, 1899-1911]; hereafter *PSPREP*), for 1762-96 (*PSPR. Tsarstvovanie Ekateriny Alekseevny*, 3 vols. [St. Petersburg, 1910-15]; hereafter *PSPREA*), and for 1796-1801 (*PSPR. Tsarstvovanie Pavla Petrovicha* [St. Petersburg, 1915]; hereafter *PSPRPP*). Summaries and data for approximately one third of the eighteenth-century holdings of the Synodal archive are available in *Opisanie dokumentov i del, khraniashchikhsia v arkhive Sv. Sinoda*, 31 vols. (St. Petersburg, 1869-1917); hereafter *ODDS*. Some of the Synodal decrees, as well as other important legal documents, are to be found in *Polnoe sobranie zakonov Rossiiskoi imperii*, 1st. series, 45 vols. (St. Petersburg, 1830); hereafter *PSZ*. In all the documentary serials (*PSPR, PSPREP, PSPREA, PSPRPP, ODDS*, and *PSZ*), reference is to volume and entry number (thus 24:17675 is volume 24, no. 17675).

Archival notation follows the customary Soviet form: archive, f. (*fond*), op. (*opis'*), g. (*god*), otd. (*otdelenie*), st. (*stol*), k. (*karton*), razd. (*razdel*), d. (*delo*), l., ll. (*list, listy*), ob. (*oborot*). More than a thousand archival *dela* were used in this study, and it is not feasible to cite here the long and cumbersome title of each file. The ornate, prolix, and sometimes misleading titles devised by eighteenth-century clerks would in fact add little to what will already be clear from the text or note about the nature of the document or file (e.g., petition from a priest in Vladimir in 1745; student register for Riazan seminary in 1791; judicial file for the defrocking of a Suzdal deacon in 1768).

10. Tsentral'nyi gosudarstvennyi arkhiv drevnikh aktov [hereafter TsGADA], f. 1183; other useful materials in TsGADA include Kollegiia ekonomii (f. 280) and Patriarshii kazennyi prikaz (f. 235). For an institutional history of the Moscow Synodal Chancellery, see T. V. Barsov, *Sinodal'nye uchrezhdeniia prezhnego vremeni* (St. Petersburg, 1897) and "Moskovskaia Sv. Sinoda kontora," *Moskovskie tserkovnye vedomosti*, 1904, nos. 7, 9, 17, 21, 23, 28, 31; valuable extracts from the archive are in N. A. Skvortsov, *Materialy po Moskve i moskovskoi eparkhii za XVIII v.*, 2 vols. (Moscow, 1911-14).

11. This was partly due to state law; see, for example, the decree of 1750 that forbade the use of ecclesiastical attire in comic theatre (*PSPREP*, 3:1191).

12. Diocesan archives contain much valuable, unique information. For example, an inventory of the Vladimir consistory indicates records on episcopal decrees, monastery affairs, administrative personnel, clerical ordinations and appointments, criminal investigations, education, and Old Believers (N. Malitskii, "Vladimirskie konsistorskie arkhivy XVIII v.," *Vladimirskie eparkhial'nye vedomosti* [hereafter *VEV*], 1903, no. 21:584-586; S. I. Ivashkin, ed., *Gosudarstvennyi arkhiv Vladimirskoi oblasti; putevoditel'* [Vladimir, 1959]).

13. The diocesan serials used here include the following: *Iaroslavskie eparkhial'nye vedomosti* (Iaroslavl, 1862-1917; hereafter *IaEV*); *Kaluzhskie eparkhial'nye vedomosti* (Kaluga, 1862-1917; hereafter *KEV*); *Moskovskie eparkhial'nye vedomosti* (Moscow, 1869-1900; hereafter *MEV*); *Riazanskie eparkhial'nye vedomosti* (Riazan, 1865-1918; hereafter *REV*); *Tul'skie eparkhial'nye vedomosti* (Tula, 1862-1917; hereafter *TEV*); *Vladimirskie eparkhial'nye vedomosti* (Vladimir, 1865-1917; hereafter *VEV*).

14. For an index to the publications of the provincial archival commissions, see O. I. Shvedova, "Ukazatel' 'Trudov' gubernskikh uchenykh arkhivnykh komissii i otdel'nykh ikh izdanii," *Arkheograficheskii ezhegodnik za 1957 god* (Moscow, 1958), pp. 377-433.

15. Moscow diocese is exhaustively treated in N. I. Rozanov, *Istoriia moskovskogo eparkhial'nogo upravleniia*, 3 vols. (Moscow, 1869-71). A similar work on Pereslavl diocese is N. V. Malitskii's *Istoriia pereiaslavskoi eparkhii*, 2 vols. (Vladimir, 1912-18); hereafter Malitskii, *IPE*. Useful and diverse information can also be gleaned from the various seminary histories, which are usually based on intensive research in diocesan archives.

16. For details and maps, see I. M. Pokrovskii, *Russkie eparkhii v XVI-XIX vv.*, 2 vols. (Kazan, 1897-1913); a detailed breakdown of the 1784 reforms is in *TsGIA*, f. 796, op. 69, g. 1788, d. 304.

17. See K. I. Arsen'ev, *Statisticheskii ocherk Rossii* (St. Petersburg, 1848), pp. 117-135; V. E. Den, *Naselenie Rossii po piatoi revizii* (Moscow, 1902); and V. M. Kabuzan, *Narodonaselenie Rossii v XVIII-pervoi polovine XIX v.* (Moscow, 1963), pp. 107-116.

18. Rostov was famous for its churches, as a popular proverb of the seventeenth century attests: "Satan went to Rostov, but fled from the crosses" (L. N. Pushkarev, "Poslovitsy v zapisiakh XVII v. kak istochnik po izucheniiu obshchestvennykh otnoshenii," *Istoricheskie zapiski* [hereafter *IZ*], 92 [1973], pp. 317-318). Vladimir, once the political center of the northeast, so declined in later times that by the seventeenth century it could no longer afford even to maintain the famous cathedrals, Uspenskii and Dmitrovskii, that adorned the city center (see G. Chizhev, "Kratkii ocherk goroda Vladimira-na-Kliaz'me," *VEV*, 1868, no. 14:693-694).

19. See, for instance, the case of a Vladimir church that declined for lack of land and parishioners and finally closed in 1787 (N. Malitskii, "Khristorozhdestvenskaia tserkov' v g. Vladimire," *VEV*, 1905, no. 7:204).

20. V. M. Kabuzan, *Izmeneniia v razmeshchenii naseleniia Rossii v XVIII-*

pervoi polovine XIX v. (Moscow, 1971), p. 95. By contrast, the clergy and their families (like the nobility) constituted but a small part of the population—approximately 1 percent. The clergy themselves numbered some 3,000-4,000 in each of the central dioceses (in the 1780s) and served several hundred thousand male souls. For data see Table 17 below and TsGIA, f. 796, op. 64, g. 1783, d. 580, ll. 1-284.

21. The non-blacksoil zone (or the central industrial zone) customarily includes Moscow, Vladimir, Iaroslavl, Kaluga, and some areas not included in this study; parts of Tula and Riazan, however, belong to the blacksoil zone. See V. I. Semevskii, *Krest'iane v tsarstvovanie Ekateriny II*, 2 vols. (St. Petersburg, 1901-03), 1:24-28. However, each province, even each uezd (district) included soil of diverse quality; see, for example, the description of soil variations in Vladimir uezd in "Otvety, kasaiushchiesia do zemlevladeniia na ekonomicheskie voprosy, o uezde goroda Volodimira," *Trudy Vol'nogo ekonomicheskogo obshchestva* [hereafter *TVEO*], 12 (St. Petersburg, 1769): 97; see the similar reports in the "Ekonomicheskie otvety" for Riazan and Pereslavl (ibid., 7:50-51, 83).

22. M. M. Shcherbatov, *Neizdannye proizvedeniia* (Moscow, 1935), p. 6.

23. Arcadius Kahan, "Natural Calamities and Their Effects upon the Food Supply in Russia," *Jahrbücher für Geschichte Osteuropas*, 16 (1968): 353-377.

24. See Iu. V. Got'e, *Zamoskovnyi krai v XVII veke* (2nd. ed.; Moscow, 1937).

25. Kabuzan, *Izmeneniia*, pp. 16-17; Den, *Naselenie*, 1:6.

26. One dessiatine (*desiatina*) equals 2.7 acres. In Moscow, for example, the average allotment declined from 5.1 dessiatines in 1678 to 2.4 dessiatines in 1795 (see Ia. E. Vodarskii, "Kolichestvo zemli i pashni na dushu muzhskogo pola v tsentral'no-promyshlennom raione v XVII-XIX vv.," *Ezhegodnik agrarnoi istorii vostochnoi evropy za 1965 g.* [Moscow, 1970], p. 239). For a convenient table on allotments, see N. L. Rubinshtein, *Sel'skoe khoziaistvo vo vtoroi polovine XVIII v.* (Moscow, 1957), pp. 209-210.

27. Land shortage was hardly the only factor; poor technology and mismanagement were also important; for the case of monastery economies, see A. M. Borisov, "Krizis tserkovnogo i monastyrskogo zemlevladeniia i khoziaistva v 40-60-kh godakh XVIII v.," *Istoriia SSSR*, 1968, no. 3:142-151.

28. I. I. Lepekhin, *Dnevnye zapiski puteshestviia po raznym provintsiiam Rossiiskogo gosudarstva*, 4 vols. (2nd. ed.; St. Petersburg, 1795-1805), 1:6.

29. "Otvety . . . Volodimira," *TVEO*, 12:112; similar complaints were registered in the "Ekonomicheskie otvety" for Riazan, Pereslavl, and Kaluga (ibid., 7:75, 105; 11:118).

30. Semevskii, *Krest'iane*, 1:26-27; Akademiia nauk SSSR, *Ocherki istorii SSSR; Rossiia vo vtoroi polovine XVIII v.* (Moscow, 1956), p. 64.

31. For example, Pereslavl-Zalesskii uezd had a peasant population that was primarily serf (51 percent), but also included state peasants (12 percent) and church peasants (37 percent). For a comprehensive picture, see the corrected first census in V. M. Kabuzan and M. M. Shchepukova, "Tabel' pervoi revizii narodonaseleniia Rossii, 1719-1727 gg.," *Istoricheskii arkhiv* [hereafter *IA*], 1959, no. 3:126-165.

32. Iu. R. Klokman, *Sotsial'no-ekonomicheskaia istoriia russkogo goroda;*

vtoraia polovina XVIII v. (Moscow, 1967), pp. 31-32, 207.

33. Akademiia nauk SSSR, *Istoriia Moskvy,* 6 vols. (Moscow, 1952-59), 2:143-167, 307, 475-529; Klokman, p. 210.

34. For typical descriptions, see Klokman, pp. 212-221 and passim.

35. The ubiquitous citation of factories (*fabriki*) is misleading; the term was applied virtually to any enterprise with a machine, even though few individuals were employed and production was negligible. See, for example, the data on labor in the factories of Vladimir province in 1790 in R. G. Ryndziunskii, *Gorodskoe grazhdanstvo doreformennoi Rossii* (Moscow, 1958), p. 27.

36. L. K. Bakmeister, *Topograficheskie izvestiia, sluzhashchiia dlia polnogo geograficheskogo opisaniia Rossiiskoi imperii,* 1 vol. in 4 pts. (Moscow, 1771-74), 2:139-141; see the similar picture of Vladimir, Murom, and Pereslavl-Zalesskii, all based on survey data compiled in the 1760s (1:98; 2:120, 131). For data on the amount of land cultivated by townspeople, see L. M. Maksimovich, *Novyi i polnyi geograficheskii slovar' Rossiiskogo gosudarstva,* 6 vols. (Moscow, 1788-89), 1:221, 3:258, 4:70, and passim.

37. Klokman, p. 155.

38. Bakmeister, 1:7.

39. On Ivanovo, see K. P. Shchepetov, *Krepostnoe pravo v votchinakh Sheremetevykh (1708-1885 gg.)* (Moscow, 1947); for other important commercial and industrial villages noted by contemporary observers, see Bakmeister, 2:133-134; Lepekhin, 1:47-50; and Maksimovich, 4: prilozhenie.

40. For example, Rostov had only six stone buildings out of a total of 1,110; even the prosperous Tula had but 100 out of 3,500 (Maksimovich, 4:195, 5:352).

2. Parish Clergy in a Secular Empire

1. *Cambridge Modern History,* 14 vols. (Cambridge, 1902-12), 6:628. On the evolution of absolutism, see the stimulating article by Marc Raeff, "The Well-Ordered Police State and the Development of Modernity in Seventeenth- and Eighteenth-Century Europe," *American Historical Review,* 80 (1975): 1221-1243. On the new political secularity, see the discussion and references in the following: B. Groethuysen, "Secularism," *Encyclopedia for the Social Sciences,* 15 vols. (New York, 1930-34), 13:631-645; G. Gebhardt, *Handbuch der deutschen Geschichte,* 4 vols. (8th ed.; Stuttgart, 1954-59), 2:68-71, 168-172; Fritz Hartung, *Deutsche Verfassungsgeschichte von 15. Jahrhunderts bis zur Gegenwart* (7th ed.; Stuttgart, 1959), pp. 70-73; P. V. Verkhovskoi, *Uchrezhdenie dukhovnoi kollegii i dukhovnyi reglament,* 2 vols. (Rostov, 1916), 1:247-264.

2. M. Cherniavsky, *Tsar and People* (New Haven, 1961), pp. 44-100.

3. See "Puteshestvie antiokhskogo patriarkha Makariia v Rossiiu v polovine XVII veka," *Chteniia v obshchestve istorii i drevnostei rossiiskikh* [hereafter *Chteniia OIDR*], 1897, 4:158 and passim.

4. *PSZ,* 2:826; on the Law Code of 1649, see M. Arkhangel'skii, *O sobornom ulozhenii Tsaria Alekseia Mikhailovicha 1649 g. v otnoshenii k pravoslavnoi russkoi tserkvi* (St. Petersburg, 1881), and M. Cherniavsky, "The Old Believers and the New Religion," *Slavic Review,* 25 (1966):12.

5. Cherniavsky, *Tsar and People*, pp. 72, 90-91; N. I. Pavlenko, "Idei absoliutizma v zakonodatel'stve XVIII v.," in Akademiia nauk SSSR, *Absoliutizm v Rossii* (Moscow, 1964), pp. 381-427; idem, "Petr I (K izucheniiu sotsial'no-politicheskikh vzgliadov)," in *Rossiia v period reform Petra I* (Moscow, 1973), pp. 46-48, 56-60. For the intellectual sources of Peter's principal political theoretician, Feofan Prokopovich, see G. Gurvich, *"Pravda voli monarshei" Feofana Prokopovicha i ee zapadnoevropeiskie istochniki* (Iur'ev, 1915).

6. See Cherniavsky, "The Old Believers"; R. O. Crummey, *The Old Believers and the World of Anti-Christ* (Madison, 1970); N. N. Pokrovskii, *Antifeodal'nyi protest uralo-sibirskikh staroobriadtsev v XVIII v.* (Novosibirsk, 1974), pp. 34-66.

7. *PSZ*, 5:3006, 6:3485.

8. N. A. Voskresenskii, ed., *Zakonodatel'nye akty Petra I* (Moscow and Leningrad, 1945), p. 148. For Peter's religious views, see the following: Smolitsch, *Geschichte*, pp. 66-76; R. Stupperich, *Staatsgedanke und Religionspolitik Peters des Grössen* (Königsberg, 1936); R. Wittram, *Peter I: Czar und Kaiser*, 2 vols. (Göttingen, 1964), 1:106-111, 2:170-194.

9. See Peter's Ecclesiastical Regulation (*PSPR*, 1:1; also translated into English by Alexander Muller as *The Spiritual Regulation of Peter the Great* [Seattle, 1972]) and Catherine's decree on church landholding (*PSPREA*, 1:37). For further examples, see Pavlenko, "Idei absoliutizma," and I. I. Ditiatin, *Stat'i po istorii russkogo prava* (St. Petersburg, 1896), pp. 593-594.

10. Pavlenko, "Idei absoliutizma," p. 392; Raeff, "The Well-Ordered Police State," pp. 1326-1329.

11. See A. Zav'ialov, *Vopros o tserkovnykh imeniiakh pri Imp. Ekaterine II* (St. Petersburg, 1900).

12. *PSPR*, 1:1; *PSZ*, 6:6506.

13. Verkhovskoi, 1:684; see also D. W. Treadgold, *The West in Russia and China*, 2 vols. (Cambridge, 1973), 1:83; G. V. Florovskii, *Puti russkogo bogosloviia* (Paris, 1937), pp. 82-83; Akademiia nauk SSSR, *Ocherki istorii SSSR; Rossiia v pervoi chetverti XVIII v.* (Moscow, 1954), pp. 277-278. Studies of archival materials on specific issues, in contrast to the purely juridical analyses, have suggested a revision of the traditional conception of the Church after 1721; see the analysis of I. A. Bulygin on monastic landholding ("Tserkovnaia reforma Petra I," *Voprosy istorii*, 1974, no. 5:74-93) and the remarks by Pokrovskii on Church-state conflicts over the Old-Believer question (*Antifeodal'nyi protest*, pp. 8-10, passim).

14. See Gregory L. Freeze, "Counter-Reform in the Church: Pobedonostsev and the Church Hierarchs" (Paper presented to the Annual Convention of the American Historical Association, Washington, D.C., December, 1976).

15. Verkhovskoi, 1:607.

16. Ivan Perov, *Eparkhial'nye uchrezhdeniia v russkoi tserkvi v XVI i XVII vekakh* (Riazan, 1882), pp. 155-163.

17. See, for example, such standard works as V. O. Kliuchevskii, "Istoriia soslovii v Rossii," *Sochineniia*, 8 vols. (Moscow, 1956-59), 6:276-466, and M. Vladimirskii-Budanov, *Gosudarstvo i narodnoe obrazovanie v XVIII v.* (Iaroslavl, 1874), p. 85, passim.

18. N. Lazarevskii, "Sosloviia," *Entsiklopedicheskii slovar' Brokgauza-Efrona*, 86 vols. (St. Petersburg, 1890-1907), 60:911-913.

19. For example, in 1725 Feofan Prokopovich used the term *soslovie* to refer to the entire population "of every rank" (F. Prokopovich, *Sochineniia* [Moscow, Leningrad, 1961], p. 128). A document from 1733, similarly, used "the entire Christian *soslovie*" to describe the Church as a corporate group (TsGIA, f. 796, op. 14, g. 1733, d. 206, l. 1).

20. For examples of *dukhovnyi chin* and *sviashchennyi chin*, see: TsGIA, f. 796, op. 14, g. 1733, d. 36, l. 2; *PSPREP*, 1:162; TsGIA, f. 796, op. 51, g. 1770, d. 470, l. 35 ob.

21. See F. Kaiser, "Der europäische Anteil an der russischen Rechtsterminologie der petrinischen Zeit," *Forschungen zur osteuropäischen Geschichte*, 10 (1965):75-333.

22. For the decision to omit the clergy, see S. M. Troitskii, *Russkii absoliutizm i dvorianstvo v XVIII v.* (Moscow, 1974), pp. 64-65. By the mid-nineteenth century many clergy wanted the state to define its status relative to the Table of Ranks, hoping thereby to obtain the corresponding honors, legal rights, and pensions; see, for example, the proposal of the Kiev committee on reform in the clergy in TsGIA, f. 804, op. 1, razd. 1, d. 59, ll. 53-59.

23. The mechanics of bureaucratic correspondence reinforced this transference of basic terms; the Senate or appropriate government organ ordinarily heard out the Synodal memorandum or decree and then recopied it as part of the introduction to its own resolution.

24. Ia. P. Shakhovskoi, *Zapiski* (St. Petersburg, 1872), pp. 40-41.

25. See Pokrovskii, *Antifeodal'nyi protest*, p. 28.

26. For a typical case where a runaway priest's son in Suzdal was returned to the Synodal command, see TsGADA, f. 1183, op. 1, g. 1734, d. 322, ll. 1-4.

27. See, for instance, *PSPR*, 2:466 and *PSZ*, 11:8481.

28. On the Church's role in the Legislative Commission, see I. M. Pokrovskii, *Ekaterinskaia komissiia o sostavlenii novogo ulozheniia i tserkovnye voprosy o nei (1766-1771 gg.)* (Kazan, 1910) and B. V. Titlinov, *Gavriil Petrov, mitropolit novgorodskii i sankt-peterburgskii (1730-1801 gg.)* (St. Petersburg, 1916), pp. 165-266.

29. Another possible factor was Catherine's low regard for canon law, which she traced to slavish "southern" Roman origins (Rukopisnyi otdel, Gosudarstvennaia biblioteka im. V. I. Lenina [hereafter GBL], f. 222 [N. I. Panin], k. XVII, d. 1, l. 21 ob.). I am grateful to Marc Raeff for the use of his microfilm of this last archival item; for the negative import of Catherine's remark, see Marc Raeff, "The Empress Reads the Vinerian Professor," *Oxford Slavonic Papers*, 7 (1974):18-41.

30. *Sbornik Imperatorskogo russkogo istoricheskogo obshchestva*, 148 vols. (St. Petersburg, 1867-1916), 36:185-189; hereafter *SIRIO*.

31. William Tooke, *View of the Russian Empire*, 3 vols. (2nd. ed.; London, 1800), 2:114-115.

32. On Dubianskii, see V. Kolachev, *O polozhenii pridvornogo dukhovenstva v XVIII v.* (Petrograd, 1914), p. 16. For a chance admission of ownership of house-serfs, see the complaint by a Moscow sacristan that his "serf,

Petr Iakimov, ran away after stealing my possessions" ("Opisanie dokumentov sysknogo prikaza," *Opisanie dokumentov i bumag Ministerstva iustitsii*, 21 vols. [St. Petersburg, 1869-1916], 4:84; hereafter *ODBMIu*). For a report of a Moscow priest who sold a serf in 1766 for ten rubles, see Rozanov, *Istoriia*, 2, pt. 2:n.465.

33. See the 1729 case involving a Vladimir priest who sold three poll-tax registrants (formerly in the clerical estate) to a landlord for twenty rubles in *ODDS*, 9:228; a similar case in 1731 ended in the suspension of a priest making such a sale (*ODDS*, 11:238).

34. *PSPREP*, 2:810; *PSZ*, 12:9106.

35. *SIRIO*, 43:49 (Synodal proposal) and 417 (Gavriil's proposal).

36. Semevskii, *Krest'iane*, 1:5.

37. M. N. Tikhomirov and P. P. Epifanov, eds., *Sobornoe ulozhenie 1649 g.* (Moscow, 1961), ch. 19, arts. 3; reiterated in the Moscow Church Council of 1667 (*PSZ*, 1:412).

38. *ODDS*, 23:503.

39. Rozanov, *Istoriia*, 2, pt. 2:341-342. Loans by clergy, as one might expect, were not common; a 1732 list shows they held only 4 percent of all loans registered (representing 1 percent of the value of all loans); see N. I. Pavlenko, "O rostovshchichestve dvorian v XVIII v.," in *Dvorianstvo i krepostnoi stroi Rossii v XVIII v.* (Moscow, 1975), p. 269.

40. TsGIA, f. 796, op. 50, g. 1769, d. 271, ll. 20 ob.-23 ob.

41. *O dolzhnostiakh presviterov prikhodskikh ot slova Bozhiia, sobrannykh pravil i uchitelei tserkvi sostavlennoe* (St. Petersburg, 1776), p. 101.

42. Whereas a priest might be demoted to the rank of churchman, for the same offense a churchman was expelled from the clerical estate and sent into the army or serfdom; see, for example, a case in Vladimir in 1781 (TsGIA, f. 796, op. 62, g. 1781, d. 426, ll. 1-54) and another in Moscow in 1765 (Skvortsov, *Materialy*, 1:56-57).

43. Znamenskii, *PDPV*, p. 5.

44. *PSZ*, 2:1325.

45. *PSZ*, 4:2015.

46. See Kliuchevskii, *Sochineniia*, 4:127-146, 7:318-402.

47. *PSZ*, 6:3481; *ODDS*, 1: prilozhenie 23; *PSZ*, 6:3492.

48. *ODDS*, 1:275 and prilozhenie 23; *PSZ*, 6:3802.

49. *ODDS*, 1:275 and prilozhenie 23; *PSPR*, 1:175.

50. See, for instance, a Senate decree of 1744 in *PSZ*, 12:8981.

51. *PSZ*, 14:10650.

52. "Nakaznaia gramota Mitropolita Makariia po stoglavnomu soboru," *Pravoslavnyi sobesednik* [hereafter *PS*], 1863, no. 1:88; Perov, pp. 155-163.

53. *PSZ*, 4:1818, 1876; M. Gorchakov, *Monastyrskii prikaz* (St. Petersburg, 1868), pp. 123-128. When the clergy's former judicial privilege was restored, some bishops complained that state officials were so accustomed to exercising control over the clergy that it was difficult to secure clerical rights (*ODDS*, 1:321, 531).

54. *PSPR*, 1:76; *PSZ*, 6:3761; *ODDS*, 1:310.

55. *PSPR*, 1:150. For local reports of abuse and violation, see *ODDS*,

1:321, 531; *PSPR*, 1:213, 215; 2:544. For examples of vigorous attempts by the Synod to safeguard clerical privilege, see *PSPR*, 1:312; 2:532; 3:996.

56. *ODDS*, 11:109. For further cases, see TsGIA, f. 796, op. 48, g. 1757, d. 119, ll. 1-16 and TsGADA, f. 1183, op. 1, g. 1751, d. 287, ll. 1-6.

57. TsGADA, f. 1183, op. 1, g. 1758, d. 204, ll. 1-50; TsGIA, f. 796, op. 39, g. 1758, d. 310, ll. 1-9. A similar incident, likewise ending with an apparent defeat for the Church, occurred in Vladimir uezd (TsGADA, f. 1183, op. 1, g. 1758, d. 297, ll. 1-6).

58. See, for example, *ODDS*, 7:276, 8:399, and *PSPR*, 6:2240.

59. *PSZ*, 11:8360; *PSPREP*, 1:152; 3:980.

60. *PSPREP*, 2:780; *PSZ*, 12:9079.

61. *PSZ*, 14:10293, 10650.

62. At most, the Synod asked for an oral description of the alleged offenses but made no attempt to investigate the case (see *PSPR*, 5:1514).

63. See the curious exchange in *ODDS*, 12:54 and *PSPR*, 7:2550.

64. TsGADA, f. 1183, op. 1, g. 1746, d. 242, ll. 1-6.

65. See N. Novombergskii, *Slovo i delo gosudarevo*, 2 vols. (Tomsk, 1909-11) and N. B. Golikova, "Organy politicheskogo syska i ikh razvitie v XVII-XVIII vv.," in *Absoliutizm v Rossii*, pp. 243-280.

66. *ODDS*, 2, pt. 1:211.

67. See the decrees of 1722 and 1733 in *PSPR*, 2:547, 8:2715.

68. The priest was flogged for this stunt (Malitskii, *IPE*, 1:74-75).

69. For example, one priest detained by the consistory of Vladimir diocese in a witchcraft case declared word and deed in hopes of better justice; after an interrogation by the Secret Chancellery, he was promptly returned to the consistory (TsGADA, f. 1183, op. 1, g. 1760, d. 39, ll. 1-18).

70. *PSZ*, 15:11445; Rozanov, *Istoriia*, 2, pt. 2:127-128.

71. *PSZ*, 17:12606.

72. TsGIA, f. 796, op. 71, g. 1790, d. 386, ll. 1-159.

73. *PSZ*, 18:12909, 19:13609.

74. Pavlenko, "Petr I," pp. 42, 60-82.

75. See S. M. Troitskii, "Finansovaia politika russkogo absoliutizma vo vtoroi polovine XVII-XVIII v.," in *Absoliutizm v Rossii*, pp. 281-319.

76. Znamenskii, *PDR*, pp. 101-113.

77. *PSZ*, 4:2011, 2130, 2263.

78. Gorchakov, pp. 224-225.

79. See the collective petitions and the reports on the clergy of Suzdal (*ODDS*, 1:369), Kostroma (*ODDS*, 1:394; *PSPR*, 1:155), Riazan (*ODDS*, 2, pt. 1:211; pt. 2:838), Moscow (*ODDS*, 2, pt. 2:1236), Voronezh (*ODDS*, 2, pt. 1:261), Tver (*ODDS*, 2, pt. 1:345), and Rostov (*ODDS*, 6:244).

80. Gorchakov, p. 225.

81. *ODDS*, 4:132.

82. After Peter's death the distressed condition of the general population impelled the government to suspend and reduce tax levies; see E. V. Anisimov, "Materialy Komissii D. M. Golitsyna o podati (1727-1730 gg.)," *IZ*, 91 (1973):338-352, and the literature cited therein.

83. [F. C. Weber], "Zapiski Vebera o Petre Velikom i ego preobrazovaniiakh," *Russkii arkhiv* [hereafter *RA*], 1872, p. 1131.

84. I. Chistovich, *Feofan Prokopovich i ego vremia* (St. Petersburg, 1868), p. 189; for a similar report by the bishop of Rostov, see *ODDS*, 8:244.

85. *PSPR*, 8:2685.

86. *PSPR*, 6:1984; *ODDS*, 6:282. On the burden of quartering, see Klokman, p. 69. Demands by the laity that clergy bear civic responsibilities were most intense in Moscow, where some clergy owned several buildings; in 1738 Anna declared that such wealthy priests should indeed share these burdens (*PSPR*, 10:3230).

87. Tikhomirov, *Sobornoe ulozhenie 1649 g.*, ch. 14, art. 10.

88. P. N. Miliukov, *Gosudarstvennoe khoziaistvo Rossii v pervoi chetverti XVIII v. i reforma Petra Velikogo* (2nd. ed.; St. Petersburg, 1905), pp. 457-461; on the duties of Swedish clergy, see M. Roberts, "The Swedish Church," in *Sweden's Age of Greatness*, ed. M. Roberts (New York, 1973), p. 134.

89. V. A. Petrov, "K voprosu o roli dukhovenstva v bor'be s antifeodal'nymi vosstaniiami (o nerazyskannom ukaze 1708 g.)," *IA*, 1955, no. 4:198-199.

90. Kozlov, "Tserkovnaia reforma," pp. 123-128.

91. *PSZ*, 6:4012; a copy of the original is in GBL, Otdel redkikh knig, attached to *Prisiaga sviashchennicheskaia* (Moscow, 1722).

92. *PSPR*, 2:596; see also ibid, 4:1350. For a further instance of Feofan Prokopovich's intertwining of faith and politics, see the discussion of his *Pervoe uchenie otrokom* in James Cracraft, "Feofan Prokopovich," in *The Eighteenth Century in Russia*, ed. J. G. Garrard (Oxford, 1973), pp. 95-101.

93. *Prisiaga khotiashchim vzyti na stepen' sviashchenstva* (Moscow, 1679), pp. 1-18.

94. *Prisiaga sviashchennicheskaia* (Moscow, 1722), p. 1.

95. TsGIA, f. 796, op. 18, g. 1737, d. 127, l. 3; *Prisiaga sviashchennicheskaia* (Moscow, 1747); a late eighteenth-century oath is appended to *Sokrashchennyi katekhizis dlia sviashchenno-i-terkovnosluzhitelei* (Moscow, 1777), pp. 47-47 ob. For an interesting case where a cleric demanded and received a reward for informing on the political misconduct of a retired officer, see *SIRIO*, 101:51-52.

96. *PSPR*, 1:105.

97. *PSPR*, 2:865; *PSZ*, 6:4113; *PSPR*, 2:880.

98. *ODDS*, 3:590; see also the cases of individual priests in Kaluga and Pereslavl who failed to inform in *ODDS*, 1:208; 2, pt. 2:1110.

99. *PSZ*, 4:1908; see also Rozanov, *Istoriia*, 1:108-109; 3, pt. 1:120.

100. *PSPR*, 3:1143; the decree was reiterated in 1724 (*PSPR*, 4:1218).

101. Rozanov, *Istoriia*, 1:n.291. In a case on Vladimir, the clergy who failed to comply were fined, but the authorities later returned the assessments (*ODDS*, 10:112).

102. *PSPR*, 5:1656, 1712; *ODDS*, 6:21.

103. *Prisiaga khotiashchim vzyti na stepen' sviashchenstva; Akty istoricheskie* [hereafter *AI*], 5 vols. (St. Petersburg, 1841), 5:244; *PSZ*, 3:1612.

104. *PSZ*, 5:3168, 3183; see also Rozanov, *Istoriia*, 1:106-108 and *ODDS*, 1:35, 180, 260.

105. Pokrovskii, *Antifeodal'nyi protest*, pp. 42-66.

106. *PSPR*, 2:453, 454, 721; this was reaffirmed in 1726 (ibid., 5:1730).

107. *PSZ*, 5:3169.

108. *PSZ*, 6:3515; *ODDS*, 2, pt. 1:91, 528; 4:52; *PSPR*, 5:1565.

109. For explicit authorization by the Synod to sign for illiterate parishioners, see the Novgorod case of 1722 in *ODDS*, 2, pt. 2:873 and *PSPR*, 2:768.

110. Pokrovskii, *Antifeodal'nyi protest*, pp. 25-27.

111. TsGIA, f. 796, op. 56, g. 1775, d. 87, ll. 2 ob.-5. For other instances of forged documents, see the case of a Riazan priest in 1746 (TsGADA, f. 1183, op. 1, g. 1746, d. 380, l. 1) and a Kolomna priest in 1770 (*ODDS*, 50:392).

112. See Robert E. Jones, *The Emancipation of the Russian Nobility, 1762-1785* (Princeton, 1973).

113. *PSPR*, 6:2122 and 8:2685.

114. See Troitskii, "Finansovaia politika," and idem, *Finansovaia politika russkogo absoliutizma v XVIII v.* (Moscow, 1966).

115. The Synod won formal annulment of the civic duties in 1742, but some city authorities ignored the new law, provoking indignant protests from the clergy. For the cases of Moscow in 1769 and Riazan in 1783, see *PSPREA*, 1:477 and TsGIA, f. 796, op. 64, g. 1783, d. 219, ll. 4, 7-8; for the Synod's fight to obtain and secure the privilege, see *ODDS*, 6:282. Because townsmen continued to violate this privilege, Emperor Paul in 1798 reaffirmed that "the personal dwellings of ordained clergy and churchmen are free from levies and police duties, with the exception, however, of those which are rented out or bring in an income" (*PSPRPP*, 304).

116. See Pokrovskii, *Antifeodal'nyi protest*, pp. 9-10, 205-207, 286.

117. *PSPREA*, 1:375, 2:1002.

118. See Gregory L. Freeze, "P. A. Valuyev and the Politics of Church Reform (1861-62)," forthcoming in *Slavonic and East European Review*.

119. See N. F. Demidova, "Biurokratizatsiia gosudarstvennogo apparata absoliutizma XVII-XVIII vv.," in *Absoliutizm v Rossii*, pp. 206-242, and idem, "Prikaznye liudi XVII v. (Sotsial'nyi sostav i istochniki formirovaniia)," *IZ*, 90 (1972):332-354.

120. See M. M. Bogoslovskii, *Oblastnaia reforma Petra Velikogo* (Moscow, 1902), pp. 270-281, and Iu. V. Got'e, *Istoriia oblastnogo upravleniia v Rossii ot Petra I do Ekateriny II*, 2 vols. (Moscow, 1913-41), 1:285-290.

121. *ODDS*, 1:300; 2, pt. 1:378; 2, pt. 2:1089; *PSPR*, 2:624, 648; for data on the numbers of clerical children in the cipher schools (where they composed 46 percent of all those enrolled), see TsGIA, f. 796, op. 16, g. 1735, d. 382, l. 5; *ODDS*, 15:prilozhenie 22.

122. *PSPR*, 1:1; Muller, *Spritual Regulation*, p. 41.

123. *PSZ*, 5:2978.

124. *ODDS*, 1:628; *PSPR*, 4:1209.

125. *PSZ*, 7:4499; *PSPR*, 4:1252; *ODDS*, 4:220.

126. Troitskii, *Russkii absoliutizm*, pp. 213-214.

127. *ODDS*, 12:76; *PSPR*, 7:2552, 3237; *PSPREA*, 1:62, 131.

128. *ODDS*, 7:54, 8:39, 9:413, 50:91; *PSPR*, 5:1910, 6:2106, 2263; *PSPREP*, 4:1465, 1468.

129. TsGIA, f. 796, op. 36, g. 1755, d. 150, ll. 1-2; *PSPR*, 9:2933.

130. *PSZ*, 20:14831. This decree followed a government study of the clerical estate; the administration required 9,688 seminarians and found that 27,949 educated clerical youths were idle (Titlinov, *Gavriil*, p. 539). Subsequently, during the conscription of 1784, Catherine ordered the release of seminarians "inclined" toward secular service (*PSZ*, 22:15978).

131. K. Nadezhdin, "Materialy dlia istorii Vladimirskoi seminarii," *VEV*, 1877, no. 20:1021.

132. Titlinov, *Gavriil*, p. 540.

133. Rozanov, *Istoriia*, 3, pt. 1:46-47.

134. Walter Pintner, "The Social Characteristics of the Early Nineteenth-Century Russian Bureaucracy," *Slavic Review*, 29 (1970):435. Mr. Pintner has kindly shared unpublished data showing that clerical youths in Vladimir composed 34 percent of the officials in the *gubernskoe pravlenie*, 43 percent in the *kazennaia palata*, and 34 percent in the *sudebnaia palata*. According to the data, the proportion of clerical offspring was roughly similar in Kursk and Vologda and somewhat less in Penza and Kostroma.

135. I. Prilezhaev, "Dukhovnaia shkola i seminaristy v istorii russkoi nauki i obrazovaniia," *Khristianskoe chtenie* [hereafter *Khr. cht.*], 1879, tom 2:169; see also S. K. Smirnov, *Istoriia troitskoi lavrskoi seminarii* [hereafter *ITS*] (Moscow, 1867), pp. 520-537.

136. *PSPREA*, 3:1318.

137. *PSZ*, 22:16342.

138. *Opis' dokumentov i del, khraniashchikhsia v arkhive Sv. Prav. Sinoda. Dela Komissii dukhovnykh uchilishch* [hereafter *Opis' DKU*] (St. Petersburg, 1910), p. 2.

139. The term "clerical children" includes the progeny of both ordained clergy and churchmen; lacking the protection of sacred ordination, the children of ordained clergy and churchmen received equal treatment.

140. See Peter's decree to the metropolitan of Rostov in I. A. Shliapkin, *Sv. Dimitrii Rostovskii i ego vremia* (St. Petersburg, 1891), p. 311.

141. *PSZ*, 6:4035.

142. *SIRIO*, 4:388, 68:444, 521-522; "Dnevnik gr. Alekseia Grigorovicha Bobrinskogo," *RA*, tom 3, no. 10:138; B. N. Putilov, ed., *Poslovitsy, pogovorki, zagadki v rukopisnykh sbornikakh XVIII-XX vv.* (Moscow, Leningrad, 1961), p. 106.

143. TsGIA, f. 796, op. 46, g. 1765, d. 297, l. 1 ob.; for cases of clerical youths involved in banditry, see the reports on Moscow in 1756 and Uglich in 1763 (ibid., op. 37, g. 1756, d. 28, ll. 1-5 and op. 46, g. 1765, d. 311, ll. 1-2).

144. *PSZ*, 4:2130, 2186; Gorchakov, pp. 226-228.

145. *PSPR*, 2:745, 3:1029, 1121.

146. Kazan reported that only 64 youths (an average of 0.1 per church) were inscribed in the poll-tax population, and Velikii Ustiug reported only 68 youths (0.2 per church). See TsGIA, f. 796, op. 20, g. 1739, d. 14, ll. 171, 173; *ODDS*, 19: prilozhenie 1.

147. TsGIA, f. 796, op. 20, g. 1739, d. 14, ll. 232 ob.-233, 310 ob.-311.

148. The number drafted here is compared to the size of the estate in the mid-1730s, since no data on the latter are available in the early 1720s (*ODDS*,

19: prilozhenie 1; TsGIA, f. 796, op. 20, g. 1739, d. 14, ll. 232 ob.-223, 310 ob.-311). This figure is much less than the 60 to 70 percent estimate given in L. G. Beskrovnyi, *Russkaia armiia i flot v XVIII v.* (Moscow, 1958), and Kartashev, 2:527.

149. *PSZ*, 9:7070; for details, see B. V. Titlinov, *Pravitel'stvo Anny Ioannovny v ego otnoshenii k delam pravoslavnoi tserkvi* (Vil'na, 1905), pp. 200-271.

150. For the eleven dioceses which reported, there were 6,146 conscripts; this does not include the massive Synodal region with almost 5,000 churches (*ODDS*, 19: prilozhenie 1).

151. The number drafted, as measured against the total number of churchmen and clerical children, constituted 12 percent in Arkhangel'sk, 13 percent in Belgorod, 17 percent in Kazan, 13 percent in Kolomna, 21 percent in Nizhnii-Novgorod, 15 percent in Pskov, 6 percent in Riazan, 25 percent in Rostov, 4 percent in Smolensk, 12 percent in Suzdal, and 18 percent in Velikii Ustiug (ibid.).

152. TsGADA, f. 1183, op. 1, g. 1737, d. 32, ll. 2-2 ob.

153. Ibid., d. 117, ll. 1-40.

154. TsGIA, f. 796, op. 18, g. 1737, d. 32, chast' 2, ll. 148-151 ob., 641-650 ob. In 1744 the Senate granted a blanket exemption for seminarians (see ibid., op. 25, g. 1744, d. 134, l. 15).

155. N. A. Popov, "Pridvornye propovedi v tsarstvovanie Elizavety Petrovny," *Letopis' russkoi literatury i drevnosti*, 1859, tom 2, otd. 3:1-33.

156. *PSZ*, 11:8836; for subsequent modifications achieved through the efforts of the Synod, see *PSPREP*, 2:741 and 894.

157. *PSZ*, 12:9483.

158. On the forcible assignment of draftees to landlords, see *PSZ*, 12:9548.

159. Some nobles were so eager for additional factory labor that they simply seized churchmen, especially in the Iaroslavl area, according to a complaint in 1755 by the metropolitan of Rostov (TsGIA, f. 796, op. 36, g. 1755, d. 344, ll. 404-407 ob.). When a factory in the province was auctioned in 1778, the advertisement noted that 36 of 112 workers were "former churchmen" (*Moskovskie vedomosti*, 1778, no. 46 [July 9], *pribavlenie*). The Synod complained bitterly about the unseemly enserfment of former clerical people, but the Senate turned aside its remonstrations (TsGIA, f. 796, op. 43, g. 1762, d. 411, ll. 1-99). Later, at the Legislative Commission in 1767 Metropolitan Gavriil requested that the draftees be assigned to any status but "do not give churchmen unfit for the clerical rank to landlords" (*SIRIO*, 43:418).

160. See the data compiled for 1747-53 in TsGIA, f. 796, op. 25, g. 1744, d. 179, ll. 26-26 ob.

161. *PSZ*, 17:12575, 18:12861.

162. *PSZ*, 18:13236; a memorandum of 1777 noted that 8,961 were drafted in the conscription of 1769 (TsGIA, f. 796, op. 58, g. 1777, d. 143, l. 1).

163. After receiving reports about excessive churchmen and youths in Kaluga and Tula dioceses, the Senate proposed a rigorous conscription (ibid., op. 62, g. 1781, d. 588, l. 1/b). For the Synod's efforts to limit the conscription, see *PSPREA*, 2:1157, 1161; TsGIA, f. 796, op. 65, g. 1784, d. 443, ll. 1-

20 ob.; *PSZ*, 22:15978, 15981.

164. The total drafted numbered 1,845 in Kolomna diocese, 275 in Moscow, 690 in Pereslavl, 3,250 in Riazan, 593 in Rostov, 254 in Suzdal, 783 in Vladimir, and 32,259 for the whole empire. Of these, the seminarians removed for "obtuseness" or "bad conduct" were a small number: 81 in Kolomna diocese, 83 in Moscow, 84 in Pereslavl, 22 in Riazan, 65 in Rostov, 13 in Suzdal, 24 in Vladimir, and 1,455 for the Empire (TsGIA, f. 796, op. 62, g. 1781, d. 588, ll. 431-432). For an example of a churchman who had eluded previous conscriptions only to be caught in 1784, see ibid., op. 66, g. 1785, d. 256, ll. 1-2; for other evidence on the conscription's impact, see Metropolitan Platon's report of 1786 on Moscow diocese in Rozanov, *Istoriia*, 3, pt. 1:137.

165. TsGIA, f. 558 (Ekspeditsiia dlia svidetel'stvovaniia gosudarstvennykh schetov), op. 2, d. 127, ll. 239-240 ob.

166. *PSZ*, 22:16646; *PSPREA*, 3:1378.

167. TsGIA, f. 796, op. 71, g. 1790, d. 55, ll. 1-156. The data here were incomplete, with only preliminary reports from some dioceses and none at all from others; according to these incomplete reports, 270 were drafted in Moscow, 337 in Vladimir, 438 in Kolomna, 334 in Rostov, and 5 in Riazan.

168. Titlinov, *Gavriil*, pp. 545-546.

169. *PSZ*, 24:17675; *PSPRPP*, 38, 56; TsGIA, f. 796, op. 77, g. 1796, d. 670, ll. 1-8; Titlinov, *Gavriil*, p. 555.

170. For some interesting observations on the deleterious effect of conscriptions on clerical status, see the *zapiski* of the early 1850s in the personal archive of Metropolitan Filaret (GBL, f. 316, papka 65, dd. 14, 15, 16, 17, 18).

171. N. B. Golikova, *Politicheskie protsessy pri Petre I* (Moscow, 1957), p. 130. Some clergy were involved in the Astrakhan revolt of 1705-06: one cathedral priest supported the rebels, and a sacristan warmly praised a book against Peter's mandatory beard shaving, adding that "it would be a good thing to stand up for this, even if you had to die for it" (N. B. Golikova, *Astrakhanskoe vosstanie 1705-6 gg.* [Moscow, 1975], pp. 81, 307).

172. Kozlov, "Tserkovnaia reforma," pp. 237, 242, 248-256.

173. TsGIA, f. 796, op. 2, g. 1721, d. 272, ll. 1-1 ob.

174. *SIRIO*, 94:228-229, 523.

175. *ODDS*, 9:390 and 493.

176. For a comprehensive treatment, see Titlinov, *Pravitel'stvo*, ch. 2-4.

177. *ODDS*, 15:272.

178. TsGADA, f. 1183, op. 1, g. 1737, d. 320, ll. 1-2 and g. 1738, d. 440, ll. 1-117.

179. Kozlov, "Tserkovnaia reforma," pp. 306-316.

180. *ODDS*, 16:307.

181. TsGIA, f. 796, op. 17, g. 1736, d. 439, l. 1 ob.; *ODDS*, 19: prilozhenie 1; *ODDS*, 18: prilozhenie 16.

182. See the statements of "unsworn clergy" in Murom uezd in *ODDS*, 10:230; for legislation, see Titlinov, *Pravitel'stvo*, pp. 202-207.

183. *PSPR*, 7:2298, 2518; 9:2853; 10:3417. That lower officials heeded the injunction is evident from their requests for confirmation that clerical candidates had signed the oaths (TsGADA, f. 1183, op. 1, g. 1737, d. 78, ll. 1-2;

d. 179, ll. 1-3; d. 180, ll. 1-2).

184. *PSZ*, 9:7133.

185. *PSZ*, 11:8130; see also, for earlier policy, *PSPR*, 10:3251, 3383.

186. For cases of such returning clergy, see: *PSPREP*, 1:324, 405; TsGIA, f. 796, op. 25, g. 1744, d. 441, l. 1.

187. TsGADA, f. 1183, op. 1, g. 1736, d. 198, ll. 1-111.

188. Ibid., d. 158, l. 1; similar cases were reported in Rostov in 1733 and Suzdal in 1738 (ibid., g. 1733, d. 171, ll. 1-4; *ODDS*, 18:324).

189. TsGADA, f. 1183, op. 1, g. 1736, d. 188, ll. 1-2. The Secret Chancellery adopted an analogous policy of limiting investigation of Old Believers to real political cases (see Pokrovskii, *Antifeodal'nyi protest*, p. 31).

190. TsGIA, f. 796, op. 36, g. 1755, d. 87, ll. 1-3.

191. Ibid., op. 42, g. 1761, d. 81, ll. 1-11 ob.

192. See K. V. Sivkov, "Podpol'naia politicheskaia literatura v Rossii v poslednei treti XVIII v.," *IZ*, 19 (1946):63-101 (esp. 86-87), and idem, "Obshchestvennaia mysl' i obshchestvennye dvizheniia v Rossii v kontse XVIII v.," *Voprosy istorii*, 1946, no. 5/6: 90-95.

3. The Hierarchy and the Parish Clergy

1. The episcopacy or hierarchy (*arkhiereistvo*) of the Russian Church consisted of three descending offices: metropolitan (*mitropolit*), archbishop (*arkhiepiskop*), and bishop (*episkop*). Although each office enjoyed special signs of status, all were considered part of the same hierarchical rank. A particular diocese tended to confer a particular title, in accordance with the stature of the diocese; yet there was no firm rule, and changes were frequent. For a list of individual hierarchs, see P. Stroev, *Spiski ierarkhov i nastoiatelei monastyrei* (St. Petersburg, 1877) and Iu. Tolstoi, *Spiski arkhiereev i arkhiereiskikh kafedr, ierarkhii vserossiiskoi, so vremeni uchrezhdeniia Sv. Prav. Sinoda, 1721-1872 gg.* (St. Petersburg, 1872).

2. *PSPR*, 1:76; *PSZ*, 6:3761; *ODDS*, 1:310.

3. See, for example, A. Lebedev, "Primenenie nakazanii v srede dukhovenstva," *Russkaia starina* [hereafter *RS*], 73 (February 1872):313-338. Even so astute a historian as Znamenskii exaggerated the problem of episcopal abuse and disregarded the important changes occuring within the Church administration (see his *PDPV*, pp. 507, 617-619, 627-628, and passim).

4. [I. S. Belliustin], *Opisanie sel'skogo dukhovenstva* (Leipzig, 1858); [D. Rostislavov], *O chernom i belom pravoslavnom dukhovenstve*, 2 vols. (Leipzig, 1863).

5. Dobrynin's memoirs describing his service in the Sevsk consistory were published as "Istinnoe povestvovanie ili zhizn' Gavriila Dobrynina, im samim napisannaia," *Russkaia starina*, 1871, February-October. It was no accident that they appeared in *Russkaia starina*, which had a distinctly liberal, populist bias under the editorship of M. I. Semevskii. But Dobrynin's experiences were exceptional: Kirill was indeed a scoundrel but actually one of the very few after 1764 who merited (and received) a formal trial and investiga-

tion. After a priest complained that Kirill violated the new law of 1765 that set limits on ordination fees, the Synod and Senate opened a formal investigation (TsGIA, f. 796, op. 53, g. 1772, d. 420; op. 55, g. 1774, d. 537). Dobrynin's account clearly does not depict the typical pattern in the episcopacy; see the perceptive comments by N. D. Chechulin, *Russkoe provintsial'noe obshchestvo vo vtoroi polovine XVIII veka* (St. Petersburg, 1889), pp. 83-84.

6. See Max Weber, "Bureaucracy," in *From Max Weber: Essays in Sociology* (New York, 1946), pp. 196-244.

7. Pokrovskii, *Russkie eparkhii*, 1:275-279, 314-365.

8. See Igor Smolitsch, *Russisches Mönchtum; Entstehung, Entwicklung und Wesen 988-1917* (Würzburg, 1953), pp. 119-382, and the literature cited therein.

9. Pokrovskii, *Russkie eparkhii*, 1:95, 260-262, 314-365.

10. I. I. Shimko, *Patriarshii kazennyi prikaz* (Moscow, 1894), p. 158.

11. *ODDS*, 28:70.

12. In the second quarter of the seventeenth century Patriarch Filaret borrowed the *prikaz* (chancellery) structure for his own administration; nevertheless, his version was chaotic and riddled with informality (see Shimko, pp. 1-2). For complaints of abuse by parish clergy, see the petition quoted in S. M. Solov'ev, *Istoriia Rossii s drevneishikh vremen*, 15 vols. (Moscow, 1959-66), 6:207-210.

13. These districts were once under lay *desiatil'niki* (see N. Kapterev, *Svetskie arkhiereiskie chinovniki v drevnei Rusi* [Moscow, 1874], pp. 114-179, and V. Samuilov, "Desiatil'niki i popovskie starosty," *Tserkovnye vedomosti*, 1900, no. 35:1392-1396). By the late seventeenth century, however, bishops routinely relied upon abbots; see Patriarch Adrian's "instructions" to the abbot of a monastery in Vladimir (*PSZ*, 3:1612). Where a reliable abbot was unavailable, Adrian assigned these tasks to the archpriest of the district cathedral; see, for instance, his charge to the archpriest of a cathedral in Iaropol'ch in the same Vladimir province ("Instruktsiia starostam popovskim," *Drevniaia rossiiskaia vivliofika*, 15 [2nd. ed.; Moscow, 1790]:373-374; hereafter *DRV*).

14. *PSZ*, 3:1612; "Ustavnaia gramota Patriarkha Adriana," *Vremennik obshchestva istorii i drevnostei rossiiskikh* [hereafter *Vremennik OIDR*], 11 (1851), pt. 3:30-46; "Instruktsiia," *DRV*, 15:373-405.

15. This basic structure remained in the Synodal region until the 1740s; see Rozanov, *Istoriia*, 1:58-62; for a list of 22 such administrators in 1745, see TsGADA, f. 1183, op. 1, g. 1745, d. 293, ll. 7 ob.-8 ob.

16. Perov, pp. 106-110; Samuilov, "Desiatil'niki," pp. 1393-1396; "Blagochinnye," *Pravoslavnaia bogoslovskaia entsiklopediia*, 6 vols. (St. Petersburg, 1900-11), 2:490 [hereafter *PBE*]; Znamenskii, *PDR*, pp. 145-146.

17. *PSZ*, 3:1612.

18. Patriarch Adrian's "Instructions to Clerical Elders" contained 72 articles in the main section: 15 on general supervision of the church and clergy, 20 articles on the parishioners, and 37 detailed articles on tax collection and delivery.

19. TsGADA, f. 235, op. 2, d. 6436, l. 5; op. 4, g. 1703, d. 87, ll. 1-2.

20. V. M. Undol'skii, "Gramoty ob uchrezhdenii popovskikh starost i o tserkovnom blagochinii v Moskve," *Vremennik OIDR*, 14 (1852):21-28; see also *AI*, 4:184 and 188, and D. Vvedenskii, *Kresttsovoe dukhovenstvo v staroi Moskve* (Moscow, 1899).

21. Shakhovskoi, p. 39.

22. See, for example, a decree of the Patriarch in 1687 that attempted to establish uniform ordination fees for all dioceses (*ODBMIu*, 1, pt. 3, no. 1).

23. *PSPR*, 1:1, 22, 151; 5:1903, 1937; *ODDS*, 7:30. Over-Procurator Shakhovskoi, hoping to assert firm control over the diocesan bishops, yearned to reestablish the *fiskal* system in the 1740s; see his proposals to the Synod in his *Zapiski*, pp. 280-281, 296-297.

24. Before mid-century, bishops sometimes neglected to reply to Synod decrees; see Shakhovskoi's complaint in his *Zapiski*, pp. 296-297. Thereafter, however, nonfeasance did not go unnoticed; in 1756, for example, Bishop Platon of Vladimir was curtly reminded by the Synod to reply by the next post (TsGIA, f. 796, op. 37, g. 1756, d. 204, ll. 1-35).

25. See, for example, the Synod's investigation of a Suzdal bishop who had exceeded the number of clerical appointments permitted by government regulations (TsGIA, f. 796, op. 62, g. 1781, d. 195, ll. 1-140).

26. Such steps were taken, for example, in Suzdal in 1737 and Riazan in 1757 (TsGADA, f. 1183, op. 1, g. 1737, d. 357, l. 1; TsGIA, f. 796, op. 38, g. 1757, d. 417, ll. 1-2 ob.).

27. Voskresenskii, pp. 411-513.

28. At first the collegial boards were randomly called *dikasteriia* and *konsistoriia*, but in 1744 the Synod made the latter term standard and subsequently defined its structure as well (*PSPREP*, 2:667, 685; *PSPREA*, 1:450); for its order to the bishop of Tambov to establish a consistory after the pattern of other dioceses, see *PSPREP*, 4:1599.

29. Rozanov, *Istoriia*, 2, pt. 2:51.

30. *PSPR*, 1:1.

31. See the fascinating accounts of episcopal visitations in the 1750s in Moscow (Rozanov, *Istoriia*, 2, pt. 1:63-64; 2, pt. 2:19-20), Riazan in 1753-54 ("Dmitrii Sechenov," *REV*, 1916, no. 11/12:481-482), Pereslavl (Malitskii, *IPE*, 1:318-320), Vladimir (K. Nadezhdin, "Ocherk istorii Vladimirskoi seminarii," *VEV*, 1865, no. 14:771; A. I., "Episkop vladimirskii Pavel," *VEV*, 1910, no. 32:581), and Rostov in the late 1770s (*Ierarkhiia rostovsko-iaroslavskoi pastvy* [Iaroslav, 1862], pp. 259-260).

32. Of 127 bishops appointed in the period 1700-62, 70 (55 percent) were Ukrainian or White Russian, 10 (8 percent) were foreigners (Greek, Rumanian, Serbian, and Georgian), and 47 (37 percent) were Great Russian. The prelates usually brought along trusted aides from the Ukraine, thereby significantly magnifying Kiev's total impact. See K. V. Kharlampovich, *Malorossiiskoe vliianie na velikorusskuiu tserkovnuiu zhizn'* (Kazan, 1914), pp. 459 and passim.

33. Illustrative was the case of a Georgian, Antonii, who knew no Russian and allowed an *administrator* to rule in his stead (*PSPREP*, 4:1573; P. Malitskii, *Istoriia Vladimirskoi dukhovnoi seminarii* [hereafter *IVS*], 3 vols. [Moscow, 1900-02], 1:64-65).

34. *PSPREP*, 4:1380; *PSZ*, 14:10216.

35. For a summary of legislation, see V. Ivanovskii, *Russkoe zakono-datel'stvo XVIII i XIX vv. v svoikh postanovleniiakh otnositel'no monashe-stvuiushchikh lits i monastyrei* (Khar'kov, 1905), pp. 23-25.

36. Smolitsch, *Russisches Mönchtum*, pp. 427, 451.

37. For testimony on the popularity of bishops, see the materials on Metropolitan Platon of Moscow (A. P. Butenev, "Vospominaniia o moem vremeni," *RA*, 1881, tom 3:11), Bishop Simon of Riazan (A. Sokolov, "Simon Lagov," *REV*, 1884, no. 8:156), Arsenii of Rostov ("Dnevnik preosv. Arseniia Vereshchagina," *IaEV*, 1895, no. 27:419-420, and passim), and the bishop of Kolomna (A. T. Bolotov, *Zapiski Andreia Timofeevicha Bolotova*, 4 vols. [St. Petersburg, 1871-73], 4:1192-1195).

38. D. I. Rostislavov, "Zapiski," *RS*, 27 (1880):8-10; see similar materials on bishops Viktor and Ksenofont in Malitskii, *IVS*, 1:124 and "Iz vospominanii i rasskazov o Ksenofonte," *VEV*, 1874, no. 8:401.

39. This sample of 26 individuals is based on signed replies to a decree of the Moscow Synodal Chancellery in 1756 (from Vladimir, Vologda, Kolomna, Voronezh, Pereslavl, Suzdal, Kazan, Kostroma, Astrakhan, Viatka, Arkhangel'sk, Tobol'sk, and Rostov) in TsGADA, f. 1183, op. 1, g. 1756, d. 1, ll. 7-39. It is likely that more abbots were formally members of the consistory but failed to sign; however, the calculation here is more meaningful for it reflects functional participation, not merely nominal membership. On formal lists the black clergy appear far more prevalent; for example, Moscow diocese rarely included white clergy before 1758 (see the lists in Rozanov, *Istoriia*, 2, pt. 1:24, 40, 53) and the Moscow Synodal Chancellery consisted overwhelmingly of monastic clergy (84 percent) in 1738-69 (see the lists in Skvortsov, *Materialy*, 2:352-354). Even after 1768, when the Synod ordered bishops to appoint at least one priest to the consistory, black clergy continued to dominate such lists; see, for example, the Rostov consistory lists in "Delo iz proshlogo stoletiia ob uchitele Iaroslavskoi dukhovnoi seminarii," *IaEV*, 1890, no. 21:324, 327.

40. TsGIA, f. 796, op. 54, g. 1773, d. 140, l. 218 ob.; for a full table on these boards, see Zav'ialov, *Vopros*, pp. 367-380.

41. TsGIA, f. 796, op. 54, g. 1773, d. 140, ll. 82-82 ob., 218-218 ob., 241 ob.-242; d. 141, ll. 10, 93-98, 161 ob.

42. *PSPR*, 1:1.

43. In 1727 the Synod ordered the appointment of such stewards to replace the "ecclesiastical inspectors" (*PSPR*, 5:1937). For orders to establish superintendents to control clerical behavior, see *PSPR*, 10:3711 and *ODDS*, 21:414; for the Synodal "instructions" to superintendents in Moscow, see *PSPR*, 10:3338.

44. Even in a single diocese, terminology varied; in Pereslavl, for example, the official was variously called clerical elder (*popovskii starosta*) and steward (*zakazchik*); see Malitskii, *IPE*, 1:31-33, 151-153, 181-185. The occupant of such offices could also vary considerably in status and rank; in one area of Suzdal diocese, the office of steward was held by an archpriest (1721-37), a priest (1737-40), an abbot (1740-57), and again a priest (after 1757); see "Letopis' ob Il'inskoi tserkvi," *VEV*, 1881, no. 11:433.

45. Rozanov, *Istoriia*, 2, pt. 1:48, 89-93, n. 237-239; N. Rozanov, "Preosviashchennyi Platon I," *MEV*, 1869, no. 23:4-6.

46. Malitskii, *IPE*, 1:144.

47. "Instruktsiia popovskim starostam ot 1743 g.," *IaEV*, 1883, no. 18:141-143.

48. Rozanov, *Istoriia*, 2, pt. 1:n.242; 2, pt. 2:116-117.

49. Platon (Levshin), *Instruktsiia blagochinnym iereiam ili protoiereiam* (Moscow, 1775), punkt 1; Rozanov, *Istoriia*, 3, pt. 1:37-38; see also the Kolomna instruction of 1779 in M. Rudnev, "K istorii Kolomenskoi eparkhii," *Chteniia OIDR*, 1903, no. 4, otd. 3:33.

50. Some areas retained the steward (*zakazchik*), although his functions were identical to those of a superintendent (see the 1778 reference in Rostov diocese in "Neumestnaia ostrota," *IaEV*, 1882, no. 9:71-72); somewhat exceptional was Suzdal diocese, which permitted the election of this official as late as 1773 (TsGIA, f. 796, op. 54, g. 1773, d. 141, l. 45 ob.). Impetus for appointing superintendents came from a Synodal decree of 1782 (*PSPREA*, 2:1065) and a specific order from Paul in 1797 (*PSPRPP*, 91); in 1799-1800 Platon's "Instructions" became standard for all dioceses ("Blagochinnye," *PBE*, 2:685).

51. On the uneven distribution of resources, see A. A. Novosel'skii, "Rospis' krest'ianskikh dvorov," *IA*, 4 (1949):88-149; *ODDS*, 19: prilozhenie 5.

52. The marriage license yielded a small fee that traditionally went to the Church (*AI*, 1:155, 4:151, 5:244; *PSZ*, 3:1612); from 1714, however, the state utilized these funds for canal construction, military expenditures, and especially hospitals (Gorchakov, pp. 211-215, 227, 240).

53. *Dukhovnyi shtat* (St. Petersburg, 1764); *PSZ*, Kniga shtatov, 43, otd. 3; *PSPREA*, 1:167.

54. Malitskii, *IPE*, 2:17-25, 55-68; Rozanov, *Istoriia*, 2, pt. 2:54.

55. *PSPRPP*, 161.

56. Rozanov, *Istoriia*, 3, pt. 1:30 and n.86.

57. V. I. Semevskii, "Sel'skii sviashchennik vo vtoroi polovine XVIII v.," *RS*, 1877, no. 8:527.

58. TsGIA, f. 796, op. 54, g. 1773, d. 140, ll. 12-12 ob., 84, 96, 153, 162; Rozanov, *Istoriia*, 3, pt. 1:36, n.108.

59. Malitskii, *IPE*, 1:169.

60. "Dmitrii Sechenov," *REV*, 1916, no. 13/14:534-535.

61. For a 1793 Synodal decree requiring that all consistory clerks be chosen from seminarians, see *PSPREA*, 3:1549.

62. See the complaint of a Murom cleric in 1794 that the local superintendent, a relative of the bishop, was committing various abuses, in Titlinov, *Gavriil*, p. 376.

63. Malitskii, *IPE*, 1:9-10, 151; 2:6-8.

64. See, for example, the request by Amvrosii and Dmitrii in TsGIA, f. 796, op. 48, g. 1757, d. 224, ll. 1-8 and op. 44, g. 1753, d. 62, ll. 1-4.

65. *OLDS*, 34:242; *PSPREP*, 4:1382.

66. Nadezhdin, "Ocherk," *VEV*, 1865, no. 14:771.

67. Malitskii, *IPE*, 1:181-182.

68. Rozanov, *Istoriia*, 2, pt. 1:63-64; 2, pt. 2:19-20.

69. "Dnevnik preosv. Arseniia," *IaEV*, 1895, no. 7:108 and passim.

70. Bolotov, 4:1192-1195.

71. Sokolov, "Simon Lagov," *REV*, 1884, no. 13:249-252.

72. *PSPR*, 8:2774; *ODDS*, 14:20.

73. TsGIA, f. 796, op. 53, g. 1772, d. 452, l. 8.

74. On internal conflict in the Western Church, see the cases of Sweden, France, and England in: Roberts, "The Swedish Church," pp. 160-161; John McManners, *French Ecclesiastical Society under the Ancien Régime* (Manchester, 1960), and *Cambridge Modern History*, 6:78-79.

75. "Tserkovnye postanovleniia o sviashchenstve," *PS*, 1859, no. 2:255-263.

76. For the cases of Sweden and England, see C. Hallendorff and A. Schück, *History of Sweden* (Stockholm, 1929), p. 132, and Emma Mason, "The Role of the English Parishioner, 1100-1500," *Journal of Ecclesiastical History*, 27 (1976):18-19.

77. On the candidate's interrogation in Moscow in the 1640s (where merely a witness is used to confirm that the candidate is not a bonded person or socially disqualified), see the materials in N. A. Skvortsov, *Dukhovenstvo Moskovskoi eparkhii v XVII veke* (Moscow, 1916), p. 10.

78. Rozanov, *Istoriia*, 1:66-67.

79. *PSPR*, 5:1661; *PSZ*, 7:4802.

80. "Rasporiazheniia Arseniia Matseevicha po upravleniiu rostovsko-iaroslavskoiu pastvoiu," *IaEV*, 1868, no. 31:263-264.

81. K. Glebov, "Materialy k biografii preosv. Simona Lagova," *REV*, 1897, no. 6:183; Platon, *Instruktsii*, punkt 40.

82. For examples of the ordination charter, see a charter from 1501 (in Amvrosii, *Istoriia rossiiskoi ierarkhii*, 6 vols. [Moscow, 1807-15] 4:659-660), from the mid-seventeenth century ("Stavlennaia gramota ot 1656 g.," *IaEV*, 1893, no. 33:520-521), from the late seventeenth century (TsGADA, f. 1183, op. 1, g. 1735, d. 175, ll. 3-4), and Synodal charters from the 1720s and 1740s (GBL, Otdel redkikh knig, Sbornik 65, *list* 1; TsGIA, f. 796, op. 21, g. 1740, d. 43, ll. 3 ob.-4).

83. *AI*, 4:259. Here data are cited only for the appointment from sacristan to priest; for promotion from sacristan to deacon, or deacon to priest, the cost was approximately one half. For a seventeenth-century satirical tale about the extortion of funds from candidates, see "Khozhdenie popa Savvy," in *Russkaia demokraticheskaia satira XVII v.*, ed. V. P. Adrianova-Peretts (Moscow, 1954), pp. 70-72.

84. *PSZ*, 6:3870; *PSPR*, 1:63, 3:1138; *ODDS*, 1:224; 2, pt. 2:940.

85. Rozanov, *Istoriia*, 1:33; I. T. Pososhkov, *Kniga o skudosti i bogatstve* (Moscow, 1951), pp. 15, 30.

86. See the case of Archbishop Georgii (Dashkov) of Rostov in *ODDS*, 10:422.

87. *PSPR*, 7:2547, 8:2848.

88. Shakhovskoi, pp. 265-266; *ODDS*, 22:236.

89. "O sviashchenno-sluzhitel'skikh stavlennykh gramotakh," *RSP*, 1899, no. 27:229-234.

90. The Synod's verification of documents in 1746 uncovered a number of

clergy in each district without proper documents; see TsGADA, f. 1183, op. 1, g. 1746, d. 407, l. 6 ob. and d. 406, ll. 12-17, 20-20 ob., 26-30. See also similar reports for Vladimir (*ODDS*, 32:60), Pereslavl (Malitskii, *IPE*, 1:212), and Moscow (Rozanov, *Istoriia*, 2, pt. 1:47-48).

91. Malitskii, *IPE*, 1:216-217.

92. *PSPR*, 2:439.

93. *PSZ*, 10:7734; *PSPR*, 10:3454; *ODDS*, 19:14; TsGADA, f. 1183, op. 1, g. 1739, d. 38, ll. 6 ob.-7; Malitskii, *IPE*, 1:290-294.

94. Rozanov, *Istoriia*, 3, pt. 1:51.

95. TsGIA, f. 796, op. 46, g. 1765, d. 58, ll. 2-3 ob.; *PSPREA*, 1:225.

96. TsGIA, f. 796, op. 53, g. 1772, d. 420, ll. 15-20 ob., 24; op. 55, g. 1774, d. 537, ll. 1-66.

97. Shimko, pp. 121-158; Perov, pp. 76-79.

98. *ODBMIu*, 1, pt. 3, no. 3.

99. Shimko, p. 158.

100. *ODBMIu*, 1, pt. 3, no. 3; Shimko, p. 196; Perov, p. 89.

101. "Materialy dlia istorii Vladimirskoi eparkhii," *VEV*, 1892-94 (pribavleniia); *ODDS*, 29:220.

102. Rozanov, *Istoriia*, 2, pt. 1:n.425; Malitskii, *IPE*, 1:216.

103. *PSPR*, 1:1.

104. Malitskii, *IPE*, 1:222-223.

105. D. Agntsev, *Istoriia Riazanskoi dukhovnoi seminarii* [hereafter *IRS*] (Riazan, 1889), pp. 35-36.

106. Nadezhdin, "Ocherk," *VEV*, 1868, no. 23:1110-1111.

107. Malitskii, *IPE*, 1:223.

108. Shimko, p. 312.

109. Malitskii, *IVS*, 1:75-76.

110. Nadezhdin, "Ocherk," *VEV*, 1866, no. 4:171, 174-175.

111. *PSZ*, 16:12060; *PSPREA*, 1:167.

112. See M. S. Popov, *Arsenii Matseevich, mitropolit rostovskii i iaroslavskii* (St. Petersburg, 1905).

113. For example, 93 percent of the students in the Vladimir seminary in 1793 paid their own way; see the student register in TsGIA, f. 796, op. 74, g. 1793, d. 94, ll. 349-421.

114. I. V. Malinovskii, "Otkrytie Vladimirskogo dukhovnogo uchilishcha i pervye gody ego sushchestvovaniia, 1790-1800 gg.," *TVUAK*, 3 (1901):168.

115. See Adrian's ordination charter in TsGADA, f. 1183, op. 1, g. 1735, d. 175, ll. 3-4.

116. See, for example, the clerical instruction manual from the 1770s, *O dolzhnostiakh presviterov prikhodskikh*, pp. 70-80.

117. *PSPR*, 3:1054; *ODDS*, 2, pt. 2:940.

118. TsGIA, f. 796, op. 53, g. 1772, d. 171, l. 14.

119. Ibid., op. 61, g. 1780, d. 236, l. 4.

120. For an example of a superstition case in Suzdal, see *PSPR*, 10:3225.

121. TsGADA, f. 1183, op. 1, g. 1732, d. 732, l. 1; TsGIA, f. 796, op. 14, g. 1733, d. 257, ll. 1-8.

122. *PSPREA*, 1:666, 2:1065.

123. For the procedures in Moscow, see Rozanov, *Istoriia*, 2, pt. 1:123-132; 3, pt. 1:62-64.

124. TsGIA, f. 796, op. 48, g. 1767, d. 505, ll. 1-4 contains a typical request to expedite the investigation and trial.

125. Typical was a 1781 case in Vladimir (ibid., op. 62, g. 1781, d. 194, l. 28).

126. See the case in Vladimir diocese in 1763 in TsGIA, f. 796, op. 44, g. 1763, d. 66, ll. 3-3 ob.

127. TsGADA, f. 1183, op. 1, g. 1736, d. 198, l. 81.

128. TsGIA, f. 796, op. 53, g. 1772, d. 54, ll. 1-17; *ODDS*, 21:107.

129. TsGIA, f. 796, op. 50, g. 1769, d. 271, ll. 55-55 ob.

130. Ibid., op. 42, g. 1761, d. 65, ll. 18 ob.-19.

131. One Suzdal priest was sentenced to five years' confinement in the monastery for service errors (see TsGADA, f. 1183, op. 3, g. 1758, d. 358, l. 1). For the case of a Suzdal priest who had been suspended in 1729 for service mistakes, see his pleas in 1732 for reinstatement in ibid., op. 1, g. 1732, d. 732, l. 1.

132. For the case of a Suzdal priest and deacon defrocked in 1733 for brawling and spilling the Elements, see TsGIA, f. 796, op. 14, g. 1733, d. 257, ll. 1-8.

133. See A. F. Lavrov, "Vdovye sviashchennosluzhiteli," *Khr. Cht.*, 1870, pt. 2, no. 12:1019-1056; 1871, pt. 1, no. 2:343-382; no. 7:75-125.

134. *PSPR*, 3:997; 4:1197, 1202; 5:1492; 8:2802; 10:3415.

135. See the Synod's complaint in 1727 (*PSPR*, 6:2076) and 1739 (*PSPR*, 10:3464), and its attempt to modify Peter's policy under the Supreme Privy Council (*SIRIO*, 94:831). Shortages in fact persisted throughout the eighteenth century; see the table on vacancies in 1789 in Titlinov, *Gavriil*, pp. 709-711.

136. *PSPR*, 10:3447.

137. TsGIA, f. 796, op. 37, g. 1756, d. 446, l. 2.

138. Ibid., op. 36, g. 1755, d. 344, l. 341. See also Metropolitan Arsenii's order to tonsure educated churchmen in 1763 ("Ukaznoe predpisanie Iaroslavskogo dukhovnogo pravleniia," *IaEV*, 1890, no. 5:69-72). For another case, see I. Ia. Moroshkin, "Iz del XVIII st.," *Drevniaia i novaia Rossiia*, 4 (1878), pt. 1:278.

139. *PSPR*, 1:1.

140. TsGIA, f. 796, op. 39, g. 1758, d. 97, ll. 1-32.

141. *ODDS*, 9:131, 11:79.

142. TsGIA, f. 796, op. 43, g. 1762, d. 223, l. 9 ob.

143. "Neskol'ko neizvestnykh ukazov i pisem Imperatora Petra III," *Zaria*, 3 (1871), no. 2:17.

144. After the Synod ordered a review of Arsenii's decisions (TsGIA, f. 796, op. 43, g. 1762, d. 223, l. 11), he was upheld in one case but reversed in seven others (ibid., op. 46, g. 1765, d. 311, ll. 1-2; d. 369, l. 1). For the condemnation of Arsenii in the newspaper, see *Moskovskie vedomosti*, 1763, no. 31, *pribavlenie*.

145. TsGIA, f. 796, op. 46, g. 1765, d. 241, ll. 1-2; *PSPREA*, 1:260.

146. See also Titlinov, *Gavriil*, p. 349.

147. TsGIA, f. 796, op. 54, g. 1773, d. 425, ll. 43-46 ob.

148. *PSPREA*, 1:654.

149. TsGIA, f. 796, op. 54, g. 1773, d. 425, l. 11; a similar case involve´
Riazan priest in 1780 (ibid., op. 61, g. 1780, d. 477, ll. 4-4 ob., 9-13 ob.).

150. Ibid., op. 55, g. 1774, d. 131, ll. 1-7.

151. See Titlinov, *Gavriil*, pp. 165-266, and Pokrovskii, *Ekaterinskaia komissiia*.

152. TsGIA, f. 796, op. 47, g. 1766, d. 120, l. 7 ob.

153. *PSPREA*, 1:349; *PSZ*, 18:12909.

154. *PSPRPP*, 20, 83; see also Titlinov, *Gavriil*, pp. 599-600.

155. Rozanov, *Istoriia*, 2, pt. 2:41.

156. *PSPREA*, 1:615.

157. TsGIA, f. 796, op. 52, g. 1771, d. 169, ll. 1-11.

158. Ibid., op. 54, g. 1773, d. 292, ll. 1-21.

159. For instance, after the Moscow plague heightened concern over vagrant clergy in Moscow and, especially, the public service of rites, the Synod
changed the original punishment of one offender from demotion to defrocking
(ibid., op. 53, g. 1772, d. 90, ll. 1-14).

160. Ibid., op. 57, g. 1776, d. 148, ll. 1-6 ob.

161. Ibid., d. 150, ll. 1-4.

162. Ibid.. op. 58, g. 1777, d. 47, ll. 1-2.

163. Ibid., op. 63, g. 1782, d. 322, ll. 1-6, 10.

164. M. Nazar'in, "Prikhodskoe dukhovenstvo v pravlenie Elizavety Petrovny (1741-1761 gg.)," *Strannik*, 1904, no. 6:931-932.

165. See, for instance, TsGIA, f. 796, op. 57, g. 1776, d. 313, ll. 5-6, 7-7
ob., 19-21 ob.

166. Ibid., op. 46, g. 1765, d. 241, ll. 1-2; *PSPREA*, 1:260.

167. A. I., "Episkop vladimirskii Pavel," *VEV*, 1910, no. 32:584.

168. TsGIA, f. 796, op. 65, g. 1784, d. 274, ll. 11-11 ob., 16, 23, 31.

169. Titlinov, *Gavriil*, pp. 374-375.

170. TsGIA, f. 796, op. 71, g. 1790, d. 36, ll. 9-10.

171. Ibid., op. 72, g. 1791, d. 173, ll. 3-4; see also Titlinov, *Gavriil*, p. 369.

172. A. A. Iakovlev, "Zapiski A. A. Iakovleva," *Pamiatniki novoi russkoi
istorii*, 3 (St. Petersburg, 1873), pt. 2:91.

173. *PSPR*, 1:1.

174. *Pouchenie sviatitel'skoe* (St. Petersburg, 1774), p. 7.

175. *PSPREP*, 3:1062.

176. TsGIA, f. 796, op. 65, g. 1784, d. 275, ll. 23-29.

177. "Iz bumag imp. protoiereia Ioanna Pamfilova," *RA*, 1871, no. 1:231.

178. Widowed priests who took monastic vows could become hierarchs,
but in the eighteenth century few did so. In Vladimir province, for example,
only three of twenty-four bishops (in Suzdal, Pereslavl and Vladimir dioceses)
were formerly widowed priests. Yet none of them was likely to grasp the
problems of the average clergyman: Afanasii (bishop of Suzdal, 1735-37) was
previously a cathedral archpriest, while Sil'vestr (bishop of Pereslavl, 1761-
68) and Pavel (bishop of Vladimir, 1763-70) had court connections (see Tolstoi, pp. 7, 15, and V. Orlov, "Kratkie biograficheskie svedeniia," *VEV*, 1886,
no. 19:509-510).

179. Petr Alekseev, "Rassuzhdenie na vopros: mozhno li dostoinomu svia-

shchenniku, minovav monashestvo, proizvedenu byt' vo episkopa?" *Chteniia OIDR*, 1867, kniga 3, otd. 5:17-26; V. I. Savva, ed., *Sochineniia protiv episkopov XVIII v.* (St. Petersburg, 1910).

180. Shimko, pp. 312-313.

181. Malitskii, *IVS*, 1:19-21. See similar materials on Pereslavl diocese (Malitskii *IPE*, 1:44-46, 224-225), Suzdal diocese (Malitskii *ISS*, p. 10), and Riazan diocese (Agntsev, *IRS*, p. 37).

182. *ODDS*, 8:456.

183. TsGIA, f. 796, op. 14, g. 1733, d. 268, l. 1.

184. Malitskii, *IPE*, 1:175-176.

185. See the cases of an impertinent deacon of Kolomna diocese in 1777 and a Riazan cleric in 1784 (TsGIA, f. 796, op. 58, g. 1777, d. 204, ll. 1-81 and op. 65, g. 1784, d. 275, ll. 1-29).

186. Nadezhdin, "Ocherk," *VEV*, 1868, no. 23:1111-1112; Malitskii, *IVS*, 1:106-108.

187. Rozanov, *Istoriia*, 3, pt. 1:62-63.

188. For the case of a priest defrocked for cursing his bishop, see TsGIA, f. 796, op. 61, g. 1780, d. 22, ll. 1-25 ob.

189. *PSPREA*, 1:666.

190. *PSPR*, 1:208.

191. *PSPREP*, 2:683; see similar cases in 1729 (*ODBMIu*, 4:88-89), 1731 (*ODDS*, 11:79), 1761 (TsGIA, f. 796, op. 42, g. 1761, d. 65, ll. 18 ob.-19), and 1742 (*PSPREP*, 1:221).

192. Malitskii, *IPE*, 1:175.

193. *ODDS*, 21:106.

194. The complaint by Peter III about the Synod's improper review of appeals originated with petitions from two priests ("Neskol'ko neizvestnykh ukazov," *Zaria*, 3 (1871), kn. 2:17-18). Catherine II also liked to play the role of "little mother"; see her intervention on behalf of some "unfortunate churchmen" in TsGIA, f. 796, op. 56, g. 1775, d. 142, ll. 1-191). Paul's access to the throne in 1796 likewise aroused great hopes among the white clergy as well as peasantry, eliciting a spurt of clerical petitions to the Emperor (Titlinov, *Gavriil*, p. 417).

195. Znamenskii, *PDPV*, p. 613.

4. The New World of the Seminary

1. See the rough estimates in A. I. Sobolevskii, "Obrazovannost' Moskovskoi Rusi XVI-XVII vv.," *Otchet o sostoianii i deiatel'nosti Imperatorskogo S.-Peterburgskogo universiteta za 1891 god* (St. Petersburg, 1892), prilozhenie, pp. 5-12.

2. See S. A. Kniaz'kov and N. I. Serbov, *Ocherk istorii narodnogo obrazovaniia v Rossii do epokhi reform Aleksandra II* (Moscow, 1910), pp. 9-19.

3. See the decrees of the Church Council of 1551 (*Akty, sobrannye v bibliotekakh i arkhivakh Rossiiskoi imperii Arkheograficheskoiu ekspeditsieiu*, 4 vols. [St. Petersburg, 1836], 1:229) and the Moscow Church Council of 1667 (*PSZ*, 1:412).

4. See Pososhkov, p. 34, and an anonymous project (by a contemporary

of Peter the Great) that condemns the clergy's ignorance in philosophy and theology (S. V. Rozhdestvenskii, *Ocherki po istorii sistem narodnogo prosveshcheniia v Rossii v XVIII-XIX vv.*, 1 vol. [St. Petersburg, 1912], prilozhenie 2, pp. 10-11); for further references, see P. Pekarskii, *Vvedenie v istoriiu prosveshcheniia v Rossii pri Petre Velikom*, 2 vols. (St. Petersburg, 1862), 1:135, 178, 326; 2:521. As Denis Fonvizin's "The Minor" and S. T. Aksakov's *Family Chronicle* show, however, many of the nobility were as boorish as the worst priest. As late as 1767, in the local noble "instructions" to the Legislative Commission, 17 percent (160 of 951) could not even sign their own names; the rates of functional illiteracy no doubt were significantly higher (Jones, p. 58).

5. *Zhivopisets*, 1772 (2nd. ed.; St. Petersburg, 1773), *chast'* 1, *list* 3, p. 15.

6. Voskresenskii, p. 33; *PSPR*, 2:596.

7. Voskresenskii, pp. 33-34.

8. *PSPR*, 10:3296.

9. *PSPREA*, 1:76.

10. See, for example, Anna's decree of 1740 (*PSZ*, 11:8130).

11. *PSPR*, 1:1; *PSPRPP*, 91.

12. Voskresenskii, pp. 33-34.

13. *PSPREA*, 3:1250.

14. See, for instance, "Po povodu pechataemogo nizhe 'Uchrezhdeniia' Simona," *REV*, 1866, no. 20:580.

15. G. Istomin, "Postanovleniia Imperatritsy Ekateriny II otnositel'no obrazovaniia dukhovenstva," *TKDA*, 1867, tom 3, no. 9:588-601; for the 1766 project, see S. M. Rozhdestvenskii, ed., *Materialy dlia istorii uchebnykh reform v Rossii v XVIII-XIX vv.* (St. Petersburg, 1910), pp. 270-271.

16. Titlinov, *Gavriil*, pp. 758-779; *PSPREA*, 1:245 and 253.

17. *PSPR*, 10:3408, 3638, and *ODDS*, 17:32; see a similar resolution by the bishop of Vladimir in 1753 (Malitskii, *IPE*, 1:53-54). For a discussion of primers, see Max Okenfuss, "Education in Russia during the First Half of the Eighteenth Century" (Ph.D. diss., Harvard University, 1970), pp. 173-212.

18. Rozhdestvenskii, *Materialy*, p. 276. Bishop Simon of Riazan likewise stressed that Latin is "not merely the foundation, but also the building (*zdanie*) of learning" ("Po povodu pechataemogo nizhe 'Uchrezhdeniia,' " *REV*, 1866, no. 17:505).

19. See, for example, H. C. Barnard, *A History of English Education from 1760* (London, 1961), p. 17, and W. A. L. Vincent, *The Grammar Schools: Their Continuing Tradition* (London, 1969), esp. pp. 93-108.

20. *PSPREP*, 1:459.

21. Smirnov, *ITS*, pp. 340-341.

22. Catherine specifically enjoined the hierarchs to expel poor students and to matriculate only competent youths (*PSPREA*, 1:76).

23. Shliapkin, p. 314.

24. *PSZ*, 4:2186; see also 4:2308, 5:3175.

25. For the best overview, see P. V. Znamenskii, *Dukhovnye shkoly v Rossii do reformy 1808 g.* (Kazan, 1881), pp. 21-42; hereafter *DSh*. On the impressive school in Novgorod, see E. I. Prilezhaev, "Novgorodskie epar-

khial'nye shkoly v petrovskuiu epokhu," *Khr. Cht.*, 1877, tom 1:331-370, and also the student register in TsGIA, f. 796, op. 8, g. 1727, d. 223 and *ODDS*, 7:223.

26. S. K. Smirnov, *Istoriia Moskovskoi slaviano-greko-latinskoi akademii* (Moscow, 1855), pp. 3-254.

27. "Rostovskoe uchilishche pri Sv. Dmitrie mitropolite," *IaEV*, 1863, nos. 24-25, and Shliapkin, pp. 327-353.

28. *PSPR*, 1:192, 2:648, 3:1131.

29. For a survey of progress achieved by 1727, see the reports to the Supreme Privy Council in Pekarskii, 1:109-121.

30. Makarii, *Istoriko-statisticheskoe opisanie Riazanskoi dukhovnoi seminarii*, pp. 7-9; Agntsev, *IRS*, pp. 11-12.

31. Malitskii, *ISS*, pp. 5-10; TsGIA, f. 796, op. 18, g. 1737, d. 32, chast' 1, ll. 197-211 ob. (register of pupils for 1723-26); Nadezhdin, "Materialy," *VEV*, 1874, no. 20:1019.

32. Amvrosii, 1:426; Pekarskii, 1:114-115.

33. TsGIA, f. 796, op. 18, g. 1737, d. 32, chast' 1, ll. 197-211 ob.

34. Amvrosii, 1:430; Pekarskii, 1:114.

35. For abundant evidence of financial problems, see the reports from Riazan in 1725 (*ODDS*, 5:17 and 163; *PSPR*, 5:1586), and various dioceses in 1727 (Pekarskii, 1:109-121).

36. *PSPR*, 1:1.

37. Typical was the plight of the Suzdal seminary: in 1722 the bishop gathered only 636 bushels of rye and oats from 500 churches, and by 1726 failed to collect even this amount (*ODDS*, 18: prilozhenie 15); see the record of annual budgets in TsGIA, f. 796, op. 19, g. 1738, d. 274, ll. 46-50 ob.

38. Makarii, pp. 8-9; see also "Sredstva soderzhaniia grammaticheskikh shkol i Iaroslavskoi seminarii v polovine XVIII st.," *IaEV*, 1872, no. 13:100-101.

39. *PSPR*, 2:648; for an attempt to train teachers at the advanced Novgorod seminary, see ibid., 3:1131.

40. See, for instance, the cases described in *PSPR*, 2:648, 3:1108.

41. Obscurantist bishops became the butt of A. D. Kantemir's satirical poem, "Satira I: Na khuliashchikh ucheniia," reprinted in *Russkaia literatura XVIII v.*, ed. G. P. Makogonenko (Leningrad, 1970), p. 60.

42. *PSPR*, 10:3540; see also Agntsev, *IRS*, pp. 18-21. The Synod took similar measures against the bishops of Rostov; see the warning to Ioakim in 1739 (*PSPR*, 10:3475) and Arsenii Matseevich in 1745 (*PSPREP*, 2:903; "Piatiletniaia vakatsiia dlia bezuspeshnykh uchenikov Iaroslavskoi dukhovnoi seminarii," *IaEV*, 1887, no. 34:545-556, no. 35:573-575).

43. The enrollment in Riazan increased sharply; it reported 140 pupils in 1740, 156 pupils in 1746, 100 pupils in 1749, 232 pupils in 1753, and 328 pupils in 1763 (TsGIA, f. 796, op. 18, g. 1737, d. 32, chast' 3, ll. 73-84; Agntsev, *IRS*, pp. 28, 99).

44. The seminary in Suzdal closed frequently (1726-35, 1737-39, 1741-43, 1745-55), but finally became stable after 1755 (TsGIA, f. 796, op. 18, g. 1737, d. 32, chast' 1, ll. 197-211 ob.; chast' 2, ll. 148-151 ob.; chast' 3, ll. 86-90 ob.;

op. 25, g. 1744, d. 134, ll. 49-51 ob.; Malitskii, *ISS*, pp. 5-7). On Iaroslavl, see "Posylka v 1756 g. uchenikov iz Iaroslavskoi seminarii v Moskovskuiu zaikonospasskuiu akademiiu," *IaEV*, 1895, no. 26:415-416.

45. Smirnov, *ITS*, pp. 35 and passim.

46. Malitskii, *IVS*, 1:1-63; Nadezhdin, "Ocherk," *VEV*, 1865-68; Malitskii, *IPE*, 1:52-54.

47. TsGIA, f. 796, op. 36, g. 1755, d. 344, ll. 380 ob.-403.

48. N. P. Travchetov, "Delo o bogoprotivnom sne," *TVUAK*, 2 (1900): 72.

49. For example, in Kolomna seminary in 1733, 93 percent of the pupils came from Kolomna and Kolomna uezd; in Rostov diocese in 1730-38, 91 percent of the pupils came from Rostov and Rostov uezd; in Suzdal diocese in 1736, 88 percent came from Suzdal or Suzdal uezd (TsGIA, f. 796, op. 14, g. 1733, d. 386, l. 22; op. 18, g. 1737, d. 32, chast' 2, ll. 148-151 ob., 641-650 ob.). The only exception was Riazan, where (for unknown reasons) a student register of 1744 shows that only 23 percent came from Riazan and Riazan uezd, and the remainder came from many parts of the diocese (ibid., op. 25, g. 1744, d. 134, ll. 64-81 ob.).

50. A Synod investigation of 1755 revealed few students even in the middle grade of *ritorika* (rhetoric); authorities reported 43 pupils in the Moscow Academy, but elsewhere far fewer—11 in Rostov, 10 in Kolomna, 19 in Riazan, 25 in Pereslavl (probably the Trinity-Sergius Seminary), and none in Suzdal or Vladimir (TsGIA, f. 796, op. 36, g. 1755, d. 150, l. 6).

51. Shakhovskoi, prilozhenie 27, p. 273.

52. Malitskii, *IVS*, 1:9-24, 66-77, 106-108; Agntsev, *IRS*, pp. 60-61. On peasant complaints about the seminary tax, see the Iaroslavl incident of 1757 described in "Uravnenie v 1757 g. Spaso-Iaroslavskogo monastyria s drugimi monastyriami v nesenii tiagostei po soderzhaniiu seminarii," *IaEV*, 1895, no. 26:401-410.

53. In 1759 the bishop of Riazan set rates for landless churches (0.5 to 0.75 kopecks per parish household) and those owning arable land (7.5 kopecks per *chetvert'*); a similar scheme was devised in Rostov (Agntsev, *IRS*, pp. 56-59; "Sredstva soderzhaniia," *IaEV*, 1872, no. 14:107-109).

54. On the difficulty of finding teachers, see petitions from Kolomna in 1733 (TsGIA, f. 796, op. 14, g. 1733, d. 386, ll. 1-22), and Riazan in 1739 (ibid., op. 20, g. 1739, d. 14, l. 76 ob.; TsGADA, f. 1183, op. 1, g. 1739, d. 721, ll. 1-3); on the Synod's admission of an "extreme dearth" of teachers, see *PSPREP*, 2:595.

55. Kharlampovich, p. 708.

56. In 1767 Trinity-Sergius Seminary reported pupils mainly from Pereslavl diocese but youths from nine other dioceses also studied there. In the Moscow Academy, of its total enrollment of 275 pupils, 24 were from other dioceses; though a small figure, the outsiders nevertheless composed 38 percent (14 of 37) of the uppermost classes, philosophy and theology (TsGIA, f. 796, op. 48, g. 1767, d. 547, ll. 428-429 ob.; see also Smirnov, *ITS*, pp. 228, 480-482). Even this was a burden; to pay the costs of maintaining two seminarians at the Moscow Academy in 1757, the bishop of Rostov had to reduce

his seminary from fifty to forty pupils ("Posylka v 1756 g. uchenikov," *IaEV*, 1895, no. 26:415-416).

57. See, for example, the case of the Riazan seminary, which replaced an expensive Academy teacher with its own seminary graduate (Agntsev, *IRS*, pp. 30-33).

58. See, for instance, the complaints of the bishop of Kolomna in 1744 (*PSPREP*, 2:530) and the Synod in 1742 (*PSPREP*, 1:187); see also the reports on Riazan (Agntsev, *IRS*, pp. 21-27), Suzdal (Malitskii, *ISS*, pp. 92-93), Vladimir (Malitskii, *IVS*, 1:8, 49-62), and Trinity-Sergius (Smirnov, *ITS*, pp. 24-25).

59. For submitting false reports about their sons, see the cases of a priest in Vladimir in 1737 (TsGIA, f. 796, op. 18, g. 1737, d. 378, ll. 1-13) and of priests in Suzdal in 1741 (*ODDS*, 21:106).

60. Nadezhdin, "Ocherk," *VEV*, 1867, no. 9:430-431. For similar problems in Trinity-Sergius Seminary, see Smirnov, *ITS*, p. 27.

61. Agntsev, *IRS*, pp. 26-27.

62. Malitskii, *IVS*, 1:89; Nadezhdin, "Ocherk," *VEV*, 1865, no. 14:777-781.

63. Nadezhdin, "Ocherk," *VEV*, 1865, no. 14:779.

64. In 1744 the metropolitan of Rostov promulgated a formal schedule of fines for clergy who concealed their sons from the seminary; the bishop of Riazan followed suit and for 1750-52 alone he assessed 791.50 rubles (of which, however, he managed to collect little). More impetuous, the bishop of Suzdal ordered in 1765 that offenders be flogged. ("Ukaznoe predpisanie Iaroslavskogo dukhovnogo pravleniia," *IaEV*, 1890, no. 13:201-203; Agntsev, *IRS*, pp. 37-38; N. Malitskii, "Beguny v Suzdal'skoi dukhovnoi seminarii," *VEV*, 1905, no. 13:364).

65. N. Malitskii, "Pervye kanikuly vo Vladimirskoi dukhovnoi seminarii," *VEV*, 1899, no. 3:120.

66. For the printing and distribution of the 1722 primer, see *PSPR*, 2:913; for the measures of 1742-44 on the primer and catechism, see the following: *PSPREP*, 1:128 and 377; Nadezhdin, "Ocherk," *VEV*, 1865, no. 1:63, n.1. In 1759 the price of a catechism was 36 kopecks, a primer 32 kopecks, and a "trilingual lexicon" (presumably Latin-Greek-Russian) was 1.50 rubles (*ODDS*, 39:96). The high cost of religious books provoked the Senate in 1744 to question the Synod why they were so expensive (*PSPREP*, 2:548). Little wonder, then, that the clergy rarely owned printed books, apart from the mandatory catechism; see S. P. Luppov, *Kniga v Rossii v pervoi chetverti XVIII v.* (Leningrad, 1973), pp. 161-163.

67. TsGIA, f. 796, op. 18, g. 1737, d. 253, ll. 66 ob.-67; *ODDS*, 18: prilozhenie 15.

68. *PSPR*, 10:3342. These schools were of very modest dimensions, however; ordinarily, a special examiner provided intensive instruction to the youths awaiting ordination. The Synod made appointments of examiners in 1741 (*ODDS*, 21:6) and they were later reported performing their duties in Trinity-Sergius Seminary and Pereslavl diocese (Smirnov, *ITS*, p. 63; Malitskii, *IPE*, 1:290-294).

69. N. Malitskii, "Obuchenie pereiaslavskikh sviashchenno-tserkovno-sluzhitelei katekhizisu," *VEV*, 1905, no. 5:135-139; Smirnov, *ITS*, pp. 58-62.

70. Rozanov, *Istoriia*, 2, pt. 1:65.

71. I. Dobroliubov, "Ukazatel' materialov dlia istoriko-statisticheskogo opisaniia Riazanskoi eparkhii, khraniashchikhsia v arkhive dukhovnoi konsistorii (1720-1830 gg.)," *TRUAK*, 16 (1901), pt. 2:177; Rozanov, *Istoriia*, 2, pt. 1: n.188, n.338; TsGADA, f. 1183, op. 1, g. 1737, d. 390, l. 5 ob.

72. *PSPREA*, 1:219; TsGIA, f. 796, op. 46, g. 1765, d. 19, ll. 1-4 ob.

73. Malitskii, *IVS*, 105-112; N. Malitskii, "K istorii Vladimirskoi dukhovnoi seminarii pri episkope Pavle," *VEV*, 1907, no. 6:87-89. However, in fairness to Catherine, it should be noted that at least two seminaries obtained larger budgets: the Rostov seminary's budget increased from 1,290 to 1,524 rubles, and the Riazan seminary budget increased from 1,315 rubles (average income of 1758-63) to 1,633 rubles (TsGIA, f. 796, op. 46, g. 1765, d. 19, ll. 98-100, 190-191 ob.; Agntsev, *IRS*, pp. 58-59).

74. For examples of declining enrollments, see Malitskii, *ISS*, pp. 104-105, 130, and Malitskii, *IPE*, 2:74, 92.

75. Total enrollment dropped from 5,844 pupils (in 1762) to 4,673 pupils (in 1766); see Zav'ialov, *Vopros*, p. 347, and TsGIA, f. 796, op. 51, g. 1770, d. 470, ll. 11-12.

76. In Riazan, for example, the population grew steadily: 217 pupils in 1767, 289 in 1778, 531 in 1790, and 790 in 1800 (Agntsev, *IRS*, p. 100 n.; N. I. Kuleshov, "Shkola i obrazovanie v Riazanskoi gubernii v poslednei chetverti XVIII v." [Diplomnaia rabota, Moscow State University, 1967], p. 29; Sokolov, "Simon Lagov," *REV*, 1883, no. 21:551; TsGIA, f. 796, op. 71, g. 1790, d. 417, ll. 486-519).

77. Only Platon's schools received a state budget (Rozanov, *Istoriia*, 3, pt. 1:19 and nn.44-46). For the rise of district schools in Vladimir province, see Malitskii, *IVS*, 1:130-131; N. Vinogradov, "Istoricheskaia zapiska o Pereiaslavl'-Zalesskom dukhovnom uchilishche," *VEV*, 1888, nos. 16-21; V. Dobronravov, "Viaznikovskoe dukhovnoe uchilishche," *VEV*, 1905, no. 18:523-531; no. 21:613-621.

78. See the lists for Riazan in 1790 and Vladimir in 1793 (TsGIA, f. 796, op. 71, g. 1790, d. 417, ll. 486-519; op. 74, g. 1793, d. 94, ll. 349-421 ob.).

79. Malitskii, *IVS*, 1:124-185.

80. *PSPREA*, 1:567; see the similar measures of Platon in Moscow and Simon in Riazan (Rozanov, *Istoriia*, 3, pt. 1:19; Dobroliubov, "Ukazatel'," *TRUAK*, 16, pt. 2:188). On implementation, see the reports to the Synod from the early 1780s (TsGIA, f. 796, op. 65, g. 1784, d. 443, l. 5; op. 63, g. 1782, d. 543, ll. 13-21 ob., 67-132; op. 64, g. 1783, d. 217, ll. 65-66 ob.).

81. TsGIA, f. 796, op. 66, g. 1785, d. 214, ll. 1-1 ob. For a case where churchmen were replaced by seminarians, see ibid., d. 297, ll. 1-1 ob.

82. *PSZ*, 22:15978; 24:17675. A list of Vladimir seminarians conscripted in 1784 confirms that those drafted were considered "obtuse" (Malitskii, *IVS*, 3:5-11).

83. *PSPREA*, 1:219.

84. Znamenskii, *DSh*, p. 496. To solicit increases, hierarchs plied the em-

press with ingratiating ceremony; see, for example, the efforts of Trinity-Sergius Seminary in Smirnov, *ITS*, pp. 440-441.

85. *PSPRPP*, 161.

86. *PSZ*, 17:12060; *PSPREA*, 1:167.

87. In Vladimir priests had to give 12 kopecks, churchmen 6 kopecks (Malitskii, *IVS*, 1:116-117); on Riazan, see Agntsev, *IRS*, p. 63.

88. Catherine, through the Moscow governor, ordered Platon to cease such collections and to return the money ("Pis'ma i reskripty Ekateriny II-oi k moskovskim glavnokomanduiushchim," *RA*, 10 [1872], pp. 302-303). Moscow archpriest Petr Alekseev, who heartily disliked the Metropolitan, relates the affair with undisguised glee (see "Iz bumag imp. protoiereia Ioanna Pamfilova," *RA*, 1871, no. 1:225-226).

89. Malitskii, *IVS*, 1:130; I. V. Malinovskii, "Otkrytie Vladimirskogo dukhovnogo uchilishcha i pervye gody ego sushchestvovaniia," *TVUAK*, 3 (1901): 168.

90. Seminarians, who ordinarily had a right to one half the income of the reserved position, often had difficulty collecting their share, and some bishops set standard rates to avoid controversy (Nadezhdin, "Ocherk," *VEV*, 1868, no. 23:1117-1118; Agntsev, *IRS*, pp. 73-74).

91. Chistovich, *Istoriia*, pp. 51-52; see also the Synod's approval of a seminarian's request for a "reserved position" in 1789 (TsGIA, f. 796, op. 70, g. 1789, d. 387, l. 4 ob.).

92. Seminary registers of 1790-93 show the use of reserved positions, mainly for upper-class students. Bishops were loath to make exceptions, but the bishop of Vladimir did so in the case of M. M. Speranskii, later a famed bureaucrat; as a young pupil, he was awarded the position of a deacon because of his excellent grades, but this was "not to be an example for others" (N. Malitskii, "K biografii gr. M. M. Speranskogo," *VEV*, 1904, no. 17:492-496).

93. Rostov seminary reported 102 reserved positions, of which 13 were priests' positions, 17 deacons' positions, and 72 churchmen's positions. Most reserved positions were given to pupils in the upper forms; 76 percent of all positions, in fact, were held by students in the upper three forms. Every position given to pupils in the lower forms was that of churchman (TsGIA, f. 796, op. 71, g. 1790, d. 417, ll. 385-454).

94. In Riazan the clergy had to pay various fines—50 kopecks for failing to teach their children, 1.50 rubles for tardiness in delivering the youth to the seminary, and 1 ruble for concealing a truant (Agntsev, *IRS*, pp. 66-70).

95. Ibid., pp. 64-66.

96. In 1794, for example, the Riazan seminary devoted 36.8 percent of its budget to plant maintenance and supplies, 28.8 percent to teachers' salaries, 10.8 percent to administrative costs, and 23.6 percent to student support (Kuleshov, "Shkola," p. 31). Similar was the budget of the Iaroslavl seminary in 1798, just before Paul increased the budgets: 19.5 percent for plant maintenance and supplies, 42.9 percent for teachers' salaries, 3.4 percent for administration, and 34.2 percent for student support. After the budget increases, the support for students grew from 650 to 1930 rubles (now 49 percent of the

budget); see TsGIA, f. 796, op. 79, g. 1798, d. 35, ll. 460-461, 463-464.

97. In Vladimir, for example, 87 percent paid their way in the seminary; in the church schools, 98 to 99 percent depended upon their fathers for support (with only a handful in the church schools holding reserved positions). TsGIA, f. 796, op. 74, g. 1793, d. 94, ll. 349-421.

98. N. I. Petrov, *Kievskaia akademiia vo vtoroi polovine XVII v.* (Kiev, 1895), pp. 110-111.

99. Kharlampovich, pp. 633-740. Moscow Academy shows the magnitude of Ukrainian influence: Kiev provided 21 of 23 rectors, 17 of 21 prefects, and 95 of 125 instructors (ibid., pp. 649-666).

100. For a comparison of the European and Kievan models, see Okenfuss, "Education," pp. 118-119, and idem, "The Jesuit Origins of Petrine Education," in *The Eighteenth Century in Russia*, ed. J. G. Garrard (Oxford, 1973), pp. 110-111.

101. *PSPR*, 1:1. This system also reflected Prokopovich's dissatisfaction with "Latin" education in Kiev; see the summary discussion in A. Arkhangel'-skii, *Dukhovnoe obrazovanie i dukhovnaia shkola v Rossii pri Petre Velikom* (Kazan, 1883), pp. 16-26.

102. See Znamenskii, *DSh*, pp. 436-465, and Smirnov, *ITS*, pp. 37-53.

103. Znamenskii, *DSh*, p. 437.

104. Ibid., pp. 445-450.

105. Exceptional was the Trinity-Sergius seminary, where the instructor used the writings of Feofan Prokopovich (Smirnov, *ITS*, pp. 37-38).

106. The dissident nobleman A. N. Radishchev put such a critique in the mouth of a seminarian in his *Journey from St. Petersburg to Moscow* (Cambridge, Mass., 1955), p. 78. See also the later scholarly critiques by D. Agn-tsev ("Sostoianie uchilishch pri Ekaterine II," *REV*, 1877, no. 1:49) and Znamenskii (*DSh*, pp. 119-121, 464-465).

107. Smirnov, *ITS*, pp. 58-62.

108. Znamenskii, *DSh*, pp. 445-448.

109. Smirnov, *ITS*, pp. 63-94.

110. Znamenskii, *DSh*, pp. 456-462.

111. *PSPREA*, 1:76.

112. Znamenskii, *DSh*, pp. 409-429; Agntsev, *IRS*, pp. 30-33.

113. Agntsev, *IRS*, pp. 33-34; Malitskii, *ISS*, p. 109. In 1764 the Rostov seminary allocated 10 rubles for new books, a sum sufficient for the purchase of only a few books at most (TsGIA, f. 796, op. 46, g. 1765, d. 19, ll. 98-100).

114. Malitskii, *IVS*, 1:90-91.

115. Smirnov, *ITS*, pp. 54-56; the seminary inherited, it should be noted, a large monastery library numbering 1,677 volumes from the time of Peter the Great (see Luppov, p. 280).

116. See Znamenskii, *DSh*, pp. 729-783; Agntsev, "Sostoianie," *REV*, 1876-81, provides a useful analysis of the new textbooks.

117. For instance, in most seminaries the lower courses were reorganized into "lower" and "upper" grammar (*nizshaia grammatika; vysshaia grammatika*); many schools combined poesy (*piitika*) and rhetoric (*ritorika*) into a single course.

118. The Commission on Church Estates instructed bishops "not to use Alvarez but to use Lebedev's grammar" (Rozhdestvenskii, *Materialy*, p. 314).

119. Baumeister's textbook (*Elementa philosophiae recentioris usibus juventutis scholasticae recentioris* [Leipzig, 1755]), as indeed other of his writings that popularized the philosophy of Christian Wolff, were subsequently translated into Russian between the 1760s and the 1780s; see the list of translated works in *Svodnyi katalog russkoi knigi grazhdanskoi pechati XVIII v. (1725-1800 gg.)*, 5 vols. (Moscow, 1963-67), 1:80-81. On the adoption of Baumeister's textbook, see the reform project of 1766 in Rozhdestvenskii, *Materialy*, p. 315; for specific seminaries, see the materials on Vladimir (Malitskii, *IVS*, 1:163-164), Suzdal (Malitskii, *ISS*, p. 111), and Iaroslavl (TsGIA, f. 796, op. 79, g. 1798, d. 35, ll. 127-127 ob.). For a close analysis of Baumeister's textbook, see Agntsev, "Sostoianie," *REV*, 1878, no. 9:300-303, no. 13:406-408; no. 15:456-459; no. 20:566-567; 1880, no. 9:260-269; no. 10: 279-283.

120. Znamenskii, *DSh*, pp. 756-767; Malitskii, *ISS*, p. 111. The most commonly used textbook was Ioann Karpinskii's work, *Compendium orthodoxae theologicae doctrinae* (see, for example, Malitskii, *IVS*, 1:163). Metropolitan Platon's textbook, recommended by a commission in 1766, was in fact used by the Iaroslavl seminary in 1798, but in the class of rhetoric, not theology (Rozhdestvenskii, *Materialy*, p. 315; TsGIA, f. 796, op. 79, g. 1798, d. 35, ll. 127-127 ob.).

121. Seminary reports on curriculum in 1798 indicate the inclusion of some supplementary religious instruction; see the Iaroslavl report in TsGIA, f. 796, op. 79, g. 1798, d. 35, ll. 127-127 ob.

122. *PSPREA*, 3:1250; Malitskii, *IVS*, 1:161-163.

123. Smirnov, *ITS*, p. 310.

124. Malitskii, *IVS*, 1:166-167.

125. Titlinov, *Gavriil*, p. 786.

126. On the abortive attempt to establish "Russian schools," see the original decree (*PSZ*, 27:20670) and B. N. Titlinov, *Dukhovnaia shkola v Rossii v XIX v.*, 2 vols. (Vil'na, 1908-1909), 1:12.

127. Catherine required all seminaries to offer Greek in 1784 (*PSPREA*, 2:1180, 1182). However, few seminarians studied Greek or Hebrew; even at Trinity-Sergius Seminary, only 6 percent studied Hebrew and 9 percent Greek, while 19 percent studied German and 20 percent French (Smirnov, *ITS*, pp. 238-240). An important exception (outside the central dioceses) was the new seminary in Ekaterinoslav, where the Greek prelate Evgenii Bulgaris gave priority to the study of Greek. See Stephen K. Batalden, "Eugenios Voulgaris in Russia, 1771-1806" (Ph.D. diss., University of Minnesota, 1975), pp. 132-141.

128. In 1798 all seminaries reported the study of secular subjects; the report on Riazan even referred to "Russian experimental physics" among others. See the reports of Iaroslavl, Moscow, and Riazan in TsGIA, f. 796, op. 79, g. 1798, d. 35, ll. 78, 127-127 ob., 143-144.

129. N. Rudnev, "Tul'skaia dukhovnaia seminariia," *TEV*, 1862, no. 9:488-489.

130. Pupils in theology and philosophy represented 9 percent of the seminary in Kolomna (1790), 11 percent in Riazan (1790), 12 percent in Rostov (1790), 11 percent in Vladimir-Suzdal (1793), and 11 percent in the Moscow Academy (1790) (TsGIA, f. 796, op. 71, g. 1790, d. 417, ll. 152-187, 385-454, 486-519; d. 418, ll. 517-590; op. 74, g. 1793, d. 94, ll. 349-381).

131. Malitskii, *ISS*, p. 110.

132. See the bleak descriptions of the seminaries in Riazan and Vladimir (Agntsev, *IRS*, pp. 118-119; Malitskii, *IVS*, 1:169).

133. Agntsev, *IRS*, pp. 122-123; see also Malitskii, *ISS*, pp. 97-98.

134. *Opis' DKU*, p. 5.

135. Znamenskii, *DSh*, pp. 680-706; Agntsev, *IRS*, pp. 102-109; Malitskii, *ISS*, pp. 77-92.

136. Smirnov, *ITS*, p. 147.

137. In 1798 the seminaries of Suzdal, Iaroslavl, Kolomna and Riazan reported that their teaching staffs consisted of 18 white clergy, 16 unordained instructors (most probably, recent seminary graduates teaching until a good position became available), and only 3 monks (TsGIA, f. 796, op. 79, g. 1798, d. 35, ll. 129 ob.-131, 144-146, 194, 280 ob.). Monastic staff were common only in the higher academies; Moscow Academy, for instance, reported in 1790 that five of its ten instructors were monks (ibid., op. 71, g. 1790, d. 417, ll. 81 ob.-86).

138. Titlinov, *Dukhovnaia shkola*, 1:13.

139. See the descriptions of the seminary library in Vladimir and Riazan (Malitskii, *IVS*, 1:176-180; Agntsev, *IRS*, pp. 131-134). The plight of seminary libraries aroused the interest of the Freemason and philanthropist, N. I. Novikov, who donated 300 rubles worth of books to the Suzdal seminary (Malitskii, *ISS*, pp. 111-112).

140. Titlinov, *Gavriil*, p. 7; Znamenskii, *DSh*, pp. 786-787.

141. See "Nekrolog Giliarova-Platonova," *Vestnik evropy*, 1887, no. 11:452.

142. "Arsenii Matseevich, byvshii mitropolit rostovskii," *Chteniia OIDR*, 41 (1862), kn. 2, chast' 5:32.

143. I. Bogoslovskii, "Istoricheskaia zapiska o Rostovskom dmitrievskom dukhovnom uchilischche," *IaEV*, 1899, no. 24:357.

144. N. K., "Arsenii Matseevich kak propovednik," *IaEV*, 1864, no. 52: 508-509.

145. Radishchev, pp. 77-82; Smirnov, *ITS*, pp. 455-456; Sokolov, "Simon Lagov," *REV*, 1884, no. 3:65.

146. The Ecclesiastical Regulation provided for an age group of ten to fifteen (*PSPR*, 1:1), a group which Petrine pedagogy viewed as amenable to specialized, professional education. But seminary lists from the 1730s and 1740s show that the range in student age was considerable—from six or seven up to twenty or more (TsGIA, f. 796, op. 25, g. 1744, d. 134, ll. 49-51 ob., 64-81 ob., 82-88, 107-121).

147. For a revealing picture of the seminary experience from the early nineteenth century, see N. P. Giliarov-Platonov, *Iz perezhitogo*, 2 vols. (Moscow, 1886). From all accounts, it seems that the abrupt changes from home to

school, from freedom to service rigors, from Russian to an alien culture were not unlike the experiences of the Westernizing nobility. Compare the account in Marc Raeff, *Origins of the Russian Intelligentsia: The Eighteenth-Century Nobility* (New York, 1966), pp. 122-147.

148. In 1787 Platon instructed the seminarians to inform the prefect if they were insulted in the marketplace; with tactical forethought, Platon also urged them to travel in groups of five or six (Smirnov, *ITS*, p. 463).

149. See, for example, the comments by Alexander Herzen about the seminarians who speak "another language" at the university; in the famous novel by I. S. Turgenev, *Fathers and Sons*, the aristocratic Pavel Petrovich declares that he is "not a seminary rat" (A. Herzen, *My Past and My Thoughts*, 4 vols. [New York, 1968], 1:97; I. S. Turgenev, *Fathers and Sons* [New York, 1966], p. 121).

150. Vissarion Belinskii, whose grandfather was a deacon and whose father was probably once a seminarian, used "seminarian" as a pejorative term. He once wrote a letter to Botkin, upbraiding "that cad, that pig, the seminarist Nikitenko"—who had of course never been in a seminary (V. G. Belinskii, *Selected Philosophical Works* [Moscow, 1948], p. 152).

151. *PSPR*, 1:1; Muller, *Spiritual Regulation*, pp. 40-41.

152. For Peter's view of education as the first stage of service, see Vladimirskii-Budanov, *Gosudarstvo*, pp. vi, 188-245.

153. *PSPR*, 1:1; Smirnov, *ITS*, pp. 14-15.

154. See copies of a typical *attestat* in Smirnov, *ITS*, p. 102, and TsGIA, f. 796, op. 44, g. 1763, d. 79, l. 8.

155. Malitskii, *IVS*, 1:52.

156. Nadezhdin, "Ocherk," *VEV*, 1867, no. 9:437-438; Malitskii, *ISS*, pp. 48-60; "Delo iz proshlogo stoletiia ob uchitele Iaroslavskoi dukhovnoi seminarii i bibliotekare Petre Kotsinskom," *IaEV*, 1890, no. 21:329-332.

157. Agntsev, *IRS*, pp. 46-47.

158. Malitskii, *IVS*, 1:81-82.

159. See Nadezhdin, "Ocherk," *VEV*, 1867, no. 9:1069.

160. Ibid., 1868, no. 16:784-792.

161. Malitskii, *ISS*, pp. 31-33.

162. Nadezhdin, "Ocherk," *VEV*, 1868, no. 16:794; see also Pekarskii, 1:454.

163. See Giliarov-Platonov, 1:97, and "Rasskazy sviashchennika," *RS*, 24 (1879), no. 3:554-555.

164. *PSPR*, 1:1.

165. See Catherine's complaint about this in 1762 (*PSPREA*, 1:76); for an example of the bishop's reluctance to expel pupils, see the reports on Suzdal and Vladimir (Malitskii, *ISS*, pp. 101-102, and idem, *IVS*, 1:173-174). Indeed, after the 1808 seminary reforms, the enrollment in Moscow schools dropped from 2,456 to 1,923 pupils by expelling such unfit youths (Titlinov, *Dukhovnaia shkola*, 1:13).

166. Malitskii, *IVS*, 1:168-171.

167. Giliarov-Platonov, 1:115-118.

168. Agntsev, *IRS*, p. 113.

169. Ibid., pp. 40-41.
170. Nadezhdin, "Ocherk," *VEV*, 1866, no. 4:173.
171. Agntsev, *IRS*, pp. 28, 48. One seminary outside the central area, Viatka, reported that in 1735-38 more than half its pupils (253 of 491) had fled (TsGIA, f. 796, op. 18, g. 1737, d. 32, chast' 2, ll. 537-537 ob.).
172. See the cases of Vladimir and Suzdal in Malitskii, *IVS*, 1:58-62, 91-99, and idem, *ISS*, pp. 130-135.
173. For the request of a Iaroslavl seminarian to become a peasant in 1781 and the case of a Suzdal seminarian who sought to enlist in the army in 1769, see Vladimirskii-Budanov, *Gosudarstvo*, p. 232, and Malitskii, *ISS*, pp. 132-133.
174. TsGADA, f. 1183, op. 1, g. 1755, d. 401, ll. 3-3 ob.; see also Nadezhdin, "Ocherk," *VEV*, 1868, no. 17:834-840, and Malitskii, *IVS*, 1:58-61.
175. See Kniaz'kov and Serbov, pp. 61-79.
176. In 1785 Catherine directed the bishops to study the new question-and-answer methods used in state schools; because of the bishops' skepticism and the rapid turnover in teaching staff, however, her order had scant effect (*PSPREA*, 3:1221, 1250; Znamenskii, *DSh*, pp. 787-794; Malitskii, *IVS*, 1:161-163).
177. Istomin, "Postanovleniia," pp. 597-598; Rozhdestvenskii, *Materialy*, pp. 288, 318.
178. Malitskii, "Beguny," *VEV*, 1905, no. 13:362; see also Malitskii, *IVS*, 1:161.
179. See the comprehensive instructions issued for Trinity-Sergius Seminary in 1767 and 1786 (Smirnov, *ITS*, pp. 452-464) and Riazan Seminary in 1779 ("Po povodu pechataemogo nizhe 'Uchrezhdeniia,' " *REV*, 1866, no. 17:527-528).
180. "Po povodu pechataemogo nizhe 'Uchrezhdeniia,' " *REV*, 1866, no. 17:527-528.
181. Nadezhdin, "Ocherk," *VEV*, 1868, no. 23:1119; Malitskii, *IVS*, 1:180-182.
182. Resistance, if less obtrusive, did not cease entirely, however. See reports on the 1790s in Riazan, Vladimir, and Murom (Sokolov, "Simon Lagov," *REV*, 1884, no. 2:42-43; "Nekrolog: Protoierei P. I. Pevnitskii," *VEV*, 1866, no. 7:336; Travchetov, "Delo," *TVUAK*, 2:74).
183. Smirnov, *ITS*, p. 138.
184. Ibid., pp. 476-478.
185. Malitskii, *ISS*, pp. 115-116; see also Rudnev, "Tul'skaia dukhovnaia seminariia," *TEV*, 1863, no. 15:144.
186. Smirnov, *ITS*, pp. 149-152, 452-464.
187. Giliarov-Platonov, 2:8-9.
188. Agntsev, "Sostoianie," *REV*, 1878, no. 3:100.
189. See, for example, the discussion of theological questions in a debate at the Vladimir seminary in 1791 (Malitskii, *IVS*, 1:165-166).
190. For fascinating descriptions of "debates" in Riazan and Vladimir, see: Agntsev, *IRS*, 127-130; Sokolov, "Simon Lagov," *REV*, 1884, no. 6:116; I. V. Dobroliubov, "Seminarskoe torzhestvo 1797 g.," *Istoricheskii vestnik*, 1880, no. 3:646-647; Malitskii, *IVS*, 1:165-166.

191. See Agntsev, *IRS*, pp. 150-158.

192. For a general description of the material hardships, see Znamenskii, *DSh*, pp. 639-665. For reports of students in Pereslavl begging alms in the 1790s, see Vinogradov, "Istoricheskaia zapiska," *VEV*, 1888, no. 16:562-563. See also the grim description of student life in Suzdal and Vladimir in Malitskii, *ISS*, pp. 20-21, and idem, *IVS*, 1:131-132.

193. Students in Riazan were crowded into fifteen cottages, where a single room served as bedroom, dining room, and classroom (Agntsev, *IRS*, pp. 51-56). The problem of overcrowding was emphasized in the bishops' reports on the condition of their seminaries; see, for instance, the comments on Iaroslavl, Kolomna, Moscow, Riazan, and Vladimir-Suzdal in TsGIA, f. 796, op. 79, g. 1798, d. 35, ll. 77-77 ob., 125 ob.-127, 142-142 ob., 193 ob., 279 ob.-280.

194. See, for example, the description of Pereslavl in the 1790s in Vinogradov, "Istoricheskaia zapiska," *VEV*, 1888, no. 16:562-563.

195. Malitskii, *ISS*, pp. 48-63; Malitskii, "Beguny," *VEV*, 1905, no. 3:362.

196. *PSPREA*, 1:567.

197. See, for example, the reports on Suzdal and Trinity-Sergius seminaries (Malitskii, *ISS*, p. 104; Smirnov, *ITS*, pp. 159, 541-542).

198. Malitskii, *IVS*, 1:174.

199. The Synod implicitly authorized this practice in a decree of 1770 (*PSPREA*, 1:571); for an account of such a policy, see the case of Pereslavl in Malitskii, *IPE*, 2:117.

200. See the interesting comments by Giliarov-Platonov, 2:3-15. It is not possible to make a precise comparison of student enrollment and the whole population of clerical children, for authorities did not maintain a list of the clergy's children not in the seminary. But a rough comparison is possible between the students' origins and the breakdown of ordained clergy and churchmen. In general, the number of churchmen usually exceeded the ordained clergy by the end of the century; in Vladimir, for example, a report of 1782 shows 1,606 priests and deacons (46 percent) and 1,909 churchmen (54 percent). But the seminary registers consistently show more children of ordained clergy: 54 percent were the sons of ordained clergy in Kaluga, 70 percent in Kolomna, 65 percent in Riazan, and 72 percent in Suzdal (TsGIA, f. 796, op. 63, g. 1782, d. 543, ll. 3 ob.-12; op. 62, g. 1781, d. 585, ll. 455-456; op. 71, g. 1790, d. 417, ll. 486-519; d. 418, ll. 517-590; op. 79, g. 1798, d. 958, ll. 4-20). A note of caution is in order: this is a crude approximation, since the more prosperous ordained clergy may have had a lower rate of infant mortality and churchmen were sometimes too young to have school-age children; on the other hand, many priests were probably too old to have sons aged 7 to 15.

201. The term "learned clergy" referred at mid-century to one who had completed the rhetoric class; later, it generally referred to a graduate of the philosophy or theology class. See Skvortsov, *Materialy*, 1:165; Rozanov, *Istoriia*, 3, pt. 1:90.

202. "Learned clergy" constituted 50 percent of all archpriests, 20 percent of all priests, and 10 percent of all deacons in Moscow in 1774 (Skvortsov, *Materialy*, 1:151-152).

203. Malitskii, "Obuchenie," *VEV*, 1905, no. 5:135; Travchetov, "Delo," *TVUAK*, 2:72-73.

204. In 1785 a city priest, aged 58, resisted a bishop's orders to relocate to a rural parish, arguing that "in view of my old age I cannot become accustomed to farming" (TsGIA, f. 796, op. 66, g. 1785, d. 256, l. 1 ob.). See also the description of hardships suffered by one priest as he adjusted to a village parish and field labor in Giliarov-Platonov, 1:47.

205. Tooke, 2:120n.

206. Malitskii, *IPE*, 1:290.

207. *SIRIO*, 43:421; see the similar comment by Metropolitan Platon in "Pis'ma Platona," *PO*, 1870, no. 10:81.

208. See the bishops' reports to the Synod in the early 1780s in TsGIA, f. 796, op. 63, g. 1782, d. 543, ll. 13-21 ob., 67-132; op. 64, g. 1783, d. 217, ll. 65-66 ob.; op. 65, g. 1784, d. 443, l. 5.

209. On the proposals to exclude churchmen's sons, see *SIRIO*, 113:50, 113, 116; for data on unplaced seminarians, see the reports for 1849 and 1853-54 in TsGIA, f. 796, op. 131, g. 1850, d. 1998 and f. 802 (Uchebnyi komitet), op. 6, d. 16114.

210. Bolotov, 4:877; see also his comments on the local clergy (3:462-463, 4:465, 1103, 1124, 1191, 1293-1294).

211. M. P. Poludenskii, "Rasskazy Kn. Sergeia Mikhailovicha Golitsyna," *RA*, 7 (1869), no. 4:630.

212. As early as 1779, Bishop Simon of Riazan ordered his seminarians to study medicine, though there is no evidence that they did so ("Po povodu pechataemogo nizhe 'Uchrezhdeniia,' " *REV*, 1866, no. 18:532). The bishop of Iaroslavl similarly proposed to introduce the study of medicine in 1798, arguing that such training would enable the priest to render practical assistance to the ignorant peasantry (TsGIA, f. 796, op. 79, g. 1798, d. 35, ll. 127-127 ob.). In 1802 the study of medicine was in fact made a formal obligation for all seminaries (*PSZ*, 27:20346).

213. See Arcadius Kahan, "The Costs of Westernization: The Gentry and the Economy in the Eighteenth Century," *Slavic Review*, 25 (1966):40-66.

5. The Structure and Economics of Clerical Service

1. Similar data for 1747 and 1776 are to be found in TsGIA, f. 796, op. 28, g. 1747, d. 216, and op. 57, g. 1776, d. 362, ll. 25-30 ob.

2. *AAE*, 1:229.

3. Pokrovskii, *Russkie eparkhii*, 1:174-175, n.2; 1:234-235.

4. V. Kholmogorov and G. Kholmogorov, *Istoricheskie materialy dlia sostavleniia tserkovnykh letopisei Moskovskoi eparkhii* [vols. 2-11 entitled: *Istoricheskie materialy o tserkvakh i selakh XVI-XVIII st.*], 11 vols. (Moscow, 1881-1911), 1:255-256; hereafter *IM*.

5. Pokrovskii, *Russkie eparkhii*, 2:28-29.

6. *PSZ*, 1:288, 289, 291.

7. See Pokrovskii, *Russkie eparkhii*, 1:357.

8. Shliapkin, p. 314.

9. Local officials and noblemen shared this outlook; see the statement by a local official in Shatsk, and the noble "instructions" to the Legislative Commission (*ODDS*, 16:149; *SIRIO*, 4:338; 68:444, 521-522).

10. See Hugo Hantsch, *Die Geschichte Österreichs*, 2 vols. (Graz, 1968-1969), 2:221.

11. Kotoshikhin estimated the number of endowed churches at 1,500 in the mid-seventeenth century; although the total number of churches at that time is unknown, it was surely less than the 10,781 reported in 1700 (Pokrovskii, *Russkie eparkhii*, 2:28, n.1); thus endowed churches probably represented 15 to 20 percent of all churches in the mid-seventeenth century.

12. *PSZ*, 22:16448.

13. For an estimate of some 5,000 chapels (though obviously without a resident priest in most of them), see E. Golubinskii, *Istoriia russkoi tserkvi*, 2 vols. (2nd. ed.; Moscow, 1901-10), 2, pt. 2:80-81.

14. See, for example, the case of England: John Moorman, *Church Life in England in the Thirteenth Century* (Cambridge, 1945), pp. 15-18, and Mason, "Role of the English Parishioner," p. 22.

15. The vagrant, free-lance priests numbered approximately two hundred in Moscow—or roughly one vagrant priest for each parish in the city (*ODDS*, 2, pt. 1:492. Because the vagrant clergy conducted themselves outrageously and gave religious services without authorization from local diocesan authorities, the Church forbade clergy to travel without passports and set fines for magnates who gave them refuge (see *PSPR*, 7:2570).

16. Giliarov-Platonov, 1:19-20.

17. *PSZ*, 5:3171.

18. *PSPR*, 2:533 and 902. Peter did, however, authorize chapels for high officials or magnates (*znatnye liudi*).

19. *PSPR*, 3:1120, 4:1295.

20. *PSPR*, 5:1672, 1771; *ODDS*, 3:521; 6:66.

21. Skvortsov, *Materialy*, 2:690; see also 2:691, 700, 714.

22. *PSZ*, 15:11460.

23. *PSPREA*, 1:27.

24. In a 1764 ruling the Synod gave a narrow interpretation to Catherine's decree, defining "magnate" to include only those holding the first two ranks (a tiny segment of the nobility) and restricting permission to cases where a chapel was physically necessary (*PSPREA*, 1:211). Later, on its own initiative, the Synod collected data on such chapels, with the clear intent of restricting their number (*PSPREA*, 1:620). Diocesan authorities were no less hostile to opening such chapels. For example, one aristocrat recalled that Metropolitan Platon so disliked private chapels that only high connections sufficed to obtain permission (Kn. I. M. Dolgorukov, *Povest' o rozhdenii moem, prois-khozhdenii i vsei zhizni* [Petrograd, 1916], p. 25).

25. *PSZ*, 5:2985.

26. *PSZ*, 5:3171.

27. *PSZ*, 6:3991; *PSPR*, 2:586, 662.

28. *PSPR*, 3:1054, 1029.

29. *PSPR*, 5:1848, 7:2435; *ODDS*, 6:110.

30. For cases where permission was granted after investigations, see the report on Suzdal in 1730, Murom uezd in 1747, and Romanov uezd in 1745 (*ODDS*, 10:14; TsGADA, f. 1183, op. 1, g. 1747, d. 284, ll. 1-1 ob.; A. Sokolov, "Selo Tikhonovo," *IaEV*, 1890, no. 1:4-14).

31. See the rejection of applications in 1742 and 1775 in *PSPREP*, 1:225 and Skvortsov, *Materialy*, 1:217.

32. *PSZ*, 19:13541.

33. Data here for urban churches include not only parishes but also cathedrals, endowed churches, and other miscellaneous types; reductions affected primarily endowed churches, not parish churches. A more refined analysis, however, is impossible, for the data from 1783 give only the sum total of churches, not each category. However, the later data show that in all cities the average parish was over 20 households: 27 in Moscow, 64 in Iaroslavl, and 135 in Kaluga. Even in the traditional religious cities the averages exceeded the norm: 37 households per parish in Suzdal, 54 in Murom, 43 in Pereslavl, 32 in Rostov, and 55 in Riazan (TsGIA, f. 796, op. 64, g. 1783, d. 580, ll. 1-284).

34. Kabuzan, *Izmeneniia*, pp. 52-53.

35. *PSZ*, 4:2352; *ODDS*, 1: prilozhenie.

36. *ODDS*, 2, pt. 1:495.

37. *PSZ*, 4:2352, 5:3171.

38. *PSPR*, 2:674; *PSZ*, 6:4035.

39. *PSPR*, 2:745; *ODDS*, 2, pt. 1:756.

40. In 1740, for example, the average household (including males and females) had 8.76 individuals in Suzdal, 8.92 in Rostov, 9.94 in Riazan, and 12.43 in Kolomna dioceses, variations that reflected both the amorphousness of the "household unit" and the different social topographies of each area (*ODDS*, 20: prilozhenie 10).

41. Only minor changes were made. For example, in 1725 the Synod authorized the bishop to ordain a second priest instead of a deacon where the parish encompassed a large territory and a single priest could not handle all the rites and sacraments by himself (*PSPR*, 5:1677; *ODDS*, 5:345).

42. *PSZ*, 14:10665, 10780.

43. Rozanov, *Istoriia*, 1:n.375; 2, pt. 1:47.

44. *ODDS*, 18: prilozhenie 16.

45. *PSPREA*, 1:436.

46. *PSZ*, 20:14807; *PSPREA*, 2:889.

47. See the Synodal admonitions of 1778 and 1784 in TsGIA, f. 796, op. 59, g. 1778, d. 356, ll. 1-2 ob. and *PSPREA*, 2:1167.

48. TsGIA, f. 796, op. 62, g. 1781, d. 195, ll. 1-153.

49. Ibid., op. 76, g. 1795, d. 75, ll. 46-47 ob.

50. Skvortsov, *Materialy*, 2:723; TsGIA, f. 796, op. 62, g. 1781, d. 195, ll. 67-140 ob.

51. *PSPR*, 1:1, 2:596; Muller, *Spiritual Regulation*, pp. 55, 69.

52. Verkhovskoi, 2:91.

53. See Voskresenskii, pp. 57, 60-61, and Troitskii, *Russkii absoliutizm*, pp. 48-77.

54. *PSPR*, 4:1396; *ODDS*, 4:474.

55. Pososhkov, p. 34.

56. Iu. V. Got'e, "Proekt o popravlenii gosudarstvennykh del Artemiia Petrovicha Volynskogo," *Dela i Dni*, 3 (1922):22; "Zapiska ob Artemii Volynskom," *Chteniia OIDR*, 1858, kn. 2, chast' 5:155.

57. N. A. Popov, *Tatishchev i ego vremia* (Moscow, 1861), p. 226.

58. *SIRIO*, 43:49, 421; see also Titlinov, *Gavriil*, p. 174, and E. M. Prilezhaev, "Nakaz i punkty deputatu ot Sv. Sinoda v Ekaterinskuiu komissiiu o sochinenii proekta novogo ulozheniia," *Khr. Cht.*, 1876, tom 2:223-265.

59. Titlinov, *Gavriil*, pp. 230-237, 608-609.

60. See D. Ilovaiskii, "Graf Iakov Sivers," *Russkii vestnik*, 1865, no. 1:46-47.

61. *SIRIO*, 6:150.

62. GBL, f. 222, k. XVII, d. 1, l. 21; S. N. Kologrivov, "Novonaidennyi trud Ekateriny Velikoi," *RA*, 1908, no. 6:176.

63. Pokrovskii, *Russkie eparkhii*, 2:541.

64. Titlinov, *Gavriil*, pp. 620-653; Pokrovskii, *Russkie eparkhii*, 2:555-556.

65. *PSZ*, 25:18316; Titlinov, *Gavriil*, pp. 655-676.

66. Got'e, *Istoriia oblastnogo upravleniia*, 1:187-188, 292; see also Troitskii, *Russkii absoliutizm*, pp. 253-267.

67. Kahan, "Costs of Westernization," pp. 41-47.

68. The Synod confirmed in 1744 the monopoly of clergy in Uspenskii Cathedral over marriage licenses; they also had the right to consecrate churches. This privileged status nettled Metropolitan Platon (Levshin), who claimed that the exclusive status of the Kremlin clergy made it impossible for him to correct "disorders" among them (*PSPREP*, 2:781; Rozanov, *Istoriia*, 3, pt. 1:41).

69. Zav'ialov, *Vopros*, pp. 284-285.

70. TsGADA, f. 280, op. 3, d. 145, ll. 7-13, 83-86.

71. TsGIA, f. 796, op. 24, g. 1743, d. 496, chast' 1, ll. 143-147 ob.

72. Rozanov, *Istoriia*, 2, pt. 1:179.

73. *PSPREA*, 1:167; Rozanov, *Istoriia*, 3, pt. 1:n.607.

74. P. Znamenskii, "O sposobakh soderzhaniia russkogo dukhovenstva v XVII-XVIII st.," *PS*, 1865, no. 3:149-152.

75. Malitskii, *IPE*, 1:212.

76. TsGADA, f. 280, op. 3, d. 145, ll. 27-32 ob., 34-48; 20-20 ob. Interestingly, when the state tried to improve the condition of clergy at the Uspenskii Cathedral by reducing the size of the staff, its clergy opposed the change by citing seventeenth-century charters (TsGIA, f. 796, op. 25, g. 1744, d. 321, ll. 1-2).

77. Malitskii, *IPE*, 2:172. It is difficult to judge the degree of deliberate falsification, especially in cases where the clergy claimed destitution in hope of some aid or concession from the bishop. But it seems that reports were roughly accurate, especially in the larger churches, where petitioners' claims were subject to comparison with the records of income that were maintained for determining each cleric's share of parish revenues.

78. Cf. Got'e, *Istoriia oblastnogo upravleniia*, 1:273-277.

79. *Dukhovnyi shtat*, pp. 47-52, 85-86; *PSPREA*, 1:167.

80. TsGIA, f. 796, op. 79, g. 1798, d. 35, l. 460.

81. Ibid., op. 25, g. 1744, d. 321, ll. 12-13. Similar was the plight of cathedral clergy in Mozhaisk, where the twelve clerics reported a total income of only 74.20 rubles per year (Malitskii, *IPE*, 2:166-167).

82. *ODDS*, 16:122.

83. Beginning in 1688 the cathedral clergy of Murom had difficulty collecting dues from their peasants and after a prolonged struggle finally obtained a writ in 1700 ordering the cathedral's peasants "to be obedient to him, Archpriest Fedor, in all matters, to do all the work, and to pay the money obligations without any resistance." More troubles erupted in the 1730s and by 1740 the peasants had completely ceased paying their quitrent, leaving the cathedral clergy in desperate straits. The squabbling was not resolved until 1759, when the civil authorities in Vladimir decided the case against the peasants, ordered them to pay the back quitrent, and had the "ringleaders" flogged. (S. N. Vvedenskii, "Iz tserkovnoi stariny muromskogo kraia," *TVUAK*, 11 [1909]: 3-22; *ODDS*, 20:312, 21:688, 31:63; "Dmitrii Sechenov," *REV*, 1916, no. 18/19:723-728; 1917, no. 6:156.)

84. TsGADA, f. 280, op. 3, d. 743, ll. 14-27; TsGIA, f. 796, op. 28, g. 1747, d. 216, ll. 140 ob.-145.

85. Data for 1747 show that most positions were occupied in the main district cathedrals, though occasionally vacancies would exist in churchmen's ranks; in general, however, the district cathedrals were relatively well-staffed (TsGIA, f. 796, op. 28, g. 1747, d. 216, ll. 140 ob.-143, 346 ob.-347, 173 ob.-175).

86. *Dukhovnyi shtat*, pp. 87-88; *PSPREA*, 1:167.

87. *PSPREA*, 3:1255.

88. Skvortsov, *Materialy*, 2:717.

89. Znamenskii, "O sposobakh," pp. 160-166; as a typical endowment grant, see the charter given by the tsar to a Suzdal church in 1651 allotting a subsidy of 23 rubles per annum (*AI*, 4:47).

90. *PSZ*, 3:1664.

91. *PSPR*, 5:1720, provides a typical example.

92. *ODDS*, 16:49, 20:559.

93. TsGIA, f. 796, op. 55, g. 1774, d. 362, ll. 14-14 ob.; Rozanov, *Istoriia*, 2, pt. 2:110-111.

94. TsGIA, f. 796, op. 55, g. 1774, d. 362, ll. 14-14 ob.

95. For diocesan reports in 1781-82, see ibid., op. 62, g. 1781, d. 586, ll. 202-270 ob.

96. GBL, f. 222, k. XVII, d. 1, l. 21.

97. TsGIA, f. 796, op. 28, g. 1747, d. 216, ll. 482 ob.-486.

98. Ibid., op. 62, g. 1781, d. 586, ll. 202-270 ob.

99. *PSPREA*, 2:814.

100. TsGIA, f. 796, op. 28, g. 1747, d. 216, ll. 124 ob.-125.

101. Ibid., op. 62, g. 1781, d. 586, ll. 15-16, 202-270 ob.

102. Ibid., op. 28, g. 1747, d. 216, ll. 180 ob.-182; op. 48, g. 1767, d. 547, ll. 444-498; op. 60, g. 1779, d. 162, ll. 1-10; op. 62, g. 1781, d. 586, ll. 7-9.

103. On the attempt of petty noblemen (ranks 6 and lower) to obtain private chapels, see the material on Moscow in the 1760s and the Synod's opposition (Rozanov, *Istoriia*, 2, pt. 2:39-40; *PSPREA*, 1:211).

104. TsGIA, f. 796, op. 52, g. 1771, d. 240, ll. 174-181 ob., 193-203.

105. All four chapels in Pereslavl and Vladimir dioceses, for example, employed full-time priests (ibid.).

106. Giliarov-Platonov, 1:19-20.

107. See, for instance, the data on chapels in Moscow in 1771-73 after the plague (Skvortsov, *Materialy*, 2:514-533).

108. Zav'ialov, *Vopros*, pp. 284-285.

109. TsGADA, f. 280, op. 3, d. 145, ll. 50-145 ob.

110. Ibid., d. 743, ll. 1-13, 28-59.

111. Ibid., d. 311, ll. 1-245; d. 508, ll. 1-139.

112. V. Lestvitsyn, "Tserkvi g. Iaroslavlia v 1781 g.," *IaEV*, 1874, nos. 38-51; for an example of a merchant's bequest, see "Vkladnaia zapis' ot 1693 g.," *IaEV*, 1894, no. 21:331-332.

113. The term *ruga* was applied both to the tsar's endowment for churches and to a landlord's grant to his parish church. They were quite different, however; unlike the tsar's benefice, the landlord's stipend was a salary or supplement, often based on short-term contracts.

114. Skvortsov, *Materialy*, 1:178. For supplements in kind, see the *ruga* contracts in *ODDS*, 21:38 and Skvortsov, *Materialy*, 1:79, 214, 229.

115. Shchepetov, pp. 160-161.

116. Skvortsov, *Materialy*, 1:183. See also Sokolov, "Selo Tikhonovo," *IaEV*, 1890, no. 1:12-13.

117. Skvortsov, *Materialy*, 1:73; TsGIA, f. 796, op. 62, g. 1781, d. 51, ll. 15 ob.-16. See also Skvortsov, *Materialy*, 1:214, 228, 229; 2:714-716; M. V. Dovnar-Zapol'skii, "Materialy dlia istorii votchinnogo upravleniia v Rossii," *Universitetskie izvestiia* [hereafter *UI*], 43 (1903), no. 12:6.

118. Skortsov, *Materialy*, 1:73, 178, 182.

119. TsGADA, f. 1183, op. 1, g. 1739, d. 38, ll. 15-16.

120. Ibid., g. 1746, d. 194, l. 4.

121. Rozanov, *Istoriia*, 2, pt. 1:n.124. For other examples, see Skvortsov, *Materialy*, 1:79-80, 228, and *ODDS*, 3:182, 7:111.

122. *PSPREP*, 4:1359; see also *ODDS*, 21:38.

123. Shimko, pp. 107-109.

124. A. P. Dobroklonskii, *Rukovodstvo po istorii russkoi tserkvi*, 4 vols. (Riazan, Moscow, 1889-1893), 3:57; P. V. Znamenskii, "Zakonodatel'stvo Petra Velikogo otnositel'no dukhovenstva," *PS*, 1863, no. 10:127.

125. *ODBMIu*, 1, pt. 3, no. 3.

126. Znamenskii, "Zakonodatel'stvo Petra," p. 127; see also A. Lototskii, "Material'naia obespechennost' prikhodskogo dukhovenstva v proshlom veke," *RSP*, 1899, no. 37:57-58. For a picture of this insufficient landholding, see the tax records of the Patriarchal Treasury in "Opisanie knig dozornykh, perepisnykh, opisnykh, mezhevykh, doimochnykh, razdel'nykh, otdel'nykh, obysknykh i rospisnykh, sostavlennykh po patriarshim ukazam 1620-1703 godov," *ODBMIu*, 2, pt. 2:1-209. For an example of clergy losing land, see "Votchinnye vladeniia," *IaEV*, 1878, no. 42:334.

127. *PSPR*, 1:1, 3:1071; *PSZ*, 11:8625.

128. TsGADA, f. 1183, op. 1, g. 1747, d. 284, l. 1 ob.

129. TsGIA, f. 796, op. 44, g. 1763, d. 79, l. 1.

130. M. I. Smirnov, "Bol'she-brembol'skii d'iakon Mikhail Mikhailov," *TVUAK*, 15 (1913):13.

131. The raw numbers were as follows: 51 of 500 churches in Suzdal diocese reported no land, 280 of 1,215 churches in Riazan, and 93 of 784 in Kolomna. Very little of the landlessness can be attributed to city churches, for most urban parishes actually possessed land. In Murom, for example, the five city parishes had an average of 14 dessiatines—less than the norm, but more than most rural parishes in the surrounding uezd (*ODDS*, 18:288 and prilozhenie 16).

132. Sokolov, "Selo Tikhonovo," *IaEV*, 1890, no. 1:12-13.

133. *PSPR*, 3:1054; *ODDS*, 2, pt. 2:940.

134. *ODDS*, 2, pt. 1:58.

135. "Neskol'ko ukaznykh predpisanii prezhnikh dukhovnykh pravlenii," *IaEV*, 1889, no. 50:787-790.

136. For example, see Malitskii, *IVS*, 1:75 and Nadezhdin, "Ocherk," *VEV*, 1866, no. 4:171-172.

137. *PSPREP*, 4:1359; *ODDS*, 34:174.

138. *PSZ*, 14:10237.

139. L. V. Milov, *Issledovaniia ob "Ekonomicheskikh primechaniiakh" k general'nomu mezhevaniiu* (Moscow, 1965), pp. 11-15.

140. *PSPREA*, 1:293, 312; see also Milov, pp. 15-17.

141. *PSZ*, 18:12925.

142. *PSPREA*, 2:811; see also the reports in *PSPREA*, 2:888.

143. TSGIA, f. 796, op. 66, g. 1785, d. 221, ll. 1-41; *PSPREA*, 3:1238, 1319, 1327; for other cases in 1780 and 1799, see Ia. O. Kuznetsov, "Iz perepiski pomeshchika s krest'ianami vo vtoroi polovine XVIII st.," *TVUAK*, 6 (1904):37; and A. V. Selivanov, "Opis' del arkhiva Vladimirskogo gubernskogo pravleniia," ibid., 6:46. For cases of townspeople encroaching on parish land, see: Petropavlovskii, "Kratkaia istoricheskaia zapiska," *MEV*, 1895, no. 20:206; A. Romanov, "Tul'skaia kazanskaia tserkov'," *TEV*, 1862, no. 13:19-20.

144. *PSZ*, 18:12925, 20:14377, 14750; TsGIA, f. 796, op. 59, g. 1778, d. 465, ll. 1-2.

145. *PSPRPP*, 167; *PSZ*, 25:18316; Rozanov, 3, pt. 1:261-262; Titlinov, *Gavriil*, pp. 655-674. For an impressive picture of landholding diversity, see the data compiled on Novgorod and Tikhvin districts in the mid-1780s (Titlinov, *Gavriil*, pp. 636-653).

146. *Opis' DKU*, p. 15, n.1.

147. See, for example, TsGIA, f. 804, op. 1, razd. III, dd. 10-21 on Vladimir diocese.

148. See a Suzdal case in 1758 in TsGIA, f. 796, op. 39, g. 1758, d. 97, l. 1 ob.

149. Rozanov, *Istoriia*, 2, pt. 1:171, and 2, pt. 2:n.338, 341; Semevskii, "Sel'skii sviashchennik," pp. 511-514; Lototskii, "Material'naia obespechennost'," *RSP*, 1899, no. 38:45.

150. See the bishop's notations on a Suzdal list of 1781 in TsGIA, f. 796, op. 62, g. 1781, d. 195, ll. 67-70.

151. The Synod emphasized the variation in parishes (with many having less than 15 or 20 households) in 1733, when it tried to free the clergy from the

bathhouse tax (*PSPR*, 8:2685). In 1743, when it proposed to establish a schedule of fines on parishes (for procrastination in the selection of new clergy), it designed a "graduated" system that would take into account the differences in parish size and economy (*PSPREP*, 1:457).

152. See "Materialy dlia istorii Vladimirskoi eparkhii," *VEV*, 1892-94, pribavleniia.

153. V. Lestvitsyn, "Polozhenie iaroslavskogo dukhovenstva vo vtorom desiatiletii XVIII v.," *IaEV*, 1873, nos. 49-51; 1874, nos. 7, 10-13, 18-24, 34-35. Most churches belonged to a middling range of 50 kopecks to 1.50 rubles.

154. S. Arkhangel'skii, "Selo Vasil'evskoe Shuiskogo uezda," *VEV*, 1911, no. 7:184-185.

155. Semevskii, "Sel'skii sviashchennik," pp. 511-514.

156. Malitskii, *IVS*, 1:114-115. The only comprehensive picture available pertains to an area outside the central Moscow region—Novgorod and Tikhvin districts. According to data compiled there in the 1780s, the average clerical income for priests and churchmen was 60 rubles in Novgorod uezd, 30 rubles in Tikhvin uezd. In both cases the priest's share would be higher, with his two churchmen receiving one half that amount. For complete tables, see Titlinov, *Gavriil*, pp. 636-653.

157. Dobroliubov, "Opis' pridanogo, dannogo za docher'iu sviashchennika v XVIII st.," *TRUAK*, 1, pt. 2:36-37.

158. "Opisanie dokumentov sysknogo prikaza," *ODBMIu*, 4:84-85.

159. *ODDS*, 18: prilozhenie 16.

160. TsGIA, f. 796, op. 28, g. 1747, d. 216, ll. 126-138.

161. Malitskii, *IPE*, 1:383.

162. Ibid., 1:380-382; see also N. Malitskii, "Uprazdnennaia Khristorozhdestvenskaia tserkov'," *VEV*, 1913, no. 48:970.

163. TsGIA, f. 796, op. 17, g. 1736, d. 439, ll. 181, 187 ob., 188 ob., 190 ob.

164. Nadezhdin, "Ocherk," *VEV*, 1866, no. 4:172.

165. TsGADA, f. 1183, op. 1, g. 1736, d. 198, ll. 5-6 ob.; *ODDS*, 2, pt.1:492. See also the report of "starving clergy" in Riazan diocese as late as 1787 in Sokolov, "Simon Lagov," *REV*, 1884, no. 2:337.

166. *Opis' DKU*, p. 9, n.1.

167. TsGADA, f. 1183, op. 1, g. 1735, d. 181, ll. 5-5 ob.

168. Skvortsov, *Materialy*, 2:106.

169. *Opis' DKU*, p. 10.

170. See, for instance, a dispute over land in a 1703 case in TsGADA, f. 235, op. 1, chast' 2, d. 6271, ll. 1-16.

171. The Suzdal schedule of 1732 is summarized in a 1789 report in TsGIA, f. 796, op. 70, g. 1789, d. 40, ll. 33-33 ob.

172. Malitskii, *IPE*, 1:68-69.

173. TsGIA, f. 796, op. 70, g. 1789, d. 40, l. 33 ob.

174. Semevskii, "Sel'skii sviashchennik," p. 513.

175. Rozanov, *Istoriia*, 3, pt. 1:127-128.

176. Malitskii, *IVS*, 1:114-115; Semevskii, "Sel'skii sviashchennik," pp. 511-514.

177. TsGIA, f. 796, op. 55, g. 1774, d. 131, l. 16.

178. P. V. Il'inskii, "Otdelenie arkhiva starykh del Vladimirskoi dukhov-noi konsistorii," *TVUAK,* 4:100; Rostislavov, "Zapiski," *RS,* 27 (1880):8.

179. Kuznetsov, "Iz perepiski pomeshchika," *TVUAK,* 6:23, 27.

180. TsGIA, f. 796, op. 70, g. 1789, d. 40, ll. 1-1 ob.

181. Putilov, p. 51.

182. Malitskii, *IPE,* 1:323-324.

183. TsGIA, f. 796, op. 70, g. 1789, d. 40, ll. 1-39.

184. Platon, *Instruktsii,* punkt 30.

185. Malitskii, "Zaboty," *VEV,* 1907, no. 5:66-67.

186. TsGIA, f. 796, op. 65, g. 1784, d. 274, l. 38, 94; see also TsGADA, f. 1183, op. 1, g. 1738, d. 440, ll. 49-49 ob.

187. TsGIA, f. 796, op. 54, g. 1773, d. 425, l. 1; op. 79, g. 1798, d. 160, l. 8.

188. See, for example, the far-reaching proposal in an anonymous *zapiska* (actually authored by a minor official, P. N. Batiushkov) and ensuing debate in the Church (TsGIA, f. 796, op. 205, d. 361, ll. 19-26 ob.; f. 797, op. 29, III otd., 1 st., d. 148, chast' 1, ll. 60-75).

189. See, for example, the clashes between the Senate and Synod in the 1740s (*PSPREP,* 1:248, 2:894) and in the 1780s (TsGIA, f. 796, op. 62, g. 1781. d. 588, ll. 1-2, and op. 65, g. 1784, d. 443, ll. 1-20).

190. *PSPR,* 10:3330.

191. The vacancies numbered 679 (in 1738), 625 (in 1739), 623 (in 1740), 591 (in 1741), 639 (in 1742), 532 (in 1743), 465 (in 1744), 345 (in 1747), and 1068 (in 1752). *ODDS,* 18: prilozhenie 16; TsGIA, f. 796, op. 28, g. 1747, d. 216, ll. 124 ob.-125; op. 25, g. 1744, d. 179, ll. 26-26 ob.

192. TsGIA, f. 796, op. 28, g. 1747, d. 216, ll. 180 ob.-182; op. 36, g. 1755, d. 344, ll. 380 ob.-403; op. 48, g. 1767, d. 547, ll. 444-498.

193. *ODDS,* 18: prilozhenie 16.

194. TsGIA, f. 796, op. 17, g. 1736, d. 439, ll. 1-2.

195. Shakhovskoi, pp. 264-265.

196. *ODDS,* 18: prilozhenie 16.

197. TsGIA, f. 796, op. 28, g. 1747, d. 216, ll. 124 ob.-125, 140 ob.-143, 173 ob.-175, 180 ob.-182, 346 ob.-353, 484 ob.-486.

198. Rozanov, *Istoriia,* 3, pt. 1:125.

199. *ODDS,* 9:214.

200. Typical was a case in 1774, where a *d'iachok* exposed the misdeeds of the local priest and demanded the latter's position as a reward (TsGIA, f. 796, op. 55, g. 1774, d. 131, ll. 2, 32 ob.).

201. *PSPREP,* 1:248, 457.

202. Ibid., 4:1444.

203. TsGIA, f. 796, op. 65, g. 1784, d. 443, ll. 71-85, and op. 62, g. 1781, d. 588, ll. 117-124, 127-131.

204. Ibid., op. 65, g. 1784, d. 443, ll. 71-83.

205. See the resolutions on the petitions of churchmen from various dio-ceses in ibid., op. 65, g. 1784, d. 274, ll. 11-11 ob., 16, 23, 31.

206. See explicit statements by several bishops in ibid., op. 63, g. 1782, d. 543, ll. 13-21 ob.; op. 64, g. 1783, d. 217, ll. 65-66 ob.; op. 65, g. 1784, d. 443, l. 5.

207. In Rostov a deacon who brawled with his priest and accidentally killed him was defrocked for the crime (ibid., op. 50, g. 1769, d. 157, ll. 1-31). More premeditated was the murder of a Pereslavl priest by members of a competing clan in 1774 (ibid., op. 55, g. 1774, d. 212, ll. 1-19). Murders or manslaughter were rare; in most cases the underlying factor was a long-standing feud.

208. Diocesan records fully confirm the frequency of internal clerical conflict. See, for example, the archival inventory of Riazan diocese in Dobroliubov, "Ukazatel'," *TRUAK*, 17, pt. 2:107-110, 114-116, 123. This problem is vividly depicted in the diary of a St. Petersburg ecclesiastical superintendent; see N. Barsov, "Peterburgskii prikhodskoi sviashchennik vo vtoroi polovine XVIII i nachale XIX st.," *Khr. Cht.*, 1876, tom 2:662.

209. Cases of such abuse abound. For example, in 1776 a priest in Vladimir beat and cursed his *d'iachok* and then expelled him from the parish (TsGIA, f. 796, op. 57, g. 1776, d. 150, l. 1). In 1782 one priest in Suzdal diocese flew into a rage when the *ponomar'* failed to unlock the church for him, and gave him a severe thrashing (TsGIA, f. 796, op. 63, g. 1782, d. 277, l. 1). See also the description of brawls inside the church in *ODDS*, 10:381 and TsGIA, f. 796, op. 54, g. 1773, d. 292, l. 3 ob.

210. Arkhangel'skii, "Selo Vasil'evskoe," *VEV*, 1911, no. 7:185.

211. Platon, *Instruktsii*, punkt 31.

212. See, for example, the disputes over income in Murom (*Opis' del Riazanskogo istoricheskogo arkhiva* [Riazan, 1899], 1:10, 11, 25), Vladimir (TsGIA, f. 796, op. 62, g. 1781, d. 508, ll. 1-39), and Iur'ev-Pol'skii (ibid., op. 50, g. 1769, d. 271, ll. 17-41 ob.)

213. TsGIA, f. 796, op. 44, g. 1763, d. 344, ll. 1-1 ob.

214. Smirnov, "Bol'she-brembol'skii d'iakon," *TVUAK*, 15:14-17.

215. TsGIA, f. 796, op. 79, g. 1798, d. 951, l. 6.

216. Sokolov, "Simon Lagov," *REV*, 1884, no. 10:188-190.

217. Bolotov, 1:149.

6. The Clergy and the Parish Community

1. Znamenskii, *PDPV*, pp. 65-66; see also Smolitsch, *Geschichte*, pp. 428-458 and Kartashev, 2:501-542.

2. Znamenskii, *PDPV*, p. 46. A similar note is struck by M. Bogoslovskii in his account of parish life in northern Russia at the end of the seventeenth century (*Zemskoe samoupravlenie na russkom severe XVII v.*, 2 vols. [Moscow, 1909-1912], 2:45-46).

3. Besides the discussion in Znamenskii, the only monograph that treats the eighteenth-century parish at length is A. A. Papkov's work, *Upadok pravoslavnogo prikhoda XVIII-XIX vv.* (Moscow, 1899); however, it is little more than a summary of the familiar laws in *PSZ*.

4. See, for example, the standard works on the townspeople (Kizevetter, *Posadskaia obshchina*) and peasantry (Semevskii, *Krest'iane*).

5. Znamenskii, *PDR*, p. 9; see also Bogoslovskii, *Zemskoe samoupravlenie*, 2:52.

6. On this earlier coincidence of community and parish in France, En-

gland, and Sweden, see Jerome Blum, "The Internal Structure of the European Village Community from the Fifteenth to the Nineteenth Century," *Journal of Modern History*, 43 (1971):548 and M. Roberts, *Essays in Swedish History* (Minneapolis, 1967), p. 7.

7. Znamenskii, *PDR*, p. 14; Bogoslovskii, *Zemskoe samoupravlenie*, 2:21-23.

8. Golubinskii, 1, pt. 1:463-467. Examples of such clerkship are common; see, for instance, a document where the priest signed for an illiterate noblewoman ("Razdel'naia zapis'," *IaEV*, 1894, no. 23:358-359). See also Sheremetev's instruction of 1727 regarding this duty and, especially, his use of the term *zemskie d'iachki* (Shchepetov, p. 265).

9. Znamenskii, *PDR*, p. 15.

10. Even in the eighteenth century, such trade fairs were still convened on church holidays; for a listing, see Maksimovich, 4: prilozhenie, pp. iii-xciv, and Bakmeister, passim.

11. Bogoslovskii, *Zemskoe samoupravlenie*, 2:39. The parish church was also used for the safekeeping of personal property, especially icons; see, for instance, the list of deposits in a Rostov church in "Rospiska ot 1666 g.," *IaEV*, 1894, no. 21:332.

12. On the role of the parish church in education, see M. Vladimirskii-Budanov, "Gosudarstvo i narodnoe obrazovanie v Rossii s XVII v. do uchrezhdeniia ministerstv," *Zhurnal ministerstva narodnogo prosveshcheniia* [hereafter ZhMNP], 169 (October 1873):182-190, 215-216.

13. Znamenskii, *PDR*, pp. 16ff.; Bogoslovskii, *Zemskoe samoupravlenie*, 2:22.

14. Bogoslovskii, *Zemskoe samoupravlenie*, 2:23.

15. Golubinskii, 1, pt. 1:341.

16. See *AAE*, 1:229.

17. Bogoslovskii, *Zemskoe samoupravlenie*, 2:40-46. The church elder (*tserkovnyi starosta*), a layman elected as overseer of each church, is not to be confused with the clerical elder (*popovskii starosta*), a priest elected as overseer of a district with many churches.

18. *AI*, 5:122.

19. On the reforms by Joseph II, see V.-L. Tapié, *Rise and Fall of the Habsburg Monarchy* (New York, 1972), p. 221; on the Russian parish reforms of the 1870s, see N. Runovskii, *Tserkovno-grazhdanskie zakonopolozheniia otnositel'no pravoslavnogo dukhovenstva v tsarstvovanie Imp. Aleksandra II* (Kazan, 1898).

20. Skvortsov, *Materialy*, 2:603.

21. Rozanov, *Istoriia*, 2, pt. 2:104.

22. Platon, *Instruktsii*, punkt 13.

23. For the decline in 1740-83, see Table 9 above.

24. Rozanov, *Istoriia*, 3, pt. 1:116-117, 186.

25. Malitskii, *IPE*, 1:380-382. Because reorganization was technically much easier in towns, bishops concentrated efforts there. Gavriil, in his background document for the Legislative Commission, suggested reorganization of parishes only in cities and said nothing about rural parishes (*SIRIO*, 43:417).

26. Skvortsov, *Materialy*, 2:717. The angry parishioners then filed a protest at the Moscow Synodal Chancellery: "They, the *iamshchiki*, having buried their forebears and relatives at their church and having made improvements [in the church] at their own expense, do not want to relocate to another parish, allegedly by force and for no good reason."

27. In Suzdal, for instance, the range in parish size was still considerable in 1781; of 20 churches, 2 had fewer than 20 households (TsGIA, f. 796, op. 62, g. 1781, d. 195, ll. 67-140 ob.). Similarly, in Iaroslavl, 7 of 43 churches had fewer than 20 households (V. Lestvitsyn, "Tserkvi g. Iaroslavlia v 1781 g.," *IaEV*, 1874, nos. 38-41). Thus both cities had a number of parishes falling below the legal minimum for an urban church—twenty households (*PSZ*, 20:13541). Such nominally "undersized" parishes were actually quite viable, however; they included the more prosperous townsmen as parishioners—merchants, officials, and noblemen.

28. Johann Falk, *Beyträge zur topografischen Kenntniss des russischen Reichs*, 3 vols. (St. Petersburg, 1785), 1:58. For similar data on other provincial towns, see *Materialy dlia istorii gorodov XVI-XVIII vv.; Pereiaslavl'-Zalesskii* (Moscow, 1884), p. 28, and *Materialy dlia istorii gorodov XVI-XVIII vv.; Rostov* (Moscow, 1884), pp. 87-88. For a full picture of the pace of stone church construction, see V. G. Dobronravov and V. Berezin, *Istoriko-statisticheskoe opisanie tserkvei i prikhodov Vladimirskoi eparkhii* [hereafter *ISOVE*], 4 vols. (Vladimir, 1893-97).

29. See, for example, the materials on Riazan (TsGIA, f. 796, op. 64, g. 1783, d. 219, ll. 1-111) and Iaroslavl ("Dela namestnika Mel'gunova v pol'zu tserkvi v 1783-1787 godakh," *IaEV*, 1884, no. 7:49-54).

30. For a table showing the structure of rural Russia, see Gregory L. Freeze, "The Disintegration of Traditional Communities: The Parish in Eighteenth-Century Russia," *Journal of Modern History*, 48 (1976):39.

31. Appeals to establish a new parish routinely used this argument. For example, a landowner in Murom uezd won permission to open a new church by stressing religious needs: "Because of the distant location of the [other] church and the separation by streams, the peasants of my village Fedorkovo are deprived of sacred rites and die without penance" (TsGADA, f. 1183, op. 1, g. 1747, d. 284, ll. 1-1 ob.).

32. This attitude found expression, for example, in a 1730 petition from a landlord in Murom, who sought to establish a separate parish for his serfs in order to provide "better supervision of the peasants in the performance of their Christian duties" (*ODDS*, 10:140). He no doubt interpreted those "Christian duties" broadly.

33. See the table in Freeze, "Disintegration," p. 40.

34. Maksimovich, 4:218-220; 5:355. But it was not always thus; in Rostov uezd, there were only 56 noble residences for 81 parishes (ibid., 4:198).

35. Predictably, the presence of several noblemen gave rise to disputes over the control of a parish church; see, for example, the interesting case in Suzdal in 1781 in TsGIA, f. 796, op. 62, g. 1781, d. 51, ll. 1-2 ob., 11-12, 22-23 ob.

36. Rozanov, *Istoriia*, 3, pt. 1:116-117.

37. Rudnev, "K istorii," p. 35.

38. TsGIA, f. 796, op. 74, g. 1793, d. 366, ll. 57-58 ob.

39. V. G. Dobronravov, "Sviatoezerskaia pustyn'," *TVUAK*, 11 (1909): 30-32. In 1769, when the bishop of Vladimir established a new parish church in the place of an old hermitage, he transferred twenty households from a local parish to supplement its income (N. Malitskii, "Nikolaevskaia pushchugova pustyn'," *VEV*, 1910, no. 39:719-723). See also cases where parishes were abolished, as in Pereslavl in 1764 and Rostov in 1780 (N. Malitskii, "Uprazdnennaia Khristorozhdestvenskaia tserkov'," *VEV*, 1913, no. 48:971; "Uprazdnenie v 1780 g. v g. Rostove vo imenovanie sv. ottsov tserkvi," *IaEV*, 1895, no. 31:483-487).

40. For the classic treatment, see Kizevetter, pp. 618-795.

41. On the problem of unrecorded peasant migrants, see P. G. Ryndziunskii, "Novye goroda Rossii kontsa XVIII v.," in *Problemy obshchestvenno-politicheskoi istorii Rossii i slavianskikh stran* (Moscow, 1963), pp. 365-366.

42. *Pereiaslavl'-Zalesskii; materialy dlia istorii Danilovskogo monastyria i naseleniia goroda XVIII st.* (Moscow, 1891), pp. 30-110. Similarly, a church in Vladimir in 1794 included 3 merchant households, 22 townsmen of various ranks (*meshchane, iamshchiki,* and *raznochintsy*), and 35 peasant households (*ISOVE*, 1:84).

43. Semevskii, *Krest'iane*, 1:163.

44. See, for example, the report of peasant entrepreneurs and hired laborers in "Otvety . . . o uezde g. Volodimira," *TVEO*, 12:112.

45. Semevskii, *Krest'iane*, 1:238-239.

46. Ibid., 1:162-359; Jones, pp. 18-36.

47. Semevskii, *Krest'iane*, 2:92-107, 154-155, 271-273.

48. See the discussion and references in Jones, pp. 210-243, and M. P. Pavlova-Sil'vanskaia, "Sotsial'naia sushchnost' oblastnoi reformy Ekateriny II," in *Absoliutizm v Rossii*, pp. 460-491.

49. Maksimovich, 1:249, 5:353, and passim; see also Bakmeister, 1, pt. 2:99, 120, 132-133, 138. Only the most backward towns (such as Zvenigorod) and landlord estates still had trade limited to Sundays (Bakmeister, 1, pt. 1:7; Shchepetov, p. 45).

50. The Synod prohibited the practice in 1723 (*PSPR*, 3:999, and *ODDS*, 3:106). The metropolitan of Rostov, Arsenii, reiterated this ban in 1746 to protect the parish clergy from bearing financial responsibility ("Ukaznoe predpisanie Iaroslavskogo dukhovnogo pravleniia," *IaEV*, 1890, no. 6:87-90).

51. *PSPR*, 1:17; *ODDS*, 1:131; *PSPR*, 2:931, 5:1708; *ODDS*, 5:9.

52. TsGIA, f. 796, op. 14, g. 1733, d. 128, ll. 1-4.

53. Ibid., ll. 5-5 ob.

54. Ibid., ll. 13-14; for similar efforts in Pereslavl in the 1750s, see Malitskii, *IPE*, 1:321-323.

55. N. Malitskii, "Prodazha tserkovnykh svech v XVIII v.," *VEV*, 1904, no. 16:469-473; see also *Opis' DKU*, p. 17.

56. See Vladimirskii-Budanov, *Gosudarstvo*. The traditional parish instruction, however, was preserved in some towns; see the description of the

19 parish schools in Tula in the 1790s and of a school in Kolomna in the 1820s in A. Ivanov, "Iz istorii prikhodskikh shkol v Tul'skoi eparkhii," *TEV*, 1862, no. 16:219; Giliarov-Platonov, 1:86-87.

57. For references on the gentry proposals, see Semevskii, *Krest'iane*, 1:276-286; see also M. D. Kurmacheva, "Problemy obrazovaniia v Ulozhennoi Komissii 1767 g.," in Akademiia nauk SSSR, *Dvorianstvo i krepostnoi stroi Rossii XVI-XVIII vv.* (Moscow, 1975), pp. 240-264. For the bishop's proposals, see *SIRIO*, 43:418, 422; for the proposal of the Commission on Church Estates, see Rozhdestvenskii, *Materialy*, pp. 326-339.

58. Malitskii, *ISS*, pp. 106-107. The governor of Tula issued a similar order; see A. I., "Materialy dlia istoriko-statisticheskogo opisaniie Tul'skoi eparkhii," TEV, 1881, no. 15:104-105.

59. *PSPREP*, 1:400, 442, 494; 3:1003.

60. Proclamation of Stefan Iavorskii in 1705 (Rozanov, *Istoriia*, 1:73).

61. Two parishes in Rostov diocese reported the theft of more than 500 rubles in 1798 (TsGIA, f. 796, op. 79, g. 1798, d. 421, ll. 29, 55); see similar reports in "O tserkovnom khoziaistve prikhodskikh tserkvei Iaroslavskoi eparkhii v proshlom stoletii," *IaEV*, 1899, no. 28:422.

62. A Moscow priest in the 1740s secretly sold a silver censer and other service instruments "to pay off debts on his priest's position" (Skvortsov, *Materialy*, 1:53). A priest in Rostov embezzled candle revenues for his own use ("O tserkovnom khoziaistve," *IaEV*, 1899, no. 28:421-422), and a priest in Murom was accused of stealing church property (Dobroliubov, "Ukazatel'," *TRUAK*, 17, pt. 2:109). The Synod in 1740 complained of widespread peculation by parish clergy and ordered the election of church elders to see that the clergy "do not use these revenues for their own benefit" (*PSPR*, 10:3607).

63. *PSZ*, 5:3171; *PSPR*, 1:17, 9:2984, 10:3607. Landlords too ordered the election of church elders; see, for instance, the instructions by Rumiantsev in the 1750s and Shuvalov in the 1790s (Dovnar-Zapol'skii, "Materialy," *UI*, 43 [1903], no. 12:7; 49 [1909], no. 7:224).

64. Rozanov, *Istoriia*, 2, pt. 1:120-123; 2, pt. 2:285-286.

65. "Eshche ukaznoe predpisanie Iaroslavskogo dukhovnogo pravleniia," *IaEV*, 1889, no. 51:812-814; Glebov, "Materialy," *REV*, 1897, no. 5:149.

66. Znamenskii, *PDPV*, pp. 65-66; see also Smolitsch, *Geschichte*, 1:430 and Kartashev, 2:506.

67. See the epistle by Gennadii from the late fifteenth century (*AI*, 1:104) and a Pskov bishop in the late seventeenth century (*AI*, 5:122).

68. *PSZ*, 5:3171; *PSPR*, 1:1.

69. See, for example, the Synod resolutions of 1721, 1739, and 1742 (*PSPR*, 1:109; *ODDS*, 19:14; *PSPREP*, 1:248).

70. Bolotov, 3:462-463.

71. Znamenskii, *PDPV*, p. 51.

72. *AAE*, 1:229; see also the 1667 Moscow Church Council in *PSZ*, 1:412.

73. *PSPR*, 1:1.

74. *PSPR*, 2:439, 10:3342; *PSPREP*, 1:248.

75. TsGIA, f. 796, op. 38, g. 1757, d. 136, ll. 2-2 ob.

76. For examples of nonlandlord parishes, see the case in Suzdal in 1780

(ibid., op. 61, g. 1780, d. 117, ll. 19-19 ob.) and Iur'ev-Pol'skii in 1783 (ibid., op. 64, g. 1783, d. 231, l. 3). For examples of landlords' petitions in Vladimir in 1781-82, see ibid., op. 62, g. 1781, d. 51, ll. 1-30, and op. 63, g. 1782, d. 543, l. 70.

77. See the certification of good conduct for a Pereslavl churchman in 1763, a cleric of Arzamas in 1777, and a priest from Shui in 1793 (ibid., op. 44, g. 1763, d. 344, ll. 3-4 ob.; op. 58, g. 1777, d. 390, l. 14; op. 74, g. 1793, d. 366, l. 3).

78. In 1770, when a new bishop had not yet been appointed to Novgorod, the Synod supervised all appointments for the diocese, and the archival record shows that each appointment began with an election by the parish (*ODDS*, 50:9, 31, 34, 35, 46, 47, 53, 78, 145, 158, 166, 173, 223, 274, 356, 357, 430, 485). And within the central region, the archival inventory for Riazan diocese in the 1780s and 1790s contains numerous references to parish election petitions (see Dobroliubov, "Ukazatel'," *TRUAK*, 16, pt. 2:188-189, and 17, pt. 2:121-133).

79. Malitskii, *IPE*, 1:63-65; Titlinov, *Gavriil*, pp. 69-71, 528.

80. "Ukaznye predpisaniia Iaroslavskogo dukhovnogo pravleniia," *IaEV*, 1890, no. 2:23-26.

81. *SIRIO*, 43:423-424. After Afanasii proposed a law requiring parish submission, the Synod confirmed his recommendation and directed its delegate at the Legislative Commission to seek a law requiring them to comply (ibid., 43:47). None was obtained.

82. TsGIA, f. 796, op. 62, g. 1781, d. 195, l. 47.

83. Rozanov, *Istoriia*, 1:105; 2, pt. 1:n.123; 2, pt. 2:n.297.

84. Platon, *Instruktsii*, punkt 40.

85. See, for instance, these instructions to stewards: I. F. Petrovskaia, ed., "Nakazy votchinnym prikazchikam pervoi chetverti XVIII v.," *IA*, 8 (1953): 248, and Dovnar-Zapol'skii, "Materialy," *UI*, 45 (1905), no. 8:82.

86. In one sensational case, Metropolitan Arsenii excommunicated an unrepentant landlord and his serfs as well, an act so brash that it earned a sharp rebuke from the Synod (*PSPREA*, 1:24); see also his decree in "Ukaznoe predpisanie Iaroslavskogo dukhovnogo pravleniia," *IaEV*, 1890, no. 7:108-111.

87. *PSPREA*, 1:664.

88. D. I. Rostislavov, "Zapiski," *RS*, 27 (1880):8-10.

89. For a typical case, see TsGIA, f. 796, op. 43, g. 1762, d. 223, ll. 2-2 ob.

90. Ibid., op. 44, g. 1763, d. 79, ll. 1-1 ob.

91. Rudnev, "K istorii," p. 15.

92. Sokolov, "Simon Lagov," *REV*, 1884, no. 10:191; see also Dobroliubov, "Ukazatel'," *TRUAK*, 16, pt. 2:188-199; 17, pt. 2:126-128.

93. "Zapiski o zhizni Platona, mitropolita moskovskogo," in I. M. Snegirev, *Zhizn' moskovskogo mitropolita Platona* (Moscow, 1891), pt. 2: 225; Platon, *Instruktsii*, punkt 40.

94. Malitskii, *IPE*, 1:64-65. When a cleric produced a testament from his parishioners that he was of good conduct and wanted by the parish, the bishop declared that the petition was worthless and showed only the ability of

the cleric to wheedle signatures from the laity (TsGIA, f. 796, op. 62, g. 1781, d. 380, ll. 1-2 ob., 5-5 ob.).

95. For a 1793 case where a parish was divided over an appointment, see TsGIA, f. 796, op. 74, g. 1793, d. 366, ll. 3, 47-48 ob.

96. Rozanov, *Istoriia*, 1:66-67; 2, pt. 1:102-103.

97. Platon, *Instruktsii*, punkt 40.

98. "Rasporiazheniia Arseniia Matseevicha po upravleniiu rostovsko-iaroslavskoiu pastvoiu," *IaEV*, 1868, no. 31:263-264.

99. Malitskii, *IPE*, 1:295-296, and prilozhenie, pp. liii-lv.

100. Rudnev, "K istorii," p. 15; see also the bishop's instructions of 1779 to his ecclesiastical superintendents (ibid., pp. 39-40).

101. A landlord's parish constituted a partial exception. If in residence, the landlord himself had the sole right to select candidates; if absent, then the serfs normally made the selection with their master's consent. See the instructions to stewards in the following: Petrovskaia, "Nakazy," p. 248, and Dovnar-Zapol'skii, "Materialy," *UI*, 44 (1904), no. 7:82.

102. See, for example, a parish petition from "the better parishioners" to reinstate a suspended priest in Vladimir diocese (TsGIA, f. 796, op. 58, g. 1777, d. 390, l. 14).

103. Parish petitions gave precedence to the *vkladchiki* in recognition of their special status; see, for example, a 1757 petition from a Vladimir parish that placed their signatures at the head of the list (TsGADA, f. 1183, op. 1, g. 1757, d. 438, l. 1).

104. Rozanov, *Istoriia*, 2, pt. 2:35.

105. Platon, *Instruktsii*, punkt 40.

106. "Neskol'ko ukaznykh predpisanii prezhnikh dukhovnykh pravlenii," *IaEV*, 1889, no. 50:796.

107. TsGIA, f. 796, op. 66, g. 1785, d. 256, ll. 3-4, 17 ob.-18 ob.

108. *PSPRPP*, 91, 103, 106, 149.

109. *PSPR*, 2:476.

110. Ibid., 8:2679.

111. *ODDS*, 14:172; *PSPR*, 9:2857.

112. *PSPREP*, 1:248; see also 1:497.

113. Ibid., 3:980.

114. TsGIA, f. 796, op. 74, g. 1793, d. 366, ll. 51-51 ob.

115. Ibid., op. 57, g. 1776, d. 150, l. 2.

116. Ibid., op. 56, g. 1775, d. 50, l. 10 ob.

117. Ibid., op. 34, g. 1753, d. 74, ll. 1-3.

118. Ibid., op. 48, g. 1767, d. 521, l. 9 ob.

119. *PSPREA*, 1:244.

120. *Ustav dukhovnykh konsistorii* (St. Petersburg, 1841), article 202.

121. *PSPR*, 2:476.

122. TsGIA, f. 796, op. 17, g. 1736, d. 439, l. 181 ob.

123. *ODDS*, 21:107; see also 28:57.

124. N. Bogoslovskii, "Selo Liakhi," *VEV*, 1910, no. 51/52:988.

125. TsGIA, f. 796, op. 54, g. 1773, d. 140, ll. 241 ob.-242.

126. Selivanov, "Opis' del arkhiva," *TVUAK*, 1:2.

127. *PSPR*, 2:596.

128. "Rasporiazheniia Arseniia Matseevicha po upravleniiu rostovsko-iaroslavskoiu pastvoiu," *IaEV*, 1868, no. 30:256.

129. Platon, *Instruktsii*, punkt 32.

130. For pre-Petrine legislation, see Arkhangel'skii, *O sobornom ulozhenii*, pp. 76-80; for the eighteenth century, see Semevskii, "Sel'skii sviashchennik," pp. 503-506. According to rather unreliable data compiled in the early 1780s, it seems that most made confession and slightly fewer took communion. For the entire Empire, 4.8 percent missed confession, 12.9 percent missed communion; for most of the central dioceses, the rate of deviance was considerably less (in Vladimir diocese, for example, 0.4 percent missed confession, 1.5 percent missed communion). In four of the central dioceses, however, the numbers missing communion were significant: 14.6 percent in Pereslavl diocese, 13.4 percent in Kolomna, 12.9 percent in Moscow, and 6.0 percent in Suzdal (TsGIA, f. 796, op. 63, g. 1782, d. 123, ll. 2-3).

131. Malitskii, *IPE*, 1:115-116. See also "Raporiazheniia Arseniia Matseevicha," *IaEV*, 1868, no. 34:290-292; "Ukaznoe predpisanie Iaroslavskogo dukhovnogo pravleniia," *IaEV*, 1890, no. 6:94-96; Rozanov, *Istoriia*, 3, pt. 1:182-183.

132. On monastic lands, see N. I. Pavlenko, "Monastyrskoe khoziaistvo XVIII v. po votchinnym instruktsiiam," in *Problemy obshchestvenno-politicheskoi istorii Rossii i slavianskikh stran*, p. 319. As examples of landlords' orders see Semevskii, *Krest'iane*, 1:273-274; "Nakaz upravitel'iu ili prikaz-chiku," *TVEO* 12 (1769):32; "P. M. Bestuzhev-Riumin i ego novgorodskoe pomest'e," *RA*, 1904, no. 1:28; A. I. Andreev, "Nakaz votchinnika krest'ianam 1709 g.," *IA*, 8 (1953):270. Not all instructions, however, included this order; see, for example, the 1794 instruction of Shipov in Dovnar-Zapol'skii, "Materialy," *UI*, 49 (1909), no. 7:230-240 and no. 11:241-244.

133. TsGIA, f. 796, op. 46, g. 1765, d. 59, ll. 2-3; *PSPREA*, 1:225.

134. *PSPREA*, 1:664.

135. See also Titlinov, *Gavriil*, pp. 618-632.

136. "Razgovor sviashchennika s ieromonakhom v tsarstvovanie Ekateriny II ob uluchshenii byta dukhovenstva," *Kievskie eparkhial'nye vedomosti*, 1874, no. 24:667-677.

137. *PSZ*, 27:19816. Under the new schedule, the average "legal" income of a parish staff rose for the whole empire from 3.685 rubles in 1783 to 10.805 rubles in 1824 (TsGIA, f. 797, op. 96, d. 5, ll. 1 ob.-2).

138. TsGIA, f. 796, op. 65, g. 1784, d. 275, ll. 1-2.

139. Ibid., op. 61, g. 1780, d. 118, ll. 1-24.

140. Ibid., op. 66, g. 1785, d. 65, l. 1.

141. Ibid., op. 62, g. 1781, d. 194, ll. 1-2 ob.

142. V. Dal', *Poslovitsy russkogo naroda* (Moscow, 1957), p. 707. For some seventeenth-century antecedents, see the proverb collections in P. Simoni, *Starinnye sborniki russkikh poslovits, pogovorok, zagadok, i proch. XVII-XIX st.* (St. Petersburg, 1899), pp. 132, 150, 152, 179 (proverb numbers 1:1903, 2476, 2515, and 2:192). See also Putilov, pp. 57, 106-107.

143. Rozhdestvenskii, *Ocherki*, prilozhenie 2, pp. 11-12.

144. D. Rovinskii, *Russkie narodnye kartinki*, 5 vols. (St. Petersburg, 1881-93), 3:39-40.

145. V. I. Lestvitsyn, "Krest'ianskaia gazeta iz ada," *RS*, 1875, no. 9:215-216.

146. D. I. Fonvizin, "Poslanie k slugam moim Shumilovu, Van'ke i Petrushke," in *Russkaia literatura XVIII v.*, p. 290. Equally incisive was the satirical attack on the clergy (thinly disguised as a criticism of "Roman" clergy) in F. A. Emin's "Mail from Hell" (*Adskaia pochta*, 1769, July, pp. 29-30).

147. *Opis' DKU*, p. 9.

148. "K voprosu o reforme tserkovnogo prikhoda," *VEV*, 1916, no. 14: 255.

149. Tikhomirov, *Sobornoe ulozhenie*, ch. 10, articles 85-89. The parish clergy subsequently complained to Tsar Aleksei Mikhailovich that the fine was too small: "If anyone has to pay a fine for insulting a priest or deacon, then he has nothing to fear [because] it is only a trifling sum" (Solov'ev, *Istoriia*, 6:209).

150. Tikhomirov, *Sobornoe ulozhenie*, ch. 1, articles 1-3.

151. *PSZ*, 12:9079, 18:13286.

152. *Slavianskii bukvar'* (Moscow, 1704), p. 20 ob.; Tikhon, *Nastavlenie o sobstvennykh vsiakogo khristianina dolzhnostiakh* (St. Petersburg, 1791), pp. 101-102.

153. *ODDS*, 2, pt. 1:58.

154. *Izvestiia reshitel'nyia o bedstvennykh i nedoumennykh sluchaiakh, i kako iereiu i d'iakonu i prochim v tom ispravitisia* (Moscow, 1705), pp. 5-5 ob.

155. *PSPR*, 8:2776.

156. *PSPR*, 1:1.

157. *PSPREP*, 4:1620; *PSPREA*, 1:24.

158. *SIRIO*, 43:47.

159. TsGIA, f. 796, op. 61, g. 1780, d. 123, ll. 1-2.

160. The bishops barely managed to maintain formal equality. The Synod received reports in 1746 that government offices were sending directives (*ukazy*) to bishops. Citing a Petrine decree of 1723 that made the Synod and Senate "equal" in their respective commands, the Synod formally proposed to extend this proposal to their provincial organs. The Senate agreed (*PSZ*, 12:9342).

161. TsGIA, f. 796, op. 66, g. 1785, d. 65, ll. 1-6.

162. *PSPR*, 8:2776; *ODDS*, 14:26.

163. [N. Malitskii], "Episkop vladimirskii Pavel," *VEV*, 1910, no. 31:560-561; see also the case of a priest in Murom who pronounced anathema on a parishioner (Travchetov, "Delo," *TVUAK*, 2:75-76).

164. "Opisanie dokumentov sysknogo prikaza," *ODBMIu*, 4:85.

165. Shchepetov, pp. 161-162, 271.

166. Typical were cases occurring in Pereslavl and Rostov dioceses (TsGIA, f. 796, op. 43, g. 1762, d. 411, ll. 1-2; op. 25, g. 1744, d. 165, ll. 1-8).

167. V. S. Ikonnikov, "Arsenii Matseevich," *RS*, 1879, no. 5:33-34; Ar-

senii also excommunicated a landlord and his peasants for the murder of a priest; see "Ukaznoe predpisanie Iaroslavskogo dukhovnogo pravleniia," *IaEV*, 1890, no. 7:108-111.

168. Malitskii, *IPE*, 1:355-356; for other cases, see: *ODDS*, 29:114; Malitskii, *IPE*, 1:353-354, 2:120-127; Smirnov, "Bol'she-brembol'skii d'iakon," *TVUAK*, 15:17-24.

169. Rozanov, *Istoriia*, 2, pt. 1:n.456.

170. "Dmitrii Sechenov," *REV*, 1916, no. 18/19:719-720.

171. *PSPREA*, 2:849, 857.

172. *SIRIO*, 43:49 (Synodal instruction to its deputy), 417 (Gavriil's statement), and 424 (Afanasii's statement).

173. TsGIA, f. 796, op. 54, g. 1773, d. 140, ll. 82-82 ob.

174. Ibid., op. 64, g. 1783, d. 231, ll. 13 ob.-14.

175. "Pis'ma Platona," *RA*, 1870, no. 10:81.

176. See, for example, the statements of clergy in Gorokhovets and Shui districts (TsGIA, f. 804, op. 1, razd. 3, d. 18, ll. 3-3 ob., 7-7 ob.; d. 15, ll. 4-5, 70 ob., 93-94).

177. For a discussion and references on parish reform in Protestant lands, see Hartung, pp. 70-73; Gebhardt, 2:168-172; Roberts, "The Swedish Church," p. 169. For the parallel development in Catholic lands, see John Bossy, "The Counter-reformation and the People of Catholic Europe," *Past and Present*, 47 (1970):51-70.

178. For a different view, which postulates a "Protestant Quasi-Reformation" on the basis of intellectual sources, see Treadgold, 1:84-115.

179. Hantsch, 2:221; Tapié, p. 221.

180. Russian hierarchs personally subscribed to the new secular journals, ordered their seminaries to do likewise, and no doubt encouraged the parish clergy to emulate this example. Significantly, some white clergy—mainly those in elite positions, such as archpriests and priests in diocesan cathedrals —did subscribe to the new publications. For example, the subscription lists for N. I. Novikov's *Utrennii svet* included bishops (Platon of Moscow, Samuil of Rostov, Ieronim of Vladimir, Feofilakt of Pereslavl and Simon of Riazan), a number of seminaries, and even a few archpriests and priests (*Utrennii svet*, chast' 1, November 1777, p. vi; chast' 2, January 1778, p. iii, and March 1778, pp. v-vii; chast' 3, May 1778, pp. iv-vi; August 1778, pp. iii-vi). For Metropolitan Platon's review of Novikov, see Rozanov, *Istoriia*, 3, pt. 1:100-101.

181. *PSPREP*, 1:353, 2:595; Platon, *Sokrashchennoe khristianskoe bogoslovie* (Moscow, 1765), p. 7.

182. *PSPR*, 4:1246; Rozanov, *Istoriia*, 1:90-92; *PSPREP*, 2:762; 3:1181.

183. For attempts in Moscow, see Rozanov, *Istoriia*, 2, pt. 1:48, 140-141; 3, pt. 1:86-88; for the 1751 decree by Arsenii, see "Rasporiazheniia Arseniia Matseevicha," *IaEV*, 1868, no. 36:304-305.

184. *PSPREP*, 2:679, 762, 3:1181; *PSPREA*, 3:1239.

185. Rozanov, *Istoriia*, 2, pt. 1:141-144.

186. Ibid., 3, pt. 1:89-91, 182; Sokolov, "Simon Lagov," *REV*, 1884, no. 2:41, no. 8:153-154; Mitropol'skii, "Preosv. Arsenii," *IaEV*, 1901, no. 20: 319.

187. Rozanov, *Istoriia*, 1:112-114; 2, pt. 2:320.

188. Orders to clean the church appeared in Patriarch Adrian's instructions for clerical elders in 1697 (*PSZ*, 3:1612); from the 1740s they appeared with more bureaucratic zest in the frequent resolutions of the Synod and diocesan authorities (*PSPREP*, 2:725, 4:1357; *PSPREA*, 1:644, 2:1066; Rozanov, *Istoriia*, 2, pt. 2:309-310; Platon, *Instruktsii*, punkt 11; Rudnev, "K istorii," p. 35).

189. Peter banned processions, but in 1744 the Synod declared that there was no canonical justification for the prohibition and relaxed the rules; after 1762 Catherine's government reimposed the restrictions (*PSZ*, 7:4549; *ODDS*, 2, pt. 1:244; *PSPREP*, 2:583; *PSPREA*, 1:356 and 639).

190. Rozanov, *Istoriia*, 3, pt. 1:138-140.

191. As an example of a parish contract limiting the number of processions and visitations, see Dobronravov, "Sviatoezerskaia pustyn'," *TVUAK*, 11:30-32.

192. For references to seventeenth-century descriptions, see N. Malitskii, "Denezhnye shtrafy za razgovory pri bogosluzhenii," *VEV*, 1904, 22:643.

193. See Patriarch Ioasaf's decree of 1636 (*AAE*, 3:269) and Simeon Polotskii's tract, *Pouchenie o blagogoveinom stoianii v khrame* (Moscow, 1668), pp. 1-11.

194. *PSZ*, 5:3250; see also *PSPR*, 3:974 and *ODDS*, 3:404, 557.

195. *PSPREP*, 1:98, 106, 146, 190.

196. Malitskii, *IPE*, 1:117-118; "Rasporiazheniia Arseniia Matseevicha," *IaEV*, 1868, no. 30:256.

197. N. Rozanov, "Preosviashchennyi Timofei," *MEV*, 1869, no. 27:8.

198. Malitskii, "Denezhnye shtrafy," *VEV*, 1904, no. 22:644-646.

199. N. Malitskii, "Rasporiazheniia episkopa Ieronima, kasaiushchiesia otpravleniia bogosluzheniia vo Vladimirskoi eparkhii," *VEV*, 1907, no. 4:54.

200. *PSPREP*, 1:400, 442, 494 and 3:1003; *PSPREA*, 1:640; 2:786.

201. Rozanov, *Istoriia*, 2, pt. 2:321-322.

202. Malitskii, *IPE*, 1:121; "Preosviashchennyi Ilarion," *VEV*, 1874, no. 11:562-563; see also N. Malitskii, "Rasporiazheniia episkopa Ieronima o prisutstvovanii sviashchennosluzhitelei na brachnykh torzhestvakh," *VEV*, 1907, no. 39:615-618.

203. Cases involving priests who deliberately concealed Old Believers sometimes reached the Synod. For example, a report from the Secret Chancellery in 1742 led to the discovery of clergy in Suzdal diocese who concealed Old Believers, and in 1759 a priest of Kolomna diocese, Ivan Minin, reported 26 parishioners as making confession when in fact they did not (TsGIA, f. 796, op. 25, g. 1744, d. 539, l. 7; op. 43, g. 1762, d. 449, ll. 6-9 ob.). Few indeed were reported; according to data compiled in 1740, there were only 412 registered Old Believers in Rostov, 202 in Riazan, 188 in Suzdal, and 474 in Kolomna dioceses (*ODDS*, 17:113). According to Shcherbatov's estimate later in the century, however, at least one fourth or one third of the population adhered to the Old Belief (M. M. Shcherbatov, "Statistika v rassuzhdenii Rossii," *Chteniia OIDR*, 1859, kn. 3, razdel 2:57).

204. *ODDS*, 32:60; see also Pokrovskii, *Antifeodal'nyi protest*, p. 212.

205. N. Solov'ev, "Letopis' ob Il'inskoi tserkvi, Shuiskogo uezda," *VEV*, 1912, no. 10:246-249; see also the case in Nizhnii-Novgorod described in *PSPR*, 9:3141.

206. *ODDS*, 3:233.

207. See the cases in Kaluga in the 1720s, and in Pereslavl and Gzhatsk at mid-century (*ODDS*, 9:64; Malitskii, *IPE*, 1:141-143, 390-393).

208. For the fascinating saga of a priest from Murom who finally turned up in Simbirsk, see Il'inskii, "Otdelenie arkhiva starykh del," *TVUAK*, 4:101. A similar episode involved a priest from Tambov; after peregrinations across Russia, he was eventually arrested in Shui (TsGIA, f. 796, op. 79, g. 1798, d. 470, l. 2).

209. Rozanov, *Istoriia*, 3, pt. 1:94-97.

210. Ibid., 1:110-111; 3, pt. 1:76-78.

211. One landlord's instruction, published in 1770 in a leading agricultural journal as a model for other serfowners, directed the steward to arrange "useful" marriages and, "if the young person refuses such [a proposal] to marry, or if his father and mother are for some reason weak, in such cases you must (in a proper way) compel them [to marry]." ("Sochinennyi Gospodinom statskim sovetnikom P. I. Rychkovym nakaz dlia derevenskogo upravitelia," *TVEO*, 16 [1770]:34).

212. Typical were the cases of a priest, Mikhail Vasil'ev, of Arzamas uezd in 1777, a priest, Stefan Andreev, of Serpukhov in 1778, and a priest, Mikhail Stepanov, of Tula uezd in 1784 (TsGIA, f. 796, op. 58, g. 1777, d. 390, ll. 1-1 ob.; op. 62, g. 1781, d. 448, ll. 1-4; op. 65, g. 1784, d. 148, ll. 2, 20-25).

213. The Synod learned of such cases regularly, as in the reports on offending clergy in Iaroslavl in 1744, Pereslavl in 1750, and Serpukhov in 1781 (ibid., op. 25, g. 1744, d. 496, ll. 6-6 ob.; op. 31, g. 1750, d. 142, ll. 1-7; op. 62, g. 1781, d. 25, l. 1).

214. *PSPREA*, 2:770, 795; see also Semevskii, *Krest'iane*, 1:313-314. Landlords derived little benefit from the custom, and one nobleman specifically ordered his steward to prohibit the practice on his estates, since "such a marriage, besides [causing] harm and disorder, has no usefulness" ("Sochinennyi Gospodinom statskim sovetnikom P. I. Rychkovym nakaz," *TVEO*, 16:33).

215. TsGIA, f. 796, op. 56, g. 1775, d. 280, ll. 1-2.

216. *PSPREA*, 2:1042.

217. *PSPR*, 1:1. See also the Synod's decrees of 1733 and 1741 (ibid., 8:2739, 10:3688). For an attempt to obtain periodic reports, see TsGIA, f. 796, op. 34, g. 1753, d. 6, ll. 1-67. A lively description of popular superstition is also provided in Malitskii, *IPE*, 1:132-138.

218. *PSPR*, 10:3225.

219. Skvortsov, *Materialy*, 1:56-57.

220. Rozanov, *Istoriia*, 2, pt. 2:306.

221. The authorities discovered clergy possessing "magical papers" in Rostov in 1736 and later in Pereslavl (*PSPR*, 9:2962; Malitskii, *IPE*, 1:132-138).

222. Bolotov, 2:795-796; for further references, see A. Lototskii, "Iz byta starogo dukhovenstva," *RS*, 1904, no. 4:108-116.

223. For a good summary account, see Rozanov, *Istoriia*, 2, pt. 2:82-87; see also Amvrosii's report on September 12, four days before his murder (TsGIA, f. 796, op. 52, g. 1771, d. 325) and the report of the Moscow Consistory shortly afterwards (TsGIA, f. 796, op. 52, g. 1771, d. 337).

224. *PSPR*, 8:2721; see also Skvortsov, *Materialy*, 2:642-660, and Rozanov, *Istoriia*, 1:114-115; 2, pt. 1:158-160.

225. For a summary of Catherine's legislation on the peasant problem, see M. T. Beliavskii, *Krest'ianskii vopros nakanune vosstaniia E. I. Pugacheva* (Moscow, 1965), pp. 38-54.

226. Kuznetsov, "Iz perepiski pomeshchika," *TVUAK*, 6:38-39; see also pp. 11, 27, 29, 36). In addition, see the cases described in *ODBMIu*, 4:85-87, and the Sheremetev instruction of 1727 in Shchepetov, p. 265.

227. Such was often the case; see, for instance, the landlord's instruction in Dovnar-Zapol'skii, "Materialy," *UI*, 49 (1909), no. 7:235-240; 50 (1910), no. 11:241-244.

228. Popov, *Tatishchev*, pp. 226-227.

229. *Derevenskoe zerkalo*, 1799; reprinted in *Ocherki istorii SSSR; Rossiia vo vtoroi polovine XVIII v.*, p. 83.

230. See, for instance, Nepliuev's report on a Bashkir uprising in 1755 (Ivan I. Nepliuev, *Zapiski* [St. Petersburg, 1893], pp. 144-145).

231. For two sporadic episodes, see the incidents in Riazan in 1730 (*ODDS*, 10:173 and 263) and in Vladimir province (N. Voronin, "Krest'ianskoe dvizhenie v XVIII v. po Vladimirskoi provintsii," *Iz proshlogo vladimirskogo kraia*, 1 [Vladimir, 1930]:15-16). See also an interesting case in Ostashkov uezd, where a *d'iachok* penned a manifesto on serf rights (Sivkov, "Podpol'naia," pp. 79-80).

232. For the most exhaustive analysis, see Kadson, "Krest'ianskaia voina 1773-1775 gg. i tserkov'." For a briefer analysis and references to published literature, see Dorothea Peters, "Politische und gesellschaftliche Vorstellungen in der Aufstandsbewegung unter Pugachev (1773-1775)," *Forschungen zur osteuropäischen Geschichte*, 17 (Wiesbaden, 1973):129-132.

233. Kadson, "Krest'ianskaia voina," pp. 287-291.

234. Peters, "Politische und gesellschaftliche Vorstellungen," p. 130.

235. TsGIA, f. 796, op. 205, d. 74, l. 7; Kadson, "Krest'ianskaia voina," p. 197.

236. *PSPREA*, 2:760.

237. For the exceptional area of the northwest, see N. L. Rubinshtein, "K kharakteristike votchinnogo rezhima i krest'ianskogo dvizheniia v kontse 70-kh gg. XVIII v.," *IZ*, 40 (1952):140-153; for a broader treatment, see idem, "Krest'ianskoe dvizhenie v Rossii vo vtoroi polovine XVIII v.," *Voprosy istorii*, 1956, no. 11:34-51.

238. TsGIA, f. 796, op. 62, g. 1781, d. 18, l. 1. For an incident in Penza see V. G. Dobronravov, "Dela Vladimirskogo gubernskogo pravleniia, postupivshiia v arkhiv Vladimirskoi uchenoi arkhivnoi komissii," *TVUAK*, 3 (1901):2.

239. *PSPREA*, 2:1002.

240. *PSPREA*, 1:80 and 199.

241. See E. P. Trifil'ev, *Ocherki po istorii krepostnogo prava v Rossi; Tsarstvovanie Imp. Pavla Pervogo* (Khar'kov, 1904) and the devastating cri-

tique by N. P. Pavlov-Sil'vanskii (reprinted in his *Ocherki po russkoi istorii XVIII-XIX vv.* [St. Petersburg, 1910], pp. 154-205). In addition, see M. De-Pule, "Krest'ianskoe dvizhenie pri Imp. Pavle Petroviche i dnevnik Kn. N. P. Repina," *RA*, 1869, no. 3:525-577 and Rubinshtein, "Krest'ianskoe dvizhenie," pp. 47-51.

242. Selivanov, "Opis'," *TVUAK*, 6:39-40, 5:23-24 (see also 1:31, 34-35; 4:24, 30-31; 5:22-23); in addition, see the episodes in *Krest'ianskoe dvizhenie v Rossii v 1796-1825 gg.*, ed. S. N. Valk (Moscow, 1961), pp. 34, 79.

243. Selivanov, "Opis'," *TVUAK*, 1:47, 5:23-24.

244. *PSPRPP*, 53: see also DePule, "Krest'ianskoe dvizhenie," pp. 543-545.

245. *PSPRPP*, 91; see also 103, 363.

246. Ibid., 167.

7. A Separate Society and Culture

1. See, for instance, Znamenskii, *PDPV*, pp. 120, 176, and passim; Jean Gagarin, *The Russian Clergy* (London, 1872), pp. iii, 17. Not all shared this view; some conservative Church hierarchs (such as Metropolitan Filaret of Moscow) denied that the clergy were a caste (P. A. Valuev, "Vsepoddanneishii doklad [16.XI.1861 g.]" in TsGIA, f. 908 [P. A. Valuev], op. 1, d. 112, ll. 28-31 ob.). Most observers, however, took the contrary view: government officials, the secular press (whether liberal or conservative, Westerner or Slavophile), ecclesiastical journals, and indeed many bishops shared the view that the parish clergy formed a closed, isolated caste.

2. Giliarov-Platonov, 1:vi, 2:139-143.

3. *PSZ*, 24:17675.

4. The definition of caste varies considerably, from a strict view that limits its application to India, to a broader usage suitable for comparative analysis. For the narrow view, see J. H. Hutton, *Caste in India* (London, 1951), ch. 9; for a more comparative definition, see G. D. Berreman, "Caste in India and the United States," *American Journal of Sociology*, 66 (1970): 120-127. For an introduction to the literature, see the articles on "Caste" and "Caste in India" in *International Encyclopedia of the Social Sciences*, 17 vols. (New York, 1968), 2:333-344.

5. See the resolutions of the Church Councils of 1551 and 1667 (*AAE*, 1:229 and *PSZ*, 1:412).

6. Znamenskii, *PDR*, p. 36.

7. Znamenskii concedes that access remained open but emphasizes the hereditary patterns taking shape in the seventeenth century; yet he offers little evidence for his view other than sparse juridical references. He has been sharply criticized for exaggerating the hereditary ties in pre-Petrine Russia by Vladimirskii-Budanov (*Gosudarstvo*, pp. 97-98). See the balanced assessment of this issue in Golubinskii, 2, pt. 2:83. On the admission of townsmen to the clergy, see some interesting examples from a church in Rostov ("Povest' o nachale . . . ," *IaEV*, 1872, nos. 35:277 and 36:284).

8. See Skvortsov, *Dukhovenstvo*, pp. 10, 12, and passim.

9. In his instruction on ordination procedures, a Riazan hierarch of the

mid-seventeenth century made no mention of a candidate's social origin but only required that he be of the minimum age, literate, and of good moral character. See P. Sladkopevtsev, "Preosviashchennyi Misail," *REV*, 1866, no. 13:385.

10. Materials on the Moscow area for the seventeenth century show that, while a priest often had his son serve as churchman, there were no hard lines of hereditary succession at a given church; see the numerous listings in Kholmogorov, *IM*, 3:6, 33, and passim.

11. Den, "Podatnye elementy," *IRAN*, 1918, no. 5:268-269.

12. *PSZ*, 4:2789.

13. *PSPREP*, 2:248. The Senate's response was ambiguous: it ordered a compilation of pertinent legislation but then proceeded no further (*PSPREP*, 1:457).

14. For legislation, see Vladimirskii-Budanov, *Gosudarstvo*, pp. 204-219.

15. See, for example, *ODBMIu*, 4:85-87.

16. For references, see A. Lototskii, "Na povorote," *RS*, 128 (1906):590-592.

17. Got'e, "Proekt," p. 22.

18. On the Ukraine, see Znamenskii, *PDPV*, pp. 101-102, and P. I. Poletika, "Vospominaniia," *RA*, 1885, no. 3:307.

19. Tooke, 2:119-120.

20. Den, "Podatnye elementy," *IRAN*, 1918, 5:269-270.

21. TsGIA, f. 796, op. 63, g. 1782, d. 543, ll. 3 ob.-12.

22. For regulations on minimum ages for installation and ordination, see *PSPREP*, 3:1020.

23. Rules for retiring infirm clergy, given in the medieval *Kormchaia kniga*, were reaffirmed by the Synod; for citations of canon law and a reiteration of the rule, see *Katekhizis sokrashchennyi dlia sviashchenno-i-tserkovnosluzhitelei* (Moscow, 1798), p. 19; see also "Tserkovnye postanovleniia o sviashchenstve," *PS*, 1859, no. 2:126. Bishops indeed enforced this rule. In 1757, for instance, the bishop of Vladimir forced a priest to resign because of infirmity and failing vision, and in 1791 an ecclesiastical superintendent ordered an aged, infirm priest to cease giving services (TsGADA, f. 1183, op. 1, g. 1757, d. 438, l. 1; TsGIA, f. 796, op. 72, g. 1791, d. 146, ll. 12-13).

24. Reports show that retired clergy represented 6 percent of the clergy in Suzdal in 1737, 9 percent in Pereslavl in 1767, 8 percent in Vladimir in 1782, and 9 percent in the whole Empire in 1796 (TsGIA, f. 796, op. 17, g. 1736, d. 439, ll. 167-167 ob.; op. 48, g. 1767, d. 547, d. 444-479; op. 63, g. 1782, d. 543, ll. 3 ob.-12; *PSPRPP*, 38).

25. TsGIA, f. 796, op. 62, g. 1781, d. 195, l. 38; for other such cases, see ibid., ll. 21-21 ob. (Suzdal), *ODDS*, 10:150 (Moscow), and Il'inskii, "Arkhiv," *TVUAK*, 2:10-11 (Pereslavl).

26. See government complaints and orders to cease such deception in 1711 (*PSZ*, 4:2352), 1724 (*PSPR*, 4:1312), and 1778 (*PSZ*, 20:14807). Another practice common in Moscow was the appointment of a cleric's son as an assistant (*v zastavku*): the elderly priest received the income, the son helped perform services, and both were protected from relocation or conscription. After

1765 diocesan authorities ceased making such appointments and observed the formal rules of the *shtat* (Rozanov, *Istoriia*, 2, pt. 1:114, n.279; 2, p. 2:274-275, nn. 304-305).

27. *PSPR*, 2:596.

28. TsGIA, f. 796, op. 62, g. 1781, d. 195, ll. 63-64.

29. Ibid., op. 55, g. 1774, d. 131, l. 1 ob.

30. Bolotov, 1:149, 2:794.

31. Typical was the suspension of a cleric in Vladimir in 1777 (TsGIA, f. 796, op. 58, g. 1777, d. 390, l. 23 ob.).

32. Ibid., op. 65, g. 1784, d. 274, ll. 11-11 ob., 16, 23, 31, 76-78 ob., 192-192 ob.; op. 65, g. 1784, d. 237, ll. 1-12.

33. Bolotov, 4:1080.

34. TsGIA, f. 796, op. 48, g. 1767, d. 467, l. 2 ob.

35. Ibid., op. 58, g. 1777, d. 204, ll. 37-37 ob. One cleric in Iaroslavl, who had been ordered by the bishop to move to a new parish, complained that because he had once received "punishment with the lash," no parish was willing to accept him (ibid., op. 48, g. 1767, d. 521, l. 3).

36. *PSPREA*, 1:653. This system of promotion was also implicit in the installation charters given to churchmen, which obliged a *ponomar'* or *d'iachok* to serve zealously "so that you will be worthy of advancement to the ordained clergy" (TsGIA, f. 796, op. 65, g. 1784, d. 274, l. 94). The bishops of Moscow and Kolomna even required that special explanations be provided if seniority in promotions was violated (Rozanov, *Istoriia*, 3, pt. 1:125-126; Rudnev, "K istorii," p. 15).

37. See the interesting case of a Moscow priest who lost his position in 1774 because of debts (70 rubles to a merchant) in Skvortsov, *Materialy*, 1:49.

38. See the assessments (up to several hundred rubles) on clerical property and positions in Moscow (Rozanov, *Istoriia*, 1:135, n.459; 2, pt. 2:33-34, 69; Skvortsov, *Materialy*, 1:78, 100; 2:499).

39. Rozanov, *Istoriia*, 2, pt. 1:n.274.

40. Petitions from widows were exceedingly common, invariably drawing a picture of utter destitution and starving children; see, for instance, the petitions from Moscow in 1721, 1726, 1730, and 1764, and from Vladimir in 1729 (TsGIA, f. 796, op. 2, g. 1721, d. 225, ll. 1-2; *ODDS*, 6:109, 10:21; Rozanov, *Istoriia*, 2, pt. 2:n.304; *ODDS*, 9:214).

41. *Katekhizis sokrashchennyi dlia sviashchenno-i-tserkovnosluzhitelei*, p. 19.

42. Smirnov, *ITS*, p. 540.

43. Thus in 1723 the Synod declared that "for appointment to the positions of deceased priests and deacons, do not wait until their children have attained the proper age, but appoint those who have studied in the schools in accordance with the existing laws" (*ODDS*, 2, pt. 2:940); for similar statements in 1721, 1722, 1739, and 1742, see *PSPR*, 1:109, 2:371; *ODDS*, 19:14; *PSPREP*, 1:248.

44. *PSPR*, 2:596.

45. *Istoriko-statisticheskie svedeniia o S.-Peterburgskoi eparkhii*, 10 vols. (St. Petersburg, 1869-1885), 2:204-205.

46. Znamenskii, *PDPV*, pp. 122-123.

47. Rudnev, "K istorii," p. 15.

48. *ODDS*, 28:20.

49. TsGIA, f. 796, op. 79, g. 1798, d. 429, l. 3 ob.

50. Ibid., op. 42, g. 1761, d. 65, ll. 19-19 ob.

51. Ibid., op. 69, g. 1788, d. 127, l. 1 ob.

52. *PSZ*, 1:412.

53. Ibid., 5:3175.

54. See, for instance, the Synod's resolutions of 1721, 1722, and 1723 (*PSPR*, 1:109; *ODDS*, 2, pt. 2:940; *PSPR*, 3:1090); for the order extending this to include sacristans' homes see *PSPR*, 2:876.

55. In 1759 the empress decreed that plots set aside for clerical homes were to remain the property of the Church in perpetuity (*PSPREP*, 4:1659); a similar decree was issued in 1779 (*PSPREA*, 2:905).

56. *PSPREA*, 1:403.

57. Rozanov, *Istoriia*, 2, pt. 2:69; 3, pt. 1:23, 110-111; *PSPREA*, 2:1062.

58. TsGIA, f. 796, op. 64, g. 1783, d. 45, l. 22 ob.

59. *PSZ*, 1:412.

60. See Peter's decrees of 1708, 1710, and 1718, and the Ecclesiastical Regulation of 1721 (*PSZ*, 4:2186, 2308; 5:3175; *PSPR*, 1:1).

61. Agntsev, *IRS*, pp. 72-73.

62. *PSPR*, 1:139.

63. *ODDS*, 10:286.

64. *ODDS*, 23:41.

65. *PSPREA*, 1:403.

66. *ODDS*, 8:106 [misprinted in *ODDS* as item number 119].

67. TsGADA, f. 1183, op. 1, g. 1756, d. 176, ll. 1-26.

68. *PSPR*, 10:3217; *ODDS*, 18:129. See also the similar cases in Moscow in 1726 and 1730 (*ODDS*, 6:109, 10:21).

69. *ODDS*, 21:37.

70. *PSPREA*, 1:403.

71. For similar decisions in typical cases, see the Synod's response to petitions from Tver in 1780 (TsGIA, f. 796, op. 61, g. 1780, d. 266, ll. 1-7 ob.), Moscow in 1767 (*PSPREA*, 1:359), Suzdal in 1792 (*PSPREA*, 3:1499), and Novgorod in 1770 (*ODDS*, 50:97).

72. Rozanov, *Istoriia*, 2, pt. 2:n.304.

73. Skvortsov, *Materialy*, 2:15.

74. See, for example, the cases in Moscow in 1773 and Suzdal in 1792 (Skvortsov, *Materialy*, 2:499-500; *PSPREA*, 3:1499).

75. TsGIA, f. 796, op. 62, g. 1781, d. 195, l. 47, 67 ob.

76. Illustrative were the cases of a Vladimir cleric in 1783 and a Moscow priest in 1780 (ibid., op. 64, g. 1783, d. 302, ll. 1-1 ob.; op. 61, g. 1780, d. 236, l. 2 ob.).

77. Ibid., op. 58, g. 1777, d. 390, l. 23 ob.

78. *PSPREA*, 1:615.

79. TsGIA, f. 796, op. 57, g. 1776, d. 111, ll. 1-7; for a similar case in Novgorod in 1770, see *ODDS*, 50:426.

80. See the opinions filed in 1880-81 by bishops from Iaroslavl, Tver, Sim-

birsk, Don, Chernigov, Polotsk, Tambov, Ufa, Poltava, Tula, and Kher'son (TsGIA, f. 797, op. 50, III otd., 5 st., d. 182, chast' 2, ll. 17-17 ob., 59-59 ob., 71-71 ob., 79-79 ob., 84 ob., 113-113 ob., 132 ob.-133, 182-183, 231-232, 269 ob.-270 ob., 321 ob.-322 ob.).

81. Peter had, it seemed, touched upon the issue in 1724, when he decreed that it is permissible to "accept as priests and deacons people who till the soil [*pashennye*], if there are no other qualified people" (*PSZ*, 7:4455). The nineteenth-century editors of *PSZ* interpreted *pashennye* to mean peasants, implying that they could thus enter the parish clergy. But such was not the case. The decree actually pertained not to the parish clergy but to the monastic clergy, whom Peter had divided into "serving monks" and "farming monks" (*pashennye*) in his attempt to reduce the number of "parasitic monks." See the pertinent legislation in *PSPR*, 4:1197 (on *pashennye*) and 1202 (on monks). This explains why Peter's seemingly liberal decree was never cited by the Synod, which later combed the laws for precedents to justify the appointment of poll-tax registrants. See, for example, the omission of the 1724 decree from a research note (*spravka*) on poll-tax laws that was compiled in 1775 (TsGIA, f. 796, op. 56, g. 1775, d. 142, ll. 5-6).

82. *PSPR*, 5:1661.

83. *PSZ*, 7:4802.

84. *PSPR*, 5:1693; *ODDS*, 2, pt. 1:756; 5:383.

85. *ODDS*, 7:148.

86. *ODDS*, 7:29.

87. *PSPR*, 6:2066.

88. *PSZ*, 7:5202; *PSPR*, 6:2098.

89. *PSZ*, 8:5264; for the text of such a release, see TsGIA, f. 796, op. 62, g. 1781, d. 585, l. 533.

90. For detailed data, see TsGIA, f. 796, op. 20, g. 1739, d. 14, ll. 169, 171, 173, 232 ob., 264 ob., 310-311 ob. and the extensive summaries in Den, "Podatnye elementy," *IRAN*, 1918, no. 5:271-292.

91. *PSPREP*, 1:248.

92. *PSPREP*, 1:457. But several months earlier, in January 1743, the Senate had already begun to complain about poll-tax registrants escaping into the clergy (*PSPREP*, 1:278); nevertheless, here it implicitly accepted the Synod's proposal without remonstrance.

93. *PSZ*, 12:8981; *PSPREP*, 2:677. This blunt decree immediately had a sobering effect upon the Synod, as an incident shortly afterwards made clear. The Synod received a petition from a sacristan's son in Suzdal diocese, pleading that he be released from the poll-tax registry in order to enter the clergy; the Synod circumspectly advised him to apply "in the appropriate place" because "the Holy Synod has no decrees on the removal of such people from the poll tax" (TsGIA, f. 796, op. 25, g. 1744, d. 363, l. 1).

94. TsGIA, f. 796, op. 27, g. 1746, d. 123, ll. 1-6.

95. See, for instance, the Synod's resolutions of 1747, 1754, 1756, and 1761 (*PSPREP*, 3:1000, 4:1400 and 1729). The last decree was especially important, for it permitted a brief surge of poll-tax registrants into the clergy in 1761-62 (see, for example, TsGIA, f. 796, op. 56, g. 1775, d. 142, ll. 1-1 ob.).

For firm rebuffs by the Senate, see its decrees of 1750 and 1754 (*PSPREP*, 3:1158, 4:1401; *PSZ*, 13:9781, 14:10422).

96. Den, "Podatnye elementy," *IRAN*, 1918, no. 13:1362-1363.

97. The data for Pereslavl and Vladimir are to be found in TsGIA, f. 796, op. 48, g. 1767, d. 547, ll. 454-466 ob. and op. 46, g. 1765, d. 276, ll. 176-177. The Senate also actively opposed the tonsure of poll-tax registrants into the monastic clergy (see its decrees of 1766 in *PSPREA*, 1:282 and 294). Reports show that a number of central dioceses had accepted poll-tax registrants (often former monastery peasants) into the monastic order; there were 23 such monks in Trinity-Sergius Monastery, 13 elsewhere in Pereslavl diocese, 31 in Vladimir, and 8 in Riazan, while some outlying dioceses had still larger numbers (such as 163 in Velikii Ustiug). See TsGIA, f. 796, op. 46, g. 1765, d. 276, ll. 56-57, 120, 142-142 ob.

98. See reports of routine verification in Moscow and Riazan (Rozanov, *Istoriia*, 2, pt. 1:n.266; 2, pt. 2:136-137; TsGIA, f. 796, op. 38, g. 1757, d. 417, ll. 1-2).

99. TsGIA, f. 796, op. 48, g. 1767, d. 547, ll. 454-466 ob.

100. In Pereslavl, for example, 60 percent were formerly of clerical status; in Riazan 94 percent had come from the clergy (ibid., op. 48, g. 1767, d. 547, ll. 454-466 ob.; op. 46, g. 1765, d. 276, ll. 179-190 ob.).

101. *PSPREA*, 1:188; see also the Senate memorandum of 1766 (ibid., 1:282).

102. TsGIA, f. 796, op. 50, g. 1769, d. 428, ll. 1-6.

103. *SIRIO*, 43:47; Titlinov, *Gavriil*, pp. 209-221, 240-243.

104. TsGIA, f. 796, op. 56, g. 1775, d. 119, ll. 1-1 ob.

105. Ibid., op. 56, g. 1775, d. 142, ll. 1-191; "Pis'ma Imp. Ekateriny II-oi k Ober-Prokuroram Sv. Prav. Sinoda, 1765-1796 gg.," *RA*, 8 (1870):767.

106. The Synod tried to apply the manifesto to collective petitions it had received from Pereslavl, Kolomna, Rostov, and other central dioceses (TsGIA, f. 796, op. 56, g. 1775, d. 119, ll. 1-187; d. 179, ll. 1-96). It used the same technique in the question of schismatics; see Pokrovskii, *Antifeodal'nyi protest*, pp. 166-167.

107. Senate resolution of 10 May 1776 (TsGIA, f. 796, op. 56, g. 1775, d. 119, ll. 83 ob.-84). When it distributed this decree to the subordinate bishops, it advised them to fill vacancies by requesting idle clergy from neighboring dioceses if there were too few candidates in their own (ibid., ll. 87 ob.-88; *PSPREA*, 2:827).

108. TsGIA, f. 796, op. 62, g. 1781, d. 497, l. 3.

109. Ibid., op. 56, g. 1775, d. 179, ll. 65-67 ob.; op. 58, g. 1777, d. 15, ll. 20-22.

110. Data were compiled only on sacristans, not the ordained clergy (who had received the sacrament of ordination and thus were safe from expulsion); hence the total number of poll-tax registrants in the parish clergy was somewhat higher.

111. TsGIA, f. 796, op. 63, g. 1782, d. 543, ll. 13-21 ob., 67-132.

112. Prior to the conscription, 667 sacristans were reported in all dioceses; during the conscription 1,354 sacristans and their sons were drafted. The rate

of conscription was high: 119 of 123 in Kolomna, 52 of 52 in Vladimir, and 150 of 150 in Riazan (ibid., op. 65, g. 1784, d. 443, ll. 71-85, 678-685; Den, "Podatnye elementy," *IRAN*, 1918, no. 14:1540).

113. TsGIA, f. 796, op. 62, g. 1781, d. 585, l. 385.

114. Typical were the statements by the bishops of Riazan, Pereslavl, and Rostov (ibid., op. 64, g. 1783, d. 338, ll. 33-34 ob.; op. 64, g. 1783, d. 566, ll. 1-1 ob.; op. 64, g. 1783, d. 375, ll. 1-1 ob.).

115. Den, "Podatnye elementy," *IRAN*, 1918, no. 14:1541.

116. See J. T. Flint, "The Secularization of Norwegian Society," *Comparative Studies in Society and History*, 7 (1963-64):339.

117. *ODDS*, 1:300; 2, pt. 1:378; *PSPR*, 2:624 and 648.

118. *PSPR*, 1:1 (italics mine). Appropriate for such a policy, Prokopovich favored a generalized curriculum; for his attempt to include jurisprudence in the seminary at Aleksandro-Nevskii Monastery in St. Petersburg, see Chistovich, *Feofan*, p. 135.

119. Vladimirskii-Budanov, *Gosudarstvo*, pp. 117-142.

120. TsGIA, f. 796, op. 18, g. 1737, d. 32, chast' 2, ll. 148-151 ob.

121. See the student registers in ibid., chast' 2, ll. 110-111 ob., 324-360 ob., 641-650 ob.; chast' 3, ll. 73-84. Radically different were the seminaries in the Ukraine, where the clergy's sons were a minority in the 1730s—composing only 30 percent of the pupils in the Kiev Academy and Chernigov seminary (see Rozhdestvenskii, *Ocherki*, pp. 47-56).

122. TsGIA, f. 796, op. 25, g. 1744, d. 134, ll. 107-121; see also Smirnov, *ITS*, pp. 26, 101, 104. A similarly high proportion of monastery employees' sons were enrolled in the Aleksandro-Nevskii Monastery of St. Petersburg (Chistovich, *Istoriia*, pp. 7, 11, 45).

123. For data on the Moscow Academy, see *ODDS*, 9:571; *PSPR*, 6:2135; for data on 1730, see *ODDS*, 10:378 or Rozhdestvenskii, *Ocherki*, p. 60.

124. *PSPREP*, 2:580; *PSZ*, 12:8904.

125. TsGIA, f. 796, op. 24, g. 1743, d. 496, chast' 2, ll. 124-134 ob.

126. For the legislation, see Vladimirskii-Budanov, *Gosudarstvo*, pp. 117-142.

127. *PSPR*, 3:1097.

128. The authorities were well aware of this factor; a 1766 education project, for example, specified that seminary education was free to the clergy's children, but others would have to pay (Rozhdestvenskii, *Materialy*, pp. 279-280).

129. See the Synod's "doubts" about a common curriculum in a 1726 memorandum to the Supreme Privy Council (*SIRIO*, 69:67; *PSPR*, 5:1858). It subsequently adduced a further argument that probably caused even greater concern—lack of resources; see its resolution of 9 January 1727 in *PSPR*, 5:1887.

130. *PSPR*, 4:1189.

131. Smirnov, *IMA*, p. 179.

132. Ibid., pp. 179-180; Amvrosii, 1:429; *PSPR*, 6:2135.

133. Agntsev, *IRS*, p. 98; see a similar case in Makarii, p. 2.

134. Even in Riazan three of the four "outsiders" were the sons of ecclesiastical officials, and only one pupil was listed in the registry as a peasant

(TsGIA, f. 796, op. 74, g. 1793, d. 94, ll. 349-421; op. 71, g. 1790, d. 417, ll. 385-454, 486-519; op. 71, g. 1790, d. 418, ll. 517-590).

135. Ibid., op. 71, g. 1790, d. 417, ll. 87-152.

136. See the reports by the bishops of Moscow, Rostov, Riazan, and Pereslavl (ibid., op. 64, g. 1783, d. 375, ll. 1-1 ob.; op. 64, g. 1783, d. 338, ll. 1-4, 33-34 ob.; op. 64, g. 1783, d. 566, ll. 1-1 ob.).

137. For canon law, see "Tserkovnye postanovleniia," PS, 1859, tom 2:262-277.

138. The main difficulty concerns fugitives. It is, however, a moot point whether they departed voluntarily, for many were under suspicion for criminal offenses and some had escaped from diocesan jails and monastery detention. This is evident from the frequent search warrants issued for their arrest and return to their home dioceses. See, for example, such warrants issued for clergy from Suzdal, Vladimir, and Pereslavl dioceses in TsGADA, f. 1183, op. 3, g. 1758, d. 358, ll. 1-3; op. 1, g. 1755, d. 66, ll. 1-2; op. 1, g. 1759, d. 259, ll. 1-2; TsGIA, f. 796, op. 34, g. 1753, d. 541, ll. 1-4.

139. TsGIA, f. 796, op. 17, g. 1736, d. 439, ll. 195-196 ob.

140. Ibid., op. 36, g. 1755, d. 344, ll. 380 ob.-403. The bishop had reported 4,278 clergy and sons in the second reviziia of the 1740s; from this group, 730 had died, leaving a balance of 3,548. All were still in the clerical estate in 1756 with these exceptions: 2 transferred to Moscow University, 1 to a Moscow typography, and 43 ran away (total: 1.2 percent); another 20 were expelled from the clerical estate after committing various crimes (0.7 percent). For similar data on the succeeding period (1756-66), see ibid., op. 48, g. 1767, d. 547, ll. 452-452 ob.

141. Student registers from the 1790s show that only a small percentage of the students transferred to the secular command, although these were compactly concentrated in the uppermost classes. In 1793 the seminary of Vladimir reported that of 149 students withdrawing from the seminary, 17 (11.7 percent) had transferred to the secular command—10 to the medical school, 3 to the civil service, 2 to Moscow University, 1 to a Moscow typography, and 1 became a lay seminary teacher. Even lower rates were recorded by other dioceses (ibid., op. 71, g. 1790, d. 417 and d. 418; op. 74, g. 1793, d. 94).

142. Kizevetter, Posadskaia obshchina, pp. 75-76.

143. In Riazan, for example, the students in state schools (both the maloe narodnoe uchilishche and glavnoe narodnoe uchilishche) totaled only 29, whereas the seminary enrollment was 531 (Kuleshov, pp. 63-64; TsGIA, f. 796, op. 71, g. 1790, d. 417, ll. 486-519). A similar picture is to be found in Moscow; see the data on state schools in Moscow in L. A. Lepskaia, "Sostav uchashchikhsia narodnykh uchilishch Moskvy v kontse XVIII v.," Vestnik MGU, Seriia: istoriia, 1973, no. 5:92, 96. At the same time, the clergy's sons constituted a small proportion of the enrollment in the secular schools; for all schools in 1802 they represented only 2 percent of the pupils (Kniaz'kov and Serbov, p. 154). According to the data on Riazan and Moscow, the clergy's sons constituted a larger percentage in the maloe narodnoe uchilishche than in the glavnoe narodnoe uchilishche but their total numbers were still small (Kuleshov, pp. 63-64; Lepskaia, "Sostav," pp. 92, 96).

144. Troitskii, Russkii absoliutizm, pp. 213-214.

145. TsGIA, f. 796, op. 65, g. 1784, d. 274, l. 30. Only in major towns in the last quarter of the century did the clergy's sons possess (or borrow) sufficient capital to declare themselves merchants. Thus in 1784 during the conscription in Moscow 102 youths became merchants with an average capital of 415.75 rubles (ibid., f. 558, op. 2, d. 127, ll. 241-243 ob.). On a smaller scale, several churchmen in Tula in the 1770s and 1780s asked permission to transfer to the merchant class, and a Kolomna report of 1797 also showed a number of such transfers (ibid., f. 796, op. 66, g. 1775, d. 141, ll. 1-5; ODDS, 50:418; TsGIA, f. 796, op. 64, g. 1783, d. 89, ll. 1-7; op. 77, g. 1796, d. 670, ll. 1-8). If the merchant guilds offered a relatively enticing alternative, the status of common townsman certainly did not; see the bleak descriptions in Bakmeister, 1, pt. 2:120, 125, 131, 141.

146. That the chancellery employees provided the main source of new bureaucrats is evident in the 1755 census of civil service officials (see Troitskii, *Russkii absoliutizm*, pp. 213-214); on the development of the "estate" of *prikaznye liudi*, see Vladimirskii-Budanov, *Gosudarstvo*, pp. 174-187. For comparative data on the clergy's offspring (who numbered into the thousands in each diocese), see TsGIA, f. 796, op. 64, g. 1783, d. 375 and d. 566.

147. Thus 10 of 17 pupils leaving the Vladimir seminary in 1793 for secular careers studied medicine; a similar pattern prevailed in other seminaries (TsGIA, f. 796, op. 74, g. 1793, d. 94, ll. 349-421).

148. For the Moscow data, see ibid., op. 62, g. 1781, d. 588, ll. 117-124 ob.

149. See, for example, the Synodal decree of 1732 in *PSPR*, 7:2570.

150. For example, see *ODDS*, 2, pt. 1:492 and pt. 2:902.

151. See, for instance, the decrees of 1721, 1722, 1732, 1742, 1765, and 1798 (*PSPR*, 1:116, 2:596, 7:2570; *PSPREP*, 1:71; *PSPREA*, 1:266; *PSPRPP*, 182).

152. See the forcible return of clerical youths in the following: TsGADA, f. 1183, op. 1, g. 1734, d. 322, ll. 1-4; Malitskii, *ISS*, pp. 132-133; Malitskii, *IVS*, 1:58-61.

153. *PSZ*, 7:4499; *PSPR*, 4:1252; *ODDS*, 4:220.

154. TsGIA, f. 796, op. 64, g. 1783, d. 89, ll. 1-7; d. 236, ll. 1-2 ob.

155. *ODDS*, 50:291.

156. TsGIA, f. 796, op. 67, g. 1786, d. 185, ll. 1-1 ob.

157. See, for instance, the Synod's rulings in a Viatka case of 1780 and Vladimir in 1785 (ibid., op. 61, g. 1780, d. 196, ll. 1-2 ob.; op. 66, g. 1785, d. 62, ll. 1-6 ob.).

158. *PSPR*, 1:120; *ODDS*, 2, pt. 1:378; PSPR, 2:624, 850, 890.

159. *PSPR*, 7:2488; see also *ODDS*, 10:378 and *PSPR*, 7:2627.

160. *PSZ*, 8:6066.

161. *PSPR*, 9:3139 and 3140.

162. See, for instance, the Synodal resolutions of 1747-49 and 1755 in *PSPREP*, 3:1002, 1055, 1124; 4:1423.

163. See Znamenskii, *DSh*, pp. 597-601.

164. TsGIA, f. 796, op. 48, g. 1767, d. 547, l. 14 ob.; *PSPREA*, 1:360.

165. *PSZ*, 18:13306.

166. *ODDS*, 50:69; see similar action in two other cases in *ODDS*, 50:91.

167. TsGIA, f. 796, op. 56, g. 1775, d. 594, l. 2; see also *PSPREA*, 2:792.

168. TsGIA, f. 796, op. 73, g. 1792, d. 5, ll. 1-43.

169. *PSPRPP*, 335, 342, 423, 473.

170. Smirnov, *ITS*, p. 552.

171. Ibid., pp. 578-583.

172. The bishop of Rostov displayed uncommon zeal in executing Catherine's decree of 1779 urging seminarians to enter the bureaucracy. He organized a systematic examination of youths in his diocese and gave this instruction to the examiners: "The persons [conducting the examination] are to encourage the fathers and relatives and children themselves that they should not display stubborn opposition to leaving for appointment to the chancelleries. Rather, feeling Her Imperial Majesty's compassion for their benefit and advantage, they themselves should strive to make themselves fit for this." And in an ominous allusion to the state conscriptions, the bishop added that "those who remain in excess, over appointment [norms], . . . in time will not be left without the appropriate review." ("Meropriiatiia so storony Sv. Sinoda v 1775-1779 gg. k utverzhdeniiu gramotnosti mezhdu det'mi dukhovenstva i vypusk ikh iz dukhovnogo vedomstva v namestnichestvo," *IaEV*, 1895, no. 45:416-417.)

173. "Po povodu pechataemogo nizhe 'Uchrezhdeniia,' " *REV*, 1866, no. 19:543-544.

174. Sokolov, "Simon Lagov," *REV*, 1884, no. 10:183.

175. See, for example, "Sv. Tikhon," *IaEV*, 1861, no. 34:327-328.

176. See, for instance, the petition of a priest in Vladimir uezd in 1737 (TsGADA, f. 1183, op. 1, g. 1737, d. 32, ll. 2-2 ob.).

177. Pososhkov, p. 34; Popov, *Tatishchev*, pp. 226-227.

178. See Rostislavov's interesting sketch of a Riazan family at the beginning of the nineteenth century in his "Zapiski," *RS*, 27 (1880):545-549.

179. See the general treatment in Hans Rogger, *National Consciousness in Eighteenth-Century Russia* (Cambridge, Mass., 1960), pp. 45-84; for vivid descriptions of the changing life-style, see Bolotov's *Zapiski* and Baturin's memoirs ("Zapiski P. S. Baturina," *Golos minuvshego*, 1918, no. 1:67, 74-78).

180. The "manuscript miscellanies" were hand-copied, nonaristocratic literary works; they often included religious, historical, or simply entertaining tales. The parish clergy had dominated this genre in the seventeenth century but ceased to do so in the eighteenth; though some clergy still possessed miscellanies, theirs were curiously old-fashioned, seventeenth-century in content (see M. Speranskii, *Rukopisnye sborniki XVIII v.* [Moscow, 1963], pp. 99-102).

181. *Stavlennicheskaia gramota* (GBL, Otdel redkikh knig, Sbornik 65, l. 1); see the later ordination charter in TsGIA, f. 796, op. 22, g. 1741, d. 43, ll. 3 ob.-4.

182. *O dolzhnostiakh presviterov prikhodskikh*, pp. 88-89.

183. Rozanov, *Istoriia*, 2, pt. 1:n.448; "Dnevnik," *IaEV*, 1895, no. 1:9.

184. Malitskii, *IPE*, 1:65-69; see also Arsenii Matseevich's order to clerical elders in "Rasporiazheniia Arseniia Matseevicha," *IaEV*, 1868, no. 30:262.

185. Rozanov, *Istoriia*, 2, pt. 2:76; for similar measures by his successor Platon Levshin, see 3, pt. 1:67-68 and n.601, and Platon, *Instruktsii*, punkt 16. For Kolomna diocese, see Rudnev, "K istorii," p. 36.

186. N. Malitskii, "Zaboty ep. Ieronima o vozvyshenii nravstvennosti i blagochiniia vladimirskogo dukhovenstva," *VEV*, 1907, no. 5:65-66.

187. TsGIA, f. 796, op. 52, g. 1771, d. 396, ll. 1-36; *PSPREA*, 1:666.

188. See, for example, the brief instructional pamphlet of 1705 (reprinted in 1747 and 1753): *Izvestie reshitel'noe o bedstvennykh i nedoumennykh sluchaekh*, pp. 2-2 ob.

189. Rozanov, *Istoriia*, 1:136-137.

190. N. Rozanov, "Preosviashchennyi Iosif," *MEV*, 1869, no. 21:6.

191. "K istorii nebogosluzhebnogo odeianiia," *VEV*, 1899, no. 18:618-619; Il'inskii, "Otdelenie," *TVUAK*, 4:100.

192. Malitskii, "Zaboty," *VEV*, 1907, no. 5:68.

193. Rozanov, *Istoriia*, 3, pt. 1:n.347; Platon, *Instruktsii*, punkt 43; see also the Kolomna instruction in Rudnev, "K istorii," p. 40.

194. Glebov, "Materialy," *REV*, 1897, no. 6:179-180. Even in the early nineteenth century priests often could not afford a proper cassock; according to one source, some rural clergy had to rent the cassock of a town priest in order to appear before the bishop (Giliarov-Platonov, 1:20).

195. V. Orlov, "Kratkie biograficheskie svedeniia ob ierarkhakh Vladimirskoi eparkhii," *VEV*, 1886, no. 20:534.

196. Rozanov, *Istoriia*, 1:139.

197. *O dolzhnostiakh presviterov prikhodskikh*, p. 89.

198. Rozanov, *Istoriia*, 2, pt. 2:351-352; Skvortsov, *Materialy*, 2:373-374.

199. TsGIA, f. 796, op. 67, g. 1786, d. 185, ll. 13-15 ob.

200. Platon, *Instruktsii*, punkt 33.

201. Rudnev, "K istorii," p. 38.

202. Znamenskii, *PDPV*, p. 785.

203. For the circular questionnaire of the Special Commission, see TsGIA, f. 804, op. 1, razd. 1, d. 9, ll. 13-33.

204. Kozlov, "Tserkovnaia reforma," pp. 306-316.

205. Malitskii, *ISS*, pp. 29-41.

206. TsGIA, f. 796, op. 71, g. 1790, d. 264, l. 5 ob.

207. Archpriest Petr Alekseev of Blagoveshchenskii Cathedral asked that he be addressed as *protoierei*, not *protopop*, and complained that *pop* was a vulgar, humiliating term. Metropolitan Platon rejected his request, however, arguing that *pop* was firmly rooted in Church tradition ("Iz bumag imp. protoiereia Ioanna Pamfilova," *RA*, 1871, no. 1:229).

208. See the episode involving a Viatka priest in Titlinov, *Gavriil*, pp. 360-369. Later, Emperor Paul initiated the practice of awarding medals and honors to the white clergy; see *PSPRPP*, 276 and 314.

209. Giliarov-Platonov, 1:v-vii.

210. Before the mid-eighteenth century, marriage to a serf entailed enserfment, but in Catherine's reign this practice ceased (Semevskii, *Krest'iane*, 1:13-14). There were, to be sure, cases of voluntary marriage to serfs (Rostislavov, "Zapiski," *RS*, 27 [1880]:7-8); there were even occasional marriages

into the families of nobles and prosperous townspeople (Rozanov, *Istoriia*, 2, pt. 2:351; 3, pt. 1:n.605; Bolotov, 4:1297). For most clergy, however, endogamous marriages were still the rule. The fullest picture of marital patterns is provided in the detailed profiles of "the poll-tax clergy" in 1782: a few had married merchants' daughters and one had even wedded a serf woman, but most had married within the clerical estate. See the lists for Vladimir and Pereslavl dioceses in TsGIA, f. 796, op. 63, g. 1782, d. 543, ll. 13-21 ob., 67-132.

211. Rozanov, *Istoriia*, 3, pt. 2:180-181; 2, pt. 1:173-174; 2, pt. 2:342-345.

212. Znamenskii, *PDPV*, p. 120.

213. Riazan petition of 1798 (TsGIA, f. 796, op. 79, g. 1798, d. 428, l. 7). Of many other examples, see the following typical statements: a Kolomna petitioner of 1784 declared that "my father, grandfather, and forefathers were all from the clergy (ibid., op. 65, g. 1784, d. 274, ll. 78-78 ob.); faced with conscription, churchmen frequently claimed to be "of clerical birthright" (ibid., op. 56, g. 1775, d. 142, l. 1; op. 58, g. 1777, d. 15, 1. 20 ob.).

214. TsGADA, f. 1183, op. 1, g. 1746, d. 339, l. 3; V. I. Kholmogorov and G. I. Kholmogorov, *Materialy dlia istorii, arkheologii i statistiki moskovskikh tserkvei* (Moscow, 1884), p. 632.

Selected Bibliography

The best single guide to sources and secondary literature is Igor Smolitsch, *Geschichte der russischen Kirche* (Leiden, 1964), pp. xv-liii. For additional references, see G. V. Florovskii, *Puti russkogo bogosloviia* (Paris, 1937), pp. 521-574; Gregory L. Freeze, "N. P. Giliarov-Platonov: A View of the Clergy and Church Education," in N. P. Giliarov-Platonov, *Iz perezhitogo* (forthcoming reprint; Cambridge, 1977); A. P. Dobroklonskii, *Rukovodstvo po istorii russkoi tserkvi*, 4 vols. (Riazan, Moscow, 1886-1893); and P. N. Berkov, ed., *Istoriia russkoi literatury XVIII veka; bibliograficheskii ukazatel'* (Leningrad, 1968), pp. 56-100, 203-206. Much valuable material is also listed in the library catalogues of the main theological academies: Leningradskaia dukhovnaia akademiia, *Katalog sistematicheskii (po distsiplinam) russkikh knig, nakhodiashchikhsia v biblioteke Leningradskoi dukhovnoi akademii*, 3 vols. (Leningrad, 1954); Moskovskaia dukhovnaia akademiia, *Sistematicheskii katalog knig v biblioteke Moskovskoi dukhovnoi akademii*, 5 vols. (Moscow, 1881-1910); and Peterburgskaia dukhovnaia akademiia, *Alfavitnyi ukazatel' knig i rukopisei nakhodiashchikhsia v biblioteke Peterburgskoi dukhovnoi akademii*, 6 vols. (St. Petersburg, 1886-1889). For indexes to the neglected, but valuable ecclesiastical journals, see Iu. I. Masonov, et. al., *Ukazateli soderzhaniia russkikh zhurnalov i prodolzhaiushchikhsia izdanii, 1755-1970 gg.* (Moscow, 1975).

Listed below are only some of the more important works, with an emphasis upon lesser known literature on church history rather than the standard works familiar to specialists. Of the voluminous materials in the *eparkhial'nye vedomosti* and church serials, only the most essential are listed here.

I. Archival Sources

Gosudarstvennaia biblioteka im. V. I. Lenina. Rukopisnyi otdel.

    f. 222   N. I. Panin
    f. 316   Filaret (Drozdov)

Gosudarstvennaia publichnaia biblioteka im. M. E. Saltykova-Shchedrina. Rukopisnyi otdel.

    Sobranie Titova
    f. 573   S.-Peterburgskaia dukhovnaia adademiia

Tsentral'nyi gosudarstvennyi arkhiv drevnikh aktov.

    f. 235   Patriarshii kazennyi prikaz
    f. 280   Kollegiia ekonomii
    f. 1183 Moskovskaia sinodal'naia kontora

Tsentral'nyi gosudarstvennyi istoricheskii arkhiv SSSR.

    f. 558   Ekspeditsiia dlia svidetel'stvovaniia gosudarstvennykh schetov
    f. 571   Departament raznykh podatei i sborov
    f. 796   Kantseliariia Sv. Sinoda
    f. 797   Kantseliariia Ober-Prokurora
    f. 802   Uchebnyi komitet
    f. 804   Osoboe prisutstvie po delam pravoslavnogo dukhovenstva

II. Published Sources

Akty istoricheskie. 5 vols. St. Petersburg, 1841.

Akty, sobrannye v bibliotekakh i arkhivakh Rossiiskoi Imperii Arkheograficheskoi ekspeditsieiu. 4 vols. St. Petersburg, 1836.

Alekseev, Petr. "Rassuzhdenie na vopros: Mozhno li dostoinomu sviashchenniku, minovav monashestvo, proizvedenu byt' vo episkopa?" *Chteniia OIDR,* 1867, kn. 3, otd. 5:17-26.

———— *Rech' o dostoinstve i pol'ze katekhizisa.* Moscow, 1759.

———— *Tserkovnyi slovar'.* 3 vols. St. Petersburg, 1794.

Andreev, A. I. "Nakaz votchinnika krest'ianam 1709 g.," *IA,* 8 (1953): 269-277.

Arkhivy po Vladimirskoi gubernii. 2 vols. Vladimir, 1916.

"Arsenii Matseevich, byvshii mitropolit rostovskii," *Chteniia OIDR,*

41 (1862), kn. 2, chast' 5:1-44.

Bakmeister, L. I. *Topograficheskie izvestiia, sluzhashchiia dlia polnogo geograficheskogo opisaniia Rossiiskoi imperii.* 4 pts. Moscow, 1771-74.

"Blagoslovennaia gramota ot 1705 g.," *IaEV*, 1895, no. 18:286-287.

Bobrov, A. A. "O nadzore za prodavaemymi ikonami," *TVUAK*, 2 (1900):64.

Bolotov, A. T. *Zapiski Andreia Timofeevicha Bolotova.* 4 vols. St. Petersburg, 1871-73.

Bychkov, F. A. *Akty, otnosiashchiesia k istorii Iaroslavskoi gubernii.* Iaroslavl, 1889.

Coxe, William. *Travels into Poland, Russia, Sweden and Denmark.* 2 vols. 2nd. ed. London, 1785.

Dal', V. *Poslovitsy russkogo naroda.* Moscow, 1957.

Danilov, M. V. *Zapiski.* Moscow, 1842.

"Dela namestnika Mel'gunova v pol'zu tserkvi v 1783-87 godakh," *IaEV*, 1884, no. 7:49-54.

"Dnevnik Preosv. Arseniia Vereshchagina," *IaEV*, 1894, nos. 43-49; 1895, nos. 1-7, 9, 11, 13-15, 18-19, 27-29, 40-42.

Dobroliubov, I. "Opis' pridanogo, dannogo za docher'iu sviashchennika v XVIII st.," *TRUAK*, 1(1887), pt. 2:36-37.

——— "Seminarskoe torzhestvo 1797 g.," *Istoricheskii vestnik*, 1880, no. 3:646-647.

——— "Ukazatel' materialov dlia istoriko-statisticheskogo opisaniia Riazanskoi eparkhii, khraniashchikhsia v arkhive dukhovnoi konsistorii (1720-1830 gg.)," *TRUAK*, 16 (1901), pt. 2:176-222; 17 (1902), pt. 1:11-24, pt. 2:91-160.

Dobronravov, V. G. "Dela Vladimirskogo gubernskogo pravleniia," *TVUAK*, 3 (1901):1-58.

Dobrynin, G. I. "Istinnoe povestvovanie o zhizni Gavriila Dobrynina," *RA*, 1871, nos. 2-4, 6-10.

"Doklad Sv. Sinoda Imp. Elizavete Petrovne o knigakh, protivnykh vere i nravstvennosti," *Chteniia OIDR*, 1866, kn. 4, otd. 5:7-8.

Dovnar-Zapol'skii, M. V. "Materialy dlia istorii votchinnogo upravleniia v Rossii," *Universiteskie izvestiia*, 43 (1903), no. 12:1-32; 44 (1904), no. 6:33-64, no. 7: 65-96; 45 (1905), no. 8:97-128; 49 (1909), no. 7:193-240; 50 (1910), no. 11:241-288.

"Dukhovnoe zaveshchanie sviashchennika XVIII v.," *RA*, 27 (1889), kn. 1:523-526.

"Dva pis'ma ot 1797 i 1798 gg. kniazia A. Golitsyna k tserkovnomu staroste," *IaEV*, 1894, no. 28:443-445.

Eleonskii, S., ed. "Khozhdenie popa Savvy," *Literaturnoe nasledstvo*, 9/10 (1933):106-111.

"Epitrakhil'naia gramota ot 1686 g.," *IaEV*, 1893, no. 33:519-520.

"Epitrakhil'naia gramota v Pereslavskoi eparkhii," *VEV,* 1912, no. 16:356-358.

"Eshche ukaznoe predpisanie Iaroslavskogo dukhovnogo pravleniia," *IaEV,* 1889, no. 51:809-814.

Falck, Johann. *Beyträge zur topografischen Kenntniss des russischen Reichs.* 3 vols. St. Petersburg, 1785.

Giliarov-Platonov, N. P. *Iz perezhitogo.* 2 vols. Moscow, 1886.

Glebov, K. "Materialy k biografii preosv. Simona Lagova," *REV,* 1897, no. 1:8-12, no. 2:53-61, no. 4:110-116, no. 5:148-150, no. 6:178-186.

Got'e, Iu. V., ed. "Proekt o popravlenii gosudarstvennykh del Artemiia Petrovicha Volynskogo," *Dela i Dni,* 3 (1922):1-31.

"Gramoty o uchrezhdenii popovskikh starost i o tserkovnom blagochinii v Moskve," *Vremennik OIDR,* 14 (1852):21-28.

Iakovlev, A. A. "Zapiski A. A. Iakovleva," *Pamiatniki novoi russkoi istorii,* 3 (1873):87-112.

Il'inskii, P. V. "Arkhiv Pereiaslavskogo dukhovnogo pravleniia," *TVUAK,* 2 (1900):3-16.

———— "Otdelenie arkhiva starykh del Vladimirskoi dukhovnoi konsistorii," *TVUAK,*4 (1902):91-102.

Innokentii. *Kratkiia nastavleniia ot pastyria sviashchenniku pri otpravlenii k dolzhnosti.* St. Petersburg, 1791.

———— *Nastavleniia ot pastyria k sviashchenniku.* St. Petersburg, 1790.

"Instruktsiia iz Rostovskoi dukhovnoi konsistorii prokuraturu Spaso-Iaroslavskoi dukhovnoi seminarii Vasiliiu Igumenu ot 1757 g.," *IaEV,* 1895, no. 17:261-271.

"Instruktsiia popovskim starostam ot 1743 g.," *IaEV,* 1883, no. 18:141-143.

"Instruktsiia starostam popovskim," *DRV,* 15 (1790):373-405.

"Istoricheskaia zapiska o nachale Iaroslavskoi dukhovnoi seminarii," *IaEV,* 1896, no. 18:273-279.

Istoricheskoe i topograficheskoe opisanie gorodov Moskovskoi gubernii s ikh uezdami. Moscow, 1787.

"Iz bumag imp. protoiereia Ioanna Pamfilova," *RA,* 1871, no. 1:201-240.

Izvestie reshitel'noe o bedstvennykh i nedoumennykh sluchaekh, i kako iereiu i d'iakonu i prochim v tom ispravitisia. Moscow, 1705.

Katekhizis dlia obucheniia stavlennikov. St. Petersburg, 1779.

Katekhizis sokrashchennyi. Moscow, 1776.

Katekhizis sokrashchennyi dlia sviashchenno-i-tserkovnosluzhitelei. Moscow, 1798.

Kholmogorov, G., and Kholmogorov, V. *Istoricheskie materialy o tserkvakh i selakh XVI-XVIII st.* 11 vols. Moscow, 1881-1911.

———— *Materialy dlia istorii, arkheologii i statistiki moskovskikh tserkvei.* Moscow, 1884.

"Khramozdatel'naia gramota s. Makarova," *IaEV,* 1882, no. 47:379-380.

Kozlov, O. F. "Dva neizvestnykh sochineniia XVIII v. o Sinode i monastyrskikh dokhodakh," *Sovetskie arkhivy,* 1972, no. 3:76-82.

Kuznetsov, Ia. O. "Iz perepiski pomeshchika s krest'ianami vo vtoroi polovine XVIII st.," *TVUAK,* 6 (1904):1-95.

Lavrov, N. F. "Odno iz sledstvennykh dukhovnykh del nachala XVIII v.," *IaEV,* 1872, no. 18:142-146.

Lepekhin, I. I. *Dnevnye zapiski puteshestviia doktora i Akademii nauk ad'iutanta I. Lepekhina po raznym provintsiiam Rossiiskogo gosudarstva.* 4 vols. 2nd. ed. St. Petersburg, 1795-1814.

Lestvitsyn, V. I. "Krest'ianskaia gazeta iz ada," *RS,* 1875, no. 9:213-216.

———— "Polozhenie iaroslavskogo dukhovenstva vo vtorom desiatiletii XVIII v.," *IaEV,* 1873, nos. 49-51; 1874, nos. 7, 10-13, 18-24, 34-35.

———— "Stavlennicheskaia tetrad'ka vremeni Mitr. Arseniia Matseevicha," *IaEV,* 1881, no. 13:97-102; no. 14:106-109.

———— "Tserkvi g. Iaroslavlia v 1781 g.," *IaEV,* 1874, nos. 38-51.

Lomonosov, M. "Ob ob"iazannostiakh dukhovenstva," *Letopis' russkoi literatury i drevnosti,* 1 (1859):197-198.

Makogonenko, G. P., ed. *Russkaia literatura XVIII v.* Leningrad, 1970.

Maksimovich, L. M. *Novyi i polnyi geograficheskii slovar' Rossiiskogo gosudarstva.* 6 pts. Moscow, 1788-89.

Malitskii, N. V. "K biografii gr. M. M. Speranskogo," *VEV,* 1904, no. 17:492-496.

———— "K istorii ikonopisaniia vo Vladimirskoi gubernii," *VEV,* 1904, no. 13:391-396.

———— "Materialy po istorii Suzdal'skoi seminarii," *VEV,* 1899, no. 15:526-534.

———— "Rasporiazheniia ep. Viktora o prisutstvovanii sviashchennosluzhitelei na brachnykh torzhestvakh," *VEV,* 1907, no. 39:615-618.

"Materialy dlia istorii biblioteki Iaroslavskoi dukhovnoi seminarii proshlogo stoletiia," *IaEV,* 1882, no. 18:140-142; no. 19:149-151.

Materialy dlia istorii goroda XVII i XVIII st.; Maloiaroslavets. Moscow, 1884.

Materialy dlia istorii goroda XVII i XVIII st.; Pereiaslavl'-Zalesskii. Moscow, 1884.

Materialy dlia istorii goroda XVII i XVIII st.; Riazan'. Moscow, 1884.
Materialy dlia istorii goroda XVII i XVIII st.; Rostov. Moscow, 1884.
Materialy dlia istorii goroda XVII i XVIII st.; Zaraisk. Moscow, 1883.
"Materialy dlia istorii uchilishcha Sv. Dimitriia Rostovskogo," *IaEV*, 1883, nos. 44-46.
"Materialy dlia istorii Vladimirskoi eparkhii," *VEV*, 1892-1900 (special supplement).
Materialy dlia istorii tserkvei Vladimirskoi gubernii. Vyp. 6. Vladimir, 1896.
Moskovskie vedomosti. Moscow, 1755-1800.
Muller, A. V. *The Spiritual Regulation of Peter the Great.* Seattle, 1972.
Nadezhdin, K. "Materialy dlia istorii Vladimirskoi seminarii," *VEV*, 1874, no. 20:1019-1024, no. 23:1179-1184.
———— "Seminaristy v svoikh stikhotvoreniiakh," *TVUAK*, 10 (1908): 1-60.
"Nakaz upravitel'iu ili zakazchiku," *TVEO*, 12 (1769):1-57.
"Neskol'ko ukaznykh predpisanii prezhnikh dukhovnykh pravlenii," *IaEV*, 1889, no. 50: 787-798.
"Neumestnaia ostrota," *IaEV*, 1882, no. 9:71-72.
Novosel'skii, A. A. "Rospis' krest'ianskikh dvorov," *IA*, 4 (1949):88-149.
"Odezhda iaroslavskikh seminaristov v seredine proshlogo stoletiia," *IaEV*, 1895, no. 31:493-495.
Opis' del Riazanskogo istoricheskogo arkhiva. Riazan, 1899.
Opis' dokumentov i del, khraniashchikhsia v arkhive Sv. Prav. Sinoda. Dela Komissii dukhovnykh uchilishch (1808-1839 gg.). St. Petersburg, 1910.
Opisanie dokumentov i del, khraniashchikhsia v arkhive Sv. Prav. Sinoda. 31 vols. St. Petersburg, 1869-1916.
Opisanie dokumentov i bumag Ministerstva iustitsii. 21 vols. Moscow, 1869-1916.
"Otvety, kasaiushchiesia do zemlevladeniia na ekonomicheskie voprosy, o uezde g. Volodimira," *TVEO*, 12 (1769):97-115.
"Otvety po Kaluzhskoi provintsii," *TVEO*, 11 (1768):86-120.
Pallas, P. S. *Puteshestvie po raznym provintsiiam Rossiiskoi imperii.* 3 pts. St. Petersburg, 1773-86.
———— *Reise durch verschiedene Provinzen des russischen Reiches.* 3 vols. St. Petersburg, 1771-76.
Parfenii [Sopkovskii] and Georgii [Konisskii]. *O dolzhnostiakh presviterov prikhodskikh ot slova Bozhiia, sobrannykh pravil i uchitelei tserkvi sostavlennoe.* St. Petersburg, 1776.
Pereiaslavl'-Zalesskii. Materialy dlia istorii Danilova monastyria i naseleniia goroda XVIII st. Moscow, 1891.

"P. M. Bestuzhev-Riumin i ego novgorodskoe pomest'e," *RA*, 1904, no. 1:5-42.

Petrov, V. A. "K voprosu o role dukhovenstva v bor'be s antifeodal'nymi vosstaniiami," *IA*, 1955, no. 4:196-200.

Petrovskaia, I. F. "Nakazy votchinnym prikazchikam pervoi chetverti XVIII v.," *IA*, 8 (1953):221-268.

"Piat' pisem ot 1786-87 gg., d'iakona rostovskoi Vvedenskoi tserkvi V. Ivanova o shkol'nykh uspekhakh svoego syna," *IaEV*, 1894, no. 33:520-524.

"Piatiletniaia vakatsiia dlia bezuspeshnykh uchenikov Iaroslavskoi dukhovnoi seminarii (1742-46 gg.)," *IaEV*, 1887, no. 34:545-556; no. 35:573-575.

Piskarev, I. *Drevnie gramoty i akty Riazanskogo kraia.* St. Petersburg, 1854.

"Pis'ma i reskripty Ekateriny II k moskovskim glavnokomanduiushchim," *RA*, 10 (1872):217-236.

"Pis'ma Imp. Ekateriny II-oi k Ober-Prokuroram Sv. Sinoda 1765-96 gg.," *RA*, 8 (1870):744-768.

Platon [Levshin]. *Instruktsiia blagochinnym iereiam ili protoiereiam.* Moscow, 1775.

——— *Pouchitel'nye slova pri vysochaishem dvore* e. i. v. . . . . gosudaryni Ekateriny Alekseevny. 20 vols. Moscow, 1779-1806.

"Po povodu pechataemogo nizhe 'Uchrezhdeniia' Simona," *REV*, 1866, no. 17:501-510; no. 18:527-536; no. 19:543-551; no. 20: 575-581; no. 21:612-621; no. 22:648-656; no. 23:687-694.

Polikarpov, F. *Bukvar' slaveno-greko-latinskii.* Moscow, 1701.

Polnoe sobranie postanovlenii i rasporiazhenii po vedomstvu pravoslavnogo ispovedaniia. 10 vols. St. Petersburg, 1869-1916. Vol. 1; 2nd. ed. St. Petersburg, 1879.

Polnoe sobranie postanovlenii i rasporiazhenii po vedomstvu pravoslavnogo ispovedaniia. Tsarstvovanie Imp. Ekateriny Alekseevny. 3 vols. St. Petersburg, 1910-15.

Polnoe sobranie postanovlenii i rasporiazhenii po vedomstvu pravoslavnogo ispovedaniia. Tsarstvovanie Imp. Elizavety Petrovny. 4 vols. St. Petersburg, 1899-1911.

Polnoe sobranie postanovlenii i rasporiazhenii po vedomstvu pravoslavnogo ispovedaniia. Tsarstvovanie Imp. Pavla Petrovicha. St. Petersburg, 1915.

Polnoe sobranie zakonov Rossiiskoi imperii. 1st series. 45 vols. St. Petersburg, 1830.

Polotskii, S. *Pouchenie o blagogoveinom stoianii v khrame.* Moscow, 1668.

——— *Pouchenie ot iereov sushchim pod nimi v pastve ikh.* Moscow, 1668.

Polunin, F. A. *Geograficheskii leksikon Rossiiskogo gosudarstva.* Moscow, 1773.

Pososhkov, I. T. *Kniga o skudosti i bogatstve.* Moscow, 1951.

Pouchenie sviatitel'skoe k novopostavlennomu iereiu. Moscow, 1670.

"Prikhodskie tserkvi Rostovsko-iaroslavskoi eparkhii za koimi v l-oi polovine XVIII st. imelis' krepostnye krest'iane," *IaEV,* 1895, no. 8:126-128.

Prokhodtsoe, I. "Materialy dlia biografii arkh. riazanskogo Simona Lagova (1778-1804 gg.)," *REV,* 1897, no. 10:309-312.

———— "Materialy dlia istorii Riazanskogo eparkhial'nogo upravleniia," *REV,* 1898, no. 3:90-95.

Putilov, B. N., ed. *Poslovitsy, pogovorki, zagadki v rukopisnykh sbornikakh XVIII-XX vekov.* Moscow, Leningrad, 1961.

Radishchev, A. N. *Journey from St. Petersburg to Moscow.* Cambridge, Mass., 1955.

"Raspisanie predmetov i uchebnykh chasov v Pereiaslavskoi dukhovnoi seminarii v 60-kh godakh XVIII st.," *VEV,* 1912, no. 29/30: 607-612.

"Rasporiazheniia Arseniia Matseevicha po upravleniiu rostovsko-iaroslavskoiu pastvoiu," *IaEV,* 1868, nos. 28-29, 30-36.

"Rech' Gosudaryni Imp. Ekateriny II," *Chteniia OIDR,* 1862, kn. 2, otd. 5:187-188.

"Rechi, sochinennyia i govorennyia pri sluchae byvshikh v Iaroslavskoi seminarii publichnykh bogoslovskikh i filosofskikh sostiazanii," *IaEV,* 1890, no. 18:273-288; no. 19:289-299.

"Reestr uchinennoi v seminarskoi kontore, kolikoe chislo v imeiushcheisia vo onom monastyre seminarii imeetsia kazennykh knig rossiiskikh, latinskikh i prochikh," *IaEV,* 1888, no. 10:78-80; no. 11:86-88; no. 14:108-112.

Rostislavov, D. I. "Zapiski," *RS,* 1880-93.

Rozhdestvenskii, S. *Materialy dlia istorii uchebnykh reform v Rossii.* St. Petersburg, 1910.

Rudnev, M. "K istorii Kolomenskoi eparkhii," *Chteniia OIDR,* 1903, kn. 4:13-52.

Savva, V. "Sochineniia protiv episkopov XVIII v.," *Chteniia OIDR,* 1910, kn. 1:3-35.

Sbornik Imperatorskogo russkogo istoricheskogo obshchestva. 148 vols. St. Petersburg, 1867-1916.

"Sekretari Rostovskoi dukhovnoi konsistorii," *IaEV,* 1895, no. 49: 777-784.

Selivanov, A. V. "Opis' del arkhiva Vladimirskogo gubernskogo pravleniia," *TVUAK,* 1 (1899):1-48; 4 (1902):1-64; 5 (1903):1-48; 6 (1904):1-49.

Serebriankov, S. "Kratkiia ekonomicheskiia do derevni sleduiushchiia zapiski, sostavlennym V. N. Tatishchevym (1742 g.)," *Vremennik OIDR*, 12 (1852):12-32.

Shakhovskoi, Ia. P. *Zapiski*. St. Petersburg, 1872.

Shcherbatov, M. M. *On the Corruption of Morals in Russia*. Cambridge, 1969.

Simon (Lagov). *Pouchenie kratkoe, kako podobaet stoiati v tserkvi bozhiei vo vremia sluzhby*. Moscow, 1786.

Skvortsov, N. A. *Dukhovenstvo Moskovskoi eparkhii v XVII v.* Moscow, 1916.

——— *Materialy po Moskve i Moskovskoi eparkhii za XVIII v.* 2 vols. Moscow, 1911-14.

Smirnov, A. V. *Materialy dlia istorii Vladimirskoi gubernii*. 3 vols. Vladimir, 1901-04.

"Sochinennyi Gospodinom statskim sovetnikom P. I. Rychkovym nakaz dlia derevenskogo upravitelia," *TVEO*, 16 (1770):13-68.

Stavlennaia gramota (dlia d'iakonov). St. Petersburg, 1765.

Stavlennaia gramota (dlia iereev). St. Petersburg, 1765.

Stavlennaia gramota (dlia prichetnikov). St. Petersburg, 1787.

"Stavlennaia gramota ot 1656 g.," *IaEV*, 1893, no. 33:520-521.

Tikhomirov, M. N., and Epifanov, P. P., eds. *Sobornoe ulozhenie 1649 g*. Moscow, 1961.

Tikhon. *Nastavlenie o sobstvennykh vsiakogo khristianina dolzhnostiakh*. St. Petersburg, 1791.

Tooke, William. *View of the Russian Empire during the Reign of Catherine the Second and to the Close of the Eighteenth Century*. 3 vols. 2nd. ed. London, 1800.

Travchetov, N. P. "Delo o bogoprotivnom sne," *TVUAK*, 2 (1900): 69-86.

——— "Svedeniia ob arkhive byvshego Muromskogo dukhovnogo pravleniia," *TVUAK*, 4 (1902):43-50.

"Ukaz Mitropolita Arseniia Matseevicha," *IaEV*, 1872, no. 7:54-56.

"Ukaz E. I. V. Elizavety Petrovny . . . preosv. Arseniiu," *IaEV*, 1872, no. 3:22-23.

"Ukaz Imp. Petra Velikgo k. Sv. Dmitriiu Rostovskomu," *IaEV*, 1890, no. 29:460-461.

"Ukaznoe predpisanie Iaroslavskogo dukhovnogo pravleniia," *IaEV*, 1890, no. 2:23-29; no. 5:65-73; no. 6:81-96; no. 7:104-112; no. 8:113-126; no. 13:199-206.

"Ukaznye predpisaniia Iaroslavskogo dukhovnogo pravleniia," *IaEV*, 1899, no. 41:641-656; no. 49:779-781.

"Ukazy Imp. Petra Velikogo ot 1702 g. v Rostov po delam tserkovnym," *IaEV*, 1890, no. 23:357-366.

"Ustavnaia gramota Patriarkha Adriana," *Vremennik OIDR*, 11 (1851):30-46.

Ustiugov, V. N. "Instruktsiia votchinnomu prikazchiku pervoi chet-
verti XVIII v.," *IA*, 4 (1949):150-183.
"Venechnyia pamiati Iaroslavskoi Dimitrie-Selunskoi tserkvi," *IaEV*,
1894, no. 25:395-400; no. 26:409-415.
"Vkladnaia zapis' ot 1693 g.," *IaEV*, 1894, no. 21:331-332.
Volkov, S. I. "Instruktsiia upraviteliam dvortsovykh volostei 1731
g.," *IA*, 6 (1951):156-198.
Voskresenskii, N. A., ed. *Zakonodatel'nye akty Petra I*. Moscow,
Leningrad, 1945.
Vvedenskii, S. N. "Iz tserkovnoi stariny muromskogo kraia,"
TVUAK, 11 (1909):3-22.
"Vysylka sviashchenno-tserkovno-sluzhitel'skikh detei Rostovskoi
eparkhii v Troitse-Sergievu seminariiu (1756-58 gg.)," *IaEV*,
1895, no. 25:394-400.
Weber, F. C. "Zapiski Vebera," *RA*, 10 (1872):1057-1068, 1334-1457,
1613-1708.
Zagorskii, M. V. "Razbor i opisanie del Pereslavskogo dukhovnogo
pravleniia," *TVUAK*, 4 (1902):1-42; 5 (1903):129-210.
"Zapiska ob Artemii Volynskom," *Chteniia OIDR*, 1858, kn. 2, chast'
5:135-170.
"Zapiska, uchinennaia v Rostovskoi dukhovnoi konsistorii, kogda v
eparkhii Rostovskoi seminariia nachalas' . . . ," *IaEV*, 1895, no.
27:427-429.
"Zapiska, uchinennaia v 1780 g. v Rostovskoi dukhovnoi konsistorii,"
IaEV, 1893, no. 6:89-90.
"Zhilye i pustye tserkvi g. Rostova," *IaEV*, 1895, no. 43:673-679.
"Zhizn' vdovogo sviashchennika," *IaEV*, 1883, no. 11:81-88; no. 13:
97-103; no. 16:121-124.

III. Secondary Works

A. I. "Episkop vladimirskii Pavel (1763-69 gg.)," *VEV*, 1910, no.
31:557-562; no. 32:580-585.
Agntsev, D. *Istoriia Riazanskoi dukhovnoi seminarii, 1724-1840 gg.*
Riazan, 1889.
———— "Sostoianie dukhovnykh uchilishch pri Ekaterine II," *REV*,
1876-81.
Akademiia nauk SSSR. *Absoliutizm v Rossii*. Moscow, 1964.
Aleksandrov, V. A. "Sel'skaia obshchina i votchina v Rossii (XVII-
nachalo XIX v.)," *IZ*, 89 (1972):231-294.
———— *Sel'skaia obshchina v Rossii*. Moscow, 1976.
Amvrosii, *Istoriia rossiiskoi ierarkhii*. 6 vols. Moscow, 1807-15.
Arkhangel'skii, A. *Dukhovnoe obrazovanie i dukhovnaia shkola v
Rossii pri Petre Velikom*. Kazan, 1883.

Arkhangel'skii, M. *O sobornom ulozhenii Tsaria Alekseia Mikhailovicha 1649 g. v otnoshenii k pravoslavnoi russkoi tserkvi.* St. Petersburg, 1881.

Arsen'ev, K. I. *Statisticheskie ocherki Rossii.* St. Petersburg, 1848.

Barsov, N. I. "K kharakteristike tserkovno-prikhodskoi propovedi v S.-Peterburge v tsarstvovanie Ekaterine II," *Khr. Cht.,* 1878, tom 1:841-886.

———— "Peterburgskii prikhodskoi sviashchennik vo vtoroi polovine XVIII i nachale XIX st.," *Khr. Cht.,* 1876, tom 2:643-673.

Barsov, T. V. *Sinodal'nye uchrezhdeniia prezhnego vremeni.* St. Petersburg, 1897.

Batalden, Stephen K. "Eugenios Voulgaris in Russia, 1771-1806." Ph.D. diss., University of Minnesota, 1975.

Becker, Christopher B. "The Church School in Tsarist Social and Educational Policy from Peter to the Great Reforms." Ph.D. diss., Harvard University, 1964.

Beliavskii, M. T. "Shkola i sistema obrazovaniia v Rossii v kontse XVIII v.," *Vestnik MGU,* Istoriko-filologicheskaia seriia, 1959, no. 2:105-120.

Belikov, V. "Otnoshenie gosudarstvennoi vlasti k tserkvi i dukhovenstvu v tsarstvovanie Ekateriny II," *Chteniia OLDP,* 1874, tom 1:96-163, 467-507, 972-1016; tom 2:152-196, 445-487, 618-651, 837-952; 1875, tom 1:203-223, 350-371, 721-762; tom 2:70-85, 247-270, 310-344.

Bissonnette, G. L. "Pufendorf and the Church Reforms of Peter the Great." Ph.D. diss., Columbia University, 1962.

Blagovidov, F. V. *Ober-prokurory Sv. Sinoda v XVIII i pervoi polovine XIX st.* Kazan, 1899; 2nd. ed., Kazan, 1900.

Bogoslovskii, I. "Istoricheskaia zapiska o Rostovskom Dmitrievskom dukhovnom uchilishche," *IaEV,* 1899, no. 17:248-251; no. 19: 277-281; no. 21:305-311; no. 24:353-357; no. 25:369-373; no. 31: 465-470; no. 32:481-485; no. 41:625-631; no. 49:753-759; no. 50:776-781; no. 51/52:791-798.

Bogoslovskii, M. M. *Oblastnaia reforma Petra Velikogo.* Moscow, 1902.

———— *Zemskoe samoupravlenie na russkom severe XVIII v.* 2 vols. Moscow, 1909-12.

Bulygin, I. A. "Tserkovnaia reforma Petra I," *Voprosy istorii,* 1974, no. 5:79-93.

Chechulin, N. D. *Russkoe provintsial'noe obshchestvo vo vtoroi polovine XVIII v.* St. Petersburg, 1889.

Chistovich, I. *Feofan Prokopovich i ego vremia.* St. Petersburg, 1868.

———— *Istoriia S.-Peterburgskoi dukhovnoi akademii.* St. Petersburg, 1857.

Chto takoe tserkovnyi starosta? St. Petersburg, 1902.

Cracraft, James. *The Church Reforms of Peter the Great.* London, 1971.

―――― "Feofan Prokopovich" in *The Eighteenth Century in Russia*, ed. J. G. Garrard (Oxford, 1973), pp. 75-105.

"Delo o pokupke latinskikh ritorik," *VEV*, 1899, no. 2:63-67.

Demidova, N. F. "Prikaznye liudi XVII v.," *IZ*, 90 (1972):332-354.

Den, F. E. "Podatnye elementy sredi dukhovenstva Rossii v XVIII v.," *IRAN*, 1918, nos. 5-7, 13-14.

Dianin, A. "Malorossiiskoe dukhovenstvo vo vtoroi polovine XVIII v.," *TDKA*, 1904, no. 8:589-628; no. 9:109-159.

"Dmitrievskaia tserkov' v g. Suzdale," *VEV*, 1874, no. 2:68-74; no. 5:262-271; no. 7:363-373.

"Dmitrii Sechenov," *REV*, 1898, no. 22:779-785; no. 24:823-829; 1899, no. 13/14:411-429.

"Dmitrii Sechenov," *REV*, 1916, no. 10:424-430; no. 11/12:479-486; no. 13/14:534-543; no. 15:601-607; no. 16:648-652; no. 18/19: 719-728; no. 20:769-775; 1917, no. 6:154-161; no. 7/8:211-216.

Dobroliubov, I. *Istoriko-statisticheskoe opisanie tserkvei i prikhodov Riazanskoi gubernii.* 4 vols. Zaraisk-Riazan, 1884-91.

Dobronravov, V. G. "Viaznikovskoe dukhovnoe uchilishche," *VEV*, 1905, no. 18:523-531, no. 21:613-621.

―――― and Berezin, V. *Istoriko-statisticheskoe opisanie tserkvei i prikhodov Vladimirskoi eparkhii.* 4 vols. Vladimir, 1893-97.

"Dukhovnye shkoly v Rostovskoi eparkhii vo vremena preosv. arkhiereia Georgiia Dashkova," *IaEV*, 1895, no. 33:513-520.

"Dukhovnye shkoly v Rostovskoi eparkhii vo vremena preosv. Ioakima," *IaEV*, 1895, no. 36:561-570.

Ekzempliarskii, P. "Rekrutskie nabory russkogo prikhodskogo dukhovenstva," *RSP*, 1863, tom 2:22-36.

―――― "Usloviia postupleniia molodykh liudei dukhovnogo zvaniia na prikhod i priniatiia sviashchennogo sana," *RSP*, 1863, tom 3:632-647, 674-684.

Ezhov, A. "O tserkovno-religioznom obrazovanii v Rossii v XVIII v.," *Strannik*, 1895, no. 9-12; 1896, no. 1-6.

Gavrilov, A. V. *Ocherk istorii S.-Peterburgskoi Sinodal'noi tipografii.* St. Petersburg, 1911.

Golikova, N. B. *Politicheskie protsessy pri Petr I.* Moscow, 1957.

Golubinskii, E. *Istoriia russkoi tserkvi.* 2 vols. 2nd. ed. Moscow, 1901-10.

Gorchakov, M. *Monastyrskii prikaz.* St. Petersburg, 1868.

Got'e, Iu. V. *Istoriia oblastnogo upravleniia v Rossii ot Petra I do Ekateriny II.* 2 vols. Moscow, 1913-41.

―――― *Zamoskovnyi krai v XVII v.* 2nd. ed. Moscow, 1937.

Grigorovich, I. *Obzor obshchikh zakonopolozhenii o soderzhanii pravoslavnogo dukhovenstva v Rossii.* St. Petersburg, 1867.

———— *Obzor uchrezhdeniia v Rossii arkhiereiskikh pravoslavnykh kafedr i sposobov soderzhaniia ikh.* St. Petersburg, 1866.

Ierarkhiia rostovsko-iaroslavskoi pastvy. Iaroslavl, 1862.

Ikonnikov, V. S. "Arsenii Matseevich," *RS,* 1879, no. 4:731-752; no. 5:1-34; no. 8:577-608; no. 9:1-34; no. 10:177-198.

Istomin, G. "Postanovleniia Imp. Ekateriny II otnositel'no obrazovaniia dukhovenstva," *TKDA,* 1867, tom 3, no. 9:580-624.

Istoriko-statisticheskie svedeniia o S.-Peterburgskoi eparkhii. 10 vols. St. Petersburg, 1869-85.

Iuzhkov, S. V. *Ocherki iz istorii prikhodskoi zhizni na severe Rossii v XV-XVII vv.* St. Petersburg, 1913.

Ivanovskii, V. *Russkoe zakonodatel'stvo XVIII i XIX vv. v svoikh postanovleniiakh otnositel'no monastyrei i monashestvuiushchikh.* Khar'kov, 1905.

Iz proshlogo Vladimirskogo kraia. Vladimir, 1930.

Jones, Robert E. *The Emancipation of the Russian Nobility, 1762-85.* Princeton, 1973.

"K istorii nebogosluzhebnogo odeianiia Vladimirskogo dukhovenstva," *VEV,* 1899, no. 18:617-621.

"K istorii razborov dukhovenstva v XVIII v.," *RSP,* 1882, tom 2:1-22.

"K istorii Vladimirskogo dukhovnogo uchilishcha v pervye gody ego sushchestvovaniia (1790-1800 gg.)," *VEV,* 1907, no. 18:271-276; no. 19:291-296.

"K kharakteristike Arseniia Matseevicha," *IaEV,* 1868, no. 25:206-209.

"K zhizneopisaniiu Arseniia Matseevicha," *IaEV,* 1868, no. 4:31-36; no. 6:50-53; no. 7:58-62; no. 8:67-69; no. 10:79-83; no. 11:91-94; no. 12:98-101; no. 13:103-106; no. 14:111-114.

Kabuzan, V. M. *Izmeneniia v razmeshchenii naseleniia Rossii v XVIII-pervoi polovine XIX vv.* Moscow, 1971.

———— *Narodonaselenie Rossii.* Moscow, 1963.

Kadson, I. Z. "Krest'ianskaia voina 1773-1775 gg. i tserkov'." Kandidatskaia dissertatsiia. Leningradskoe otdelenie Instituta istorii, 1963.

Kahan, Arcadius. "The Costs of Westernization: The Gentry and the Economy in the Eighteenth Century," *Slavic Review,* 25 (1966): 40-66.

Kamen'eva, T. N. *Svodnyi katalog russkoi knigi kirillovskoi pechati XVIII v.* Moscow, 1968.

Kapterev, N. *Svetskie arkhiereiskie chinovniki v drevnei Rusi.* Moscow, 1874.

Kartashev, A. *Ocherki po istorii russkoi tserkvi.* 2 vols. Paris, 1959.

Kataev, I. *Ocherk istorii tserkovnoi propovedi.* Odessa, 1883.

Kedrov, N. I. "Zaboty [Petra Velikogo] otnositel'no ustroistva i polozheniia belogo dukhovenstva," *PO*, 1885, no. 10:219-279.

Kharlampovich, K. V. *Malorossiiskoe vliianie na velikorusskuiu tserkovnuiu zhizn'.* Kazan, 1914.

Khitrov, I. "Nashe beloe dukhovenstvo v XVIII st. i ego predstaviteli," *Strannik,* 1896, nos. 8-10, 11; 1897, nos. 1, 2, 6.

Kholmogorov, G. I. *Starosty popovskie.* Moscow, 1911.

Klimov, N. *Postanovleniia po delam pravoslavnogo dukhovenstva i tserkvi v tsarstvovanie Imp. Ekateriny II.* St. Petersburg, 1902.

Klokman, Iu. R. *Sotsial'no-ekonomicheskaia istoriia russkogo goroda.* Moscow, 1967.

Kogan, Iu. Ia., Grekulov, E. F. and Milovidov, V. F. "Tserkov' i russkii absoliutizm v XVIII v.," in *Tserkov' v istorii Rossii (IX v.-1917 g.),* ed. N. A. Smirnov (Moscow, 1967), pp. 162-205.

Kolachev, V. *O polozhenii pridvornogo dukhovenstva v XVIII v.* St. Petersburg, 1914.

Korol'kov, K. *Ob otkrytii i zakrytii eparkhii russkoi tserkvi.* Kazan, 1876.

Kozlov, O. F. "Reforma tserkvi Petra I i otkliki na nee v russkom obshchestve v pervoi polovine XVIII v.," *Vestnik MGU,* Seriia IX (Istoriia), 1968, no. 5:86-92.

———— "Tserkovnaia reforma pervoi chetverti XVIII v." Kandidatskaia dissertatsiia. Moscow State University, 1970.

"Kratkii ocherk eparkhial'nogo upravleniia i dukhovnykh prisutstvennykh mest v Rostove," *IaEV,* 1877, no. 15:113-119; no. 16:123-128; no. 19:151; no. 20:159.

Krylov, A. "Ierarkhi rostovsko-iaroslavskoi pastvy," *IaEV,* 1862, nos. 1-48.

Krylov, V. "Ekaterinskaia komissiia v eia otnoshenii k dukhovenstvu kak sosloviiu," *Vera i razum,* 1903, tom 1:467-483, 553-584, 622-639, 695-723, 758-771.

Kryzhanovskii, E. *Sobranie sochinenii.* 3 vols. Kiev, 1890.

Ksanf, M. E. "Organy eparkhial'nogo upravleniia v drevnei Rusi," *PO*, 1874, nos. 7-12.

Kuleshov, N. I. "Shkola i obrazovanie v Riazanskoi gubernii v poslednei chetverti XVIII v." Diplomnaia rabota, Moscow State University, 1967.

Lavrov, A. F. "Vdovye sviashchennosluzhiteli," *Khr. Cht.,* 1870, no. 12:1019-1056; 1871, no. 2:343-382; no. 7:75-125.

Lebedev, A. "Primenenie nakazanii v srede dukhovenstva," *RS,* 73 (1872):313-338.

Lepskaia, L. A. "Sostav uchashchikhsia narodynkh uchilishch Moskvy v kontse XVIII v.," *Vestnik MGU*, Seriia IX (Istoriia), 1973, no. 5:88-97.

Liubimov, G. *Obozrenie sposobov soderzhaniia khristianskogo dukhovenstva ot vremen apostolov do XVII-XVIII veka.* St. Petersburg, 1851.

Lototskii, A. "Dukhovnoe obrazovanie v Rossii," *Strannik*, 1904, no. 8:149-169, no. 9:331-350.

———— "Iz byta starogo dukhovenstva," *RS*, 1904, no. 4:102-129.

———— "Material'noe obespechenie prikhodskogo dukhovenstva v proshlom veke," *RSP*, 1899, tom 3:28-39, 57-67, 86-96.

———— "Religiozno-prosvetitel'naia deiatel'nost' prikhodskogo dukhovenstva v proshlom veke," *RSP*, 1897, tom 2:241-248, 370-380, 392-396.

Lübbe, Herman. *Säkularisierung. Geschichte eines ideenpolitischen Begriffs.* Freiburg, 1965.

Luppov, S. P. *Kniga v Rossii v pervoi chetverti XVIII v.* Leningrad, 1973.

Makarii. *Istoriko-statisticheskoe opisanie Riazanskoi dukhovnoi seminarii.* Novgorod, 1864.

Makkaveev, P. "Religiozno-tserkovnye vozzreniia Ekateriny II," *Strannik*, 1904, no. 12:785-799.

Malinovskii, I. V. "Otkrytie Vladimirskogo dukhovnogo uchilishcha i pervye gody ego sushchestvovaniia 1790-1800 gg.," *TVUAK*, 3 (1901):159-172.

Malitskii, N. "Denezhnye shtrafy za razgovory pri bogosluzhenii," *VEV*, 1904, no. 22:642-648.

———— *Istoriia Pereiaslavskoi eparkhii.* 2 vols. Vladimir, 1912-18.

———— *Istoriia Suzdal'skoi dukhovnoi seminarii (1723-88 gg.).* Vladimir, 1905.

———— *Istoriia Vladimirskoi dukhovnoi seminarii.* 3 vols. Moscow, 1900-02.

———— *Iz proshlogo Vladimirskoi eparkhii.* Vyp. 2-3 only. Vladimir, 1907-12.

———— "K istorii Vladimirskoi dukhovnoi seminarii pri episkope Pavle," *VEV*, 1907, no. 6:87-89.

———— "Obuchenie pereiaslavskikh sviashchenno-tserkovno-sluzhitelei katekhizisu," *VEV*, 1905, no. 5:135-139.

———— "Rasporiazheniia ep. Ieronima kasaiushchiesia otpravleniia bogosluzheniia vo Vladimirskoi eparkhii," *VEV*, 1907, no. 4:50-55.

———— "Vladimirskie konsistorskie arkhivy XVIII v.," *VEV*, 1903, no. 19:518-526; no. 21:581-586.

———— "Zaboty ep. Ieronima o vozvyshenii nravstvennosti i blagochiniia vladimirskogo dukhovenstva," *VEV*, 1907, no. 5:65-69.

Markevich, G. "Vybornoe nachalo v dukhovenstve v drevnerusskoi tserkvi (preimushchestvenno iugo-zapadnoi) do reformy Petra I," *TKDA*, 1871, no. 8:225-273; no. 9:484-550.

Markov, N. "Deti dukhovenstva," *Strannik*, 1900, tom 1:386-411, 592-620; tom 2:60-76, 570-594; tom 3:44-63, 590-607.

[Milovidov, A. I.] "Dukhovnaia shkola v Petrovskoe vremia i postanovka ee pod vliianiem pedagogicheskikh vozzrenii Imp. Ekateriny II," *Strannik*, 1897, no. 10:271-280; no. 11:457-480.

Mitropol'skii, A. "Preosv. Arsenii (Vereshchagin)," *REV*, 1901, no. 15:221-225; no. 16:239-243; no. 17:254-259; no. 18:277-282; no. 19:289-295; no. 20:316-320; no. 21:327-330; no. 22:342-348; no. 23:358-364.

Muller, Alexander V. "The Historical Antecedents of the Petrine Ecclesiastical Reform." Ph.D. diss., University of Washington, 1973.

N. T. "K istorii Muromskogo dukhovnogo uchilishcha," *VEV*, 1897, no. 2:49-54.

Nadezhdin, K. "Ocherk istorii Vladimirskoi seminarii," *VEV*, 1865-68. Also published as *Istoriia Vladimirskoi dukhovnoi seminarii s 1740 po 1840 god.* Vladimir, 1875.

"O tserkovnom khoziaistve prikhodskikh tserkvei Iaroslavskoi eparkhii v proshlom stoletii," *IaEV*, 1899, no. 27:401-405; no. 28:420-426.

Okenfuss, Max. "Education in Russia in the First Half of the Eighteenth Century." Ph.D. diss., Harvard University, 1970.

―――― "The Jesuit Origins of Petrine Education," in *The Eighteenth Century in Russia*, ed. J. G. Garrard (Oxford, 1973), pp. 106-130.

Papkov, A. A. *Drevnerusskii prikhod.* Sergiev-Posad, 1897.

―――― *Upadok pravoslavnogo prikhoda (XVIII-XIX vv.).* Moscow, 1899.

Pavlenko, N. I. "Idei absoliutizma v zakonodatel'stve XVIII v.," in *Absoliutizm v Rossii* (Moscow, 1964), pp. 381-427.

―――― "Petr I (K izucheniiu sotsial'no-politicheskikh vzgliadov)," in *Rossiia v period reform Petra I* (Moscow, 1973), pp. 40-102.

Pekarskii, P. *Vvedenie v istoriiu prosveshcheniia v Rossii XVIII st.* 2 vols. St. Petersburg, 1862.

Perov, I. *Eparkhial'nye uchrezhdeniia v russkoi tserkvi v XVI i XVII vv.* Riazan, 1882.

Petrov, N. I. *Kievskaia akademiia vo vtoroi polovine XVII v.* Kiev, 1895.

Petrov, P. *Ocherki tserkovno-obshchestvennoi zhizni v epokhu Petra Velikogo.* Khar'kov, 1912.

Pintner, Walter. "The Social Characteristics of the Early Nineteenth-

Century Bureaucracy," *Slavic Review*, 29 (1970):429-443.

Pokrovskii, I. M. *Ekaterinskaia komissiia o sostavlenii novogo ulozheniia i tserkovnye voprosy o nei (1766-1777 gg.)*. Kazan, 1910.

────── *Russkie eparkhii v XVI-XIX, ikh otkrytie, sostav i predely*. 2 vols. Kazan, 1897-1913.

────── *Sredstva i shtaty velikorusskikh arkhiereiskikh domov so vremeni Petra I do uchrezhdeniia dukhovnykh shtatov 1764 g.* Kazan, 1907.

Pokrovskii, N. N. *Antifeodal'nyi protest uralo-sibirskikh krest'ianstaroobriadtsev v XVIII v.* Novosibirsk, 1974.

Popov, M. S. *Arsenii Matseevich, mitr. Rostovskii i Iaroslavskii*. St. Petersburg, 1905.

Popov, N. A. *Tatishchev i ego vremia*. Moscow, 1861.

Prilezhaev, E. M. "Dukhovnaia shkola i seminaristy v istorii russkoi nauki i obrazovaniia," *Khr. cht.*, 1879, tom 2:161-191.

────── "Nakaz i punkty deputatu ot Sv. Sinoda v Ekaterinskuiu komissiiu o sochinenii proekta novogo ulozheniia," *Khr. Cht.*, 1876, tom 2:223-265.

Pushkarev, L. N. "Poslovitsy v zapisiakh XVII v. kak istochnik po izucheniiu obshchestvennykh otnoshenii," *IZ*, 92 (1973):312-335.

────── "Russkie poslovitsy XVII v. o tserkvi i ee sluzhiteliakh," *Voprosy istorii religii i ateizma*, 6 (1958):153-168.

Raeff, Marc. *Origins of the Russian Intelligentsia: The Eighteenth-Century Nobility*. New York, 1966.

────── "The Well-Ordered Police State and the Development of Modernity in Seventeenth- and Eighteenth-Century Europe," *American Historical Review*, 80 (1975):1221-1243.

Razmukhin, A. I. *Istoriia russkoi propovedi*. Moscow, 1904.

"Rostovskoe uchilishche pri Sv. Dmitrie Mitropolite," *IaEV*, 1863, nos. 24-45.

"Rostovsko-Iaroslavskie ierarkhi," *IaEV*, 1893, nos. 44-47; 1894, nos. 6-12, 20-30.

Rozanov, N. *Istoriia moskovskogo eparkhial'nogo upravleniia*. 3 vols. Moscow, 1869-71.

────── "Ob arkhive Moskovskoi dukhovnoi konsistorii," *Chteniia OLDP*, 1869, kn. 6:42-104.

────── "Preosviashchennyi Iosif," *MEV*, 1869, no. 21:4-7.

────── "Preosviashchennyi Platon I," *MEV*, 1869, no. 22:6-8; no. 23:4-6.

────── "Preosviashchennyi Timofei," *MEV*, 1869, no. 27:6-8; no. 28:6-7.

Rozhdestvenskii, S. V. *Ocherki po istorii sistem narodnogo prosveshcheniia v Rossii v XVIII-XIX vekakh*. St. Petersburg, 1912.

Runovskii, N. "Soslovnaia zamknutost' belogo dukhovenstva v Rossii," *Strannik*, 1897, no. 3:438-455; no. 4:602-617; no. 5:57-90; no. 10:281-299; no. 11:488-497.

Ryndziunskii, P. G. "Antitserkovnoe dvizhenie v Tambovskom krae v 60-kh godakh XVIII v.," *Voprosy istorii religii i ateizma*, 2 (1954):154-193.

S. S. "Russkoe propovednichestvo pri Petre I," *RSP*, 1870, tom 3:13-28, 119-129, 206-220, 290-304, 487-494, 628-644.

Samuilov, V. "Blagochinnye prikhodskikh tserkvei," *Tserkovnye vedomosti*, pribavleniia, 1900, no. 36:1438-1441.

————— "Desiatil'niki i popovskie starosty," *Tserkovnye vedomosti*, pribavleniia, 1900, no. 35:1392-1396.

Semevskii, V. I. *Krest'iane v tsarstvovanie Imperatritsy Ekateriny II.* 2 vols. St. Petersburg, 1901-03.

————— "Sel'skii sviashchennik vo vtoroi polovine XVIII v.," *RS*, 1877, no. 8:501-538.

[Shchapov, A.] "Sostoianie russkogo dukhovenstva v XVIII v.," *PS*, 1862, no. 5:16-40; no. 6:173-206.

Shchepetov, K. P. *Krepostnoe pravo v votchinakh Sheremetevykh (1708-1885 gg.).* Moscow, 1947.

Shimko, I. I. *Patriarshii kazennyi prikaz.* Moscow, 1894.

Shliapkin, I. A. *Sv. Dimitrii Rostovskii i ego vremia.* St. Petersburg, 1891.

Skvortsov, V. "Afanasii Kondoidi," *VEV*, 1878, no. 6:129-146; no. 8:181-199.

————— "Varlaam (Linitskii)," *VEV*, 1879, no. 23:668-672; no. 24:681-685; 1880, no. 1:1-15; no. 8:241-251; no. 11:344-351.

Sladkopevtsev, P. "Preosv. Misail," *REV*, 1866, no. 13:378-387; no. 14:407-416; no. 15:427-440.

Smirnov, M. I. "Bol'she-brembol'skii d'iakon Mikhail Mikhailov," *TVUAK*, 15 (1913):1-39.

————— "Selo Bol'shaia Brembola," *TVUAK*, 9 (1907):1-110.

Smirnov, S. K. *Istoriia Moskovskoi slaviano-greko-latinskoi akademii.* Moscow, 1855.

————— *Istoriia Troitskoi lavrskoi seminarii.* Moscow, 1867.

Smolitsch, Igor. *Geschichte der russischen Kirche.* Leiden, 1964.

————— *Russisches Mönchtum: Entstehung, Entwicklung and Wesen 988-1917.* Würzburg, 1953.

Snegirev, I. M. *Zhizn' Moskovskogo mitropolita Platona.* 2nd. ed. Moscow, 1856.

Sokolov, A. "Simon Lagov," *REV*, 1883, nos. 20-21, 24; 1884, nos. 1-3, 6, 8, 10, 12-13.

Sokolov, V. "O podsudnosti russkogo dukhovenstva ot izdaniia sobornogo ulozheniia do Petra I," *RSP*, 1871, tom 2:255-266, 287-298, 334-347, 394-407, 430-437.

Solov'ev, N. "Letopis' ob Il'inskoi tserkvi," *VEV*, 1881, no. 10:273-279; no. 15:430-435; 1882, no. 19:540-547; no. 20:576-582.

"Sostoianie Spaso-iaroslavskoi seminarii pri mitropolite Arsenii Matseeviche (1743-63 gg.)," *IaEv*, 1895, no. 25:385-388.

"Sostoianie Spaso-iaroslavskoi dukhovnoi seminarii vo vremena preosv. Afanasiia, episkopa (1763-76 gg.)," *IaEV*, 1895, no. 23: 353-356.

Titlinov, B. *Dukhovnaia shkola v Rossii v XIX v.* 2 vols. Vil'na, 1908-09.

―――― *Gavriil Petrov, mitropolit novgorodskii i sanktpeterburgskii (1730-1801 gg.).* St. Petersburg, 1916.

―――― *Pravitel'stvo Anny Ioannovny v ego otnoshenii k delam pravoslavnoi tserkvi.* Vil'na, 1905.

Titov, A. A. *Suzdal'skie ierarkhi.* Moscow, 1882.

Tolstoi, Iu. *Spiski arkhiereev i arkhiereiskikh kafedr.* St. Petersburg, 1872.

Trefolev, L. "Vozzvanie iaroslavskogo episkopa Afanasiia k iaroslavskomu magistratu v 1765 g.," *IaEV*, 1883, no. 6:42-44.

Troitskii, S. M. *Russkii absoliutizm i dvorianstvo v XVIII v.* Moscow, 1974.

―――― "Sotsial'nyi sostav i chislennost' biurokratii Rossii v seredine XVIII v.," *IZ*, 89 (1972):295-352.

Tsarevskii, A. A. *Pravoslavnoe russkoe dukhovenstvo po myslam i idealam I. T. Pososhkova.* Kazan, 1898.

"Tserkovnye postanovleniia o sviashchenstve," *PS*, 1859, tom 2:121-161, 241-288.

Ushakov, N. N. "Istoricheskie svedeniia ob ikonopisanii i ikonopistsakh vladimirskoi gubernii," *TVUAK*, 8 (1906):1-56.

Vedeniapin, P. "Zakonodatel'stvo Imp. Elizavety Petrovny otnositel'no pravoslavnogo dukhovenstva," *PO*, 1865, no. 5:69-117; no. 7:296-334; no. 10:217-231.

"Vedomost', kogda zavedeny byli v eparkhii Rostovskoi uchilishcha i pri kom i kakie ucheniia vo onykh prepodavalis'," *IaEV*, 1895, no. 28:442-446.

Verkhovskoi, P. V. *Uchrezhdenie Dukhovnoi kollegii i dukhovnyi reglament.* 2 vols. Rostov-na-Donu, 1916.

Vinogradov, N. "Istoricheskaia zapiska o Pereiaslavl'-Zalesskom dukhovnom uchilishche," *VEV*, 1888, no. 16:560-575; no. 17:613-626; no. 18:658-672; no. 19:713-724; no. 20:750-769; no. 21:805-823.

Vladimirskii-Budanov, M. "Gosudarstvo i narodnoe obrazovanie v

Rossii s XVII do uchrezhdeniia ministerstv," *ZhMNP*, 169 (October 1873):165-220; 170 (November 1873):36-70.

—— *Gosudarstvo i narodnoe obrazovanie XVIII v.* Iaroslavl, 1874.

Vozdvizhenskii, T. *Istoricheskoe obozrenie riazanskoi ierarkhii i tserkovnykh del ee.* Moscow, 1820.

Vvedenskii, D. *Kresttsovoe dukhovenstvo v staroi Moskve.* Moscow, 1899.

Zav'ialov, A. A. *K voprosu ob imushchestvakh tserkovnykh.* St. Petersburg, 1901.

—— *Vopros o tserkovnykh imeniiakh pri Imp. Ekateriny II.* St. Petersburg, 1900.

Zernova, A. S. *Knigi kirillovskoi pechati, izdannye v Moskve v XVI-XVII vv.* Moscow, 1958.

Znamenskii, I. *Polozhenie dukhovenstva v tsarstvovanie Ekateriny II i Pavla I.* Moscow, 1880.

Znamenskii, P. V. "Chteniia iz istorii russkoi tserkvi za tsarstvovanie Ekateriny II," *PS*, 1875, no. 1:3-22; no. 2:99-143; no. 4:392-418; no. 5/6:3-44; no. 8:327-347; no. 9:87-109; no. 11/12:354-411.

—— *Dukhovnye shkoly v Rossii do reformy 1808 g.* Kazan, 1881.

—— "Ob otnoshenii grazhdanskoi vlasti k russkomu dukhovenstvu v XVII i XVIII st.," *PS*, 1865, no. 4:290-302.

—— "Ob otnosheniiakh russkikh sviashchenno-tserkovno-sluzhitelei k prikhodam v XVII i XVIII st.," *PS*, 1867, no. 1:6-27.

—— "O postuplenii v Rossii na tserkovnye dolzhnosti v XVII i XVIII v.," *PS*, 1866, no. 6:124-136.

—— "O sborakh s nizshego dukhovenstva v kaznu eparkhial'nykh arkhiereev v XVII i XVIII st.," *PS*, 1866, no. 1:37-55.

—— "O sposobakh soderzhaniia russkogo dukhovenstva v XVII i XVIII v.," *PS*, 1865, no. 3:145-188.

—— *Prikhodskoe dukhovenstvo na Rusi.* Moscow, 1867.

—— *Prikhodskoe dukhovenstvo v Rossii so vremeni reformy Petra Velikogo.* Kazan, 1873.

—— "Tserkovnye votchiny pri Petre Velikom," *PS*, 1864, no. 2: 127-152; no. 3:247-279.

—— "Zakonodatel'stvo Petra Velikogo otnositel'no chistoty very i blagochiniia tserkovnogo," *PS*, 1864, no. 10:97-131; no. 11:201-231; no. 12:290-340.

—— "Zakonodatel'stvo Petra Velikogo otnositel'no dukhovenstva," *PS*, 1863, no. 7:377-414; no. 9:45-77; no. 10:125-158; no. 12:372-405.

Index

Academy of Sciences, 35, 36

Adrian, patriarch, 22, 31, 50, 114, 243, 282

Afanas'ev, Fedor, priest, 189

Afanasii (Kondoidi), bishop of Suzdal, 140

Afanasii (Vol'khovskii), bishop of Rostov, 158, 278, 282

Aksakov, S. T., 252

Alekseev, Petr, archpriest, 74-75, 194, 257, 296

Aleksei, metropolitan of Moscow, 46

Aleksei Mikhailovich, tsar, 14-15, 281

Alexander I, 71, 120, 131

Alvarez, Emmanuel, 92, 259

Amvrosii (Zertis-Kamenskii), bishop of Pereslavl and archbishop of Moscow, 56-57, 151, 172, 212, 246, 285

Andreev, priest, 74

Anna, empress, 33, 38-39, 42-44, 61, 68, 79, 139, 143, 237

Antonii (Kartalinskii), archbishop of Vladimir, 53, 212, 244

Aquinas, Thomas, 93

Arkhangel'sk, 240, 245

Arsenii (Matseevich), metropolitan of Rostov, 54, 59, 64, 68-69, 96, 129, 154, 158-160, 164-165, 170-171, 249, 253, 276, 278, 282, 294

Arsenii (Vereshchagin), archbishop of Rostov, 53, 118, 245

Arzamas, 72, 278, 284

Astrakhan, 245

Avraamov, Fedor, priest, 44

Batiushkov, P. N., 272

Baumeister, F. C., 94, 259

Belgorod, 240

Belinskii, V. G., 97, 261

Belliustin, I. S., 47

Bishops, 46-49, 52-53, 56-57; clerical resistance to, 74-77; judicial roles of, 65-74; and seminaries, 80-82, 253; status anxieties of, 65-66, 70-71, 81, 172-174, 211; structure of, 242; visitations of, 49, 52, 56-57. *See also* Diocesan Administration; Monastic Clergy

Bolotov, A. T., 104, 145, 157, 159, 178, 186, 189

Bulavin Revolt, 29

Bureaucracy, of Church, 48, 51; of state, 1, 17, 34-36, 40-41, 147-148, 206; recruitment of seminarians for, 34-36, 205-209

Caste, 184-185, 286

Cathedrals, 107-108, 111, 121-124

Catherine I, empress, 112

Catherine the Great (II), empress: as secular ruler, 8, 18-19, 25-26, 57, 64; and ecclesiastical justice, 69, 71, 76, 251; and education of clergy, 79-80, 87, 89, 94, 100, 252, 257, 259, 261-262; and mobility in clerical estate, 198-199, 208-209; and parish, 154, 165, 179, 181, 283, 285; and reform of clerical economy, 118-119; and service structure of clergy, 112, 116, 124, 130-131; and staffing problems of churches, 142-143; and state service of clergy, 18-19, 25-26, 36-37, 39-40

Cemetery churches, 108

Central State Archive of Ancient Acts, 6

Central State Historical Archive, 6

Chancellery for Monastery Affairs, 22

Chancellery of Foreign Affairs, 35

Chin, 17-18, 22-23, 45, 218

Church: administrative system, 48-58; finances, 62-65, 121-122; governance of parish clergy, 58-77; lands and secularization, 2, 9, 15, 55, 76, 87, 121-123, 126; publications, 7, 169. *See also* Diocesan Administration

Church Council of 1551, 109, 157, 251

Church Council of 1666-67, 191-192, 235, 251, 277

Church elder (*tserkovnyi starosta*), 150, 154-156, 274, 277

Church-State relations: and administrative reorganization of dioceses, 8; and judicial status of clergy, 22-26; and operational autonomy of Church, 2, 16, 46-47, 233-234; and poll-tax policies, 21-22, 195-200, 290; in provinces, 170-172, 281; and Synodal vigilance, 76, 236; theory of, 13-16. *See also* State

Churches: controls on, 111-114; numbers of, 8, 109-110; types of, 107-

108, 121-136
Cipher schools, 35, 203, 239
Cities, types of, 11-12
Clergy. *See* Parish Clergy; Monastic
    Clergy
Clerical elder (*popovskii starosta*), 50-
    51, 54, 59-60, 113, 128, 161, 274; in-
    structions to, 7, 31, 50, 54, 59, 164-
    165
Clerical soslovie. See *Dukhovnoe Sos-
    lovie*
Commission on Church Estates, 64,
    118-119, 155, 165, 259, 277
Confession, data on omission of, 280;
    and political duties of priest, 29
Consistory. *See* Diocesan Administra-
    tion
Convent churches, 108

Desiatina (tax district), 50
D'iachok, definition of, 3
Diocesan administration: consistories
    in, 52-53, 55-56, 66-67, 245; and ec-
    clesiastical justice, 65-74, 235; orga-
    nization and development of, 48-58;
    and taxes on clergy, 50-51, 54-55, 62-
    65, 121-122; territorial divisions of,
    7-8, 49-50, 52
District church school (*dukhovnoe
    uchilishche*), 64, 89
District ecclesiastical board (*dukhov-
    noe pravlenie*), 53-54, 171
Dmitrii (Sechenov), bishop of Riazan,
    56, 246
Dmitrii (Tuptalo), metropolitan of
    Rostov, 83
Dmitrov, 123
Dobrynin, G. I., 47, 62, 242
Dubianskii, F. Ia., archpriest, 19
Dugin, Savva, 42-43, 214
Dukhovnoe soslovie (clerical estate), 3-
    4, 17, 36, 98, 185, 193, 215-218
Dukhovnyi shtat (clerical registry), 114-
    117, 194, 219

Ecclesiastical Regulation and Supple-
    ment, 23, 29, 51-52, 54, 56-57, 60,
    63, 66, 68, 74, 79, 83, 90-91, 93, 97-
    99, 117, 128, 157, 164, 169, 173, 178,
    188, 190-191, 201-202, 207-208
Ecclesiastical stewards (*zakazchiki*), 54

Ecclesiastical superintendents (*blago-
    chinnye*), 54-56, 59, 66, 161, 191,
    245; instructions to, 7, 151-152, 160-
    161, 214
Ekaterinoslav, 259
Elizabeth, empress, 24-25, 39, 44, 124,
    130, 143, 208
Emin, F. A., 281
Endowed churches, 108, 111, 124-125
Evgenii (Bulgaris), archbishop of
    Kherson, 259

Fedorov, Vasilii, priest, 135
Feodosii (Golosnitskii), bishop of Tam-
    bov, 57
Feodosii (Ianovskii), archbishop of
    Novgorod, 202
Feofilakt, (Gorskii), bishop of Pere-
    slavl, 282
Filaret (Drozdov), metropolitan of
    Moscow, 241, 286
Filaret (Romanov), patriarch, 243
Filipp (Kolychev), metropolitan of
    Moscow, 16, 46
Fonvizin, D. I., 168, 252
Free Economic Society, 10

Gavriil (Petrov), metropolitan of St.
    Petersburg, 118-119, 240, 274, 282
Gavrilov, Ivan, priest, 71, 170
Gennadii (Gonozov), archbishop of
    Novgorod, 277
Georgii (Dashkov), archbishop of
    Rostov, 247
Giliarov-Platonov, N. P., 215
Golovashkin, Ksenofont, 67
Gorokhovets, 282
Government. *See* Church-State Rela-
    tions; State
Grachevs, 12
Great Reforms of the Church, 4, 74, 274
Gzhatsk, 284

Herald-Master, office of, 30, 203
Herzen, A. I., 261

Iakovlev, A. A., 74
Iaroslavl, 113, 123, 126, 128, 132, 166,
    231, 240, 266, 275, 284, 288-289. *See
    also* Rostov (diocese)
Iavorskii, Stefan, metropolitan of Ria-

zan, 91, 277

Ieronim (Formakovskii), bishop of Vladimir, 53, 282

Instruction manuals for clergy, 7, 20, 74, 169, 190, 213

Ioakim, patriarch, 60, 127

Ioakim, archbishop of Rostov, 253

Ioasaf, patriarch, 283

Iosif (Volchanskii), archbishop of Moscow, 212

Iur'ev-pol'skii, 20, 123, 278

Ivanov, Boris, priest, 72

Ivanov, Fedor, priest, 43-44

Ivanov, Vasilii, priest, 166

Ivanovo, 12

Joseph II, Habsburg emperor, 8, 13, 110, 173

Kadson, I. Z., 5

Kaluga, 5, 10-11, 113, 136-137, 139-140, 231, 237, 240, 266, 284; seminary in, 39

Kantemir, A. D., 253

Karpinskii, I., 259

Kazan, 38, 239-240, 245

Kiev Academy, 49, 82, 85, 91, 292

Kirill (Florinskii), vicar-bishop of Sevsk, 62, 242-243

Kizevetter, A. A., 205

Klin, 151

Kologrivov, Petr, 44

Kolomna, 7, 43, 70-71, 108-110, 114, 116, 122, 125, 128-129, 133, 138, 142, 152, 154, 160-161, 167, 189, 191, 200, 207, 214-215, 240-241, 245, 251, 270, 277, 283, 288, 291-292, 294, 296-297; seminary of, 83-84, 88, 90-91, 201-202, 204, 254, 260, 263

Kormchaia kniga, 23, 196, 287

Kostroma, 236, 239, 245

Kozlov, O. F., 5

Kresttosovye popy, 51, 265

Ksenofont (Troepol'skii), bishop of Vladimir, 245

Kursk, 239

Land, of parish churches, 127-131; shortage of, 10, 131; surveys of, 10, 130-131, 154; use by parish clergy, 117-120

Law Code of 1649, 19-20, 25, 28, 42, 169

Lebedev, Vasilii, 94, 259

Legislative Commission of 1767-68, 18-19, 37, 70, 118, 155, 170-171, 198, 240, 264, 278

Lepekhin, I. I., 10

Levshin, Aleksandr, archpriest, 135

Marriage, licenses for, 246; violation of laws on, 66, 72, 167, 177-178

Medical College, 208

Menshikov, A. D., 30-31

Military churches, 108

Mohila, Peter, 96

Monastic clergy; definition of, 3; and diocesan administration, 46-47, 49-50, 53, 63, 68, 75, 249; poll-tax policy on, 290-291; and seminaries, 83, 96, 260

Moscow, 5-9, 11-12, 20, 30, 36, 40, 43, 49, 51-52, 54-55, 57, 59-61, 63, 65, 69-70, 74-76, 103, 108-109, 112-113, 116, 121, 124-127, 132, 135-136, 138-143, 151-152, 154, 156, 160-161, 166-167, 174, 178-179, 189, 191, 200, 206-207, 214-215, 230-231, 234-239, 241, 244, 247, 249-250, 256-257, 266-267, 277, 282, 286-289, 291, 293-294

Moscow (Slavonic-Greek-Latin) Academy, 35, 49, 53, 80-83, 85, 88, 90-93, 101, 103, 135, 158, 201-204, 207-208, 254, 258-261, 292

Moscow Synodal Chancellery, 6, 44, 56, 67-68, 163, 193, 245

Moscow University, 11, 35-36, 208-209, 293

Murom, 113, 123, 126, 135-136, 188, 232, 241, 246, 265-266, 268, 270, 273, 275, 277, 281, 284

Muscovy: appointment of clergy in, 58-61; Church administration in, 46-51; Church and clergy in, 2, 14, 22, 34; Church role in, 2; clerical education in, 78; clerical economy in, 127; clerical service in, 109-110; parishes in, 149-150; mobility of clergy in, 185-186

Nepliuev, I. I., 285

Nikon, patriarch, 2, 16
Nizhnii-Novgorod, 201, 240
Novgorod, 82, 162, 252, 270-271, 278,
    289
Novikov, N. I., 78, 174, 260, 282

Old Belief (schism), 29, 31-34, 48, 66,
    78, 165, 170, 173, 176-177, 190, 217,
    233, 242, 291; data on, 283
Ordained clergy, definition of, 3; legal
    status of, 20-22
Over-procurator, 2, 18, 47, 51, 73-74,
    85, 140, 154, 213

Parish: development of, 149-156; eco-
    nomics of, 117-138; historiography
    of, 147-149; number of clergy in,
    114-117; and relationship to clergy,
    156-172; religious reform in, 173-
    179; and revolt, 179-183; and selec-
    tion of clergy, 58-59, 141, 148,
    150, 156-162, 189, 192; social types
    of, 11
Parish churches, 108, 112-114, 125-136
Parish-church tax (dannye den'gi), 62-
    64, 75-76, 112, 127, 132
Parish clergy: and conflict with dioce-
    san superiors, 46-47, 74-77; conflict
    within, 144-146; and conscription,
    37-41, 89, 142, 188-189, 190, 200,
    208, 256, 291-292, 297; controls on
    appointment of, 109-111, 114-117;
    corporal punishment of 26, 41-45,
    53, 67, 70-71, 76, 168-172, 187; and
    dependence upon parish, 156-172;
    economic support of, 107-109, 117-
    138, 144-145, 164-168, 182, 187; edu-
    cational requirements for, 61, 82, 89;
    as factory conscripts, 240; families
    of, 18, 34-41, 67, 72-73, 132, 187-
    195, 231; juridical status of, 17-26;
    infirmity of, 187-188, 287; legal
    composition of, 20-22; marriages in,
    215, 296-297; ordination and in-
    stallation of, 58-62, 65, 128, 186,
    247; parish selection of, 58-59,
    141, 148, 150, 156-162; and personal
    conduct norms, 66, 211-215; registry
    system for, 114-117, 194, 219; reli-
    gious role of, 65, 172-179; and role in
    peasant uprisings, 179-183; serf

ownership by, 19, 234-235; service
    performance of, 65-74, 172-179; ser-
    mons of, 93-95, 174; social mobility
    of, 185-210; staffing problems of,
    138-143; state service of, 26-34, 179-
    183; structure and ranks of, 3; sub-
    culture of, 210-215; tonsure of wid-
    owed, 68, 205, 207, 250; travel re-
    strictions on, 70, 206
Parish registers (metricheskie knigi),
    30-31, 33
Parish schools, 150, 155, 185-186
Patriarch, 50-51
Patriarchal region, 7, 49-50, 62
Paul, emperor, 40-41, 55, 71, 76, 80,
    89, 119-120, 131, 162, 181-182, 208,
    238, 251, 296
Pavel, bishop of Vladimir, 175, 207
Penza, 239
Pereslavl, 8, 24-25, 54-56, 63, 72, 75-
    76, 85, 94, 104, 108, 113, 122, 124-
    125, 128, 131-133, 135-142, 145, 151,
    153, 159, 160-161, 165-167, 171, 175-
    176, 193, 198, 200, 205, 211, 230-
    232, 237, 241, 244-245, 250-251, 266-
    267, 273, 276, 278, 281, 284, 287,
    291-293, 297; seminary of, 85, 245,
    263
Peter the Great (I), emperor: and
    Church, 48-49, 51-53, 61, 68; and
    clerical economy, 117-120, 124, 144;
    and clerical service system, 109-112,
    114; as emperor, 1-2, 14-17, 26, 233;
    and parish, 147, 150, 153-154, 157,
    283; and religious-social roles of
    clergy, 173, 175, 178-179; and semi-
    naries, 79-80, 82, 91, 97-98; and so-
    cial mobility of clergy, 186, 191,
    195, 200-207, 290; and state service
    of clergy, 17-18, 22-24, 26-35, 37-38,
    41-42, 44-45, 219, 221
Peter II, emperor, 42,
Peter III, emperor, 25, 69, 76, 112, 180-
    181, 251
Petrov, Mikhail, deacon, 32
Priest, definition of, 3
Platon I (Malinovskii), archbishop of
    Moscow, 53, 87, 116, 127
Platon (Levshin), metropolitan of
    Moscow, 54-55, 59, 61, 65, 74, 81,
    89, 95-96, 101, 124, 136, 138, 141,

145, 151-152, 158, 160-161, 165, 172, 174-175, 192-193, 195, 200, 208-209, 213-214, 245, 256-257, 259, 261, 264-265, 267, 282, 296

Platon (Petrunkevich), bishop of Vladimir, 56, 69, 74, 245

Pobedonostsev, K. P., 16

Pokrov, 12

Poll-tax registry, 19, 21-22, 30-31, 33, 37-40, 42, 59, 143, 187, 195-200, 208, 290, 297

Ponomar', definition of, 3

Population: growth of, 9-10; and average household size, 266

Pososhkov, I. T., 60, 118, 210

Pravezh' (coercive tax collection), 28, 33

Preobrazhenskii prikaz, 24, 41

Private chapel, 108, 111-112, 125, 265

Prokopovich, Feofan, archbishop of Novgorod, 94, 98, 233-234, 237, 258, 292

Protasov, N. A., 16

Provincial reforms of 1775, 8, 12, 33, 35, 154, 206

Pskov, 196, 240

Pufendorf, Samuel, 14, 80

Pugachev Rebellion, 34, 119, 167, 179-181

Radishchev, A. N., 96, 258

Reformation: in Europe, 13, 173; in Russia, 173-179

Registry (*shtat*) of clerical positions, 114-117

Reserved positions (*zachislennye mesta*), 89-90, 257-258

Riazan, 5-6, 23, 25, 38, 42, 56-57, 59, 63, 65, 69, 73-75, 89, 95, 108, 113-114, 122, 128-129, 133, 139, 140, 142, 145, 151-152, 160, 167, 171, 192, 196, 199-200, 209, 231, 236, 240-241, 244, 250-251, 256, 266, 270, 273, 275, 285-287, 291-293, 295, 297; seminary of, 83-84, 86, 88-91, 94-95, 98-100, 202-204, 253-257, 259-260, 262-263

Romanov (uezd), 265

Romodanovskii, F. O., 177

Rostislavov, D. I., 47, 295

Rostov, 7, 9, 28, 32, 37-38, 44, 54-55,

59, 64, 82, 104, 108, 110, 113-114, 122-124, 126, 128-129, 132-133, 136, 139-142, 151, 158, 160-161, 163, 166-167, 170-171, 175, 177, 189, 196, 199-200, 230-231, 236, 238, 240-241, 244, 250-251, 256, 266, 270, 273, 275, 285-287, 291-293, 295, 297; seminary of, 39, 82-84, 88-91, 201-202, 253-260, 262-264

Ruga, 9, 124-127, 269

Russian school, 95, 259

Sacristan (churchman), definition of, 3

Saint Petersburg, 69, 95, 125, 181, 292

Samuil (Mislavskii), archbishop of Rostov, 282

Schism. *See* Old Belief

Schools, government, 37, 155

Secret Chancellery, 24-25, 42-44, 283

Secular: state, 1, 3, 13-16; command, 16, 159, 196

Seminaries, 4, 6-7, 39-41, 44-45, 52-53, 63-64, 119, 122, 138, 143, 158-159, 160, 172, 174, 182, 192, 214, 241, 256; aims of, 79-82; clerical attitudes toward, 75, 83-84, 86, 89, 98-99, 262; curriculum of, 35-37, 90-96; finances of, 83, 85, 87, 89-90; growth of, 82-90, 104; impact of, 102-106; recruitment of pupils from, 34-37, 207-209; social exclusiveness of, 79, 102, 200-204; student experience in, 97-102

Senate: and clerical economy, 119, 121, 131; and clerical service system, 114, 116; and diocesan administration, 51, 57; and parish, 154, 162-163, 169-170, 176; and seminaries, 81; and social mobility in clergy, 195-199, 208, 287, 290-291; and status of clergy, 19, 21, 23-24, 30, 39

Serapion (Liatoshevich), bishop of Pereslavl, 160

Serpukhov, 11, 284

Shakhovskoi, Ia. P., 18, 51, 60, 85, 140, 244

Shcherbatov, M. M., 9, 283

Sheremetevs, 126, 132, 170, 274

Shtat, 114-117

Shui, 113, 278, 282, 284

Sievers, Ia. E., 118

Sil'vestr (Stragorodskii), bishop of

Pereslavl, 54-55
Simon (Lagov), 53, 74, 99-100, 160, 213, 245, 252, 256, 264, 282
Smolensk, 240
Smolitsch, I., 5
Soslovie, 5, 17, 33, 41, 45, 185
Speranskii, M. M., 257
State: and conscription in clerical estate, 37-41, 89, 142, 182-190, 200, 208; and controls on clerical appointments, 109-111, 114-117; and juridical status of clergy, 16-26; and political oaths of clergy, 29-30, 41-44, 75; and political opposition of clergy, 23, 41-45, 75; and recruitment of educated clerical children, 34-37, 205-209; and role of clergy in revolts, 179-183; and service duties of clergy, 26-34; and taxes on clergy, 27-28, 33, 270-271
Stepanov, *popovich*, 42
Subscription lists, clergy participation in, 282
Sudogda, 12
Supreme Privy Council, 42, 292
Suvorov, V. I., 179-180
Suzdal, 11, 20, 39, 42-43, 68, 73, 87, 108, 113-114, 116, 122-126, 128-129, 133-137, 139-142, 145, 151-152, 155, 158, 163-164, 167, 169, 172, 176, 178, 188, 191, 193-194, 196, 200, 205, 212, 214, 234, 236, 240-242, 244-246, 248-251, 255, 265-266, 270, 273, 275-277, 283, 287, 289-290; seminary of, 39, 83-84, 88, 91, 94-95, 100, 188, 201-202, 253-255, 259-263
Sviashchennosluzhiteli, definition and composition of, 3
Synod, 2, 16; and clerical economy, 124, 127-128, 130-132, 137, 266-267, 270; and clerical service system, 112-114, 116-119, 139-140, 142, 265-266, 272; and diocesan administration, 49-52, 54, 56, 59-61, 65-76, 244-250; and parish, 154-155, 157, 162-167, 169-178, 180, 276-278, 281-284; and reform of clerical economy, 117-119; and seminaries, 80-85, 87, 89, 95, 103-104, 203, 253-264, 292; and social mobility of parish clergy, 186,

189-199, 203, 206-208, 288, 290-292, 294; and state policy on clergy, 19-24, 33-37, 39-40, 46
Synodal command, definition of, 16
Synodal region, 7, 83, 128-129

Talitskii, Grigorii, 29
Tambov, 244, 284, 290
Tatishchev, V. N., 118, 180
Taxation, of Church on clergy, 62-65; of state on clergy, 27-28, 33, 270-271
Tikhon (Iakubovskii), bishop of Suzdal, 116
Tikhvin, 270-271
Timofei (Shcherbatskii), metropolitan of Moscow, 161, 175
Tobol'sk, 82, 242
Tooke, William, 19, 104, 187
Trinity-Sergius Seminary, 85, 88, 93-94, 96, 101, 103, 201-202, 209, 214, 254-255, 257-259, 262-263
Tserkovnosluzhiteli, definition and composition of, 3
Tula, 5, 95, 113, 125, 152, 231-232, 240, 277, 284, 290, 294; seminary of, 95
Turgenev, I. S., 261
Tver, 236, 289

Uglich, 239
Ukraine, 5, 52-53, 173, 186, 244, 258, 292

Vasil'ev, Mikhail, priest, 194
Velikii Ustiug, 38, 239-240, 291
Viatka, 245, 294, 296; seminary of, 262
Viazemskii, A. A., 119
Viazniki, 122
Viktor (Onisimov), bishop of Vladimir, 137, 245
Visitations, 49, 52, 56-57
Vladimir, 5-6, 8-10, 36, 39, 43, 63-64, 67, 72, 74, 76, 85-89, 103, 108, 121-122, 126, 128-129, 131-132, 134, 136-138, 141-142, 145, 152, 160, 163-164, 167, 170, 176-177, 181-182, 187-188, 194, 198-200, 207, 212-213, 230, 232, 235-237, 239, 241, 243-245, 249-250, 252, 255, 257, 263, 267, 273, 275-276, 278-279, 287-289, 291-292,

294, 297; seminary of, 85-87, 89-90, 94, 98-101, 122, 204, 248, 253-255, 259-263
Vologda, 239, 245
Volynskii, A. P., 118
Voronezh, 236, 245

War College, 37

Weber, F. C., 28
Word and Deed, 25, 100

Zaraisk, 113
Zvenigorod, 12, 105, 113, 276
Znamenskii, P. V., 4, 6, 77, 149, 156-157, 185

Russian Research Center Studies

1. *Public Opinion in Soviet Russia: A Study in Mass Persuasion*, by Alex Inkeles
2. *Soviet Politics—The Dilemma of Power: The Role of Ideas in Social Change*, by Barrington Moore, Jr.*
3. *Justice in the U.S.S.R.: An Interpretation of Soviet Law*, by Harold J. Berman*
4. *Chinese Communism and the Rise of Mao*, by Benjamin I. Schwartz
5. *Titoism and the Cominform*, by Adam B. Ulam*
6. *A Documentary History of Chinese Communism*, by Conrad Brandt, Benjamin Schwartz, and John K. Fairbank*
7. *The New Man in Soviet Psychology*, by Raymond A. Bauer
8. *Soviet Opposition to Stalin: A Case Study in World War II*, by George Fischer*
9. *Minerals: A Key to Soviet Power*, by Demitri B. Shimkin*
10. *Soviet Law in Action: The Recollected Cases of a Soviet Lawyer*, by Boris A. Konstantinovsky; edited by Harold J. Berman*
11. *How Russia Is Ruled*, by Merle Fainsod. Revised edition
12. *Terror and Progress—USSR: Some Sources of Change and Stability in the Soviet Dictatorship*, by Barrington Moore, Jr.
13. *The Formation of the Soviet Union: Communism and Nationalism, 1917-1923*, by Richard Pipes. Revised edition*
14. *Marxism: The Unity of Theory and Practice—A Critical Essay*, by Alfred G. Meyer. Reissued with a new introduction*
15. *Soviet Industrial Production, 1928-1951*, by Donald R. Hodgman*
16. *Soviet Taxation: The Fiscal and Monetary Problems of a Planned Economy*, by Franklyn D. Holzman*
17. *Soviet Military Law and Administration*, by Harold J. Berman and Miroslav Kerner*
18. *Documents on Soviet Military Law and Administration*, edited and translated by Harold J. Berman and Miroslav Kerner*
19. *The Russian Marxists and the Origins of Bolshevism*, by Leopold H. Haimson*
20. *The Permanent Purge: Politics in Soviet Totalitarianism*, by Zbigniew K. Brzezinski*

21. *Belorussia: The Making of a Nation—A Case Study*, by Nicholas P. Vakar*
22. *A Bibliographical Guide to Belorussia*, by Nicholas P. Vakar*
23. *The Balkans in Our Time*, by Robert Lee Wolff (also American Foreign Policy Library)
24. *How the Soviet System Works: Cultural, Psychological, and Social Themes*, by Raymond A. Bauer, Alex Inkeles, and Clyde Kluckhohn†*
25. *The Economics of Soviet Steel*, by M. Gardner Clark*
26. *Leninism*, by Alfred G. Meyer*
27. *Factory and Manager in the USSR*, by Joseph S. Berliner†*
28. *Soviet Transportation Policy*, by Holland Hunter*
29. *Doctor and Patient in Soviet Russia*, by Mark G. Field†*
30. *Russian Liberalism: From Gentry to Intelligentsia*, by George Fischer*
31. *Stalin's Failure in China, 1924-1927*, by Conrad Brandt*
32. *The Communist Party of Poland: An Outline of History*, by M. K. Dziewanowski. Second edition
33. *Karamzin's Memoir on Ancient and Modern Russia: A Translation and Analysis*, by Richard Pipes*
34. *A Memoir on Ancient and Modern Russia*, by N. M. Karamzin, the Russian text edited by Richard Pipes*
35. *The Soviet Citizen: Daily Life in a Totalitarian Society*, by Alex Inkeles and Raymond A. Bauer†*
36. *Pan-Turkism and Islam in Russia*, by Serge A. Zenkovsky
37. *The Soviet Bloc: Unity and Conflict*, by Zbigniew K. Brzezinski. (Sponsored jointly with the Center for International Affairs, Harvard University.) Revised and enlarged edition. Also in Harvard Paperbacks.
38. *National Consciousness in Eighteenth-Century Russia*, by Hans Rogger
39. *Alexander Herzen and the Birth of Russian Socialism, 1812-1855*, by Martin Malia*
40. *The Conscience of the Revolution: Communist Opposition in Soviet Russia*, by Robert Vincent Daniels*
41. *The Soviet Industrialization Debate, 1924-1928*, by Alexander Erlich*
42. *The Third Section: Police and Society in Russia under Nicholas I*, by Sidney Monas*
43. *Dilemmas of Progress in Tsarist Russia: Legal Marxism and Legal Populism*, by Arthur P. Mendel*
44. *Political Control of Literature in the USSR, 1946-1959*, by Harold Swayze
45. *Accounting in Soviet Planning and Management*, by Robert W. Campbell*
46. *Social Democracy and the St. Petersburg Labor Movement, 1885-1897*, by Richard Pipes*
47. *The New Face of Soviet Totalitarianism*, by Adam B. Ulam*
48. *Stalin's Foreign Policy Reappraised*, by Marshall D. Shulman*
49. *The Soviet Youth Program: Regimentation and Rebellion*, by Allen Kassof*
50. *Soviet Criminal Law and Procedure: The RSFSR Codes*, translated by Harold J. Berman and James W. Spindler; introduction and analysis by Harold J. Berman. Second edition

51. *Poland's Politics: Idealism vs. Realism*, by Adam Bromke
52. *Managerial Power and Soviet Politics*, by Jeremy R. Azrael
53. *Danilevsky: A Russian Totalitarian Philosopher*, by Robert E. Mac-Master*
54. *Russia's Protectorates in Central Asia: Bukhara and Khiva, 1865-1924*, by Seymour Becker
55. *Revolutionary Russia*, edited by Richard Pipes
56. *The Family in Soviet Russia*, by H. Kent Geiger
57. *Social Change in Soviet Russia*, by Alex Inkeles
58. *The Soviet Prefects: The Local Party Organs in Industrial Decision-making*, by Jerry F. Hough
59. *Soviet-Polish Relations, 1917-1921*, by Piotr S. Wandycz
60. *One Hundred Thousand Tractors: The MTS and the Development of Controls in Soviet Agriculture*, by Robert F. Miller
61. *The Lysenko Affair*, by David Joravsky
62. *Icon and Swastika: The Russian Orthodox Church under Nazi and Soviet Control*, by Harvey Fireside
63. *A Century of Russian Agriculture: From Alexander II to Khrushchev*, by Lazar Volin
64. *Struve: Liberal on the Left, 1870-1905*, by Richard Pipes*
65. *Nikolai Strakhov*, by Linda Gerstein
66. *The Kurbskii-Groznyi Apocrypha: The Seventeenth-Century Genesis of the "Correspondence" Attributed to Prince A. M. Kurbskii and Tsar Ivan IV*, by Edward L. Keenan
67. *Chernyshevskii: The Man and the Journalist*, by William F. Woehrlin
68. *European and Muscovite: Ivan Kiereevsky and the Origins of Slavophilism*, by Abbott Gleason
69. *Newton and Russia: The Early Influence, 1698-1796*, by Valentin Boss
70. *Pavel Axelrod and the Development of Menshevism*, by Abraham Ascher
71. *The Service Sector in Soviet Economic Growth: A Comparative Study*, by Gur Ofer (also Harvard Economic Studies)
72. *The Classroom and the Chancellery: State Educational Reform in Russia under Count Dmitry Tolstoi*, by Allen Sinel
73. *Foreign Trade under Central Planning*, by Franklyn D. Holzman
74. *Soviet Policy toward India: Ideology and Strategy*, by Robert H. Donaldson
75. *The End of Serfdom: Nobility and Bureaucracy in Russia, 1855-1861*, by Daniel Field
76. *The Dynamics of Soviet Politics*, edited by Paul Cocks, Robert V. Daniels, and Nancy Whittier Heer
77. *The Soviet Union and Social Science Theory*, by Jerry F. Hough
78. *The Russian Levites: Parish Clergy in the Eighteenth Century*, by Gregory L. Freeze

*Out of print.
†Publications of the Harvard Project on the Soviet Social System.